CONTENTS

GENERAL INTRODUCTION

This new standard edition of *The Collected Writings of John Maynard Keynes* forms the memorial to him of the Royal Economic Society. He devoted a very large share of his busy life to the Society. In 1911, at the age of twenty-eight, he became editor of the *Economic Journal* in succession to Edgeworth: two years later he was made secretary as well. He held these offices without intermittence until almost the end of his life. Edgeworth, it is true, returned to help him with the editorship from 1919 to 1925; Macgregor took Edgeworth's place until 1934, when Austin Robinson succeeded him and continued to assist Keynes down to 1945. But through all these years Keynes himself carried the major responsibility and made the principal decisions about the articles that were to appear in the *Economic Journal*, without any break save for one or two issues when he was seriously ill in 1937. It was only a few months before his death at Easter 1946 that he was elected president and handed over his editorship to Roy Harrod and the secretaryship to Austin Robinson.

In his dual capacity of editor and secretary Keynes played a major part in framing the policies of the Royal Economic Society. It was very largely due to him that some of the major publishing activities of the Society—Sraffa's edition of Ricardo, Stark's edition of the economic writings of Bentham, and Guillebaud's edition of Marshall, as well as a number of earlier publications in the 1930s—were initiated.

When Keynes died in 1946 it was natural that the Royal Economic Society should wish to commemorate him. It was perhaps equally natural that the Society chose to commemorate him by producing an edition of his collected works. Keynes himself had always taken a joy in fine printing, and the Society, with the help of Messrs Macmillan as publishers and the Cambridge University Press as printers, has been anxious to give Keynes's writings a permanent form that is wholly worthy of him.

The present edition will publish as much as is possible of his work in the field of economics. It will not include any private and personal correspondence or publish many letters in the possession of his family. The edition is concerned, that is to say, with Keynes as an economist.

Keynes's writings fall into five broad categories. First there are the books which he wrote and published as books. Second there are collections of articles and pamphlets which he himself made during his lifetime (*Essays in Persuasion* and *Essays in Biography*). Third, there is a very considerable volume of published but uncollected writings—articles written for newspapers, letters to newspapers, articles in journals that have not been included in his two volumes of collections, and various pamphlets. Fourth, there are a few hitherto unpublished writings. Fifth, there is correspondence with economists and those concerned with economics or public affairs. It is the intention of this series to publish almost completely the whole of the first four categories listed above. The only exceptions are a few syndicated articles where Keynes wrote almost the same material for publication in different newspapers or in different countries, with minor and unimportant variations. In these cases, this series will publish one only of the variations, choosing the most interesting.

The publication of Keynes's economic correspondence must inevitably be selective. In the day of the typewriter and the filing cabinet and particularly in the case of so active and busy a man, to publish every scrap of paper that he may have dictated about some unimportant or ephemeral matter is impossible. We are aiming to collect and publish as much as possible, however, of the correspondence in which Keynes developed his own ideas in argument with his fellow economists, as well as the more significant correspondence at times when Keynes was in the middle of public affairs.

Apart from his published books, the main sources available to those preparing this series have been two. First, Keynes in his will made Richard Kahn his executor and responsible for his economic papers. They have been placed in the Marshall Library of the University of Cambridge and have been available for this edition. Until 1914 Keynes did not have a secretary and his earliest papers are in the main limited to drafts of important letters that he made in his own handwriting and retained. At that stage most of the correspondence that we possess is represented by what he received rather than by what he wrote. During the war years of 1914–18 and 1940–6 Keynes was serving in the Treasury. With the opening in 1968 of the records under the thirty-year rule, the papers that he wrote then and between the wars have become available. From 1919 onwards, throughout the rest of his life, Keynes had the help of a secretary—for many years Mrs Stephens. Thus for the last twenty-five years of his working life we have in most cases the carbon copies of his own letters as well as the originals of the letters that he received.

There were, of course, occasions during this period on which Keynes wrote himself in his own handwriting. In some of these cases, with the help of his correspondents, we have been able to collect the whole of both sides of some important interchanges and we have been anxious, in justice to both correspondents, to see that both sides of the correspondence are published in full.

The second main source of information has been a group of scrapbooks kept over a very long period of years by Keynes's mother, Florence Keynes, wife of Neville Keynes. From 1919 onwards these scrapbooks contain almost the whole of Maynard Keynes's more ephemeral writing, his letters to newspapers and a great deal of material which enables one to see not only what he wrote but the reaction of others to his writing. Without these very carefully kept scrapbooks the task of any editor or biographer of Keynes would have been immensely more difficult.

The plan of the edition, as at present intended, is this. It will total thirty volumes. Of these the first eight are Keynes's published books from *Indian Currency and Finance*, in 1913, to the *General Theory* in 1936, with the addition of his *Treatise on Probability*. There next follow, as vols. IX and X, *Essays in Persuasion* and *Essays in Biography*, representing Keynes's own collection of articles. *Essays in Persuasion* differs from the original printing into two respects: it contains the full texts of the articles or pamphlets included in it and not (as in the original printing) abbreviated versions of these articles, and it also contains two later pamphlets which are of exactly the same character as those included by Keynes in his original collection. In *Essays in Biography* there have been added a number of biographical studies that Keynes wrote both before and after 1933.

There will follow two volumes, XI–XII, of economic articles and correspondence and a further two volumes, already published, XIII–XIV, covering the development of his thinking as he moved towards the *General Theory*. There are included in these volumes such part of Keynes's economic correspondence as is closely associated with the articles that are printed in them. A supplement to these volumes, XXIX, prints some further material relating to the same issues, which has since been discovered.

The remaining fourteen volumes deal with Keynes's *Activities* during the years from the beginning of his public life in 1905 until his death. In each of the periods into which we divide this material, the volume concerned publishes his more ephemeral writings, all of it hitherto uncollected, his correspondence relating to these activities, and such other material and correspondence as is necessary to the understanding of Keynes's activities. These volumes are edited by Elizabeth Johnson and

Donald Moggridge, and it has been their task to trace and interpret Keynes's activities sufficiently to make the material fully intelligible to a later generation. Elizabeth Johnson has been responsible for vols. XV–XVIII, covering Keynes's earlier years and his activities down to the end of World War I reparations and reconstruction. Donald Moggridge is responsible for all the remaining volumes recording Keynes's other activities from 1922 until his death in 1946.

The record of Keynes's activities during World War II is now complete with the publication of volumes XXII–XXVII. It now remains to fill the gap between 1922 and 1939 with three volumes of which this is the third; to print certain of Keynes's published articles and the correspondence relating to them which have not appeared elsewhere in this edition, and to publish a volume of his social, political and literary writings.

Those responsible for this edition have been: Lord Kahn, both as Lord Keynes's executor and as a long and intimate friend of Lord Keynes; able to help in the interpreting of much that would be otherwise misunderstood; the late Sir Roy Harrod as the author of his biography; Austin Robinson as Keynes's co-editor on the *Economic Journal* and successor as Secretary of the Royal Economic Society. Austin Robinson has acted throughout as Managing Editor; Donald Moggridge is now associated with him as Joint Managing Editor.

In the early stages of the work Elizabeth Johnson was assisted by Jane Thistlethwaite, and by Mrs McDonald, who was originally responsible for the systematic ordering of the files of the Keynes papers. Judith Masterman for many years worked with Mrs Johnson on the papers. More recently Susan Wilsher, Margaret Butler and Leonora Woollam have continued the secretarial work. Barbara Lowe has been responsible for the indexing. Since 1977 Judith Allen has been responsible for much of the day-to-day management of the edition, as well as seeing the volumes through the press.

EDITORIAL NOTE

This volume is the third of three concerned with Keynes's activities between 1922 and 1939. The sources for this volume are Keynes's own surviving papers, material available in the Public Record Office and the papers of colleagues and friends. Where the material comes from the Public Record Office, the call numbers for the relevant files appear in the List of Documents Reproduced following page 594.

In this, as in all the similar volumes, in general all of Keynes's own writings are printed in larger type. Keynes's own footnotes are indicated by asterisks or other symbols to distinguish them from the editorial footnotes. All introductory matter and all writings by others than Keynes are printed in smaller type. The only exception to this general rule is that occasional short quotations from a letter from Keynes to his parents or to a friend, used in introductory passages to clarify a situation, are treated as introductory matter and are printed in the smaller type.

Most of Keynes's letters included in this and other volumes are reprinted from the carbon copies that remain among his papers. In most cases he has added his initials to the carbon in the familiar fashion in which he signed to all his friends. We have no certain means of knowing whether the top copy, sent to the recipient of the letter, carried a more formal signature.

Chapter 1

THE CURRENCY QUESTION

Once the flurry surrounding Britain's departure from the gold standard was over, Keynes settled down to what for him was a very quiet autumn. Except for spending the first half of October assembling *Essays in Persuasion* (*JMK*, vol. IX) from his writings of the previous twelve years, Keynes remained aloof from public controversy, publishing nothing of a popular sort in the last three months of the year. However, this does not mean that he was completely inactive or without influence.

As soon as Britain left gold, the authorities began to consider the appropriate currency policy under the new circumstances. At one level, the Prime Minister appointed an Advisory Committee on Financial Questions consisting of R. H. Brand, Walter Layton, Lord Macmillan, Sir Josiah Stamp and H. D. Henderson. Sir Arthur Salter joined the Committee at the end of September. At another level, the Treasury began to consider alternatives to the gold standard and an appropriate exchange rate for sterling. Keynes soon became involved at both levels.

The route by which he became involved started with a letter from Sir Frederick Leith-Ross of the Treasury.

From SIR FREDERICK LEITH-ROSS, *13 October 1931*

Private and Confidential

My dear Keynes,

There is much talk at the moment to the effect that before we go back to the gold standard we must get some better understanding with other countries as to the method on which the gold standard should be operated. It is frequently suggested that France and America do not observe 'the rules of the game' and that if those rules were properly observed the gold standard would work without any of the present economic dislocation and maldistribution of gold.

I believe that you are responsible to a considerable extent for the wide acceptance of this view and I noticed that in an article a couple of weeks back you spoke of the 'terms which must needs be strict on which we should be prepared to re-enter the system of a drastically reformed gold standard' [*JMK*, vol. IX, p. 249]. It would be of great interest to us here if you could work out for our confidential information the practical measures which you consider that France and America and other countries should take, and have not taken, to operate the gold standard fairly. Do you think that you could do something on this?

Yours sincerely,
F. W. LEITH-ROSS

To SIR FREDERICK LEITH-ROSS, *14 October 1931*

My dear Leith-Ross,

I should be delighted a little later on to let you have my ideas, both in writing and by word of mouth. There are a good many possible alternative schemes and I am not at the moment very clear in my own mind which I prefer. Also there are two rather separate problems:—

1. The question as to what general plan we ought to be working up towards;
2. The right order of procedure, and what point is best tackled first.

I am turning over both problems in my mind and I am at your service as soon as I feel ready to express myself.

Yours sincerely,
[copy not initialled or signed]

From SIR FREDERICK LEITH-ROSS, *15 October 1931*

Confidential

My dear Keynes,

Many thanks for your letter of the 14th. By all means take your time to consider both the plan and the tactics to be adopted, but as soon as you are ready I shall be very glad to have your views.

The discussions which we have had with the French indicate that they are far from being ready to do any deal on the lines discussed in the Macmillan Report. On the contrary, their general attitude is that we are now suffering the inevitable penalty for the over-liberal credit policy which the Bank of England has pursued during the last few years, and they hope that we will now be brought to see the errors of our ways. They are somewhat apprehensive as to the effects of our abandonment of the gold standard on other currencies and central banks, but they are convinced that the brunt of the difficulties will fall on us. They are exceedingly surprised that we accept the present position of sterling with such a light heart, and they appear to be genuinely afraid that if we are not careful, sterling may become a speculative counter, and in that case they believe that its depreciation might be very rapid and become unmanageable. The net effect is that there is a general readiness to help us to hold sterling and to get back to the gold standard as soon as possible, but this attitude may easily be modified if it appears that we are not doing our best to restabilise and in that case there might easily be a new flight from sterling.

I do not mean that the central banks would sell sterling if they can help it. But the fall in the gold value of sterling has, of course, entailed heavy losses to all the central banks which kept sterling balances and they are very sore about it. This experience may have serious effects in so far as it discredits the gold exchange standard and induces a general stampede from foreign *divisen* into gold. There is no doubt that this is one of the elements in the present wholesale export of gold from America, though during the past fortnight the movement has been reinforced by fear as to the position of the dollar if a policy of credit expansion is to be embarked upon. The Americans are now busily engaged in denying that any such policy is in contemplation.

Thus conditions at present do not seem to me very favourable to the initiation of any conversations for better international co-operation on the gold standard, and I fear that the French influence will be used as far as possible also to persuade the Americans to unite themselves with French policy rather than with the sort of policy that we have been advocating. It is, therefore, desirable that we should get our programme prepared, so that we can put it forward if and when a suitable opportunity occurs.

Yours sincerely,
F. W. LEITH-ROSS

To SIR FREDERICK LEITH-ROSS, *20 October 1931*

My dear Leith-Ross,

I am interested to hear what you say about the French attitude. I am not at all disposed to differ from what I take to be your attitude of some scepticism as to the utility of an international currency conference at the present stage. To some extent I think the demand for a conference is an overrun from the state of affairs which existed just before we went off gold. Today the situation is quite a new one, and, as I said before, I find it difficult to make up my mind just what to do. But I agree that it is very probable that matters are not yet ripe for an international conference and that little could result from such a gathering.

But have you considered the possibilities of an Empire conference? I am rather inclined to think that that might be the first step to take. All except Canada and South Africa have followed sterling; which gives them an interest if not a right in considering the future of sterling. Canada is half off, and one wonders how long South Africa will last. There might be great advantages in trying to concert, in the first instance, [a] common empire policy, and to establish a reputable sterling system for the Empire, before proceeding further afield.

I hope to get my ideas into writing sooner or later and will then send them on to you.

Yours sincerely,
[copy initialled] J.M.K.

Before Keynes put pen to paper for Leith-Ross, he did try his ideas out elsewhere. The first occasion was in a long letter to Walter Case setting out the general situation as he saw it.

To WALTER CASE, *2 November 1931*

My dear Case,

I think the point has now come when it might be useful that I should give you a general report on the situation as I see it.

I. *The price level*

It is remarkable to what a small extent British prices have risen so far. Up to November 1st the wholesale price index had not risen more than 5 per cent as compared with the date before we went off gold, whilst there has been no measurable change in the cost of living index number. Such rise as has taken place in the wholesale index is mainly due to the rise in cereals and textile raw materials. But even though wheat has risen about 7/- a quarter since the end of July, or approximately 30 per cent, the prices of both flour wholesale and of bread retail are absolutely unchanged. The prices of beef, mutton, and bacon have reached a record low level, and are today at the lowest figure since the War. Cheese, butter, and lard, on the other hand, have risen appreciably. Apart from pig iron, which has risen a little, the price of coal, iron and steel and other products are unchanged. Thus our exporters are getting almost the whole of the benefit of the exchange bonus and our importers of the corresponding exchange protection. Nor is there the slightest sign at present of any upward tendency of wages.

Moreover, we are to a considerable extent getting the best of both worlds, since broadly speaking the countries from which we buy our food and raw materials have followed us off gold, whilst our manufacturing competitors have remained on the old gold parity.

II. *The volume of production*

The natural result is a very high degree of optimism amongst manufacturers. The leading textile shares have on the average doubled in price, whilst a wide range of home industrials, including home rails, have risen by some 50 per cent. The extent of the rise in home industrials is somewhat veiled in the index numbers since so many companies are included of an international character. It is possible that the stock exchange enthusiasm is overdone, yet when one comes to details it is difficult to find a share which is obviously overvalued. The reason for this is that many prices had previously fallen to rubbish value. The shares were either worth nothing at all or 50 per cent to 100 per cent above the old quotation. The investing public has come to the conclusion that of the two alternatives the risk that they might be worth nothing at all is now dispelled.

When one comes to actual figures of output it is clear that by far the greatest improvement is to be found in the textile industries. The exchange depreciation has come for them at an extraordinarily convenient time of year, since this is the date at which the bulk of foreign orders are normally being placed. The result is that this country is getting a much larger share than in recent times of the normal autumn orders. I should say that the actual level of output is about 50 per cent above the lowest level reached and on average at least 25 per cent above any level of output which has been worked for some considerable time. In nearly all lines of cotton production Lancashire is probably now the cheapest producer in the world. The chief anxiety of manufacturers there is as to how long Italy, Czecho-Slovakia, and Japan will remain on gold parity. They feel confident that so long as these countries remain on gold parity they will get these dangerous competitors beaten in world markets. The same is broadly true in woollen textiles. In artificial silk on the other hand the recovery seems to be slow and my information is that such firms as Courtaulds are still making very little profit. Both for this reason and for the probable unprofitableness of the Viscose Company in America I should be inclined to pick out Courtaulds as one of the shares which is now definitely overvalued.

The coal, iron and steel industries are full of hope, but I do not think that there is yet evidence of a substantial increase in output. This is due to the intense depreciation [depression?] of the shipbuilding industry and the lack of construction activity throughout the country. However, they will greatly better their position even if consumption remains at a very low ebb provided foreign imports are not kept out. Some specialities such as galvanised sheets and tin plates are doing moderately better but are held up by the continuing extreme depression of world markets. They will get a larger share but perhaps of a diminishing volume of trade.

It is difficult to get precise information about the great mass of miscellaneous export industries. I have no reliable figures of output and can only report the spirit of optimism which prevails in provincial centres. There are undoubtedly a large number of lines in which for the first time since the War British producers find themselves in a really strong competitive position. I should not be surprised for example to see great progress in the export of motor cars. It seems to me not beyond the bounds of possibility that within two years this country will have taken the place of the United States as the leading producers of automobiles in the international market. The business of securing such a position is now being pushed forward in many quarters with the greatest energy and enthusiasm.

There has been quite an appreciable but not yet a large reduction in the number of unemployed. This is not inconsistent with the above. In recent weeks the effect of the change round in the situation has been in the first instance to bring down stocks, to fill up order books, and to lead to longer hours of work for those already in employment.

At the same time I find it very hard to estimate whether the net effect of all that has happened on the volume of employment will be really large. I should not be surprised at a reduction of perhaps as many as 250,000, but I should doubt the probability of a greater reduction unless there is either a revival of world trade or construction enterprise at home. We have still to feel the full effects on employment of the frenzied economy campaign which was in vogue during the last weeks of the late Government and which is still greatly influencing local authorities. It was impressed on every patriotic citizen and public body that it was their duty to forego any form of expenditure which could possibly be foregone. If we had continued on the gold standard the eventual effect on unemployment would have been in my judgement very large. I believe that the depreciation of sterling and the spirit of optimism should more than offset the evil effects of the economy campaign. But I should not expect a real recovery until higher authority decides to proclaim that 'patriotism' consists of a spirit of expansion and development on the part of well meaning authorities and private persons.

III. *The prospects of a tariff*

There is of course an overwhelming majority for high protection in the new Cabinet. All the same I am doubtful whether drastic measures are likely to be taken in the near future. One cannot predict confidently because the outcome depends on an almost incalculable balance of individual forces and motives. But I should be inclined to think that so far as a general tariff is concerned we shall rest content for the present with exchange depreciation, and that a general tariff, if imposed, will be moderate. It is much more likely that there will be some fairly drastic safeguarding in iron and steel, and possibly in the case of agriculture restrictions of pig and poultry imports and some kind of a wheat quota having the effect of raising the price to the British farmer above the world level without a corresponding increase to the consumer.

It may be, however, that the imperial side of production will be the predominant one. The course of events might be an imperial conference next spring followed by some sort of tariff, the prime object of which would be imperial union. The exchange depreciation having provided for the case of the British manufacturer, the imperialists are much freer than they were to mould their scheme of protection to suit imperial purposes.

IV. *The general election*

Whilst everyone expected a substantial majority for the National Government, the actual figures came, of course, as a complete surprise. As has been the case in the last three or four general elections, it is that old wretch Lord Rothermere who has been dead right. It is said that he has made a profit of the order of £100,000, buying majorities on the Stock Exchange.

The election was won not on any ordinary political arguments.

The vast mass of the general public were persuaded that some national crisis of an undefined character was upon us and that a return of the Labour Government would mean the total collapse of the currency such as occurred some years ago in Germany and Austria. General elections are always dismal affairs. But I do not think I remember any election in which more outrageous lies were told by leading statesmen. As soon as 'patriotism' is mentioned one can be sure that some roguery is afoot; and so it was in this case. Perhaps the worst example both in itself and because of the very great effect it had on the minds of the general public, was the story put about in the last days of the election by Mr Runciman and Mr Snowden that the Post Office Savings Bank was in danger. It seems that some of the funds borrowed by the Unemployment Insurance Fund had been in several years past taken from the moneys at the disposal of the Savings Bank. In actual fact there is nothing improper or dangerous in this, since they are on the guarantee of the Treasury and are on exactly the same footing as any other Government security.

Mr Snowden and Mr Runciman led the public to believe that since the insurance fund is insolvent in the sense that its assets are less than its liabilities the savings of the public had been endangered. The peculiar monstrosity of this was not only that it was untrue in itself but that the advance of funds by the Savings Bank to the unemployment fund had been actually made by Mr Snowden himself (and his Conservative predecessors) without having been reported to the Cabinet, the other members of the Government in fact being totally ignorant of the whole business. Thus Mr Snowden used for the purpose of ruining his former colleagues an episode for which he was solely responsible and which had been done by him entirely without their knowledge. But this story was put about so near the day of polling that there was no time to contradict it, and everyone agrees that it moved more votes than any other single thing. Such are politicians!

All the same one could not possibly have wished the Labour

Government to be returned. Owing to the intensive propaganda which had been raised it would have been much more difficult for them to deal satisfactorily with the currency question than the National Government. Moreover the personnel of the Labour Ministry would have been incredibly weak and their advertised policy was largely foolish. It will be good for them to go out into the wilderness for a time to find their soul again.

Meanwhile the National Party are in their hearts a little shocked at the excessive completeness of their victory and wish that they had administered a rather smaller dose of poison. There will be no effective opposition in the House of Commons and it is difficult to see how the present elements of the National Party can be held together after the first six months. However the note at present is one of moderation and reasonableness in the face of the victory. For six months at least there will be plenty to occupy Ministers without raising any extensive programme of legislation.

V. *The prospects of sterling*

I do not know how it may be in the United States but there is no doubt that in Europe the probability of any attempt on the part of Great Britain to return to the old parity or even in the near future to a new gold parity is vastly overestimated. I find that many continental observers take it as a matter of course that this country will want to be back again on gold as soon as possible. Yet I am quite convinced that this is remote from the opinion of the overwhelming majority of responsible opinion. Foreigners always underestimate the slow infiltration of what I have sometimes called [*JMK*, vol. III, pp. 3–4] 'inside opinion', whilst 'outside opinion' remains ostensibly unchanged. Then quite suddenly what was 'inside opinion' becomes 'outside opinion'. Foreigners are quite taken by surprise, but the change is really one which had been long prepared. In the later months of the old gold standard there was hardly a soul in this country who really believed in it. But it was considered that it was our duty for fairly obvious reasons to do everything we possibly could to keep where we were.

Once we had put up a fight and had nevertheless been pushed off that restored to us our complete freedom of action. And our freedom of action once regained will not be lightly abandoned.

It is much too soon to say what form the ultimate settlement will take. It is quite certain that there will be no return to the old parity. There will be no premature attempt at any settlement at all. How definite the future relationship to gold will be one cannot possibly say. Here again I fancy that the imperial aspect will predominate in the next ensuing months. I anticipate in the near future not an international currency conference but an Empire currency conference at which the whole Empire will be invited to come on to a new sterling standard and to participate in the ultimate decision as to what that new standard shall be.

There are, I think, attractions from our point of view in a new sterling standard to which the British Empire, South America, Central Europe, and Scandinavia might adhere, maintaining a definite but fluctuating (in accordance with the price level) relationship with the gold standard countries. This would have the effect of throwing the brunt of price fluctuation on the latter. When after a time the gold standard countries got tired of this, then would be the moment for evolving a new world currency. But here I am beginning to romance along the lines of my own imagination rather than of ascertained fact or existing probability.

VI. *The world situation*

I am sure that British optimism is at present carried too far by enthusiasm over the changed local situation and is paying too little attention to the continuance of depressed and dangerous conditions abroad. I read the Laval–Hoover conversations in a very pessimistic light; though I should be glad to have your views on this. The French are going to ask too much all along the line and I see nothing but trouble ahead, nor do I see any solid reason whatever as yet for expecting a recovery in the U.S.A. in 1932. Here again I should like to have your views. I do not overlook the fact that the psychological effect of some measure of recovery in Great Britain and in the great areas of the world including India, the Crown Colonies, Australia, and a large part of South America which follow in the wake of Great Britain, may acquire a considerable impetus before it is checked. Yet I can scarcely conceive that the slump will really turn round until there is a revival of construction in the U.S.A. and of international investment propagating revival of construction in the undeveloped countries of the world; and all this seems a long way off. So I expect the world depression to continue some time yet and one day Great Britain will wake up to the fact that there are strict limits to the degree of recovery which a country can gain from what is nothing but a change in its domestic circumstances and in its relationship to the rest of the world.

I might add that I have a hope that the wholesale index in terms of gold may fall no further and might even recover a little. But this will not be enough by itself to turn the tide without a genuine improvement in the construction industries.

[copy not initialled or signed]

Just over a week later, he gave fuller expression to his views when he gave a paper to the Political Economy Club in London.

Notes for a speech to the Political Economy Club, 11 November 1931

A rambling discourse—begin by reviewing events since Aug.
The lucky way in which we got off gold
State of opinion   Where there is one doubt in ten
    Ripe pear falling off the tree
    Would have been sleepy in ten minutes
    Like the bear which was 'just right'

An extraordinary example of the British way of doing things

Slow undermining of inner opinion

But it deceives the foreign observer who is perhaps becoming undeceived now but certainly believed for a few weeks after we went off that there could be no serious doubt we should go back again

This is an important factor, because it may be one of the things which has kept sterling delusively strong

The effects of going off

Must not be underestimated or judged more evanescent than they really are. It is an *enormous* event and does in my judgement probably mark the lowest point of the deflation for the world taken as a whole

First our competitive position

So far we have, in an extraordinary degree, the best of both worlds.

There is no immediate indication of our losing this. Though it is hard to believe Japan and Germany can hang on much longer.

Seasonally fortunate for Lancashire

L[ancashire] C [otton] C [orporation] report

We are now cheapest producers in world. I do not think it likely that we should pop back into our former relative position. The sense for us which kept us on gold so long will now operate to prevent the tails of the manufacturers from growing

But we must not expect too much effect on unemployment so long as the economy campaign continues

Must remember that almost every well meaning person in the country is stuffed to the teeth with intellectual error

Second, there is the effect on the price level

Here the benefit is far more widely spread.

Matter of vast importance that the price level relatively to wage level and debts has now suffered a great adjustment over a very large part of the world.

U.S.A., France, Belgium, Holland, Switzerland alone on a full gold standard

Central Europe, Japan, S. Africa, a few odd countries such as Columbia on a precarious exchange controlled basis which is rapidly strangling them.

Otherwise the whole of Asia, South America, and the British Empire is off gold and is enjoying a level price level no longer very seriously below 1929

Moreover there is no longer the same external motive on the central banks of these countries to exert deflationary pressure against domestic expansion.

The relief (e.g.) to Australia, India and to a lesser extent Canada, resulting from our action, has been greater than is yet realised by most people.

Would this benefit be lost if *everyone* came off gold?

This raises a curious and important point often overlooked.

Suppose every country had simultaneously devalued 50 per cent including the creditor countries who are exerting the deflationary strain, the benefit would have been problematical.

Explain

But more countries yet could join our club, so long as the Gold Club is not dissolved and particularly so long as creditor countries remain members

It would be *much* easier technically to stabilise sterling in terms of an index number if there were two Currency Clubs in the World – a Sterling Club and a Gold Club; for so long as the latter was not too small and had reasonably rigid wages, it could be made to bear most of the brunt of the unavoidable fluctuations.

But there is another effect which seems to me to be operating which I did not predict, though, looking back, I think I should.

Effect on gold prices

Due to inelasticity of demand

Relaxation of deflationary pressure in countries going off gold *plus* rise of prices in terms of local currency relieves position of holders of stocks of commodities and enables them to be more reluctant sellers. They can afford to hold off the market. The

weaker countries are no longer forced to sell their products at any price. Thus there is a tendency for *gold* prices to rise
And the sight of this causes replenishment of stocks by manufacturers etc.
Case of wheat and jute
But I would remind you, increase of commodity prices, without increased investment, only redistributes purchasing power and profits without increasing either
Nevertheless a more equal distribution of loss may lead to a net increase of output leading to decrease of secondary unemployment.
Indeed I should make bold to say that we were through the worst if it were not for two black spots—Germany and Central Europe in general and U.S.A.
I can see absolutely no way out of German imbroglio
French plan. Consequences of its success
Conditions of its failure
I see no real sign of break of acute deflationary conditions in U.S.A. and, even with fluctuating exchanges, that is bound to exercise deflationary influence on all of us.
As in case of Germany, I simply cannot imagine a way in which U.S.A. is to get out of the bog.
So until after the German smash and after one more disillusion in world trade, it is as well to be cautious in one's prognostications.

Now for the future of sterling
My mind not made up
I should like to see formation of a sterling club and the easiest way to start this is by Empire discussions.
What should be the rules of this club?
I have reverted to the general ideas of my *Tract on Monetary Reform* [*JMK*, vol. IV].
Take some appropriate index number
Take some appropriate normal level
Aim at stability within 5 per cent on either side

Do this by having a definite but variable gold price with wide gold points and an appropriate terms-of-credit policy.
This does the trick so long as there is a strong gold club
This seems to me to be the first stage. When the gold club gets tired of it, that would be the time for more fundamental considerations.
But if the members of the gold club come to mend their habits sufficiently to become worthy of membership of the sterling club, they would not necessarily be tired of the gold club.
If the sterling club took 1929 wholesale index as its normal, and the gold club managed its affairs so as to raise gold prices to the 1929 level, sterling would predictably rise to its old gold parity, and there would be no recriminations.
If on the contrary, then the members of the gold club will stew in their own juice until they are sufficiently stewed to be fit for rational conversation.
Appropriate normal level for sterling club
 British wages test
 War burden test
 External revenue test balanced again—volume of trade and terms of trade
 Wholesale price level for raw producing countries
If our club is to be popular, I think we should be well advised to take the last step.

Five days later he completed a paper for Leith-Ross, entitled 'Notes on the Currency Question'. As well as sending one to Leith-Ross, he sent a copy to the Governor of the Bank of England and to Hubert Henderson.

NOTES ON THE CURRENCY QUESTION

I

1. There are strong indications that the time is not yet ripe for an international currency conference. It would merely be an occasion for France to endeavour to exercise pressure to induce us to return to gold at too high a figure and at a premature date.

So far as we ourselves are concerned, we now have plenty of time. There is every reason for not taking a decision in a hurry. On the other hand, so far as the rest of the world is concerned, there is nothing to be done until the German situation has been handled, and—though this may well require a conference—it could not be primarily a currency conference.

2. On the other hand, there is a great deal to be said for an Imperial Currency Conference. No part of the British Empire is now on the gold standard except South Africa. Australia has gone farther off than we have; Canada not so far; India and the Crown Colonies are strictly on a sterling basis, and how much longer South Africa will be able to stand the racket of doubt, is open to question. The present may be an exceptional opportunity for uniting the whole Empire, or almost the whole, on a reformed sterling standard. If we had previously fixed up the broad outlines of an Empire Sterling Standard, we could then approach other countries in a vastly stronger position and very far from that of a suitor for favours. It is not unthinkable that South America, Central Europe and Scandinavia might eventually join a sterling standard, managed by the Bank of England and pivoted on London.

At the same time it is reasonable that those parts of the Empire which have linked themselves to sterling, for better and for worse, should be taken into consultation, whilst the future of sterling is being determined.

II

3. If an imperial currency conference were to be held, what general plan or what alternative plans should be brought before it for discussion? There are three principal alternatives, of which the first is only suitable for the immediate future (the next six months or year):—

1. The first is to continue as at present for some time yet; that is to say to allow frequent moderate fluctuations in the exchange round a level of about 3.85, with the Bank of England

stepping in, secretly and informally and without any definite commitment to anyone as to what its policy is or may be, to prevent extreme fluctuations in the gold value of sterling, within the limits of its available reserves.

2. The second is to choose as soon as possible a new, definitive gold parity and then, having fixed this, to return to a strict gold standard precisely as before, except with a new parity between gold and sterling.

3. The third is to endeavour to fix sterling, within certain not too narrow limits, in terms of some sort of a price standard, i.e. to stabilise the value of sterling in terms of some group of commodities. This would not be incompatible with a definite value for sterling in terms of gold at any given time.

The argument *in favour* of the first alternative is that there are still too many unknowns in the case to justify the adoption of any definitive plan whatever, at the present time. It might be held that it would be unsafe to take any definite commitments until our balance of trade is clearly on the right side; that the course of action by other countries still on the gold standard, many of whom are only hanging on by their teeth or even only pretending to hang on under cover of exchange regulations which prevent any free transactions, is unpredictable; and that the prospective commodity value of gold itself is also unpredictable. Indeed probably almost everyone would agree that it is undesirable to take any definite step until we know the answer to the German riddle.

Equally it could be maintained as *against* the second alternative that it would be quite impossible to choose a safe figure, even if we desired in principle to return eventually to a strict gold standard, so long as the behaviour of gold and the future policy of the two chief creditor gold standard countries is entirely uncertain.

The third alternative is more unfamiliar and probably requires a good deal of explanation if its implications are to be understood.

III

For the sake of illustration, let us assume that it is desired to stabilise the value of sterling in terms of an index number based on the prices of sixty of the most important articles of international or of inter-imperial commerce. (This is purely for illustration—I postpone, for the moment, the question of what price standard might be most suitable). In order to be cautious and not to promise more than could be performed, let us assume that we shall be contented, at the outset at least, if the value of sterling were kept stable, in terms of the prices of the selected group of commodities, within five percent on either side of the normal figure, i.e. that an extreme range of fluctuation of ten per cent would be permitted.

Now it is a curious point, often overlooked, that technically it is enormously easier to work such a system so long as there are some important countries remaining on a rigid gold standard, than it would be if the world as a whole were to endeavour to work such a system. Personally I believe that the world as a whole might learn to work it successfully; but unquestionably it would be much more difficult than it would be in the existing situation in which it is fairly safe to assume that France and the United States at least will remain on a rigid gold standard for some time yet.

If *every* country were to abandon gold, that would present a new problem, not quite the same as the present problem. The present problem is to evolve a system which is adapted to a world in which gold still plays a leading part as the regulator of currency and credit and as the standard of value. And, as it happens, this is the easier problem of the two.

On this assumption, namely that some important countries still adhere to a rigid gold standard, and that there are practical advantages in maintaining some definite relationship between sterling and gold, the method might be, I suggest, as follows:—

1. At any given time the Bank of England would announce

official prices at which it would be prepared to buy or sell gold or gold exchange in exchange for sterling. But these gold parities would not be intended to be immutable. On the contrary, they would be subject to change from time to time—probably by not more than one per cent at a time—in the event of a change in the value of gold relatively to the group of commodities which had been selected as the norm of sterling. In fact, just as the Bank of England is free to change its Bank rate from time to time (as a rule by moderate stages), so it would be free to change its buying and selling rates for gold—but only in prescribed circumstances which would be laid down beforehand, namely when gold itself was changing its commodity value. In ordinary circumstances the position would be much the same as formerly, except that it would probably be advisable to have a somewhat wider range between the buying and selling prices for gold ('the gold points') so as to prevent speculative anticipation when the course of prices was indicating a probability of a change in the Bank's official gold rates. E.g. if the gold points were separated by two per cent and the Bank normally changed its gold parity by not more than one per cent, speculative anticipation would not have great attractions—certainly no greater attractions than existed formerly in the case of anticipations of a change in the Bank rate. Only in the event of gold standard countries pursuing a policy which involved a material fluctuation in the commodity value of gold, would there be any material change in the gold parity of sterling or in the sterling exchange on gold standard countries. The Bank of England would be under no obligation to change its gold rates in response to every small fluctuation in terms of gold of the index number chosen as its norm, but only when the commodity value of gold seemed to be showing a definite trend away from the commodity norm of sterling.

I submit that a scheme of this kind would furnish a satisfactory compromise between different views as to the ideal ultimate solution, and would not pre-judge questions which only the future can settle satisfactorily. I claim this for the following reasons:—

(1) It is a good working compromise between the ideals of exchange stability and of price stability.

(2) It provides an anchor for sterling, which could be a complete safeguard against the 'vicious spiral' of rising wages and prices, without linking sterling irrevocably to gold in circumstances where there is no guarantee as to the future behaviour of gold.

(3) It retains gold in the same position as formerly as the ultimate reserve of the currency and credit system and as the medium for settling differences in the international balances of payments which are not settled otherwise.

(4) It is not in any way incompatible with coming ultimately to an understanding with the gold standard countries. For the link with gold is retained and if hereafter some scheme can be worked out by international co-operation for securing some reasonable measure of stability in the commodity value of gold, then sterling will automatically recover a stable value in terms of gold as well as of prices.

(5) Nor is it incompatible with an ultimate recovery of the gold value of sterling to its old parity—provided external circumstances develop in a way favourable to such a consummation. For example, assuming it to be decided that the rigidity of wages and the burden of money debts in the sterling countries require that the norm adopted for sterling should not be higher than that corresponding to the 1929 wholesale price level, then, in the event of the gold standard countries so conducting their credit policy as gradually to restore the gold price level to the 1929 level, then automatically the gold value of sterling would return *pari passu* to its old parity; whilst if on the contrary gold prices were to continue to fall or were to fail to recover, then we should be protected from the danger of having committed ourselves to something which, owing to the rigidity of wages and the burden of War debt, might be nationally disastrous. Indeed the scheme here proposed would constitute, so to speak, a declaration of the terms, laid down beforehand with adequate precision, subject to which sterling might be expected to recover

to its former relationships with the currencies which continue to adhere to the gold standard without change of parity.

IV

There remains the important and difficult question as to what norm it would be most prudent to adopt by which to determine the future commodity value of sterling.

I think that there are four leading criteria, each of which has its supporters:—

1. The first school of thought lays stress on the importance of choosing a value of sterling high enough to make it unlikely that the cost of living will rise sufficiently to provoke a not unreasonable demand for a general rise in the level of money wages. For they are afraid of the 'vicious spiral' and consider this to be the best safeguard against it. This school of thought generally has in mind some value of sterling in the neighbourhood of $4 at the existing commodity value of gold.

2. The second criterion looks chiefly to the burden of the national debt and aims at reducing this to a more manageable proportion of the national income. This would suggest a value for sterling nearer to $3 than to $4 at the existing commodity value of gold. The governing idea behind this criterion is, however, at the opposite pole from that of the first. For the relief in the burden of the national debt would only be obtained in the event of a material rise in wages and money incomes. The first criterion accepts the perpetuation of the burden of the national debt relatively to the national money income at its present heavy level (apart from relief due to conversions or to a future increase in the national real income as a result of economic progress), and all it avoids is that further aggravation of the burden which would have become necessary sooner or later if we had remained on the old gold standard and had forced down money wages and salaries to a level in equilibrium with it.

3. The third school of thought looks primarily to the balance of trade, and this tends to work out to a figure intermediate between those appropriate to the first two criteria. For this criterion naturally leads to a compromise conclusion. It remembers the £120,000,000 per annum owed us by debtor nations which is fixed in terms of sterling, and is influenced on the one hand against too high an exchange lest it put so heavy a burden on the debtors that they default, and on the other hand against too low an exchange as reducing unnecessarily the commodity value of what is owing to us. Considerations as to the visible balance of imports and exports leads to the same conclusion. For too high a rate of exchange will hinder the development of an adequate *volume* of exports, whilst too low a rate may lead to our selling our exports too cheap in terms of gold, (as happened both to France and to Germany when their currencies were heavily depreciated) and thus affect adversely their aggregate *value*. Moreover if we give an excessive bounty to our exports, we run the risk of provoking reprisals of one kind or another; whilst too great a rise in the sterling price of imports might set in operation a premature movement towards wage increases.

In fact, it is not true that, the greater the depreciation of exchange, the greater the advantage to our balance of international payments. There is an *optimum* point, given by the exchange rate, at which our exports are on a sound competitive basis and are not further cheapened beyond that point or, more precisely, where volume *x* gold price is at its maximum; as modified by calculations as to the maximum gold value of the service of sterling loans due to us arrived at by reference to the point at which a further loss of gold value by the depreciation of sterling is no longer outweighed by the better chance of avoiding default.

My impression is, as I have said, that this criterion suggests a rate of exchange intermediate between those suggested by the first and second criteria.

4. The fourth criterion looks primarily to the position of

agriculturalists and other producers of raw materials. It is of great importance to the trade and prosperity of the British Empire which includes a large body of producers of food and raw materials, that the prices of their output should return to a level approximating to that of 1929. It is also of great importance to Great Britain through its ownership of assets abroad the income of which depends on the price level of food and raw materials. Exchange depreciation will be likely, if it does not go too far, to raise the sterling prices of food and raw materials by more than it raises those of manufactured articles. Looked at narrowly this might be held to be disadvantageous to Great Britain. But from a broader standpoint the net advantage of Great Britain probably lies, and that of the British Empire certainly, in redressing the disparity of price levels which is at present so adverse to the agricultural countries. For this is the necessary condition of a substantial revival in British export trade and in the income from British-owned equities situated abroad. We have already had sufficient experience of how terms of trade unusually favourable to Great Britain (i.e. a high price for our exports relatively to that of our imports) may nevertheless work out to our great disadvantage on a balance of considerations.

On this criterion there cannot be much doubt that a return of the wholesale price of the principal foods and raw materials of international trade to the level of 1929 is greatly to be desired. With gold prices at their present level, this would probably mean a further depreciation of the sterling exchange of not less than eight to ten per cent, or in round figures a dollar exchange for sterling of (say) 3.50.

Now all these criteria deserve, in my judgement, some attention. My guess would be that the first works out, assuming the continuance of the present level of gold prices, at an exchange of 3.75 to 4, the second at an exchange of 3 or even lower, the third at an exchange of 3.50 to 3.75, and the fourth at an exchange of 3.40 to 3.50.

But I would add the following supplementary observations as bearing on the final conclusion.

The first criterion seems to me to lose most of its force as soon as sterling is given some fixed anchorage. It is mainly applicable to the transitional period when there is no firm anchorage of any kind. Thus it is an argument against 'playing about' with a very low exchange, e.g. between 3 and 3.50, during the transitional period. But as soon as the time is ripe for taking measures calculated to minimise the risk of the 'vicious spiral', then this criterion loses most of its force. Indeed it is not desirable that the country should set its face, except quite temporarily, against all wage increases. If all goes well, it is to be wished that the existing disparities of wage rates, which are conveniently but not very accurately summed up as existing between the sheltered and unsheltered industries, should be redressed by an increase of wages in the lower paid industries which have felt the full force of the slump.

The criterion of reducing the burden of the national debt as much as possible should, I think be rejected, in spite of its obvious attractions,—partly because it would be too costly in terms of the third criterion, and partly because it would be so much more satisfactory to deal with it mainly by conversions based on a fall in the rate of interest.*

As between the third and fourth criterion, the decision must largely depend on our ideas as to the extension of the field over which we would wish sterling to be the standard. If we are thinking of sterling as merely a British standard, then we might

* My own view on the latter is a little different from that usually put forward. I believe that, if we pursue a right policy, *very great* economies will be obtainable in due course from conversions. But we shall only get the full advantage if the Chancellor of the Exchequer is exceptionally patient and always thinks more of his successor than of himself. My fear is that, as soon as a tendency to a falling rate of interest sets in, the Chancellor will snatch too soon and so lose much of the full potential gain. The iron rule of the Treasury should be to issue no new loan, whether as a conversion issue or as a new loan, unless it is repayable at the issue price, at their option, within ten years, until it can be done on a three per cent basis. This is a mere *obiter dictum*, but surely the Local Loans Fund should introduce some new kind of bond and stop issuing, at present rates of interest, what is in effect a perpetual security.

take as our norm something fairly elaborate, based on the British competitive position, or the British cost of living, or the like. But if we are thinking of it as a standard applicable to most of the British Empire or even to a wider field than that, and capable of being linked up at a later date with some general international standard, then we must select some much cruder norm based on the principal articles of international trade.

It is not an easy decision to make. There are much greater advantages than most people have yet admitted in purely national currencies managed solely in the interests of domestic stability and social peace, and allowed to fluctuate if necessary in terms of other national currencies. Experience may show in the end that this is the best arrangement for everybody. But I should concede that Great Britain has more to gain than most countries from adopting a standard which is uniform over a wide field, and also that the weight of practical opinion is at present opposed to purely national currencies.

If, then, we have ambitions to make sterling a standard adopted far beyond the boundaries of this country, we are driven towards the fourth criterion. Moreover, as it happens, the fourth criterion, moderately applied, does not differ very materially in practical results from the third criterion.

The argument points, therefore, towards adopting as the norm of sterling a somewhat crude index number of the main raw commodities of international trade with its base at the 1929 figure; and then fixing a gold value for sterling (maintained as heretofore by the Bank of England's buying and selling prices for sterling in terms of gold or gold exchange), based on this norm at the outset, and modified if necessary from time to time in the event of the commodity value of gold itself (measured in terms of the above index) suffering a material fluctuation.

As to the exact composition of the index, it is sufficient to say, as a general indication of what is in view, that the production index of the Economic and Financial Section of the League of Nations comprises the following 62 commodities:—

Wheat
Rye
Barley
Oats
Maize
Rice
Potatoes
Beet sugar
Cane sugar
Beef and veal
Pork
Mutton and lamb
Coffee
Cocoa
Tea
Hops
Tobacco
Cotton-seed
Linseed
Rape-seed
Hemp-seed
Sesame-seed
Soya beans
Groundnuts
Copra
Palm and palm-kernel oil (raw)
Olive oil (raw)
Cotton
Flax
Hemp
Manila hemp
Jute

Wool
Raw silk
Artificial silk
Raw rubber
Mechanical pulp
Chemical pulp
Cement
Coal
Lignite
Petroleum
Pig-iron and ferro-alloys
Steel (ingots and castings)
Copper
Lead
Zinc
Tin
Aluminium
Nickel
Silver
Natural phosphates
Potash
Sulphur
Natural guano
Chilean nitrate of soda
Nitrate of lime (Norwegian and ammoniated)
Cyanamide of calcium
Sulphate of ammonia
Superphosphates of lime
Basic slag
Sulphate of copper

This list could form the basis of discussion; and care should be taken in the selection of weights.

V

I conceive of the sterling standard as being managed by the Bank of England. But some machinery for consultation and discussion would be desirable if the Dominions, etc., are to be invited to adopt sterling as their standard. But this and many other matters of practical detail need not be discussed in this memorandum.

16 November 1931 J. M. KEYNES

The Governor's reply on receiving Keynes's memorandum is of interest.

From MONTAGU NORMAN, *27 November 1931*

Personal

Dear Mr Keynes,

I have not yet had an opportunity of studying the secret memorandum which you kindly sent me with your note of the 20th November. But I have taken the liberty of showing it privately to one or two here who are competent to judge of these questions.

I have not received any detailed comments but they make one criticism which I may mention; to me, immersed in the practical side of the question, this criticism seems pertinent.

My friends think that you have not sufficiently considered ways and means in relation to your first alternative and have too readily taken for granted that it is within the power of the Bank of England to prevent a decline in sterling. They also emphasise that little headway can be made in formulating appropriate permanent policies until sterling has attained some semblance of stability; this will require time and depend upon the successful solution of a number of difficulties, both national and international, which occupy the attention almost exclusively at the moment.

Knowing how much discussion lies ahead of us in this connection, I forbear to mention other points which, as regards expediency or the practical side, raise awkward questions. So, for the moment, let me merely thank you for remembering me and remain,

Yours sincerely,
M. NORMAN

Keynes's memorandum had the result of his being made a member of the Prime Minister's Advisory Committee on Financial Questions, when it next met on 26 November. MacDonald also circulated Keynes's memorandum to the Committee, as well as to some members of the Cabinet. The Committee did not discuss the memorandum at any length.

This was hardly the case in the Treasury where Keynes's memorandum arrived at an important stage in their discussions.[1] It was the subject of a long memorandum by Sir Richard Hopkins which became the basis of a Treasury paper for the Cabinet on a policy for sterling which the Treasury proceeded to put into practice from the spring of 1932.

On 4 December in response to a request, he gave Walter Case further views on sterling.

To WALTER CASE, *4 December 1931*

My dear Case,

I was very grateful for your cable. I have sent a short cable rejoinder today. But my ideas are not sufficiently clear cut to lend themselves very well to expression in cablese.

1. First of all there is the question of the sterling exchange itself. On long period considerations, I have held until quite recently that sterling has been overvalued. When, however, it falls below 3.40, I am inclined to take the opposite view and to consider it undervalued. This does not mean that I should be surprised if it were to fall further in the near future. Indeed, I think it more probable than not.

For one thing, the balance of trade on income account is certainly still heavily against us. Doubtless the anticipated tariffs have stimulated imports, whilst our benefit from increased exports, which is going to be very real indeed, in the case of textiles, will take a few months to affect the exchanges. Even after the figures appear in the export return, some little time will elapse before the goods are actually paid for by the foreign

[1] For the Treasury discussions see S. Howson, *Domestic Monetary Management in Britain 1919–38* (Cambridge, 1975), pp. 82–6, Appendix 4.

purchaser. Even when the full effects of the currency depreciation are felt on the excess of our imports over our exports, it would be optimistic to expect that this would be sufficient to outweigh the great decline in our shipping activities and the almost complete disappearance of current income from British-owned equities situated abroad. It is the decline in these two elements in our national income which are at the bottom of the trouble; and they cannot be remedied except by a recovery of world trade. Thus, until world trade recovers I should consider some adverse balance of trade on income account practically inevitable. Nor should I be very much afraid of it, since the adverse balance would not be very much over a moderate period of time, in relation to our foreign resources of one kind or another.

At any rate, it is certainly not this which is mainly responsible for the weakness of [the] sterling exchange. The newspaper stories that the volume of transactions has been very small are not reliable; there have in fact been very large capital transactions both ways, far outweighing anything attributable to the balance of trade over a period of a few weeks. Both the strength and the weakness of [the] sterling exchange have been mainly attributable to the casual excess, one way or the other, of the weight of capital transactions. There is reason to believe that in the aggregate withdrawals of foreign banking and other short-term foreign balances in London have been on a very substantial scale indeed. In the long run this means a strengthening of our position. These withdrawals have been balanced by large capital transactions in the other direction,—realisation of foreign assets, repayments from Germany which have been quite large, much improved Indian and Australian balance positions, and, in the period immediately following our departure from gold, the covering of bear positions against sterling which had been built up. In the last week or two, it seems likely that bear positions have been reinstated; but this, if it is the case on any substantial scale, is again a source of strength. I do not conclude from this that a further weakening of sterling is at all improbable; but it does mean that the latent elements of strength are very great, and if there were to be very weak periods I should prefer to act on the assumption that there will be a sharp recovery, rather than a progressive deterioration.

As regards the totals of foreign balances, it is commonly said that the withdrawals are mostly European, and that America has been quite inclined of late to buy sterling. I have much more reliance on the accuracy of the former statement than of the latter, which you are in a better position to check than I.

2. The next question is as to the probable effect of the depreciation of sterling and many other currencies on the level of gold prices. My first idea was that currency depreciation in the non-gold countries would tend to depress prices in the gold countries. But I have now rather changed my opinion about this. Today in a large number of the agricultural and raw material producing countries, the producer is now getting not altogether unsatisfactory prices in terms of his local currency. The effect of this is to relieve his extreme financial stringency, and the higher prices for his product tend to make him a more reluctant [seller] and not less reluctant. In short the effect of currency depreciation is to diminish the distress selling of agriculturalists and others. There is also another influence, which will show itself perhaps more in the coming months than it has hitherto. This is the fact that when a country is no longer committed to the gold standard, its central bank is no longer under the necessity of imposing such stringent deflationary measures. I think that the fact of the various departures from gold, once the initial panic is over, will be to relieve somewhat the previous deflationary pressure in the countries affected. Both the above factors, particularly the former, by relieving the pressure on the leading markets may have some favourable influence, even on prices in gold standard countries.

All this, however, is on the assumption that nothing is

happening in the gold standard countries themselves to cause a further deterioration. It is as to this that I feel most doubtful, as I have mentioned in my cable. If American gold prices fall further it will be, I should say, primarily due to the depreciation of sterling and to the further progression of the deflationary cycle within America itself. I feel very out of date now about conditions on your side. But observing them from a distance, I simply cannot imagine what possible event can lift you out of the rut. Doubtless it will be in the nature of some quite unpredictable event. But, unluckily, it is the characteristic of unpredictable events that they cannot be predicted. On general principles I should be disposed to prophesy that the present paralytic policy of the Administration must end in some overwhelming disaster for them personally. I should not be surprised if, when the Republican Party goes to the polls a year hence, its defeat may be almost comparable with that of our Labour Party. But whether that, or the anticipation of its possibility, will make any significant difference, I do not know. Remedies will doubtless be adopted from time to time, but always too late, and in circumstances to which they are no longer appropriate. So you must, it seems to me, wait for a miracle—which will doubtless occur in due course.

I have written a letter today to Walter Stewart in Basle[2] and shall very much hope to see him before he returns to you.

Yours sincerely,
[copy initialled] J.M.K.

[2] This letter on reparations covers the same ground as Keynes's paper to the Advisory Committee on Financial Questions (*JMK*, vol. XVIII, pp. 358–63) and is not reprinted here.

On 13 December, Keynes stepped back from the currency question, but not from the preoccupations of the previous few months when he addressed the Society for Socialist Inquiry. The revised notes for his speech appeared the next spring.

From The Political Quarterly, *April–June 1932*

THE DILEMMA OF MODERN SOCIALISM

Besides two arms and two legs for oratory, gesticulation and movement, socialism has two heads and two hearts which are always at war with one another. The one is ardent to do things because they are economically sound. The other is no less ardent to do things which are admitted to be economically unsound. I mean by economically sound, improvements in organisation and so forth which are desired because they will increase the production of wealth; and by economically unsound things which will, or may, have the opposite effect.

And there is a further distinction to make. Things which are economically unsound are advocated for two widely different sorts of reasons. The first set are in pursuance of the ideal. Those who are influenced by them are ready to sacrifice economic wealth for the attainment of higher goods—justice, equality, beauty, or the greater glory of the republic. The second set are political—to get up steam, to bribe political supporters, to stir up the embers of the class war, to irritate and exasperate the powers that be and to make their task more difficult and perhaps impossible, so that the mere force of events may compel their deposition and replacement. Thus some things may be advocated *in spite of* their being economically unsound, and other things may be advocated *because of* their being economically unsound.

These three *motifs* exist, variously compounded, in the breast of every socialist. They are seen magnified, and therefore clearer, in the *politik* of the Bolshevists, the changes and vacillations in which are due to the fluctuating preponderance of one or the other *motif*. The Marxian creed, I take it, is that the third *motif*, the revolutionary, should preponderate in the first phase, the phase of attaining power; that the first, the practical, should preponderate in the second phase, when power has been used to prepare the way; and that the second, the ideal, should preponderate when the socialist republic emerges out of the blood and dust and travail, fully fledged. The Revolution, the Five Year Plan, the Ideal—that is the progression. But the distinction between the phases is not clear cut—all three *motifs* are present in some degree all the time. For English purposes one might perhaps sum the *motifs* up as the political, the practical and the ideal.

Now it is, I suggest, enormously important to know what one is doing, in what phase one is dwelling and in what proportions the *motifs* are mixed.

For my part I should like to define the socialist programme as aiming at political power, with a view to doing in the first instance what is economically sound, in order that, later on, the community may become rich enough to *afford* what is economically unsound.

My goal is the ideal; my object is to put economic considerations into a back seat; but my method at this moment of economic and social evolution would be to advance towards the goal by concentrating on doing what is economically sound. But there are others, I know, who would prefer, even today, to advocate what is economically unsound, because they believe that this is the best way to gain political power (which in any case is the first step), and that to render the existing system unworkable is the only means of reaching a new system. In my judgement both these notions are false; because the ruin of the old system, so far from making the construction of the new technically easier, may, on the contrary, make it impossible. For it will have to be on the basis of increased resources, not on the basis of poverty, that the grand experiment of the ideal republic will have to be made. I do not overlook the difficulty of getting up steam when things are going reasonably well. But I consider that precisely *that* is the problem to be solved. To be sufficiently deep-founded on the best intelligences and finest and strongest emotions of the community, to be able to keep up steam when things are going reasonably well; to thrive, not on the vapours of misery and discontent, but on the living energy of the passion for right construction and the right building up of a worthy society—that is the task.

This leads me to the daily perplexity of British socialism, and perhaps of socialism everywhere, as I see it. The practical problem, the problem of how to do what is economically sound, is mainly an intellectual problem and, as it happens, a very difficult intellectual problem, about which there is much disagreement. But intellectually a large element, probably the predominant element, of the Labour Party is old fashioned and even anti-intellectual. It has been the trouble for years past that the leaders of the Labour Party have differed from the leaders of the other parties chiefly in being more willing to do or to risk things which in their hearts they have believed to be economically unsound. They have not fundamentally disagreed with the other parties as to *what* is economically sound or unsound. Mr Thomas's ideas, for example, of what is economically sound are, and always have been, almost exactly the same as those of the Tory Nationalists, Mr Neville Chamberlain or Mr Amery; and Viscount Snowden's ideas have been just the same as those of liberal economists and deflationists such as Mr Runciman or Sir Herbert Samuel or Lord Grey. They have been totally out of sympathy with those who have had new notions of what is economically sound, whether the innovator has been right or wrong. And this condition of affairs goes deep into the bowels of the Labour Party. For the same is true, on the whole, of many others of the party's most respected pillars.

Now this puts the Labour Party into a feeble position when—as it happened last summer as a result of the deflation—the country has got into such a pickle that there is an overwhelming and universal demand for a practical solution, when everyone is determined that, for the time being at least, we must ensue what is economically sound. For it means that in such a conjuncture most of the Labour leaders agree at heart with their opponents; so that having a bad conscience, they become exceedingly ineffective for the practical purposes of government. The Labour Cabinet was in a hopeless position last August, because most of them conscientiously believed in the gold standard and in deflation by economy, and were not prepared to throw these things overboard. Yet at the same time they were equally unprepared to sacrifice the political and the ideal *motifs* in which they had been brought up.

Therefore the first task of the Labour Party, if it is to be effective, is, as I see it, to become intellectually emancipated as to what is economically sound, without losing either its political strength and its political organisation, which goes so deep into the social and economic life of England, or its ideals and ultimate goals. For in the modern world it has to be one thing or the other. Either the revolutionary *motif* must prevail or the practical *motif*. Nothing lands you in a sillier position or one which will draw down more certainly or more justly the contempt of the British people than not to know, when you propose something, whether the object of proposing it is because it is economically sound or because it is economically unsound. No one knew at the last election which leg the Labour Party was standing on, least of all the Party itself.

For my own part I would urge that we stand at a point in economic evolution when it is desirable to concentrate on what is economically sound. There are two good and sufficient reasons for this. In the first place it happens that the most pressing reforms which are economically sound do not, as perhaps they did in earlier days, point away from the ideal. On the contrary they point towards it. I am convinced that those things which are urgently called for on practical grounds, such as the central control of investment and the distribution of income in such a way as to provide purchasing power for the enormous potential output of modern productive technique, will also tend to produce a better kind of society on ideal grounds. There is probably less opposition today between the practical aim and the ideal than there has been hitherto.

In the second place there is so much to be hoped today from doing what is economically sound, that it is our duty to give this *motif* its opportunity. For it may be capable of solving once for all the problem of poverty. At present the world is being held back by something which would have surprised our fathers—by a failure of economic technique to exploit the possibilities of engineering and distributive technique; or, rather, engineering technique has reached a degree of perfection which is making obvious defects in economic technique which have always existed, though unnoticed, and have doubtless impoverished mankind since the days of Abraham. I mean by economic technique the means of solving the problem of the *general* organisation of resources as distinct from the *particular* problems of production and distribution which are the province of the individual business technician and engineer. For the next twenty-five years in my belief, economists, at present the most incompetent, will be nevertheless the most important, group of scientists in the world. And it is to be hoped—if they are successful—that after that they will never be important again. But during this horrid interval, when these creatures matter, it is of vast importance that they should be free to pursue their problem in an environment—for they, with their mixed subject-matter, are, of all men, the least independent, as the history of their theory shows, of the surrounding atmosphere—uninfluenced, as far as possible, by the bias of the other *motifs*.

All this has been brought to a head, or at least brought to notice, by the radical changes in modern technique, especially in the last ten years, which are so brilliantly described in Mr Fred Henderson's *Economic Consequences of Power Production.*[3] Immemorially man's muscles have been, for the vast majority

[3] (London, 1931.)

of purposes and operations, the source of power, sometimes aided by wind, water and domestic beasts. *Labour*, in the literal sense, has been the prime factor of production. It made a vast difference when, for transport and for certain limited operations, other sources of power were added. But even the addition of steam and electricity and petrol have not made, in themselves, so radical a change, as has the character of the new processes of production which have, in latter years, grown up with them. For until these latter years, the chief effort of new machines was to render *labour*, i.e. man's muscles, more efficient. Economists could plausibly argue that machinery was co-operative, not competitive with labour. But the effect of the latest types of machinery is increasingly, not to make man's muscles more efficient, but to render them *obsolete*. And the effect is two-fold, first to furnish us with the ability to produce consumption goods, as distinct from services, almost without limit; and secondly to use so little labour in the process than an ever-increasing proportion of human employment must be occupied either in the field of supplying human services or in meeting the demand for durable goods which, if the rate of interest were low enough, would be still far from satisfied.

Thus the apparatus of economic organisation is faced with a problem of readjustment of unusual difficulty in itself. If it is true that this apparatus has always been misunderstood and badly operated, if the supposed inner harmony and self-balancing characters of the economic system, in reliance on which our fathers were ready to surrender the system to *laissez-faire*, are an illusion, it is a natural result that events should be finding out where our intellectual weakness lies. Our prime task, therefore, is to discover, and then to do, what is economically sound. This temporary concentration on the practical is the best contribution which we of today can make towards the attainment of the ideal.

On 6 January 1932, Keynes travelled to Hamburg where he was to stay with Melchior. Two days later he gave a lecture to the International Economic Society of Hamburg under the title 'The Economic Prospects 1932'. Although the content of the lecture overlapped somewhat with his later Halley-Stewart lecture,[4] Keynes turned enough of it towards German conditions to make it of considerable interest.

THE ECONOMIC PROSPECTS 1932

The immediate problem for which the world needs a solution today is essentially different from the problem of a year ago.

Then it was a question of how we could lift ourselves out of the state of acute slump into which we had fallen and raise the volume of production and of employment back towards a normal figure.

But today the primary problem is how to avoid a far-reaching financial crisis. There is now no possibility of reaching a normal level of production at any reasonably early date. Our efforts are directed towards the attainment of more limited hopes. Can we prevent an almost complete collapse of the financial structure of modern capitalism? With no financial leadership left in the world and profound intellectual error as to causes and cures prevailing in the responsible seats of power, one begins to wonder and to doubt. At any rate, no one is likely to dispute that the avoidance of financial collapse, rather than the stimulation of industrial activity, is now the front-rank problem. The restoration of industry must come second in order of time.

The immediate causes of the financial panic—for that is what it is—are obvious. They are to be found in a catastrophic fall in the money value not only of commodities but of practically every kind of asset,—a fall which has proceeded to a point at which the assets, held against money debts of every kind including bank deposits, no longer have a realisable value in money equal to the amount of the debt. The 'margins' as we call them, upon confidence in the maintenance of which the debt and credit structure of the modern world depends, have 'run

[4] Below pp. 50–62.

off'. The assets of banks in very many countries—perhaps in all countries with the probable exception of Great Britain—are no longer equal, conservatively valued, to their liabilities to their depositors. Debtors of all kinds no longer have assets equal in value to their debts. Few governments still have revenues equal to the fixed money charges for which they have made themselves liable.

Moreover a collapse of this kind feeds on itself. We are now in the phase where the risk of carrying assets with borrowed money is so great that there is a competitive panic to get liquid. And each individual who succeeds in getting more liquid forces down the price of assets in the process of getting liquid, with the result that the margins of other individuals are impaired and their courage undermined. And so the process continues. It is, perhaps, in the United States that is has proceeded to the most incredible lengths. But that country only offers an example, extreme owing to the psychology of its people, of a state of affairs which exists in some degree almost everywhere.

The competitive struggle for liquidity has now extended beyond individuals and institutions to nations and to governments, each of which tries to make its international balance sheet more liquid by restricting imports and stimulating exports by every possible means, the success of each one in this direction meaning the defeat of someone else. Moreover every country tries to stop capital development within its own borders for fear of the effect on its international balance. Yet it will only be successful in its object in so far as its progress towards negation is greater than that of its neighbours.

Where and how is this ghastly internecine struggle to stop? At the moment we are living on slender hopes of some sort of a seasonal recovery in the New Year which will reverse the trend. If these hopes fail, as they well may, it would not surprise me to see a closing of stock exchanges in almost all countries and an almost universal moratorium in respect of the repayment of existing debts. But what then? Through lack of foresight and constructive imagination the financial and political authorities of the world have lacked the courage or the conviction at each stage of the decline to apply the available remedies in sufficiently drastic doses; and by now they have allowed the collapse to reach a point where the whole system may have lost its resiliency and its capacity for a rebound.

Well, I have painted the prospect in the blackest colours. What is there to be said on the other side? What elements of hope can we discern in the surrounding gloom? And what useful action does it still lie in our power to take?

The outstanding ground for cheerfulness lies, I think, in this—that the system has shown already its capacity to stand an almost inconceivable strain. If anyone had prophesied to us a year or two ago the actual state of affairs which exists today, could we have believed that we could continue to maintain that degree of normality which we actually have?

Could anyone, inside or outside of Germany, have believed beforehand that Germany could have stood such a degree of economic and financial pressure as she is now suffering, without a collapse of her political and social organisation? Could anyone, knowing the present level of commodity prices, have believed that the great majority of the debtor countries producing raw materials would still be meeting their obligations? Could anyone, told the present prices of bonds in the United States, have supposed that the banks and stock exchanges of that country could still keep their doors open?

This remarkable capacity of the system to take punishment is the best reason for hoping that we still have time to rally the constructive forces of the world.

Moreover, there has been a still recent and, in my judgement, most blessed event (though not all of you may agree with me), of which we have not yet had time to gain the full benefit. I mean Great Britain's abandonment of the gold standard. I believe that this event has been charged with beneficent significance for the whole world. If Great Britain had somehow contrived to maintain her gold parity, the position of the world as a whole today would be considerably more desperate than it is, and default much more general.

For Great Britain's action has had two signal consequences. The first has been to stop the decline of prices, measured in terms of national currencies, over a very considerable proportion of the world. Consider for a moment what an array of countries are now linked to the fortunes of sterling rather than of gold. Australasia, India, Ceylon, Malaya, East and West Africa, Egypt, Ireland and Scandinavia; and, in substance though not so literally, Canada and Japan. Outside Europe there are no countries in the whole world except South Africa and the United States which now conform to a gold standard. France and the United States are now the only countries of major importance where the gold standard is functioning freely.

This means a very great abatement of the deflationary pressure which was existing six months ago. Over wide areas producers are now obtaining prices in terms of their domestic currencies which are not so desperately unsatisfactory in relation to their costs of production and to their debts. These events have been too recent to attract all the attention they deserve. There are a good many countries of which it could be argued that their economic and financial condition may have turned the corner in the last three months. It is true, for example, of Australia. I think it might be true of Argentine and Brazil. There has been an extraordinary improvement in India, where one consequence of the discount of sterling in terms of gold, which no one predicted, has almost solved the financial problem of the Government;—I mean the export of gold, previously hoarded. Already in the last three months £24,000,000 has been exported; and the export is now proceeding, and seems likely to continue, at the rate of some £3 million a week. As regards Great Britain herself, the rest of the world has a little overlooked, I think, the change in the last three months which represents, if not an absolute, at least a relative improvement. The number of persons employed today falls very little short of the number employed a year ago,—which is true of no other industrial country. The present actual rate of expenditure on the unemployed falls well below the Budget provision; and it is probable that there is now an appreciable surplus of budget receipts over expenditure, available for the reduction of debt. I am much more afraid of the sterling exchange rising above what I should consider the optimum point in terms of gold than of its falling too low.

It would not be true to say that there is as yet in any part of the world an adequate relaxation of the deflationary pressure. But the widespread abandonment of the gold standard is preparing the way for the possibility of such a relaxation.

Moreover, I consider it most probable that further currencies will join the sterling group in the course of 1932. In particular, South Africa, Germany and the Central European countries, and quite possibly (in spite of their present determination to the contrary) Holland dragged at the heels of Java which will find economic life under the gold standard increasingly impracticable.

You will notice that I include Germany and her neighbours amongst those countries which I expect to abandon gold in the present year. From the standpoint of the competitive interests of my own country, I do not altogether welcome this prospect. But for Germany it seems to me to be an indubitable necessity. I appreciate the reasons which are at present influencing your authorities away from this decision—the fears, so natural in Germany, of another great inflation, and the weight of fiscal obligations outstanding which are fixed in terms of gold. But I doubt whether the first of these two arguments really applies to the substitution of a sterling standard for a gold standard. At any rate, when the various negotiations now afoot have reached their conclusions, some mitigation of the present strain of deflation and taxation upon the German people will surely be unavoidable. And the reliefs which will be called for must include the abandonment of the burden and the pretence of maintaining the external value of the mark at a fancy figure. I appreciate the reasons of psychology and high politics which lie behind the present insufferable pressure on the economic life of the German people. But the continuance of the existing deflationary pressure, when the necessity for so impressive a demonstration has passed away, would surely be a disastrous mistake.

But there is a second major consequence of the partition of the countries of the world into two groups on and off the gold standard respectively. For the two groups, as they now are or as I predict they soon will be, roughly correspond to those which have been exercising deflationary pressure on the rest of the world by having a *net* creditor position which causes them to draw gold and those which have been suffering this pressure. But the departure of the latter group from gold means the beginning of a process towards the restoration of economic equilibrium. It means the setting into motion of natural forces which are absolutely certain in course of time to undermine and eventually destroy the creditor position of the two leading creditor gold countries.

The working of this process will be seen most rapidly in the case of France. I should expect that France's creditor position will be undermined before the end of 1932. The cessation of reparation receipts, the loss of tourist traffic, the importation of a large proportion of the world's available gold, the competitive disadvantage of her export trades with non-gold countries, and the loss of income from foreign investments will, between them, do the work.

In the case of the United States the process may be a slower one, largely because the reduction of tourist traffic, which costs France so dear, means for the United States a large saving. But the tendency will be the same. A point will surely come when the current release of gold from India and from the mines will exceed the favourable balance of the gold countries.

The undermining of the competitive position of the export industries of these gold countries will be, in truth, in response to their own request;—or, at any rate a case of poetic justice. The rest of the world owes them money. They will not take payment in goods; they will not take it in bonds; they have already received all the gold there is. The puzzle which they have set to the rest of the world admits logically of only one solution, namely that the rest of us should find some way of doing without their exports. The expedient of continually reducing world prices failed; for prices were dragged down equally everywhere. But the expedient of exchange depreciation relatively to gold will succeed.

Thus a process has been set moving which may relieve in the end the deflationary pressure. The question is whether this will have time to happen before financial organisation and the system of international credit break under the strain.

If it does, then the way will be cleared for a concerted policy of capital expansion and price raising—which one can call inflation for short—throughout the world.

For the only alternative solution which I can envisage is one of the general default of debts and the disappearance of the existing credit system, followed by a rebuilding on quite new foundations.

Obviously it is very much more difficult to solve the position today than it would have been a year ago. But I still believe even now, as I believed then, that we still could be, if we would, the masters of our fate. The obstacles to recovery are not material. They reside in the state of knowledge, judgement and opinion of those who sit in the seats of authority. Unluckily the traditional and ingrained beliefs of those who hold responsible positions throughout the world grew out of experiences which contained no parallel to the present, and are often the opposite of what one would wish them to believe today.

There remains one great matter to which I have made so far no allusion, but which may largely decide whether the world's financial organisation survives the ensuing months. I mean reparations and War debts.

In a sense this has ceased to be a question of practical finance. For neither reparations nor War debts are being paid today; and nobody imagines that any substantial sum will be paid in the near future. The choice today has become obviously what I declared it would become in a book which I wrote more than ten years ago [*JMK*, vol. III]. It is a choice between a final settlement by a great act of international appeasement and a general default in an atmosphere of international disgust.

It is a delicate matter for a foreign visitor to enter into detail concerning a problem which is at the very moment the subject of high international negotiation. But one thing I can say emphatically. No responsible person in England today desires the continuance of the payment of reparations and War debts in any shape or form. My country stands without reserve—all parties and all interests in it—for a total cancellation. We now know that the whole system of ideas and policy for which these obligations stand was a disastrous error—one of the greatest errors of international statesmanship ever committed. The thing has become, as it always should have been, hateful in our eyes.

But we are not the only parties to the existing agreements. Is it better just to denounce the whole thing without agreement? Or to seek and obtain a settlement by agreement at the cost of retaining some modest remnant of War debt? In some moods one is very much disposed to the former. If I were a German, I am sure that that would very often be my mood. But it may be, nevertheless, that this is a mood of weakness rather than of strength, and that it is still the course of patient wisdom to seek a voluntary accommodation.

For consider what vast progress world opinion has shown in the last decade, and how far everyone has moved to the German point of view? I would think it probable that an agreed settlement could be made today for an annual payment by Germany of less than a third even of the amount which I proposed, as a lonely voice in those days, in my *Economic Consequences of the Peace*. If a final settlement could be obtained in return for a very modest annual payment commencing, say, three years hence, would it not be preferable to the shattering turmoil and disorganisation of a failure to agree?

I am making no prophecy. I do not know whether such a settlement is possible. But I would plead that it is worth trying.

I have often been doubtful during the past years about the wisdom of what you call the Policy of Fulfilment. If I had been a German statesman or economist, I think that I should probably have opposed it.

But now that this policy has been pursued so steadfastly and for so many years, would it not be a pity not to harvest the fruits now that they are ripening, and Germany's patience and endurance is capable, perhaps, of winning the reward of an agreed settlement on lines which would have been hailed with enthusiastic triumph even a year ago?

Let me say, before I sit down, how happy I am to be in Hamburg again. Hamburg for me will always be associated with the name and the friendship of your great citizen Dr Melchior.

It was exactly thirteen years ago that we two first met—in a railway carriage in the station of Trier on the occasion of the negotiations between Foch and Erzberger for the second renewal of the Armistice [*JMK*, vol. x, ch. 38]. He and I were, I think, the very first two civilians from the opposed camps to meet after the War in peaceful and honourable intercourse. When we two shook hands in that railway carriage on January 15, 1919, there began the long and seemingly interminable series of financial negotiations of which we have not yet seen the end today. *I* have long ago—thank God!—escaped from the toils of official service and have been a free individual man endeavouring, no longer to mould directly the course of events, but to influence the opinion which in the long run determines things. But he has found it his duty for these long and terrible years to wear himself out, serving his country and serving the world too in the direct negotiations between governments, preserving under all provocations and difficulties the highest human standards of patience and truth.

I remember most vividly the impression which Dr Melchior made upon us members of the Supreme Economic Council of the Allies in those early days of suspicion and distrust at Trier and at the several conferences which succeeded it before the re-victualling of starving Germany—which was our joint object—had been secured. In this man, we all felt, we met a true representative of the honour and uprightness of Germany. And that, as I know, has been the feeling of the many succeeding groups of representatives of the Allied Powers whom he has met. He has done his country and the world great services.

On 11 January Keynes had an hour's interview in Berlin with Heinrich Breuning, the German Chancellor. On his return to England, Keynes recorded some of his impressions for *The New Statesman* of 15 January (*JMK*, vol. XVIII, pp. 366–9). He cabled the same article to *The New Republic*. As well, he provided Walter Case with a bit of additional material in the form of a brief note.

THE POSITION IN GERMANY

My broad reactions to my visit, which included a very instructive hour's private conference with the Chancellor, are given in an article which I cabled to *The New Republic*.

I have been to Germany at all the times of crisis since the War but never, I think, have I found them so extraordinarily depressed. They are not starving, as they were in 1920–21. Everyone has more or less enough to eat, but everyone is reduced to a dead level of absence of pleasurable anticipation. During the great inflation plenty of people were making money. Today no one is making money; no one has an income which satisfies him and no one sees any chance of an improvement, except as a result of drastic change.

The result of this is a unanimous and overwhelming determination to pay no reparations whatever. I did not find anyone, except those in the highest and most responsible positions, who were even prepared to discuss with me the possibility of Germany paying anything whatever, in any circumstances. Any German Minister who was to make any statement inconsistent with this could not survive a week. Nevertheless I do not believe it to be true that they will not, in certain circumstances, agree to make payments. But they will only do so in response to a very moderate offer which constitutes a final settlement. I believe that the French are bound to be faced in the course of this year with the choice between final default on Germany's part or making them an exceedingly moderate offer.

We have all been working, not for an immediate solution, but for six months' delay, for four principle reasons: (1) to get over the Prussian elections and the German Presidential election, (2) to get over the French elections, (3) to allow time for further economic [and] financial pressure on France, where the economic situation is worsening at a great pace, and (4) to see if anything can come out of the Disarmament Conference, since there are many people here who are unwilling to quarrel with France so long as any hope remains of a satisfactory issue of the Disarmament Conference.

But a crisis cannot be delayed much beyond the middle of this year, and I should say that it is about even chances whether or not it results in the proclamation of default by Germany.

I discussed a good deal the question of Germany's remaining on the gold standard which, though in a sense nominal, is absolutely crushing their export trade. No one will admit in public that it is possible, or even conceivable, that a change should be made. Even in private they will scarcely admit it. But after conversations with many of the leading bankers, and those whose views would be decisive, I came away with the conviction that it is quite certain that Germany will depart from her present gold parity the moment that any suitable and convenient opportunity arises for doing so.

Meanwhile since most people know in their bones that the

present gold value of the mark is precarious, no one wishes to owe money in foreign currencies and everyone endeavours to transfer foreign loans into loans expressed in terms of marks. This leads, paradoxically, to a keen desire to discharge foreign debts, particularly sterling debts, and the Reichsbank has to struggle, with only very limited success, against too much of the available exchange being used up in this way. It also means that there is a great shortage of foreign bills, since every importer vastly prefers to finance his business, if he can, by means of a mark overdraft, or by selling some mark asset, rather than by drawing a foreign currency bill.

21 January 1932 J.M.K.

On 4 February, Keynes took part in a lecture series organised by the Halley-Stewart Trust under the general title 'The World's Economic Crisis and the Way of Escape'. For this lecture, Keynes re-worked his Hamburg lecture of 8 January. Keynes also gave his Halley-Stewart lecture in Cambridge on 18 February to the Marshall Society, the undergraduate economics club. J. N. Keynes and A. V. Hill, Keynes's father and brother-in-law, were present on that occasion.

The lecture appeared in the volume prepared by the Trust and in *The Atlantic Monthly* for May 1932.

From The World's Economic Crisis and the Way of Escape (*London, 1932*)

I

The immediate problem for which the world needs a solution today is different from the problem of a year ago. Then it was a question of how we could lift ourselves out of the state of acute slump into which we had fallen, and raise the volume of production and of employment back towards a normal figure. But today the primary problem is to avoid a far-reaching financial crisis. There is now no possibility of reaching a normal level of production in the near future. Our efforts are directed towards the attainment of more limited hopes. Can we prevent an almost complete collapse of the financial structure of modern capitalism? With no financial leadership left in the world and profound intellectual error as to causes and cures prevailing in the responsible seats of power, one begins to wonder and to doubt. At any rate, no one is likely to dispute that for the world as a whole the avoidance of financial collapse, rather than the stimulation of industrial activity, is now the front-rank problem. The restoration of industry must come second in order of time.

The immediate causes of the world financial panic—for that is what it is—are obvious. They are to be found in a catastrophic fall in the money value not only of commodities but of practically every kind of asset. The 'margins', as we call them, upon confidence in the maintenance of which the debt and credit structure of the modern world depends have 'run off'. In many countries the assets of banks—perhaps in most countries with the exception of Great Britain—are no longer equal, conservatively valued, to their liabilities to their depositors. Debtors of all kinds find that their securities are no longer the equal of their debts. Few governments still have revenues sufficient to cover the fixed money charges for which they have made themselves liable.

Moreover, a collapse of this kind feeds on itself. We are now in the phase where the risk of carrying assets with borrowed money is so great that there is a competitive panic to get liquid. And each individual who succeeds in getting more liquid forces down the price of assets in the process, with the result that the margins of other individuals are impaired and their courage undermined. And so the process continues. It is perhaps in the United States that this has proceeded to the most incredible lengths. The collapse of values there has reached astronomical dimensions. Between January 1930 and September 1931 the market value of the common stocks listed on the New York

Stock Exchange fell from $65,000 million to $45,000 million. One supposed that by that date the slump was far advanced. But the financial panic, as distinct from the industrial slump, was still to come. In the four months from September 1931 to January 1932 there was a further fall, equal in absolute amount to the former and in percentage amount much greater, namely from $45,000 million to $27,000 million. Yet this was perhaps the least part of the financial crash; for common stock values in America are notoriously volatile. The market value of bonds, which had not fallen at all between January 1930 and September 1931, declined in the next four months from $47,000 million to $38,000 million, that is to say, an *average* decline of 25 per cent. The fall in preferred stocks was greater still, and the position in real estate was not less serious. But the United States only offers an example, extreme owing to the psychology of its people, of a state of affairs which exists in some degree almost everywhere.

The competitive struggle for liquidity has now extended beyond individuals and institutions to nations and to governments, each of which endeavours to make its international balance sheet more liquid by restricting imports and stimulating exports by every possible means, the success of each one in this direction meaning the defeat of someone else. Moreover, every country discourages capital development within its own borders for fear of the effect on its international balance. Yet it will only be successful in its object in so far as its progress towards negation is greater than that of its neighbours.

We have here an extreme example of the *disharmony* of general and particular interest. Each nation, in an effort to improve its relative position, takes measures injurious to the absolute prosperity of its neighbours; and since its example is not confined to itself, it suffers more from similar action by its neighbours than it gains by such action itself. Practically all the remedies popularly advocated today are of this internecine character. Competitive wage reductions, competitive tariffs, competitive liquidation of foreign assets, competitive currency deflations, competitive economy campaigns, competitive contractions of new development—all are of this beggar-my-neighbour description. The modern capitalist is a fair-weather sailor. As soon as a storm rises he abandons the duties of navigation and even sinks the boats which might carry him to safety by his haste to push his neighbours off and himself in.

I have spoken of competitive economy campaigns and competitive contractions of new development. But perhaps this needs a little more explanation. An economy campaign, in my opinion, is a beggar-my-neighbour enterprise, just as much as competitive tariffs or competitive wage reductions, which are perhaps more obviously of this description. For one man's expenditure is another man's income. Thus whenever we refrain from expenditure, whilst we undoubtedly increase our own margin, we diminish that of someone else; and if the practice is universally followed, everyone will be worse off. An individual may be forced by his private circumstances to curtail his normal expenditure, and no one can blame him. But let no one suppose that he is performing a public duty in behaving in such a way. An individual or an institution or a public body, which voluntarily and unnecessarily curtails or postpones expenditure which is admittedly useful, is performing an anti-social act.

Unfortunately the popular mind has been educated away from the truth, away from common sense. The average man has been taught to believe what his own common sense, if he relied on it, would tell him was absurd. Even remedies of a right tendency have become discredited because of the failure of a timid and vacillating application of them at an earlier stage.

Now, at last, under the teaching of hard experience, there may be some slight movement towards wiser counsels. But through lack of foresight and constructive imagination the financial and political authorities of the world have lacked the courage or the conviction at each stage of the decline to apply the available remedies in sufficiently drastic doses; and by now they have allowed the collapse to reach a point where the whole system may have lost its resiliency and its capacity for a rebound.

Meanwhile the problem of reparations and war debts darkens the whole scene. We all know that these are now as dead as mutton, and as distasteful as stale mutton. There is no question of any substantial payments being made. The problem has ceased to be financial and has become entirely political and psychological. If in the next six months the French were to make a very moderate and reasonable proposal in final settlement, I believe that the Germans, in spite of all their present protestations to the contrary, would accept it and would be wise to accept it. But to all outward appearances the French mind appears to be hardening against such a solution and in favour of forcing a situation in which Germany will default. French politicians are feeling that it will be much easier for them, *vis-à-vis* the home political front, to get rid of reparations by a German default than to reach by agreement a moderate sum, most of which might have to be handed on to the United States. Moreover, this outcome would have what they deem to be the advantage of piling up grievances and a legal case against Germany for use in connection with the other outstanding questions created between the two countries by the Treaty of Versailles. I cannot, therefore, extract much comfort or prospective hope from developments in this sphere of international finance.

II

Well, I have painted the prospect in the blackest colours. What is there to be said on the other side? What elements of hope can we discern in the surrounding gloom? And what useful action does it still lie in our power to take?

The outstanding ground for cheerfulness lies, I think, in this—that the system has shown already its capacity to stand an almost inconceivable strain. If anyone had prophesied to us a year or two ago the actual state of affairs which exists today, could we have believed that the world could continue to maintain that even degree of normality which we actually have? Could anyone, knowing the present level of commodity prices, have believed that the great majority of the debtor countries producing raw materials would still be meeting their obligations? Could anyone, told the present prices of bonds in the United States, have supposed that the banks and stock exchanges of that country could still keep their doors open? Could anyone, inside or outside of Germany, have believed beforehand that Germany could have stood such a degree of economic and financial pressure as she is now suffering, without a collapse of her political and social organisation? This remarkable capacity of the system to take punishment is the best reason for hoping that we still have time to rally the constructive forces of the world.

Moreover, there has been a still recent and, in my judgement, most blessed event, of which we have not yet had time to gain the full benefit. I mean Great Britain's abandonment of the gold standard. I believe that this event has been charged with beneficent significance over a wide field. If Great Britain had somehow contrived to maintain her gold parity, the position of the world as a whole today would be considerably more desperate than it is, and default more general.

For Great Britain's action has had two signal consequences. The first has been to stop the decline of prices, measured in terms of national currencies, over a very considerable proportion of the world. Consider for a moment what an array of countries are now linked to the fortunes of sterling rather than of gold. Australasia, India, Ceylon, Malaya, East and West Africa, Egypt, Ireland and Scandinavia; and, in substance though not so literally, South America, Canada and Japan. Outside Europe there are no countries in the whole world except South Africa and the United States which now conform to a gold standard. France and the United States are the only remaining countries of major importance where the gold standard is functioning freely.

This means a very great abatement of the deflationary pressure which was existing six months ago. Over wide areas producers are now obtaining prices in terms of their domestic currencies which are not so desperately unsatisfactory in relation to their costs of production and to their debts. These events have been too recent to attract all the attention they deserve. There are several countries of which it could be argued that their economic and financial condition may have turned the corner in the last six months. It is true, for example, of Australia. I think it may be true of Argentine and Brazil. There has been an extraordinary improvement in India, where one consequence of the discount of sterling in terms of gold, which no one predicted, has almost solved the financial problem of the Government—I mean the export of gold previously hoarded. Already in the four months since October 1931, £36 million has been exported; and the export is now proceeding, and seems likely to continue, at the rate of above £1 million a week. As regards Great Britain herself, the rest of the world, and even we ourselves perhaps, may have a little overlooked the change since last September, which represents, if not an absolute, at least a relative, improvement. The number of persons employed today is not less than the number employed a year ago, which is true of no other industrial country. The present actual rate of expenditure on the unemployed falls well below the Budget provision. This has been achieved in spite of the fact that there has been, even during the past year, a further rise in real wages; for whilst money wages have fallen by 2 per cent, the cost of living, in spite of the depreciation of the sterling exchange, has fallen by 4 per cent. And the explanation is an encouragement for the future. For the explanation lies in the fact that over a wide field of her characteristic activities Great Britain today is once again the cheapest producer in the world. I believe that our textile industries can now produce more cheaply than their chief competitors over a wide range of qualities. I believe that we can run ships today at a lower cost than anyone else. I believe that we have an opportunity of making a bid for the best part of the world's export trade in motor cars and motor lorries. All this will tell increasingly with time. The forces set on foot last September have by no means had time as yet to work their full effect. But even today Great Britain is decidedly the most prosperous country in the world.

Perhaps you will retort that hopes based on an improvement in Great Britain's competitive position are inconsistent with what I was saying a few minutes ago about the uselessness of one country gaining at the expense of another. You may also think it an inconsistency with what I was saying then that I should have advocated a protective tariff for this country last year and am not prepared to oppose it today with any heat of conviction. The explanation is to be found in my belief that it is a necessary preliminary to world recovery that this country should regain its liberty of action and its power of international initiative. I believe, further, that we and we alone can be trusted to use that power of initiative, when once we have regained it, to the general advantage. I agree with those who think that many of the difficulties of recent years were due to the fact that the creditor balance available to finance new international investment had largely passed out of our hands into the hands of France and the United States. And I therefore welcome, and indeed require as an indispensable preliminary to a world recovery, that there should be a material strengthening of the creditor position of Great Britain.

It would not be true to say, in spite of these favourable developments, that there is as yet in any part of the world an adequate relaxation of the deflationary pressure. But the widespread abandonment of the gold standard is preparing the way for the possibility of such a relaxation. Moreover, I consider it not unlikely that further currencies will join the sterling group in the course of 1932; in particular South Africa, Germany and the Central European countries, and quite possibly (in spite of their present determination to the contrary) Holland dragged at the heels of Java which will find economic life under the gold standard increasingly impracticable.

But there is a second major consequence of the partition of the countries of the world into two groups on and off the gold standard respectively. For the two groups as they now are, or as they soon may be, roughly correspond to those which have been exercising deflationary pressure on the rest of the world by having a *net* creditor position which causes them to draw gold and those which have been suffering this pressure. Now the departure of the latter group from gold means the beginning of a process towards the restoration of economic equilibrium. It means the setting into motion of natural forces which are certain in course of time to undermine and eventually destroy the creditor position of the two leading creditor gold countries.

The process will be seen most rapidly in the case of France, whose creditor position is likely to be completely undermined before the end of 1932. The cessation of reparation receipts, the loss of tourist traffic, the competitive disadvantage of her export trades with non-gold countries, and the importation of a large proportion of the world's available gold will, between them, do the work. And, when the last gold bar in the world has been safely lodged in the Bank of France, that will be the appropriate moment for the German Government to announce that one of their chemists has just perfected his technique for making the stuff at 6d. an ounce.

In the case of the United States the process may be a slower one, largely because the reduction of tourist traffic, which costs France so dear, means for the United States a large saving. But the tendency will be the same. A point will surely come when the current release of gold from India and from the mines will exceed the favourable balance of the gold countries.

The undermining of the competitive position of the export industries of these gold countries will be, in truth, in response to their own request; or, at any rate, a case of poetic justice. The rest of the world owes them money. They will not take payment in goods; they will not take it in bonds; they have already received all the gold there is. The puzzle which they have set to the rest of the world admits logically of only one solution, namely that some way must be found of doing without their exports. The expedient of continually reducing world prices failed; for prices were dragged down equally everywhere. But the expedient of exchange depreciation relatively to gold will succeed.

Thus a process has been set moving which may relieve in the end the deflationary pressure. The question is whether this will have time to happen before financial organisation and the system of international credit break under the strain. If they do, then the way will be cleared for a concerted policy, probably under the leadership of Great Britain, of capital expansion and price raising throughout the world. For without this the only alternative solution which I can envisage is one of the general default of debts and the disappearance of the existing credit system, followed by rebuilding on quite new foundations.

The following, then, is the chapter of events which might conceivably— I will not attempt to evaluate the probability of their occurrence—lead us out of the bog. The financial crisis might wear itself out before a point of catastrophe and general default had been reached. This is perhaps happening. The greatest dangers may have been surmounted during the past few months. *Pari passu* with this, the deflationary pressure exerted on the rest to the world by the unbalanced creditor position of France and the United States may be relaxed, through their losing their creditor position, as a result of the steady operation of the forces which I have already described. If and when these things are clearly the case, we shall then enter the cheap money phase. This is the point at which, on the precedent of previous slumps, we might hope for the beginning of recovery. The end of deflationary pressure will show itself in a firm tendency for the sterling exchange. We should use this strength to cheapen money and increase the volume of credit, to restart home activity and to lend abroad to the utmost of our powers. For the impulse to world recovery will have to come from us in the first instance, and not from the United States.

I am not confident, however, that on this occasion the cheap money phase will be sufficient by itself to bring about an adequate recovery of new investment. Cheap money means that the riskless, or supposedly riskless, rate of interest will be low. But actual enterprise always involves some degree of risk. It may still be the case that the lender, with his confidence shattered by his experiences, will continue to ask for new enterprise rates of interest which the borrower cannot expect to earn. Indeed this was already the case in the moderately cheap money phase which preceded the financial crisis of last autumn.

If this proves to be so, there will be no means of escape from prolonged and perhaps interminable depression except by direct state intervention to promote and subsidise new investment. Formerly there was no expenditure out of the proceeds of borrowing, which it was thought proper for the state to incur, except war. In the past, therefore, we have not infrequently had to wait for a war to terminate a major depression. I hope that in the future we shall not adhere to this purist financial attitude, and that we shall be ready to spend on the enterprises of peace what the financial maxims of the past would only allow us to spend on the devastations of war. At any rate I predict with an assured confidence that the only way out is for us to discover *some* object which is admitted even by the dead-heads to be a legitimate excuse for largely increasing the expenditure of someone on something!

In all our thoughts and feelings and projects for the betterment of things, we should have it at the back of our heads that this is not a crisis of poverty but a crisis of abundance. It is not the harshness and the niggardliness of nature which is oppressing us, but our own incompetence and wrong-headedness which hinders us from making use of the bountifulness of inventive science and causes us to be overwhelmed by its generous fruits. The voices which—in such a conjuncture—tell us that the path of escape is to be found in strict economy and in refraining, wherever possible, from utilising the world's potential production, are the voices of fools and madmen. There is a passage from David Hume in which he says:

> Though the ancients maintained, that in order to reach the gift of prophecy, a certain divine fury or madness was requisite, one may safely affirm that, in order to deliver such prophecies as these, no more is necessary than merely to be in one's senses free from the influence of popular madness and delusion.

It is a high social duty today for everyone to use his influence, whatever it may be, in private and in public, in favour of every kind of expansion and expenditure, which is financially possible to those who incur it, and which in better times would be generally admitted to be legitimate and useful.

Obviously it is much more difficult to solve the problem today than it would have been a year ago. But I still believe even now, as I believed then, that we still could be, if we would, the masters of our fate. The obstacles to recovery are not material. They reside in the state of knowledge, judgment, and opinion of those who sit in the seats of authority. Unluckily the traditional and ingrained beliefs of those who hold responsible positions throughout the world grew out of experiences which contained no parallel to the present, and are often the opposite of what one would wish them to believe today.

In France the weight of authoritative opinion and public sentiment is genuinely and sincerely opposed to the whole line of thought which runs through what I have been saying. They think that if everyone had behaved as they have, everyone would have as much gold as they have. Their own accumulations are the reward of virtue, and the losses which the rest of us have suffered are the penalty of imprudence. They wish to go on to the grim conclusion. There is nothing to do with them but to wait for their conversion by the grinding pressure of events; though they are by nature such realists in the last resort that when the proof of experience arrives they may be unexpectedly exempt from obstinacy. In the United States it is almost inconceivable what rubbish a public man has to utter today if he is to keep respectable. Serious and sensible bankers, who as men of common sense are trying to do what they can to stem the tide of liquidation and to stimulate the forces of expansion, have to go about assuring the world of their conviction that there is no serious risk of inflation, when what they really mean is that they cannot yet see good enough grounds for daring to hope for it. In this country opinion is probably more advanced. I believe that the ideas of our statesmen and even of our bankers are on much sounder lines than those current elsewhere. What we have to fear here is timidity and a reluctance to act boldly. When once we have regained a power of initiative we must use it without hesitation or delay for expanding purchasing power ourselves and for helping others to expand. *We* must set the example. We must believe that safety lies in boldness and nowhere else. If we lack boldness and use our strength, when it begins to return to us, to consolidate our position, as the phrase goes, which means in practice assuming in our turn the role of deflating the rest of the world, then I recur to those prognostications of gloom with which I opened my remarks.

In December 1931, Wilbur Cross, the editor of *The Yale Review*, asked Keynes if he could manage an article for the March 1932 issue. Keynes said he could and began to prepare a piece under the title 'The Prospects of the Sterling Standard'. On 1 January Alwyn Parker of Lloyds Bank asked Keynes for an article for the Bank's *Monthly Review*. Keynes offered him *The Yale Review* article for publication in April, suggesting that the two articles would probably differ in detail, as Keynes had to send the American article off in the last week in January. Parker accepted.

Keynes sent his *Yale Review* copy, entitled 'The Prospects of the Sterling Exchange' to New Haven on 27 January. He then re-used the material in the article twice, once in a memorandum for the Scottish Investment Trust Company and then finally for Lloyds. Below we print the Lloyds version, which broadly follows the American version, except for updating and the *Postscriptum* (below pp. 80–2).

From Lloyds Bank Monthly Review, *April 1932*

REFLECTIONS ON THE STERLING EXCHANGE

The popular mind always rushes to extremes when something occurs to direct its attention on the exchange-value of a money. With a gold currency maintained at an unchanging parity with its neighbours, the forces which maintain these conditions are a silent piece of mechanism of which the ordinary man is quite unaware; its principles of operation are remote from his understanding. But when these forces fail to maintain precisely the old parity, then he concludes that they have lost their efficacy altogether, that the currency is entirely without real supporting forces, and that it will be the plaything of speculation and of panic psychology. He makes no distinction between a sound currency having an equilibrium value which is definite though not so high as the former nominal parity, and one which, attended by a prospect of illimitable government inflation, has slipped its anchors altogether. In short, he was quite ready to confuse Great Britain's departure from the gold standard last autumn with the post-war collapse of the Russian and Central European currencies. And if, on the other hand, sterling begins to improve a little, he is ready to conclude that there is nothing to prevent it from soaring back to par.

In fact, the course of sterling exchange since last October has been—subject to speculative intermissions—in fairly close accord with the dictates of fundamental factors to which, as usual, market psychology has adapted itself with great pliability. My object in what follows will be not so much to explain the past as to analyse the factors which will determine the prospects of sterling over the current year. Nevertheless, the story is a continuous one and the application of our principles to the immediate past will illustrate their application to the immediate future.

I

It is a necessity for a country that its international debts and credits (including those which arise out of movements of gold) should at all times be balanced. This seems a simple truth. But a great deal of what is said and written ignores it. For every seller of a country's exchange there must be a buyer. It is true that the level of value at which the balance is effected may be artificially improved by regulations which prohibit or restrict the sale of exchange. In this case the would-be seller of the exchange must be regarded as making a sort of forced loan to the economic system of the country whose currency he is not allowed to sell. But as for the transactions which actually take place, they *must* balance. Thus the momentary balancing one can take for granted. But really to understand which is happening and to know whether the rate of exchange at which the balance has been effected is a stable one, we have to segregate the flow of transactions on both sides of the account (which in the aggregate *must* balance) into three distinct sets (each of which, taken in isolation, need not balance, and in fact will not do so, unless it be by an improbable and transitory accident). The first is that which, in accordance with long traditional usuage, it is convenient to call the balance of trade (as distinct from the balance of payments, which refers to the totality of transactions); or, as we could more accurately describe it, *the balance of payments on income account*, since it includes all items of an income character. The second is *the balance of payments on capital account*, including foreign loans made or repaid and the sale or purchase of securities and other capital assets between foreigners and nationals. The third, which is not sharply distinguished from the second, may be called *the balance of payments on speculative account*, the characteristic of a 'speculative' exchange transaction lying in its being an attempt to make a profit out of a shortly anticipated change in the value of a currency and in the intention to reverse the transaction after no long interval.

Now, as I have said, the credit and debit items on all these accounts taken together must always exactly balance. For no one can sell a currency unless he can find a counterparty who will buy it from him; and whilst the buyer and the seller need not both belong to the same one of the three groups distinguished above, they must each belong to one or other of these groups. But the three sets of transactions are governed by largely independent considerations, so that we cannot reach clear conclusions as to the upshot of the whole matter in the particular case of Great Britain today, unless we discuss them separately.

A. *The balance of payments on income account*

This balance is made up of what is earned (positive or negative) on the balance of current business (i.e., shipping earnings, financial services, tourist services, sale of exports, etc., after deduction of the corresponding debit items, mainly, in the case of Great Britain, the purchase of imports) *plus* the income which is derived from past foreign investments.

For many years past it has been the normal position of Great Britain to have an *adverse* balance, estimated at £147,000,000 in 1929 and £192,000,000 in 1930, so far as concerns current business; but a very large *favourable* balance, estimated at £250,000,000 in 1929 and £220,000,000 in 1930 in respect of foreign investment income. In 1931 the Board of Trade estimated that the adverse balance in respect of current business rose to £275,000,000, whilst the favourable balance from foreign investment income fell to £165,000,000.

Thus the great deterioration, estimated at more than £200,000,000 altogether, which has come over the position in the last two years is due in roughly equal proportions to each of these two factors—our foreign income from current business has fallen by rather more, and our foreign investment income by rather less, than £100,000,000. Nevertheless, our position would have nearly balanced even in 1931 if our foreign investment income had not suffered so severe a decline. Indeed, there would, in my judgement, have been a surplus. For I feel some confidence that the Board of Trade have understated some of our sources of income, and I should be surprised if our true aggregate deficiency in 1931 was greater than £80,000,000. However this may be, in trying to remedy matters we naturally concentrate on improving the balance from current business, because that lies to a greater extent within our power, since there is little which we can do at the moment to restore our investment income. But this concentration on a practical problem must not lead us to exaggerate its importance as compared with a restoration of our foreign investment income, which may be said to be almost wholly dependent on a rise in the world price level and in world trade. And there is another statistical point where the emphasis is often wrongly placed, namely, as to the extent to which the decline in Great Britain's investment income is attributable to defaults on the part of her foreign debtors. In fact, so far, the decline in our fixed-interest receipts as the result of defaults is remarkably small. There have been no defaults within the Empire. Germany is still paying the interest due. In Argentine the bulk of the fixed payments are being met. I wish that I was in a position to quote exact figures. But my impression is that between 80 and 90 per cent of the fixed-interest payments due to Great Britain from abroad (excluding, of course, War debts) are still being paid as usual. No, the main loss has been from foreign properties which we own outright. It is in respect of income from British-owned railway companies operating abroad, tea and rubber plantations, tin and lead and copper mines, oilfields, land and development companies and so forth, that the decline in our favourable balance is mainly due. For the majority of such concerns today are making no profit whatever, and are even a drain upon our resources through having to draw on London reserves built up out of profits previously remitted to us. This loss of profits is entirely a reflection of the fall in commodity prices and can scarcely be made good in any other way than by a recovery in world prices.

As a very rough approximation to the facts, but one which is perhaps sufficient for our purposes, we may estimate that our 1929 investment income, amounting to (say) £250,000,000 or probably somewhat more, was divided about equally between our fixed-interest receipts and our profits from equities. Up to date the former have declined by perhaps 15 per cent, but the latter by 60 per cent or more.

Now the net result of all this is, in any case, very severe. Before 1930 our favourable balance from foreign investment income exceeded our adverse balance in respect of current business by (say) about £100,000,000 a year on the average. Late last summer, when we went off the gold standard, it was commonly estimated that the position was approximately reversed (and I still prefer this figure to the higher estimate now indicated by the Board of Trade); that is to say, our adverse balance on current business was running in excess of our favourable balance from investment income at a rate of £100,000,000 a year. Obviously the position was desperately unstable, quite apart from the capital and speculative transactions, which I shall come to later.

B. *The balance of payments on capital account*

The actual crisis of last August was, in fact, produced not by the growing adverse balance on income account, which, indeed, had not at that date gone far enough to be a major factor in the situation, but by the sudden development of an enormously adverse balance on capital account. The immediate cause of this was doubtless the breakdown of confidence in the ability of the London market to meet its short-term liabilities, engendered by the critical position in Central Europe and the realisation that much of London's assets there had become frozen or worse. But the more fundamental cause was the growing vulnerability of London—a new thing, a vulnerability which, in my judgement, had been non-existent at previous times of international crisis—due to the Bank of England's incautious handling of the position from 1925 onwards. By the return to the gold standard in 1925 at an unsuitable parity, the Bank had set itself a problem of adjustment so difficult as to have been well-nigh impossible. On the one hand, it was obviously impracticable to enforce by high Bank rate or by the contraction of credit a deflation sufficiently drastic to bring about a reduction in internal costs appropriate to the parity adopted. On the other hand, the maintenance of a low Bank rate, which would have rendered London unattractive to foreign short-term funds, would, in the actual circumstances of our trade balance and of our readiness to lend abroad, have led to a rapid loss of gold by the Bank and a much earlier collapse of the gold standard. It seems doubtful how far the Bank appreciated the character of its problem or the nature of the difficulties in the way of solving it. But the policy actually adopted was to preserve a middle course—with money dear enough to make London an attractive centre for foreign short-term funds but not dear enough to force an adjustment of internal costs. In this way we tided over the immediate situation by exploiting London's immense reserves of credit and prestige. We were even able to continue lending abroad on a scale almost commensurate with our former strength, in spite of our increasingly adverse balance on account of current business. But the inevitable price of this temporary ease was the accumulation of a heavy burden of short-term liabilities. The extent of this burden and the dates between which it was increasing fastest are not accurately known, since the Bank of England did not choose to enquire into the magnitude of these liabilities. But the evidence collected more recently indicates that in the six years from the middle of 1925 to the middle of 1931, the assistance obtained from this very precarious source was in the aggregate on an immense scale, as indeed many of us had at the time supposed it to be. The enquiries initiated by the Macmillan Committee discovered short-term liabilities to foreigners amounting to between £400,000,000 and £450,000,000. But these figures were not comprehensive, and subsequent events have shown that the true total was very much higher and may have amounted in June 1931, to some figure between £600,000,000 and £800,000,000 (the wide margin between the upper and the lower limit being mainly necessary to allow for the ambiguity of precisely what types of liabilities the figures are supposed to cover* and how far certain of the liabilities should be directly offset against counterclaims in respect of acceptances, etc.). On the other hand, the liquid available assets which London could mobilise rapidly to meet withdrawals did not amount to a third of this sum. Necessarily London had become, as I have said, *vulnerable*. Sooner or later, for good reasons or for bad, some loss of confidence might arise; and then, in all probability, the insecure structure had to tumble.

Much could be said concerning the period of actual crisis. But my present argument needs no more than the fact that the British balance of payments has had to face a huge withdrawal of these short-term foreign balances, not only before and during the crisis which ended in the suspension of the gold standard in September 1931, but also in the four or five months following. I surmise that between June 1931, and February, 1932, Great Britain may have repaid approximately half of her total liabilities, that is to say, an amount somewhere between £300,000,000 and £400,000,000. Certainly this has been an extraordinary feat, but it was not enough to save the gold standard.

Obviously these vast payments, occurring simultaneously with an adverse balance on income account, must have been approximately balanced by the collection of assets from abroad to a still greater amount. Thus huge capital transactions both

* For example, how are marketable foreign holdings of British War Loan to be regarded?

ways have been swamping the income balance and have been temporarily depriving it of the decisive importance which it must possess in the long run.

I have seen no attempt at an exact analysis of the resources out of which such great repayments have been effected. But it is easy to see what the major items must have been. Out of £130,000,000 which had been borrowed abroad by the Treasury and the Bank of England, £80,000,000 was still outstanding in February. The Bank of England depleted its stock of gold and foreign exchange (prior to the recent speculative movement dealt with later) by an amount not precisely stated but probably lying somewhere between £50,000,000 and £100,000,000. A considerable proportion of British acceptances on foreign account has been allowed to run off. Some substantial repayments of short-term advances to Germany have been received. Many foreigners owing debts in sterling have been quite willing to take advantage of the depreciation of sterling to discharge them. Many British investors and investment institutions have sold holdings of foreign securities in order to realise a profit in terms of sterling. And a decisive factor in supporting sterling has resulted from an event of quite first-class importance which no one foresaw. It deserves a short digression.

During the first three quarters of 1931 the financial position of the Government of India was becoming increasingly acute and was putting a serious drain on the resources of London. The catastrophic fall in the prices of India's exports and a considerable flight from the rupee were not only cutting off the Government of India from the possibility of remitting to London to meet its sterling charges, but were compelling it to realise sterling reserves and to borrow heavily in London to support the rupee. The position was so bad that one scarcely dared to contemplate what might be ahead. But the departure of Great Britain from gold, followed by India, has completely changed the face of the situation, and in a way that not a single soul anticipated. There has been, of course, one source of relief which was expected, namely, the higher value of India's exports in terms of depreciated sterling, making it so much easier to meet sterling obligations. But what we all overlooked was the psychological effect of a rise in the rupee price of gold on the minds of the tens of millions of Indians who are in possession of hoarded gold. For when it was discovered that gold could be sold for rupees at a profit in terms of rupees over the price at which it had been bought, there occurred a great and extraordinary event in the monetary history of the world—the tide of gold which had flowed from west to east for hundreds of years was suddenly reversed. Zemindars and peasants over the length and breadth of India began to sell their gold. The phenomenon became first apparent early in October. Melted ornaments of gold began to debouch from Bombay to a weekly figure of about £1,000,000, rose to £2,000,000 and then to £3,000,000. By the beginning of March the weekly rate had steadied down to somewhat above £1,000,000. The total outflow by that date had exceeded £40,000,000, and it shows no signs of drying up. Nor need it; for it is unlikely that this sum is more than one-fifteenth part of the hoarded gold of India.

Now this gold is sold forward against sterling, as soon as it is purchased, to one or other of the gold countries, mostly to France. The sterling thus obtained is paid over to the Government of India, in exchange for rupees, and used by them to replenish their sterling balances and to repay their dangerously excessive short-term sterling debt. Thus the equivalent in India's sales of gold is added immediately to the liquid resources of the London market; though a few months may elapse between the Indian zemindar bringing his ornaments to the touch-stone (still literally employed) of his up-country banker, and the arrival of defaced, refined and barren metal at its ultimate destination in the vaults of the Bank of France.

The Indian farmer and the African miner need only a little time to achieve the inevitable conclusion. The day must come, and not too far off, when our modern Midases will be filled to the teeth and choking. And that, perhaps, will be the moment which the irony of heaven will choose for granting to our chemists the final solution of the problem of manufacturing gold, and of reducing its value to that of a base metal.

> Witness the famous tale that Ovid told.
> Midas the king, as in his book appears,
> By Phœbus was endowed with asses' ears.

Meanwhile the historian may relate that our providential abandonment of gold has saved our Indian Empire, by its double effect in enhancing the value of India's produce and in leading to the realisation of her gold, from tragical and disastrous courses.

Finally, the benefit which the London market has secured from the strengthening of the position of India is a leading example of a general type. The sterling exchange today measures the financial strength, not so much of Great Britain alone, as of the whole group of countries whose banking systems are based on London. An improvement in the trade balance of India or of Australia or of the Crown Colonies or, indeed, of many other countries, gives almost as serviceable and immediate support to sterling as an improvement in our own trade balance. The competitive position of the agricultural producers of these countries, like that of our own manufacturers, has been greatly improved by the departure of sterling from gold. Thus in 1932, as compared with 1931, the improving trade balance of the sterling block is unquestionably one of the influences which is affecting favourably the strength of the sterling exchange.

C. *The balance of payments on speculative account*

There remains for the completion of the argument the action of the speculators. It is the business of a successful speculator to anticipate events a short time ahead and, by anticipating, to precipitate them. But when the anticipated event occurs he must reverse his transaction. Thus the speculative account can produce but a transitory effect unless it has the effect of changing the minds of those who are transferring capital for longer periods. Before Great Britain went off gold, speculation opposed sterling; afterwards the reversal of these transactions supplied a much-needed support. After the turn of the year some speculative support of sterling began to appear. By February the international speculator became convinced that there was little to lose and might be much to gain by supporting sterling, with the result that the avalanche began which temporarily overwhelmed the Bank of England and drove sterling from 3·50 up to a level, persisting for a few days, above 3·70.

This movement was on a colossal scale, comparable with the landslide in the opposite direction last summer, and it enabled the Bank of England to acquire very large stocks of foreign gold balances. Up to a point this was to be welcomed, as providing, first of all, funds with which to repay the Treasury's foreign short-term loans, and then to replenish the Bank's reserves of foreign currency. But a point came where the flood was in embarrassing volume. For the return of balances, etc., to London since the beginning of the year may well have amounted to something between £75,000,000 and £150,000,000. Moreover, it is exceedingly difficult to say what part of this vast sum represents the return of funds, of which London is, so to speak, the natural and normal home, and what part represents pure short-term speculation which will move the other way when the mass mind of the international speculator comes to the conclusion that there is nothing more 'to go for'. Certainly it seems probable that by the middle of March there were very large foreign balances in London of an unstable character, which might be a source of weakness and even of embarrassment later on, if it were not for the greatly increased strength of the Bank of England to meet any future reversal of trend. But we can feel some confidence that the Bank of England should now be in a position to control completely any purely speculative movement in either direction.

II

I neglect speculation, therefore, as a lasting influence. But I do not neglect the general opinion of the world as to the limits within which the gold value of sterling is likely to move. For this determines the rate of exchange at which more permanent foreign holders will be deterred from removing their sterling balances or encouraged to increase them. In fact, over the short period which has already elapsed since sterling's departure from gold, the rate of exchange has been more largely determined by the ideas of the average holder of sterling balances, including, in particular, the Bank of France, as to the rate at which it is good business to exchange sterling balances into gold balances and *vice versa*, than by the balance of transactions on income account. I fancy that one can even detect the motives and crude calculations which have resulted in the mean figure about which sterling has been actually oscillating. There was a widely spread feeling that from the competitive point of view British industry needed a depreciation of quite 20 per cent and that, if there is to be a permanent change in the future parity of sterling, it would scarcely be worth making for a lesser change than 20 per cent. Thus $3·90 to the £, which represents a depreciation of about 20 per cent, set the upper limit to people's ideas. Then, since it is not worth while to run a risk without some balancing hope of profit, the actual rate had to be somewhat lower than this to offer the necessary inducement. On the other hand, it has been felt that a depreciation of much more than 30 per cent, which corresponds to an exchange of $3.40 to the £, would be resisted by London as writing down too drastically the value of sterling debts owed by foreigners and as giving British industry an uneconomic bounty and one likely to provoke reprisals. Moreover, the removal of balances at a rate lower than this would mean that the loss which the foreign owner of the balances must cut would seem to him too great and perhaps beyond his capacity to write down, whilst on the other hand, the paper profit would become very tempting to those owing debts in sterling or to Englishmen holding foreign assets, and would thus stimulate capital movements favourable to sterling. If we take these upper and lower limits of $3.90 and $3.40, and then take something from the higher limit to provide the necessary inducement and something from the lower limit to provide for temporary scares and for the time lag before the balancing factors have time to act, we have the boundaries of sterling's oscillations. Within these limits the actual average rate has, I think, been determined by the decisions of the Bank of England as to the rate at which it is advisable to buy foreign gold currencies; and to a lesser extent by the decisions of the Bank of France as to the rate at which it is ready to cut its loss. It is as crude as this. These are the considerations which in truth settle the level of the sterling exchange over a limited period.

Now it is the character of a *capital* transaction to be, so to speak, 'once for all'. When the Bank of France has withdrawn its balances or a British investment trust has realised a dollar security, the effect happens *once*—it cannot be repeated. But it is the character of *income* transactions that they can be repeated year after year. If the improved competitive position of British producers diminishes our adverse balance on account of current business, this is a continuous, not a 'once for all' phenomenon. Thus in the long run the influence of the income transactions wears away that of the capital transactions like the drops of a waterfall upon a stone. The analogy is a good one. We can be certain that the waterfall will win in the end, but it may be a long time.

On the balance of considerations I see no sufficient reason for supposing that the adverse torrent on income account will be strong enough in the immediate future to shift the fluctuating value of sterling outside the limits which have been set, as explained above, by the ideas of those responsible for capital transactions. It is a case where a middle opinion is probably the best. I am sure it is a mistake to be bearish about sterling; for any material fall would bring into operation immensely powerful forces of resistance. On the other hand, I do not share the view, which a few hold, that a rapid appreciation of sterling might easily occur at any time; for there will certainly be for some time to come a heavy adverse balance on income account which will need a correspondingly substantial favourable balance on capital account to outweigh it.

Those who have been depressed by the existing indications of the magnitude of Great Britain's adverse balance on income account, have allowed too little, I think, for the time lag in the forces already set in motion. I have said that before the departure from gold the adverse balance was believed to be at a rate of £100,000,000 per annum. On the basis of the statistics available at the end of 1931 it was possible to maintain that the current adverse balance was then still higher. But a prediction based on this would have seriously under-estimated the prospective effect on Britain's competitive position of currency depreciation and tariffs combined. It is true that we are competing for a share of a terribly diminished aggregate of world trade. But there is still some trade to be done. And for the first time for several years Great Britain is now in many lines of production the cheapest producer in the world. The working off of old contracts, the anticipation of tariffs and the desperate but temporary efforts of competitors, especially in Germany, have rendered the current statistics of trade no satisfactory guide to what is in prospect. Our textile industries are producing 25 to 30 per cent more than they were. Our tin plate trade is almost flourishing. Our motor industry is in a position to get what export trade there is. Our heavy industries are not unlikely to improve within a few months. Our mercantile marine is now losing much less money than any of its competitors, which probably means that it will gradually secure a larger proportion of the available trade. I am hopeful, therefore, that the adverse balance on income account will soon be reduced to a figure below £50,000,000 *per annum* in place of a figure in excess of

£100,000,000; though I should scarcely expect to see any material favourable balance until, through a rise in world prices, our foreign-owned equities begin once again to yield us an income.

If these hopes are realised, we shall again have the value of sterling under our control, and we shall be free to work out our own policy as to what we want. When this position is reached—perhaps we have reached it already—it will be upon our own deliberate and voluntary decisions that the future level of sterling will depend.

III

There remains one set of considerations which are not to be neglected in a philosophic reflection on these matters. We have been arguing, so far, as if the value of sterling would be determined solely by factors directly affecting sterling itself. But the gold value of sterling is a symmetrical two-termed relation, and is as capable of being influenced by factors primarily affecting gold and the value of the currencies of the gold countries, as by factors primarily affecting sterling. In the recent past the gold value of sterling has been depreciated largely by the forces which were appreciating the value of the gold currencies. So much so that it would be truer to say that gold went off sterling than that sterling went off gold. A point came when the inherent stability of sterling prevented it from following any longer the crazy antics of gold. We tried to imitate the violent instability of gold, until the degree and rapidity of senseless change threatened so secure and stabilised an old-established social organisation as ours with danger to life and limb. Then at last we found it unavoidable to step off on to firmer earth.

But the prospects are, in my judgement, that the position of the gold currencies will soon be reversed. The strain to which they subjected the rest of the world was due to their having an unbalanced creditor position in their favour. Forces have now been set in operation which are certain to destroy that creditor position in course of time.

One has heard of a Senator from the Middle West who cried in a loud voice to Europe: 'We do not want your goods. We will not have your bonds. We have already got your gold. What we want is your money.' The Senator may be mythical, but there still remained a logical alternative left to Europe which he overlooked, namely, for the rest of the world to get on as best it can without buying the exports of those countries which have an unbalanced creditor position. The abandonment of the gold standard by a large group of countries and its restricted operation by others is an unavoidable means, adopted far from deliberately or even consciously, for destroying these unbalanced creditor positions by undermining the trade balance of the creditors. The creditors, by leaving open no other means of payment, have in effect demanded that the debtors shall find some way of destroying these creditors' own trade balance.

I believe that invincible forces have now been set in motion tending, with time, to the destruction of the unbalanced creditor positions. This will come partly by the means just described, namely, the undermining of the competititve strength of the creditor countries, and partly as a result of the very small remaining group of countries which are still functioning freely on a gold basis, being compelled to purchase as a commodity all the available supplies of gold metal. With the current output of the mines and the release of gold from India and elsewhere, a point has probably come already when these available supplies exceed the favourable balance of the creditor countries on income account; and before long they may be sufficient to more than offset capital movements also.

The forces thus set up will, therefore, tend towards the depreciation of the dollar and the franc. But since these currencies are, and will presumably remain, fixed in terms of gold, that can only show itself in a tendency of sterling and other non-gold currencies to appreciate. When this point has been reached, the future course of sterling and of the numerous currencies rigidly or loosely linked to it will depend on policy. After repaying what we have borrowed, we shall have the opportunity to use our growing relative strength to resume our functions as a foreign lender and to finance an expansion of output and credit and a revival of confidence. I hope that we shall resist an appreciation of our exchange, though this may prove none too easy, until we have raised the sterling price level at least to the level of 1929; and that, instead of chasing after that rascal gold, who is a worthless fellow anyway, we shall wait for him to come back to sterling as a result of gold prices also being raised to the 1929 level—after which he must do what he is told.

It is reasonable to hope that we are now moving out of the phase of *financial* crisis, at least so far as Great Britain is concerned. If there were to be a satisfactory settlement of reparations, even though the immediate effect on Central Europe proves disappointing, this phase would certainly be over. But it may need a prolonged interval of ultra-cheap money before the phase of *industrial* crisis begins definitely to pass away. On all precedent, I should expect after what has occurred a prolonged cheap money phase, proceeding to lengths not experienced since the eighteen-nineties, before enterprise revives towards an *optimum* level. The main object of our policy should be, I suggest, to accelerate the timetable, to reduce time lags and to hasten forward each inevitable stage. There is no longer any serious ground for fearing a collapse of sterling beyond our control. It is not sensible to be afraid of inflation, when the problem of stopping the deflation is so extraordinarily difficult to solve. The real risk lies in the recovery being too slow; and a bold policy will be the least dangerous.

Investors are a long way off lending for purposes which involve any material risk; and practically all new enterprise does, in present circumstances, involve a risk. They will have to be induced to consider reasonable risks once more by the yield on riskless bonds falling very low. I should hope to see the Bank rate reduced by rapid stages to $2\frac{1}{2}$ per cent, with Treasury bill rate at 1 or $1\frac{1}{2}$ per cent and deposit rate at $\frac{1}{2}$ per cent. I should not be surprised—though I still find that other people would—to see $3\frac{1}{2}$ per cent Conversion Loan standing at par within a year. Indeed, I can see no reason in past history or present prospects why it should not. Anyway, perhaps we may all agree that these things are devoutly to be desired. So it should be our motto to accelerate the timetable.

Postscriptum

Since the foregoing was written, the Bank of England appears to have ceased, at least for the time being, to control the sterling exchange, or to attempt to stabilise it at a level predetermined by policy. For the moment, therefore, its value is dependent on the whim of the speculator. How far this policy is deliberate and intentional on the part of the Bank, and how far the Bank has been taken by surprise by the volume of speculators' purchases of sterling and finds the handling of them technically unmanageable, has not been stated. It is obvious, however, that the technique of control needs some consideration. The Macmillan Committee pointed out that the resources normally at the disposal of the Bank are small in relation to the size of the London market and might prove inadequate in an emergency. They also suggested means for strengthening the Bank by increasing the resources at their disposal. Nevertheless, although nothing has been done to carry these recommendations into effect, it does not seem to me that the technical difficulties need be regarded as very serious. Indeed, the impediment may lie more in a hesitation to take decisions than in the difficulty of carrying them out when they have been taken. The following is a short list of some of the questions to be decided.-

(1) Large-scale transactions on the exchanges may involve in their final outcome large profits or losses. If it has not been

already decided whether these will fall upon the Bank or the Treasury, it ought to be settled. It would seem reasonable that all exchange transactions, including purchases and sales of gold, should be on account of the Issue Department, which would mean that the final outcome would go to the profit or loss of the Treasury.

(2) Should the Bank accumulate foreign exchange or gold? After the holdings of foreign exchange have reached a large figure, it might well be advisable to take gold. The possession of a large amount of gold will be no handicap later on when we are considering conversion schemes and large-scale international financial assistance. The gold will be more fruitful in our hands than in France or the United States.

(3) Should early steps be taken to bring down London short-term rates to a very low level, so as to reduce the yield on funds held in London by foreign-exchange speculators? Every argument seems to conjoin to enforce the advisability of this.

(4) Should the Bank operate on the forward exchanges as well as spot? Surely this would be wise. It would be more profitable; and it would ease the technical problem by reducing the amount of sterling cash which the Bank would have to find.

(5) If the Bank's assets are largely increased as the result of its purchase of gold and foreign exchange, should this be allowed to produce its normal effect on the volume of credit? If carried beyond the point at which Treasury bill rate has been brought as low as is desired, this might prove embarrassing. But it is easy to avoid it. The Government securities now held in the Issue Department could be replaced by gold or foreign exchange. Since these amount to £240,000,000 this expedient would suffice for a long time. But there are other ways of taking funds off the market if necessary, such as were evolved during the latter part of the War and afterwards.

(6) Should the Bank announce a pegged upper limit? It would steady the market if each Thursday, when Bank rate is

announced, the Bank were to announce a figure at which it would purchase gold until further notice. There would be an opportunity of varying this each Thursday. Nor would the pegged limit prevent the Bank from ever intervening on the market directly [if] it thought it advisable to do so.

(7) What should the initial pegged rate be? This is very much a matter of opinion. I should be inclined to start in the neighbourhood of the existing market rate and aim at working it gradually downwards until what the authorities judge to be the *optimum* rate for the time being has been reached.

(8) What is the *optimum* rate for the time being? I doubt if any responsible English authority would put it above 3·80 to 3·90. My own preference would be for a lower figure, say, 3·40 to 3·50. My main reasons for this are three. In the first place, I do not think that we ought to be carried away too much by the buoyant atmosphere brought by the foreign speculators—it is a gas which can easily escape. We need a figure which will not put too much strain on us when we are getting no benefit from repatriation of capital or speculative transactions. In the second place, British foreign trade will be brisker and the volume of employment decidedly higher if exchange is at the lower figure. An additional margin of 10 per cent makes a world of difference to a manufacturer. In the third place, it is most important that we should consider the interests of raw material producing countries which belong to the sterling bloc, particularly India, Australasia and the Crown Colonies. I feel sure that an exchange of 3·40 to 3·50 is decidedly more in the interest of these countries than 3·80 to 3·90, so long as gold prices remain low. If there were to be a substantial rise in gold prices, the question of the *optimum* level would have to be reconsidered.

In short, the popular notion, that the Bank of England is powerless and cannot fix the exchange at any figure it chooses within reason, is in my judgement, really quite groundless.

In the course of preparing his article on the sterling exchange, Keynes passed his proofs to Francis Rodd, who had returned to the Bank of England at the end of 1931 after spending twenty months at the Bank for International Settlements. Inevitably, Keynes made a suggestion.

To FRANCIS RODD, *24 March 1932*

My dear Francis,

There is one important point I forgot to mention yesterday. If it is desired to keep the exchange down without having to find large amounts of actual sterling, it is always possible to do so by operating on a forward exchange. It is, I should think, certain in present circumstances that a fair amount of purchase of forward dollars could always be kept going over and above any spot dollars which might be purchased. This is particularly so in present circumstances when a great deal of the demand for sterling is for forward rather than for spot.

There is a double advantage in proceeding by this technique. For if the Bank will sell forward sterling at a somewhat smaller premium than the market, this has the same effect as the lower Bank rate in diminishing the attractiveness of London as a depository of short-period funds. In the second place, so long as forward sterling is maintained at some premium over spot, the transaction pays for itself without any consideration of the opportunities of employing short-period funds abroad.

If it is really desired to keep the exchange down, I find it most difficult to suppose that there are not ways and means of doing it.

Yours ever,
[copy initialled] J.M.K.

From FRANCIS RODD, *3 April 1932*

My dear Maynard,

I am very doubtful whether one can in a storm trust oneself to securing a lump of 5 tons of lead on the wet deck of a ship wallowing in a heavy sea. The best one can hope for is that the lump (which is the speculator) will break through the side and go over board. If you have no luck it goes into the engine room and through the bottom.

By the way don't worry about the forward market & the heavy discount on forward $. It is too small to worry about and no one is using the discount + London int. rates to earn money. The forward discount is due to some heavy hedging—without spot sales—by U.S.A. against their own position i.e. hedging by forward purchases of £ bare—which the forward rate will neither en- nor dis-courage—because it is coming from the people who cannot sell their investments in N.Y. and yet will hedge at any rate of discount.

Sorry to be so incoherent but I am very rushed as I am just off for 3 weeks holiday.

Yours,

FRANCIS R.

As part of a series on the state and industry, on 14 March Keynes broadcast on state planning. His text appears below.

There is a new conception in the air today—a new conception of the possible functions of government; and in this discourse, the last but one of a series on the State and Industry, I must try to catch from the surrounding atmosphere, and re-deliver to it, what this new notion is.

It is called planning—state planning; something for which we had no accustomed English word even five years ago. It is not Socialism; it is not Communism. We can accept the desirability and even the necessity of *planning* without being a Communist, a Socialist or a Fascist. But whether it is going to prove possible to carry out *planning* in actual practice without a great change in the traditions and in the machinery of democratic government—that is the big question mark. It is perhaps *the* problem of problems which the post-war generation of young Englishmen, who will be in the prime of life over the next twenty years, have to solve.

The forces which are driving the notion of planning into our heads are drawn from two distinct sources. The first is the force of example. The Russian Five-Year Plan has assaulted and captured the imagination of the world. This dream is not yet a realised success—it is much too soon to say that—but it is not the preposterous failure which many wise and experienced people expected it to be. We are now—as a reaction from our mistake—much more inclined, I think, to exaggerate its success than to underestimate it. We are ready to give Bolshevism the credit for much which is, in truth, the mystery and glamour and excitement, immemorial and eternal, of—not Communism—but Russia. Russia under Stalin or Lenin may be more like Russia under Nicholas or Alexander than either Russias are like England or Germany or the United States. Moreover propaganda has produced its usual revulsion. We had been taught to think of Communism as involving so complete a destruction of human organisation, that when we learned that, after enormous sufferings and an incredible national effort of self-denial and the exercise of will, a Russian peasant can positively build a tractor of which the wheels go round and that there is a large electric power station at Leningrad, we gape with wonder and rush to the opposite conclusion that Communism is a roaring success.

And there is a second force of example—Italian Fascism which—attacking the same problem with an opposite mentality—seems to have saved Italy from chaos and to have established a modest level of material prosperity within a poor and over-populated country. Here again, when an Englishman learns that an Italian train has run to time, he gapes with wonder and is ready to accept the conclusion that Fascism is a roaring success.

For with our unmeasured arrogance, we judge the foreigner by a different and a lower standard. If the technical accomplishment of Austin or Morris or Courtauld had been achieved in Russia, if a Rolls Royce had been built in Moscow, if Sir Josiah Stamp had achieved in Siberia the reorganisation of the L[ondon] M[idland and] S[cottish] Railway, if the gold standard has been abandoned in an equal blaze of glory in some Fascist capital, then indeed we might have gaped. Thus our unmeasured national arrogance, which expects things to be done here, by whomsoever, with efficiency, but presumes that in Russia or in Italy there can be nothing but muddle, flatters the foreign experimentalists.

Nevertheless let us not belittle these magnificent experiments or refuse to learn from them. For it is a remarkable and a significant thing that the two most extraordinary political movements of the modern age, approaching their task from opposite moral and emotional poles, should agree in this vital particular—that state planning, that intelligence and deliberation at the centre must supersede the admired disorder of the 19th century.

Nor are these forces of example the only forces which are driving our minds in this direction. There is also the failure of the unplanned economic systems of the world, of those where intelligent deliberation at the centre is minimised or rejected. Not indeed a relative failure; for England or the United States with a quarter of the population and a third of the productive plant at a standstill can nevertheless support a standard of life at least twice as high, I should suppose, as any existing Bolshevist or even Fascist state. But an absolute failure in relation to their own potentialities. That is what demands our attention. To establish a *prima facie* case for planning, we do not need to seek or discover success in the planned regimes to the south or to the east. It is sufficient to apprehend failure, as compared with opportunity, in the unplanned regimes here at home or to the west of the ocean.

For what are the economic events of the modern world which must most strike the apprehension of the dullest observer? The extraordinary capacity for the production of material wealth—though it were for the purposes of subsequent destruction—which we developed during the War; and the opposite picture today of starvation amidst plenty, our incredible inability to carry to our mouths the nourishment which we have produced with our hands. For the War was the nearest thing we have ever had in this country to a planned regime. The environment was unfavourable, the haste was excessive and hurried improvisations were inevitable. Yet it showed us the potentialities of modern technique to produce. On the other hand today it is in the United States, where the national tradition is most antagonistic to the notion of planning and the forms of government least adapted to improvised planning, that the failure of the economic system, relatively to its opportunity, is most obvious.

Let us make a useful distinction. Let us mean by planning, or national economy, the problem of the *general* organisation of resources as distinct from the *particular* problems of production and distribution which are the province of the individual business technician and engineer. Now the business technician and the engineer, here and in the United States, have already carried their improvements to a point at which, if we could take full advantage of them, we should have gone far towards solving the problem of poverty altogether. Nor, in my judgement, is this failure to gather in and enjoy our harvest merely a phenomenon of the slump, of the violent periodic depression such as exists at this moment. It is at times of slump that the paradox of starving in the midst of potential plenty is most striking and outrageous. But I believe that we suffer a chronic failure to live up to the opportunities of our technical capacity to produce material goods.

To remedy this failure is the problem of planning. The problem of planning is to do those things which, from the nature of the case, it is impossible for the individual to attempt. To bring in the collective intelligence, to find a place in the economic scheme of things for central deliberation, is not to disparage the achievements of the individual mind or the initiative of the private person. Indeed it is the achievements of this initiative which have set the problem. It is the failure of the collective intelligence—I will not say to keep up with, but not to fall too disastrously behind—the achievements of the individual intelligence which we have to remedy. And we have to remedy it, if we can, without impairing the constructive energy of the individual mind, without hampering the liberty and the independence of the private person. If the England of the coming generations can solve that problem—and my proud patriotic heart harbours a hope that our national qualities may be best of all suited to do it—we shall have contributed, I think, something more valuable to civilisation than the Bolshevist or the Fascist can;—though I do not overlook that each of these movements may be capable in its way of contributing something to the dignity of human nature which transcends the field and scale of operation that I attribute to national planning however complete and however successful.

I have said that it is of the essence of state planning to do those things which in the nature of the case lie outside the scope of the individual. It differs from Socialism and from Communism in that it does not seek to aggrandise the province of the state for its own sake. It does not aim at superseding the individual within the field of operations appropriate to the individual, or of transforming the wage system, or of abolishing the profit motive. Its object is to take hold of the central controls and to govern them with deliberate foresight and thus modify and condition the environment within which the individual freely operates with and against other individuals.

I will give you a few illustrations chosen both from the things which we plan already and from those which we might, and perhaps should, plan in future. The illustrations will not always be chosen for their intrinsic importance, but rather to convey to you just what is meant.

The distribution of the burden of taxation with a view to its effect on industry and on the divisions of incomes and of wealth is an example of state planning. A choice between rating relief and income tax relief, to take a specific instance, is an exercise in the problems of state planning. Tariffs can be a signal and outstanding example of planning. So is the control of the exchanges and the appropriate management of the value of sterling money in relation to the currencies of the rest of the world. So is the regulation of transport by road and by rail.

Or to take cases where we do not yet plan, or plan inadequately. Town planning and rural preservation is a good illustration, although it is only of a semi-economic character. For it is a case both where it is impossible for the individual to take the necessary action however much he may wish to do so, and where the benefit cannot possibly accrue to the individual even if he were to act. Yet it is a case where enormous benefits can accrue to the whole community both now and hereafter, if strong powers of central direction are assumed and employed.

Deliberate planning to influence the localisation of industry is a matter to which more attention is likely to be given before long. We are at present experiencing in this country a transfer of industry, socially most wasteful, from the industrial north to the London area, owing to lower rates and other advantages to the individual in the latter location. Yet the effect, of which the individual recks nothing, will be, if it is carried far, to waste enormous outlays in housing and municipal works in the older areas, outlays which are very large compared with the cost of the factories transferred.

The exercise of deliberate influence on the conditions and the environment which determine the rate of growth of population and of emigration and immigration is another matter of the greatest possible importance entirely outside the sphere of the individual, there the state must act if there is to be action at all.

But at such a time as the present the most outstanding opportunity for state planning throughout the world is to be found in the avoidance, or in the mitigation of industrial slumps during which there is so vast a loss of the world's potentialities for the creation of wealth. Here again we have a problem which lies completely outside the scope of the individual. The individual is helpless,—disastrously so, as there are abundant examples today, strewn upon the carpet of the world, to show. There is virtually nothing that he can do, however ardent his desire and however pressing his personal interest. He is swept along, together with all his fellows, on a flood which he cannot control or direct. And nothing can be of the least avail which does not come from concerted action at the centre.

We have a poignant example today of the helplessness of the individual, however powerful and however great his genius, in the tragic death of Mr Ivar Kreuger. [See below, p. 92.] Here was a man of perhaps the greatest constructive business intelligence of his age, a man whose far-flung activities have been in the widest sense in the public interest, who had conceived it his mission in the chaos of the post-war world to furnish a channel between the countries where resources were in surplus and those where they were desperately required, one who built on solid foundations and surrounded himself with such safeguards as could be humanly devised in the circumstances,—suffering what the ignorant might mistake for the fate of the common gambler, but in truth crushed between the ice-bergs of a frozen world which no individual man could thaw and restore to the warmth of normal life. The spectacle of capitalists, striving to become liquid as it is politely called, that is to say pushing their friends and colleagues into the chilly stream, to be pushed in their turn by some yet more cautious fellow from behind, is not an edifying sight.

To my thinking—and here I am expressing what is only a personal view though many are coming to share it—state planning, directed to the maintenance of the general average of industrial production and activity at the optimum level and to the abolition of unemployment, is at the same time the most important and the most difficult of the tasks before us. It will lead us I believe to far more deliberate and far-reaching policies of credit control, to a great preoccupation with the appropriate level of the rate of interest, and in general to an attempt to control the rate at which new investment is encouraged and facilitated to take place. It used to be believed that the level of interest and the rate of investment were self-regulatory, and needed no management and no planning; and that all would be for the best if natural forces were left to discover and establish the inner harmonies. But such a view does not square with the facts of experience. As I began by saying, it is the failure of the unplanned industrial world of Western Europe and America to regulate itself to the best advantage, or to reap the fruits of the genius of its scientists and its engineers and its business organisers, which is predisposing many persons to consider without prejudice those far-reaching experimental projects of the most constructive minds of the post-war world which go, conveniently, by the name of planning.

I am coming towards the end of my discourse. But there is one perplexing matter, upon which opinions differ, still to be mentioned. It may be desirable that we should be bolder and more ambitious in choosing the fields which we bring within the scope of state planning. But is it practicable in a democratic community? May it not be a necessary price to pay for the benefits of state planning, that we also suffer those other affronts to the individual which seem to be inseparable from a Bolshevist or a Fascist state? For myself, I do not see why this need be so. At least I should like to try whether it be not possible to enjoy the advantages of both worlds. It is obvious that the task of state planning would be in many respects easier for an autocratic administration than for one dependent on parliamentary institutions and the breath of popular favour. On the other hand, the autocratic regime loses in two important respects;—it loses that consciousness of consent to secure which is one of the principal arts of government and indeed of the conduct of all business, whether on a large scale or on a small; and except in its early years, when those rule who have carved their own way to power, all experience shows that it soon loses the capacity to select and to employ the best available and most disinterested talent.

Moreover it should prove compatible with democratic and parliamentary government to introduce modern improvements and new organs of administration. Indeed this is surely most necessary, whether or not we greatly extend the existing functions of the state. State planning, as I conceive it, would not be administered or supervised in detail by democratically elected bodies. The latter would be judges, not of first, but of final instance, reserve forces to effect a change when grave mistakes had been made. The day-to-day tasks of state planning would be carried out in the same sort of way and with the same kind of instruments of administration under a democratic government, as they would be under an autocratic government. I contemplate nothing more than a further, and perhaps more conscious, step along the same path that we are already treading.

At any rate it is not unlikely that it will be along some such lines as this that English experiments will be made—not today perhaps, but tomorrow—with the object of solving the economic problems of the modern world. It may be that other countries will enjoy the rare opportunity of seeing three experiments carried on simultaneously, differing vastly on the surface yet each directed in effect to the solution of the same essential problem,—the Five Year Plan in Russia; the Corporative state in Italy; and state planning by Public Corporations responsible to a democracy in Great Britain. And as lovers of our species, let us hope that they will *all* be successful.

Two days before Keynes's broadcast Ivar Kreuger, the head of Kreuger and Toll, had committed suicide. Later inquiries revealed major irregularities in the company's financial affairs. When *The Financial News* asked Keynes for a comment on Kreuger's death, Keynes replied.

To MAJOR J. W. HILLS, *14 March 1932*

Dear Hills,

I heard from Bracken this morning that you would like a few words from me on Kreuger's most sad death.

I have been much pre-occupied today with the preparation of a broadcast for this evening at short notice, but my mind was so full of Kreuger that I inevitably found myself putting some little notice about him into my broadcast [above p. 90], where it came in not inappropriately. I enclose it with this letter. If it, or any part of it, is of use to you in writing about him, please make use of it as you care.

I shall always look back with the greatest happiness to that dinner which I had with you and him, and I had hoped that we had then formed an acquaintanceship which might have developed later on. It is a most grievous thing. There is nothing in the world like the cruel and cold-blooded beastliness of the American bankers.

Yours,

[copy initialled] J.M.K.

Keynes's broadcast brought him a letter from Harold Macmillan.

From HAROLD MACMILLAN, *23 March 1932*

Dear Keynes,

My mother sent me the manuscript of your wireless talk, which you were good enough to send to her. I have read it with the greatest interest and with a good deal of jealousy. I wish I could say some of these things half as well. I do not know whether you are going to publish it in any form, but I think it would be useful if it could be in print somewhere.

I know how busy you always are, but I hope to have the chance of seeing you sometime, if you are in London. There are many topics upon which I should like to hear your views, if you could spare the time.

I am returning the typescript herewith, and am very glad that I have had an opportunity of seeing it.

I am,

Yours sincerely,

HAROLD MACMILLAN

I venture to enclose a copy of a little pamphlet of mine.[5]

[5] *The State and Industry* (privately circulated, 1932).

On 12 March 1932 the Prime Minister of Australia asked a special committee, under the chairmanship of W. Bruce, to provide for discussion at a conference of State and Federal Premiers, a preliminary survey of the country's economic problems. The other members of the committee were G. S. Colman, L. F. Giblin, L. G. Melville, R. C. Mills and Edward Shann. When the committee's report of 12 April was made public, Keynes was asked for comment.

The report recommended that an attempt to attain equilibrium between costs and prices be the basis for restoring employment; that the Commonwealth Bank manage the exchange rate; that through the wage-setting machinery real wages be reduced by 10 per cent below the 1928 level; that the rate of interest be reduced; that budget deficits be limited; that tariffs be rationalised to maximise employment generally and not in specific industries; and that relief through public works replace sustenance.

On reading cabled reports of the report Keynes spent the weekend of 16 April preparing his comments which he sent off on 17 April. These appeared in *The Melbourne Herald* on 27 June.

THE REPORT OF THE AUSTRALIAN EXPERTS

I

It is a rash thing to write from a great distance on a matter which demands practical judgement more than theory. If I can contribute anything to the discussion, it will be by envisaging Australia's problem in the setting of the world crisis. For, whilst the imponderables of popular psychology and the conditions set by the balance of political power, which no one can weigh who is not on the spot, must govern the handling of the purely local problem, it is no less important to know the forest and the jungle outside, which those dwelling amongst their own trees can scarcely hope to see.

I sympathise intensely with the general method of approach which underlies the new proposals of the economists and Under-Treasurers. I am sure that the Premiers' Plan last year saved the economic structure of Australia. I am not prepared to dispute that another dose of the same medicine may be necessary. But there are some aspects of the Experts' Report which cause me hesitation. I am fearful lest a degree of readjustment should be attempted which is impracticable in the environment of present world conditions. What is, perhaps, a more vivid apprehension of affairs outside Australia may enable me to contribute to the discussion by shifting the emphasis a little.

It is a serious mistake, in my judgement, for any country to attempt a complete adjustment to the present level of wholesale prices, whether measured in gold or in sterling. The long continuance of this level of prices is not a practical working hypothesis. It is one of the things like the end of the world, against which, though it be possible, it is not sensible to insure. For unless prices rise, the existing financial structure between nations cannot possibly survive. Every country in the world has the same problem as Australia in some shape or form. If they were each to attempt to solve it by competitive wage reductions and competitive currency depreciations, no one would be better off. There is no exit along that route. Indeed the tendency of wage reductions must necessarily be to rivet upon us more securely the existing level of prices; for in the long run it is the wage level which mainly determines the price level, especially with currencies not rigidly linked to gold.

Do not suppose that I am so foolishly optimistic as to rely on [an] adequate, or even a material, rise in prices in the near future. I am pessimistic as to the progress of the timetable. I believe that the leading financial centres of the world will have to enjoy a prolonged period of ultra-cheap money before enterprise lifts its head again; and until enterprise puts more spending power into circulation, prices cannot rise. I am saying something different from this, namely that a prudent country will lay its plans for orderly reconstruction on the assumption of a much higher world price level than the present, because, unless this assumption is realised, so much else will happen, so many other things will be broken, and the whole structure of national and international indebtedness will have collapsed so completely that its pains will have been wasted.

If, therefore, I were an Australian economist advising Mr

Lyons today, I should be decidedly moderate in my ideas. I should recommend him to ride his difficult and suffering steed with as light a rein as he dare. I should not press for heroic measures. It is a time to chastise gently. Moreover I should have sufficient confidence to take this line, precisely because Australia has done so much already and has been relatively so successful in her programme of necessary readjustment—if only, in spite of disappointments, she could, by comparison with the state of others, know it! There is more chance of improving the profitableness of business by fostering enterprise and by such measures as public works than by a further pressure on money wages or a further forcing of exports. The problems of the Budget and of unemployment are now more pressing than that of the balance of trade. The latest figures plainly indicate that the Australian balance today is, as a result of measures already taken, not unsatisfactory in the circumstances.

II

Let me review the proposals before the Premiers in the light of these general notions. They can be examined, I think, under three main heads—(i) A further reduction of wages, (ii) a further depreciation of the exchange, and (iii) an extension of bank credits and loans for relief works and other measures to increase enterprise.

I understand that the reductions of wages so far effected have been unequal. It is of the essence of what has been happening in Australia that there should be equality of sacrifice, and it would seem obvious that New South Wales should be brought into line with the rest of the country. Indeed this must be in her own interest if she is not to suffer more than her share of unemployment. But a policy of a further general reduction in money wages would be a double-edged weapon. It would tend to curtail purchasing power and, consequently, to aggravate rather than assist the problem of the Budget. I do not clearly see in what way it would help the general situation unless it were to expand the physical volume of exports, and I should have supposed that in present circumstances it would have no considerable effect in that direction. So far as internal production and consumption are concerned, sales receipts would fall off by just about as much as costs had been cut. The Experts recognise that it is impracticable to reduce costs and debts by a further 40 per cent. But I go much further than this. I do not believe that unemployment would be remedied by measures of this kind even if they could be put into force. I was, I think, the first to propose what I have sometimes called the National Treaty, namely an all-round cut in costs and debts, such as Australia has already had the courage to adopt, and except in New South Wales to apply. But I proposed this as an alternative to exchange depreciation for remedying maladjustment between one country and the rest of the world. It has no efficacy except in improving the trade balance. Apart from local anomalies, I do not believe that a further general cut in money wages could do anything which a further exchange depreciation could not do better. Nor is the fact of an increased real wage for the employed in spite of reduced national wealth a sufficient argument for cutting money wages. For this is a worldwide phenomenon today which is indeed an inevitable accompaniment of the slump.

We come next to the proposal for a further depreciation of the exchange. I see nothing wrong in principle in this. I have not the detailed knowledge to say whether £125 or £130 or even £140 is the optimum level today. But I am clear upon what considerations the decision should depend. In the first place is it desirable to increase the trade balance further, and would a fall in the Australian exchange have much effect in this direction? As I have said, the trade balance seems now to be fairly satisfactory. But apart from this it is not safe to assume that a further exchange depreciation would much improve it. For the aggregate sterling value of Australia's exports would only be increased if the effect was to increase their physical *volume*, for which there may not be much scope, without lowering their sterling price, of which there might be some risk; whilst as for imports the existing restrictions are surely more than adequate. In the second place, what rate of exchange will create most confidence and will be most likely to discourage a flight from the Australian pound? If everyone is expecting a further depreciation and is endeavouring to anticipate it, then there is something to be said for giving way. On the other hand, each *de facto* depreciation may lead to an expectation of a further depreciation. On the whole I doubt if I should alter the exchange unless either the Australian banks and financial institutions were to tell me that it would make them feel more comfortable and more willing to expand credit, or the proposal was put forward as a substitute for tariffs. If an alteration of the exchange were accompanied by a corresponding rectification of tariffs, I should support it. For the aggravation of the existing tariff by the exchange depreciation being superimposed on it, is probably the principal cause of those remaining maladjustments which are purely Australian and not just a reflection of world conditions. The tariff should be reduced in proportion to the depreciation of the exchange.

But I hope the Australian authorities will not overlook the fact that what would really suit them is a further depreciation, not of the Australian pound, but of sterling. For this would raise export prices without increasing the burden of the external debt. It is the recent appreciation of sterling by 10 per cent which is the mischief. I suggest that the importance of consulting the interests of the Dominions in settling the value of sterling should be a major topic at the Ottawa Conference.

We come finally to a variety of suggestions put forward by the Experts for attacking directly the volume of unemployment. I am in complete agreement with these, especially with the proposed loan for relief works. They should be pushed forward as rapidly as prudence permits. Thus my counsel would be:—
Reduce the Budget deficits to the figure allowed by the experts.

Satisfy yourselves that the trade balance is adequate to meet pressing requirements. Perhaps depreciate the Australian pound by 5 or 10 per cent, unless sterling itself is allowed to fall a little. Under cover of this undertake the necessary downward readjustment of tariffs which are crippling efficiency. Above all, expand internal bank credit and stimulate capital expenditure as much as courage and prudence will allow. The substitution of wages for doles needs more credit but not necessarily much more currency.

Let me repeat that, broadly speaking, I take my stand with the Experts and against their critics. I differ from the former on two points only. The first is a matter of degree. I feel that they are inclined to be too drastic. The second is a point of theory. I suspect that they are too much under the influence of precarious statistics relating costs to prices and of dubious theory as to how the one can be made to catch up with the other. Unless fresh purchasing power is released, it may be that prices are related to costs after the same fashion as her tail to a cat.

III

One word in conclusion as to Australia's credit in London. I feel most strongly that it is immensely worth while to foster it. I believe that Australia has heavily over-borrowed in the past and I have often advised that her securities be avoided. But I do not therefore conclude that the days of Australia's overseas borrowing are over. In my opinion the intrinsic quality of Australia's credit though still very sensitive to passing events, relatively to that of other borrowers is higher today, in spite of Mr Lang, than it has been for several years. Apart from what I may think, I believe that Australian credit is rising rapidly in the estimation of the London market. Australia's heroic measures to fulfil her bond may have been apprehended in England somewhat slowly, but they have not escaped notice. The acuteness of your domestic political struggle has at least had the advantage of throwing into the limelight the quality of the intentions and principles of the Commonwealth Government, which London, though undemonstrative, profoundly appreciates. Moreover, if my prognostications are right, it may not be too long before this has a practical importance. I believe that a period of ultra-cheap money is in prospect and that a day is not far off when respectable borrowers will be greatly sought after. I should not be surprised if the first recovery from the slump begins within the British Empire. At any rate the best contribution towards world recovery which London can make will be the earliest possible resumption of her position as an overseas lender and the extension of a helping hand to those debtor countries who have shown that they deserve it. And why should not Australia be one of the first of these? It lies within her power.

J. M. KEYNES

Once Keynes had read the actual report he sent further comments to C. L. Baillieu, an Australian businessman who was one of his country's representatives on the Imperial Economic Advisory Committee. Paragraphs 3–6 of his letter appeared in *The Melbourne Herald* for 8 July.

To C. L. BAILLIEU, *24 May 1932*

Dear Baillieu,

Many thanks for sending me the Experts' Report and apologies for not dealing sooner with your question, but I have been frightfully busy for the last week in other directions and have had no time to get down to it.

If I had had the full text before me, I should have amplified my article in certain respects, but I don't know that I should have appreciably modified its general tendency. (By the way you have not let me have a copy of the final version of it, as you promised.) I feel, if anything, more strongly than before that the committee is inclined to be too drastic and is aiming at adjustments which are humanly impossible for Australia in the existing environment of the world.

There is one point in particular where the report strikes me as notably weak. The argument essentially depends on the hypothesis that export costs are 20 per cent above export prices, and the object of the proposals is largely to remedy this discrepancy. But the report does not appear to contain a shred of real statistical evidence that there is a discrepancy of the size claimed; nor is there any explanation as to what we mean by 'costs', in particuiar whether this means prime costs or costs allowing for normal profits and dividends and expansion, etc, etc.

Of course we all know that the export industries are under the weather, just as they are in every other country of the world, but if the committee mean that exporters are making an out of pocket loss of 20 per cent on their output, I should say that this is in the highest degree improbable. Probably they do not really mean quite this, but then they ought to say what they do mean, having regard to the extreme importance of this point in connection with their general diagnosis. In fact they show that output is at a greater level than it was ever at, which could hardly be the case if exporters were making such a gigantic loss as is suggested. On the other hand if the adjustment they demand is intended to bring the position of exporters back to what it would be in good times, then the aim seems to me to be in present conditions unnecessary and altogether impracticable. It would certainly represent something which is not being attempted in any other country whatsoever. My own opinion would be that an attempt to do as much as this for exporters would have a disastrous effect on the rest of the community.

In truth I am a little disappointed with the report. The reasoning in it seems to me to be too *simpliste*. The statistics seem to me to show that the position of Australia is in many respects better than that of many other countries. I should repeat my advice that the main object of statesmanship should be to stagger along somehow until the rest of the world pulls itself together, rather than run the risk of social upheavals by asking the impossible of human nature.

On the other hand there is another much milder way of reading the report. If it simply means that in those special cases where little or no wage reductions have taken place, there should be the same cuts as have already taken place elsewhere, that there is no reason to consider the present rate of exchange as sacrosanct, and that there should be a programme of public works for the reduction of unemployment;—then I am entirely in sympathy and agree with what they say. Thus, while their general approach to the problem seems to me rather frightening, their actual proposals are mild and reasonable enough.

I return your documents herewith.

Yours sincerely,
[copy initialled] J.M.K.

The British Budget of 19 April 1932, although it did not satisfy Keynes in every respect, brought one area of Keynes's concerns to a successful conclusion. For in the Budget, the Chancellor announced the formation of an Exchange Equalisation Account to manage the sterling exchange. Keynes's comments on the Budget as a whole were as follows.

From The Evening Standard, *20 April 1932*

THIS IS A BUDGET OF EXCESSIVE PRUDENCE

This Budget is one of extreme and, perhaps, excessive prudence—a sequel to the Budget of last autumn, rather than the prelude to future Budgets. Its contents, so far as they go, will command an unenthusiastic acquiescence.

But it scarcely discloses even in the barest outline what the policy of the Government is to be on the four vital issues of the coming year—protective tariffs, War debts, the management of the sterling exchange and the conversion of the debt. Mr Chamberlain has limited himself to the routine of the Budget and has reserved most of what really matters for later occasions.

We need not complain of this. They are all of them questions about which premature detail would be inadvisable. At the same time, their postponement does rob the Budget of much of its importance. The truth is that this April the Chancellor is not in a position to make normal forecasts. He has not the data to offer more than the outline of a Budget.

Indeed, it would be his best plan to admit that this Budget is nothing more than an interim statement and to repeat last year's unusual precedent of a further Budget in the autumn after the Tariff Advisory Committee, Ottawa and Lausanne have done their work and when the course of sterling exchange and the prospects of debt conversion are clearer. Meanwhile, he marks time, and one is left, in the main, to conjecture what lies behind the blinds which the Chancellor has not chosen to draw up.

Tariffs

A year ago I was maintaining that the case for a revenue tariff was made out, and the Chancellor's figures show that the same is true today. The protective tariffs on iron and steel which we all expect later in the week will be in the national interest.

But I hope that—with one exception—large-scale tariff experiments will stop there. We want as little industrial protection as possible in this country, both for our own sakes and so as not to set too bad an example to the rest of the world.

Tariffs, as they exist in the world today, are a first-class curse; and it is distasteful, though it be necessary, to be adding to them. Moreover, the depreciation of sterling readjusts British costs to world costs far more effectively than a tariff could, and has greatly weakened the case for protective duties.

The one exception is that of food taxes or analogous devices designed to protect British agriculture. We all know well enough that we could produce appreciably more of our own food, and that we should be a healthier and better balanced community if we did.

We ought to be free to set about this task in a straightforward way, without complicating it by such contraptions as the quota, which can be no real help to tender consciences or sensitive memories.

Meanwhile the Chancellor's self-restraint in raising no pæan over the fall of free trade, though perhaps a shade dry, was marvellously considerate and modest.

The sterling exchange

The Chancellor's announcement of the Exchange Equalisation Account was the most interesting and important thing in his speech. His proposal furnishes a means, supplementary to the Issue Department of the Bank of England, for acquiring resources for the management of the sterling exchange.

It also makes it clear that the ultimate profit or loss from managing a fluctuating exchange is the affair of the Treasury and not of the Bank of England, which is entirely as it should be.

The plan is excellent and should make us once more master in our own house, which in some recent weeks we were not.

The Macmillan Committee pointed out that the resources of the Bank of England might not prove large enough in an emergency for dealing with the huge globus of loose money, pertaining to exchange speculators and international safety-firsters, which flops about the world in these days, embarrassing now this banking system and now that.

But the Chancellor of the Exchequer's supplementary fund of £150,000,000 should enable us to maintain the sterling exchange at whatever figure we deliberately decide to be in our best interest, and not according to the whim of the foreign speculator.

The Chancellor was, I think, unnecessarily cautious in deprecating—if that was his meaning—the view that sterling would be henceforth under control. It would, as he indicated, be most inadvisable to peg sterling in terms of gold irrespective of events and, in particular, of the movements in gold prices.

But this does not mean that we cannot keep sterling about where we should wish it to be at any given time. At any rate, let us try. And in present circumstances I would plead for a return to the somewhat lower level which prevailed a short time ago. For this would be invaluable to our export industries, and, above all, it is desperately required by the producers of raw materials in Australia, India and the Crown Colonies, whose fortunes, no less than ours, are linked to sterling.

One criticism I have. The Chancellor seems to intend to use the Exchange Equalisation Account to veil the sales and purchases of gold and foreign exchange in an even completer secrecy than at present.

If so, it is bad and vicious practice. It will prevent rational comment and criticism on what is happening. It will lead to endless gossipings and half-leakages and special knowledge in inner circles, especially abroad, as to what the figures are. And it will be grossly unfair to foreign central banks. (Or is it intended to disclose to them what is kept a secret at home?)

Imagine the chaos if all central banks were to keep secret their holdings of gold and foreign balances.

Apart from this, the plan, and all that the Chancellor said about it, seem to me admirable. If, at the moment, the control of sterling leads to the accumulation of large sums, there is no harm in that. For it is not unlikely that the first impetus to recovery will have to come from within the British Empire, and the possession of substantial liquid reserves will give the City of London the courage to take the initiative and to reassume the position of international lender at not too distant a date.

Debt conversion

The modern practice of voting an undivided sum for the interest and sinking fund on the debt taken together has enabled the Chancellor to be exceedingly obscure as to the savings for which he hopes from cheap money and conversions.

The aggregate is to be the same as in the previous year after adjustment for War debts, which, Mr Chamberlain added, 'includes the sinking fund unchanged at £32,500,000'. But this will only be the case if the interest charge is the same as last year, which is improbable, even apart from conversions, if we consider the low prospective rate on Treasury bills.

Moreover, since the Unemployment Fund will no longer borrow, there is in effect a large increase in the sinking fund.

Mr Chamberlain's inability to give any relief to the taxpayer is, in fact, largely due to his having taken no credit for possible savings in these directions. This is a further reason for regarding the Budget as merely an interim statement until the position is clearer.

He would have done better here to have given some rein to his hopes, using the proceeds to relieve the direct taxpayer.

But I am not sorry that Mr Chamberlain has refrained from putting out a definite conversion project as a feature of his Budget. For there is more to be lost by the Treasury being premature in this matter than by its waiting too long.

There may be a long period of ultra-cheap money ahead of us before enterprise and investment revive.

Mr Chamberlain was entitled to congratulate himself on the relatively sound position in which he is placed. No other country in the world can make so good a showing. Since we abandoned gold we have begun to feel firm ground under our feet.

But we are still in grievous need of stimulus and encouragement and an expansive atmosphere. Mr Chamberlain is quite right in saying that it is too soon to be sure of anything, and he would not have been justified in basing his estimates on an anticipated recovery of trade.

But he should not be too cautious. Over-caution will postpone the date of recovery. 'Sound' finance may be right psychologically, but economically it is a depressing influence. There is nothing in this Budget to hasten the recovery of ourselves or of the world from the slump.

The best that can be said of it is that, by allaying various fears, it prepares the way for us to take our courage in both hands. But the preparation is no use unless the courage is to follow.

After the Budget, the debate on the Exchange Equalisation Account section of the Budget resolutions was scheduled for 25 April. Before the debate, Robert Boothby asked Keynes for advice.

From ROBERT BOOTHBY, *April 1932*

Dear Keynes,

I am sorry to bother you. But the debate on the Exchange Equalisation Account is to take place on Monday, and I am very anxious to try and elicit some useful information from Neville, although I feel it will be difficult.

One cannot help feeling that this may well prove to be a decisive step in the development of a rational relationship between the Treasury and the Bank of England, and indeed of a rational monetary policy. As you know, the House shies at currency like a frightened horse, but the younger generation is beginning to evince a real interest in all these questions; and therefore it would be a pity if the debate were to be as perfunctory as, for example, the debate on the original Gold Standard Bill in 1925.

If we are to sanction a loan of 150 millions we ought to know to what use it is to be put, and by whom. But I don't trust myself to talk sense on so technical a subject without guidance.

If you could find time to jot down a few of the points that occur to you in connection with this money resolution, and questions that ought to be asked, I should be deeply grateful. I shall be here all Monday morning (17 Pall Mall), so if they reached me by the second post it would be all right. Failing that, is there anywhere I can telephone to you? I feel very strongly (especially in the light of recent events) that we ought also to exercise a measure of control over investments, but I doubt if this could be dragged in on Monday.

With renewed apologies for troubling you.

Yours sincerely,

ROBERT BOOTHBY

To ROBERT BOOTHBY, *23 April 1932*

Dear Boothby,

On the whole the proposals for the Equalisation Fund seem to me excellent, and to deserve a blessing as initiating a scheme of currency management.

The outstanding features are the following:—

(1) The profit or loss on currency management is to be for account of the Treasury and not of the Bank of England. This is as it should be.

(2) It has, I think, been already stated in the House of Commons that whilst the scheme will be operated through the Bank of England, the Treasury takes the responsibility of the general policy pursued. This also is as it should be.

(3) According to the text of the resolution, the Fund is established 'for the purpose of strengthening the currency and checking undue fluctuations of the exchange value of sterling'. These are not the words I should have chosen. It would have been much better to have said that the purpose was to maintain stability so far as possible in the commodity value of sterling. In this connection and in connection with (2) above it would be a good thing to press the Government to say that their immediate objective would be to raise prices so far as lies in their power. That is the central issue.

(4) According to the Chancellor of the Exchequer's Budget Speech, not only will the day to day transactions of the Fund be private, which is reasonable, but the nature of its assets, in particular how far they consist of gold or foreign exchange, will not be disclosed. This seems to me exceedingly objectionable as I pointed out in my *Evening Standard* article. It is vital that it should be known whether or not the balance of payments is in favour of any given country, and whether that country is tending to lose or to gain gold and foreign balances. I think it would be wrong if we seek to conceal this. There should be a public statement, at least once a month, as to the holdings of

gold and foreign exchange. I used to say by way of joke, that the Bank of England would conceal the movements into and out of its gold reserve if it could. Now it would appear that this objective is being actually attained!

Yours sincerely,
[copy initialled] J.M.K.

In mid-May 1932 Harold Macmillan circulated a document entitled *The Next Step* advocating reflation through cheap money supplemented by selective protection and an Investment and Development Board.[6] On this Keynes commented.

To HAROLD MACMILLAN, *6 June 1932*

Dear Macmillan,

I like the enclosed very much. My criticisms are really due I expect to the sort of middle position you occupy. But as you ask me for them, I will give one or two for what they are worth.

1. My main feeling is that you are not nearly bold enough with your proposals for developing the investment functions of the state. You are trying it would seem to minimise the part which the state must play and you endeavour to get your results by a sort of combination of private enterprise and subsidy; and I doubt the feasibility of this at any rate in present times. If the amount of stimulus required is moderate, your devices might avail. But at the present time it would be extraordinarily difficult to bring about an adequate volume of investment even if one had the whole forces of the state behind one. The greater part of investment is concerned with building, transport and public utilities, and the scope here for private enterprise is in modern times somewhat limited. If your proposed body were to be set up, I believe that the additional investment which one might expect from it would be extremely small.

2. You do not call attention to the extent to which the present

[6] H. Macmillan, *Winds of Change 1914–1939* (London, 1966), pp. 359–62.

policy of the Government is contradictory. They are still maintaining a lot of the maxims and watchwords which date back from the deflationary period. Whilst it is now correct to say that one would wish prices to rise, most of what the Government actually does is of a contrary tendency. The Minister of Health is still discouraging local authorities from expenditure; the Chancellor of the Exchequer obviously believes that economy and a large sinking fund are sound, whereas obviously these measures are extremely deflationary and likely to exercise a much larger effect in the downward direction than your Investment Board would in the upward direction. Indeed, apart from the Prime Minister, I see very little sign that Ministers have given up thinking nonsense, though under outside pressure the catchwords they find it politic to utter are becoming much more sensible.

3. Are you clear that it is impossible that the rise of prices can come *first*? This can only appear as the result of a greater volume of purchasing power, brought about by increased business activity or development schemes. In some passages you seem to imply this. But elsewhere the reader might think that you considered it conceivable that there should be a *spontaneous* rise of prices.

4. Do not you pay far too much lip-service to economy? I consider the problem of Budget economy difficult. There are enormous psychological advantages in the *appearance* of economy. It prepares the way for the conversion of the Debt and it tends to lower the long-term rate of interest. The opposite would also be bad for business sentiment. But that does not prevent economy from being deflationary and probably injurious to business profits. The only qualification to this is that in so far as it leads to a remission of taxation the evil results will be less, because it is then in the main a redistribution of purchasing power. But even so the expenditure of the school teachers whose salaries are cut is likely to be reduced more than the expenditure of the supertax payer whose taxes are relieved will be increased.

The way I should put it would be to lay stress on the aim of reducing taxation by the abolition of the sinking fund in present circumstances. The reduction of the sinking fund out of taxation is pure, hundred per cent deflation.

But I am sorry that you should have found it necessary to say on page 19 'current expenditure on income-account should certainly be reduced as far as possible'.

Look at Roy Harrod's letter in last Saturday's *Economist*.[7] That seems to me to put the common-sense of the matter quite admirably.

Yours sincerely,

[copy not signed or initialled]

From a letter from HAROLD MACMILLAN, *9 June 1932*

I am very much obliged to you for your letter of June the 6th, and for the trouble you have taken in making some criticisms and suggestions about my memorandum.

I am in agreement with nearly all your criticisms in theory; but I am still trying the perhaps hopeless task of influencing the Government in the direction I want them to go, and, for this purpose, I have to conceal a certain amount and to preserve certain political decencies! I am going to try to make some modification in the way you suggest, if I can do it without destroying the chance of anybody in my party reading and being influenced by my pamphlet.

[7] Harrod's letter in the issue for 9 June had strongly advocated a programme of reflation supported by large open market operations and deficit financing.

Chapter 2

CHEAP MONEY, WISE SPENDING AND THE MEANS TO PROSPERITY

During the winter and spring of 1931–2 Keynes had not only been advocating the management of sterling at a relatively low level, but he had also been advocating cheap money. Such a policy was also put forward by the Prime Minister's Advisory Committee on Financial Questions in late February and early March 1932. Bank rate, which had been raised to 6 per cent when sterling left the gold standard, came down in three stages to 3½ per cent. In April, following the Budget which introduced the Exchange Equalisation Account, the rate came down to 3 per cent and on 12 May to 2½ per cent. The stage was then set for the Chancellor's dramatic flight to London from the reparations conference at Lausanne to announce to the House of Commons on 30 June the conversion of over £2 billion of 5 per cent War Loan 1939–47 to a 3½ per cent War Loan 1952 or after. The same day, Bank rate fell to 2 per cent, where it was to remain until August 1939.

Keynes's first comment came in a letter to C. L. Baillieu.

From a letter to C. L. BAILLIEU, *7 July 1932*

I consider the Conversion Scheme to be a sound stroke of policy. The Treasury are aiming at a very high percentage of conversion. I am by no means sure that they will secure this. But I should not consider it to be any reason for anxiety if, say, 25 per cent or even more were to remain unconverted, since this could be dealt with by a short-term bond issue, carrying a low rate of interest at the end of the year. For the future of the gilt-edged-market it is much more important that long-dated securities should not be in oversupply relative to the demand than that the percentage response to the present proposal should be as nearly as possible complete. The optimum arrangement from the point of view of the Treasury is to supply the different types of bonds in the proportions in which the public want them.

A number of difficult technical points are involved for the

near future. As you will have heard, the Bank of England is discouraging the money market and the banks from taking unassented War Loan as a 'floater'. I think that the Bank of England is making a mistake in this. It is not unlikely that the result may be a poor market for the stock in the near future. A good many private individual holders of War Loan are selling out simply because they cannot afford an income less than 5 per cent on their capital. But whilst this probably started the upward movement of the market as a whole, what we are observing is in the main a sudden realisation that a drastic readjustment is needed between yields and capital values.

One cannot foresee the exact degree at which this readjustment will be held. But I believe that the change is in the main reliable and durable and that it is of first-class importance in paving the way for a revival.

Meanwhile, the most striking feature of the immediate situation is the extraordinary disparity between yields in London and yields in New York of comparable securities. It seems to me quite impossible that the present situation can long persist. And I should have supposed it to be probable that the readjustment would be brought about by a substantial rise in prices of prime fixed-interest securities in New York. The present may be the chance of a lifetime for the purchase of the latter. Obviously everyone in New York is scared so stiff as to be unable to move. But that may be the opportunity of others away from any unsettling influence of the local atmosphere. No serious risk can arise unless the existing financial system in America is going to peg out altogether. I suppose that that is just possible, but I cannot believe that it is probable.

Keynes provided a more extensive comment to the Committee on Economic Information of the Economic Advisory Council on 18 July with a memorandum entitled 'A Note on the Conversion Scheme in Relation to the Long-term rate of Interest'.[1] A revised version formed an Appendix to

[1] The Committee on Economic Information was set up in July 1931 'to supervise the preparation of monthly reports to the Economic Advisory Council on the economic situation

the Committee's Fourth Report, dated 20 July 1932. With a slight change in title, some additional statistics, and a few minor changes in wording, Keynes published the memorandum as a paper in *The Economic Journal.*

From The Economic Journal, *September 1932*

A NOTE ON THE LONG-TERM RATE OF INTEREST IN RELATION TO THE CONVERSION SCHEME

1. A reduction of the long-term rate of interest to a low level is probably the most necessary of all measures if we are to escape from the slump and secure a lasting revival of enterprise. The successful conversion of the War Loan to a $3\frac{1}{2}$ per cent basis is, therefore, a constructive measure of the very first importance. For it represents a direct attack upon the long-term rate, much more effective in present circumstances than the indirect attack of cheap short-term money, useful and necessary though the latter is.

2. Indeed the effect of the conversion scheme on the prevailing standards of long-term rate[s] of interest, both in Great Britain and throughout the world, may be of more far-reaching importance than the relief to the burden of the national debt, which can be taken as a symbol of the advantages which borrowers generally may be going to obtain. But this will only be the case if the effect of the conversion scheme is not just a flash in the pan, propped up by newspaper propaganda and patriotic appeal just long enough for the Treasury to attain its immediate object, but has more or less lasting *sequelæ*. This is also important for the Treasury itself, since the opportunities for conversion are by no

and to advise as to the continuous study of economic development'. Its members were Sir Josiah Stamp (Chairman), Walter Citrine (to 1933), G. D. H. Cole, Keynes, Sir Alfred Lewis and H. D. Henderson (Secretary to 1934). Sir Arthur Salter and Sir Ernest Simon joined in 1932, as did the Chief Economic Adviser to the Government, Sir Frederick Leith-Ross. Other additions were Sir Frederick Phillips (1935), D. H. Robertson (1936), A. F. Hemming and Piers Debenham (Secretaries from 1934). The Committee began to meet regularly in March 1932 and continued to meet until the outbreak of war in 1939. For a full discussion of the Committee's work and the treatment of its advice by Whitehall, see Susan Howson and Donald Winch, *The Economic Advisory Council 1930–1939: A Study in Economic Advice during Depression and Recovery* (Cambridge, 1977), ch. 5.

means exhausted by the present operation. The aim should be, therefore, to maintain market conditions favourable to a falling long-term rate of interest, not only whilst the conversion is in progress, but also after it is over. Early this year I ventured the opinion that there was no reason why the yield of British Government long-term securities should not fall to a $3\frac{1}{2}$ per cent basis within the year.[2] There is now no reason why they should not fall gradually to a much lower basis than this, and every reason in the world why we should wish them to do so. But to achieve this will require the combination of deliberate purpose with the organised co-operation of the principal factors in the market. The following are notes on some aspects of the situation.

3. It is important that the market should be supplied with securities of different types and maturities in the proportions in which it prefers them. If a particular type of security, such as Government stocks having no fixed date of redemption, are in oversupply relatively to stocks with a definite maturity either of early or intermediate date, as measured by the relative strength of the demand for the two types, the former will tend to be a weak market, which will react unfavourably on long-term rates of interest generally.

Paradoxically the risk of this will arise if the conversion is unduly successful, so to speak, under the influence of propaganda and patriotic appeal.* For the old War Loan has been widely held by firms and by individuals as a temporary or only quasi-permanent investment for funds which would or might be needed for other purposes perhaps at a definite, perhaps at an indefinite date, in the belief that it combined a high yield with less liability to fluctuate in capital value than strictly long-dated securities. Such holders may agree to convert, but the new War Loan will not suit their purposes equally well and they will incline to sell it when the first enthusiasm is over, unless they

[2] See above p. 80.

* Since the above was written figures have been published showing a very remarkable degree of success, and the resulting oversupply has in fact shown itself in some weakness in the price of the stock.

have been suited in the meantime with a security of a type more adapted to their purpose.

This object could be attained by offering to holders of assented, as well as of unassented, War Loan a short-dated bond at a lower rate of interest than 3½ per cent some time in the autumn or winter. Indeed, a short-term bond issue would suit the Treasury in two ways. In the first place such bonds could, since this type of security is now in undersupply, be placed at a rate of interest well below 3½ per cent. In the second place it would ensure a better market for the new War Loan after December next, and thus pave the way for further conversion schemes in due course. Indeed, it must always be to the interest of the Treasury to supply the heterogeneous requirements of the market with securities of different types and maturities in the optimum proportions so as to minimise the aggregate cost of the national debt.

Popular opinion in relation to the conversion is, as I interpret it, a peculiar combination such as could only exist, perhaps, in this country, of a keen desire to make the scheme an overwhelming success, both by personal and by communal action, with an unspoken conviction or at least a suspicion that the whole thing is in truth a bit of bluff which a fortunate conjunction of circumstances is enabling us to put over ourselves and one another, and that the new War Loan may be expected to fall to a discount in due course.

I am not sure that the authorities themselves are entirely free from an idea of this kind. Nevertheless I plead for a policy based on the opposite hypothesis. For I am convinced that the conversion scheme is anything but a bluff. A great reduction in the long-term rate of interest corresponds profoundly to the character and, indeed, to the necessities of the underlying facts, and it may even be a necessary condition of the survival of the existing financial structure of society. Nor is there anything in the attendant circumstances which need prevent our achieving it. But it will not happen by itself and must be pursued with deliberate purpose. For there is a large conventional or psychological element in the market rate of interest which needs firm and skilful management. The first error to avoid, therefore, is the premature oversupply of a particular type of security.

4. The second danger arises in quite a different way. It lies in the very great disparity, which has come into existence since the conversion scheme was broached, between yields on sterling securities quoted in London and yields on comparable securities elsewhere, especially in the United States.

In view of this, the conversion scheme would certainly have been impracticable in the form it has actually taken if we had remained on the gold standard. For it is the vice, as well as the virtue, of the gold standard that it links the money markets of the world rigidly together and is a preventative of individual action. The power of one centre, even of London, to move ahead of the rest was narrowly limited by it, and, if the gold standard were still functioning, we should have had to accommodate ourselves to the common world denominator of intelligence, capacity, courage and public spirit. Moreover the power of independent action, which we gained when we freed our currency from the common international unit, has been reinforced in the actual circumstances of the moment by the extreme distrust towards the United States which was felt until quite lately, and is still felt today though not quite so strongly, by most investors and financial institutions. And these considerations do not apply to the United States alone. There are few quarters of the world where, for the time being, the British investor is prepared to venture new funds except with the temptation of a much higher yield of interest than he can obtain at home.

Thus to a certain extent the London investment market can function as a closed system and move under local influences in its own orbit. Even so, however, I should surmise that the existing disparity of yields cannot long persist without putting a great strain on the sterling exchange by stimulating a steady trickle of funds, if not a flood, to foreign markets. Since the extent of the disparity has not yet been realised except by the professional investor, the argument may be illustrated by a few examples of the quotations ruling on or about July 20:—

(i) Commonwealth of Australia sterling 5 per cents are selling in London at about 102. A similar dollar 5 per cent War loan is selling in New York at about 72, and even this price is the result of heavy buying from this side. Argentine sterling 5 per cents are selling in London at about 64, whilst dollar 6 per cents (of slightly longer maturity) are at about 42 in New York. Hungarian (League of Nations) sterling 7½ per cents fetch 48, whilst the identical dollar loan stands at 28. Indeed over a wide field foreign bonds today are priced, for a given yield and security, anything up to 50 per cent higher in London than in New York. Nor do exchange calculations enter directly into the above comparisons, since I am comparing securities of which both capital and interest are payable in sterling with similar securities of which both capital and interest are payable in dollars. Such wide disparities have never existed before, and it is unlikely that they can last. But meanwhile the whole burden of new borrowing, if and when there is any, will fall on London, whilst apart from new loans, there will be a steady stream of buying from London on the New York market. It would be imprudent not to expect this.

(ii) The above samples relate to foreign Government loans. But much the same thing is true of well secured industrial and public utility fixed-interest securities in Great Britain and the United States respectively, as is shown in the following tables:—

*Interest yields in U.S.A.**

	20 High-grade industrial preferred stocks	60† Representative bonds
June 1931	5·85	4·45
June 1932	8·52	7·03
20 July 1932	8·23	6·48
3 Aug. 1932	7·59	6·06

* Taken from Standard Statistics.

† 15 municipal, 15 industrial, 15 railroads and 15 public utility.

*Interest yields in Great Britain**

	British Govt.	Home corporations	45 Representative debentures	90 Representative preference shares	5† Dominion bonds
30 June 1931	4·16	4·43	5·72	6·43	5·26
29 Dec. 1931	4·85	5·01	6·18	6·75	6·18
28 June 1932	3·92	4·16	5·66	6·42	5·00
26 July 1932	3·67	3·63	4·89	5·16	4·30

* Taken from the Actuaries' Investment Index.

† One each from Australia, Canada, India, New Zealand and South Africa.

On reasonably well secured American preferred shares, not of the first class, it is easy to find yields of 8 to 10 per cent. And to take an average from the figures tabulated by Standard Statistics, excluding those which had suspended payment and those (not a few) which had a yield of more than 30 per cent (as representing those which were expected to suspend payment before long), the 48 preferred stocks of public utility concerns had an average yield on July 22 of 12·5 per cent, whilst the average yield on 142 preferred stocks of all classes was 11·4 per cent.

On the whole, it would not be an over-statement to say that, whereas a year ago the rates on fixed-interest securities were 30 per cent higher in Great Britain than in the United States, the position at the end of this July was reversed, yields in the United States being fully 30 per cent higher than in Great Britain. It is not to be expected that the distrust of the American situation and the risk of fluctuations in the exchange will prevent a steady stream of British purchases in America to take advantage of this unusual discrepancy.

(iii) Finally, there is the relative change here as compared with such countries as France and Holland which can be summed up in the following table:—

	Great Britain 3 per cent Local Loans	France 3 per cent Rentes	Holland 3 per cent (1898)
July 1931	66½	87	80¼
July 1932	86	76½	75½

In short, the rate of interest in Great Britain is, for the moment, widely out of line with what it is in the rest of the world. I call attention to these facts, in order that we may not be taken by surprise if we begin to experience their consequences, but not in order that we should be too much afraid of them or of the inevitable process of relative readjustment. For it is we, in this case, who are talking and acting sense, and the others who are talking and acting nonsense; and that will tell in our favour in the long run. We cannot expect to function as a closed system except within limits set by the risk of exchange fluctuations and our distrust of financial conditions elsewhere. We must hope, therefore, to infect others by our example, and perhaps even to supply the first impetus to recovery by our purchases in their markets. There is already talk of conversion schemes in Paris long overdue and held back hitherto by weak concessions to politics. It will not take much to bring about a reversal of sentiment in the United States. For the moment their markets are dominated by insane gambling to get in at the bottom, just as they were dominated in the boom by insane gambling to get out only at the top. If one is offered $20 for the price of $10, it may be foolish to refuse; but it may not seem so, if the $20 is on offer at $8 a week later. Yet positions of this kind—games of musical chairs in which all the players but one will in the end fail to get a seat—which are not based, and do not even pretend to be based, on intrinsic values and long views, change suddenly. It may be that London, if she is sane, prudent and bold, will initiate the change. But for this we must stick to our policy and be prepared if necessary, to sit quietly through a period of exchange weakness which may well be calculated to make us nervous, without seeking to redress the situation by any deflationary measures whatever.

Since the above paragraph was written (namely, July 20), there are abundant indications that the change in the United States has actually commenced. I do not so much refer to the fact, though it is truly remarkable, that the paper value of all the railways and public utilities, after having fallen to one tenth of what it had been two years previously, has then proceeded to double itself within five weeks.* For this is no more than a vivid illustration of the disadvantages of running a country's development and enterprise as a bye-product of a casino. I refer, rather, to the indications of a reversal of the upward trend of the long-term rate of interest as shown by a rise of 16 per cent in the index number of bonds between July 8 and August 19, 1932.

5. If the change in the rate of interest is to be lasting, there are many adjustments still to take place. We have seen that securities of all kinds, quoted on the Stock Exchange, have responded with extraordinary sensitiveness. Indeed, it would seem in some cases that they have over-responded. But there are still large areas where the readjustment has scarcely begun—in particular the real estate market, mortgages, and house rents. bank charges and building society charges, and, on the other hand, the rates allowed on deposits by the Post Office, the banks, building societies, municipal authorities and savings institutions are another field where adjustment to the new facts lags behind. All possible readjustments in these directions are, however, of extreme importance for the revival of constructive enterprise. In particular, it might be well if the banks, the building

* As a curiosity, I reproduce below the Dow-Jones Index of Stock Prices:—

	Rails	Industrials	Utilities
Sept. 1929	139·11	381·17	144·61
8 July 1932	13·23	41·22	16·53
11 Aug. 1932	28·63	68·90	29·15

societies and the Post Office Savings Bank would confer together with a view to reducing the rates allowed on all *new* deposits (or re-deposits) to figures (say) one-third below the present figures, which would allow corresponding abatements for charges on new advances.

The position of the banks (the Big Five) presents a difficult practical problem. Since the War they have incurred expenses, partly through generosity to their employees, partly through ostentation and partly through excessive competition for new business, which assume the permanence of relatively dear money. It is said that their expenses now amount to somewhere in the neighbourhood of 2 per cent of their total deposits. Moreover, there are many old-standing arrangements for allowing 2½ per cent on deposits which they are loth to disturb and which it might be unfair to disturb in view of the depositors having accepted this rate all through the dear money period. Thus with Treasury bills yielding ½ per cent and loans to the money market round 1 per cent, the banks are dependent on earning a high rate on their advances if they are to cover their expenses. The practical result is that, by obstinately maintaining their charges on advances at 5 per cent except to strong or favoured customers or those who threaten to go elsewhere, the banks are something of an obstruction to a decline in the rate of interest to certain types of borrowers; and it is difficult to see the way out. In the same way in the United States the fear of the Member Banks lest they should be unable to cover their expenses is an obstacle to the adoption of a whole hearted cheap money policy.

The building societies, on the other hand, are beginning to act. They have already reduced the rates which they allow on new deposits, and there are signs of a movement to reduce the rates charged on new mortgage loans. For example, the Halifax Building Society, which is one of the most important in the country, has already reduced its charges on new mortgage loans by ½ per cent. The funds administered by the building societies are now so enormous that this is a movement of the very first importance. We do not always remember the gigantic growth of these institutions since the War;—their new advances on mortgage were about £90,000,000 in each of the years 1930 and 1931, as compared with £9,000,000 in 1913 and no more than £25,000,000 even in 1920. Indeed the amount of new investment within this country, otherwise than through the building societies and public or semi-public authorities and boards, is now so paltry as to have but little effect on the total. If the rates generally charged by building societies could be brought down from their present level of 5½ to 6 per cent to (say) 4 to 4½ per cent, this would amount to a reduction of some 25 per cent in the cost of house-room for a section of the population, the elasticity of whose demand for house-room is probably considerable. I can conceive of few things more helpful to a recovery than this would be.

6. If we agree that the main object and advantage of a reduction in the long-term rate of interest is the assistance and stimulation of new enterprise, we must be careful not to sacrifice the end to the means. For a low rate of interest which was only maintained by restraining new enterprise, would be the most futile and disastrous way in which we could occupy ourselves. The market rate of interest depends much more on the psychology of the lender and on the behaviour of the banking system, than on the volume of new enterprise; and there is no necessary reason why the continued maintenance of low interest rates should not be compatible with a marked revival of new borrowing.

It is most desirable, therefore, to re-open the new issue market in London which is still closed to all new borrowers by the ban of the Treasury, as soon as possible. Indeed the ban is unusually strict, applying even to refunding operations and to companies seeking to raise funds for expansion from their own shareholders. A reversal of this state of affairs is called for urgently, and the Treasury, having tasted blood, must not get into the state of mind of wanting to make the slump permanent in the interest of yet further conversion schemes. At the same time I hope that we shall not return to complete *laissez-faire* in overseas lending. Another measure, depending upon the Treasury, which is urgently called for is a reduction in the rate for new loans charged by the Local Loans Commissioners to local authorities to a level which corresponds to the new price of Local Loans Stock. A fall of between a quarter and a third in the interest cost is the equivalent of about five shillings in the weekly rental of houses let at £1 a week. This means that even if there were to be some reduction in the subsidy, houses could be built to let at an appreciably lower rental than hitherto. Unfortunately the Ministry of Health is still issuing circulars to local authorities to discourage them from capital developments. The real obstacle here is, I think, that the minds of most people are still riddled with the fallacy that the volume of investment and the rate of interest are maintained at the right figures by some absolutely reliable automatic mechanism. It is believed that what we decide is always the direction of investment and never the volume of investment, so that to encourage investment in one direction is always to divert it from some other direction. If only this deep-seated habit of thought could be eradicated!

7. One effect of the conversion scheme has been to bring the stocks of the Dominions to a level at which they can again borrow without discredit or overburdening themselves, as shown in the above table (p. 119). If such loans can be floated, we shall have taken a step forward towards world recovery. I believe that we should use our available surplus for overseas lending more fruitfully if we were to direct it to the Dominions and China and, perhaps, South America, than to the distressed countries of Europe, as we shall doubtless be pressed to do at the forthcoming World Economic Conference. For a given sum advanced in the former directions might do more for international trade than if it goes into the latter channels. Professor Belshaw of New Zealand has suggested to me in correspondence

that there should be floated an Empire Reconstruction Loan of (say) £100,000,000, each of the Dominions guaranteeing somewhat more than its quota and Great Britain also guaranteeing an amount of the interest and sinking fund not exceeding a certain proportion, so that the loan would be quite safe unless more than (say) a third of the borrowers were to default. Projects of this kind deserve serious consideration.

Before the War Loan conversion operation James Meade and Roy Harrod attempted to devise a circular letter to *The Times* advocating expansion through private spending initiatives, expanding credit, remission of taxation (or at least no increase), encouragement of haste with sound investment schemes, and protecting the pound. On 15 June James Meade wrote to Keynes.

From J. E. MEADE, *15 June 1932*

Dear Keynes,

Hope you will forgive me for bothering you with the enclosed. Harrod and I thought it would be a very useful move if we could get a very large proportion of all those engaged in the study of economics to sign a joint letter to *The Times.* We have made the move on our own initiative mainly in order to do it as quickly as possible. I do hope therefore that if you agree in the main with what we have said, you will be willing to add your signature, as it would be very difficult for us to consider alterations in the text, which would have to be circulated to everyone.

We have all signed it here in Oxford except MacGregor, who has more or less promised to do so, and Cole who disagrees with our point slightly, but who I hope will yet consent.

It should be quite impressive in *The Times* if most of Cambridge sign as well.

Yours sincerely,

J. E. MEADE

To J. E. MEADE, *16 June 1932*

Dear Meade,

I have a general principle against signing circular letters. But I do agree completely with yours and if you can get a really formidable collection of signatures, I will join in.

The only possible ground for hesitation is that there are a set of sort of professional signers of circular letters; and the fact that I am always trying to be dragged in, has led to my trying to establish this general principle. However, I do agree that if you could get the bulk of the economists of Oxford and Cambridge with some other few from amongst the saved, it might be useful.

Yours sincerely,
[copy initialled] J.M.K.

The letter appeared in *The Times* for 5 July signed by 13 Oxford economists, 13 Cambridge economists, including Keynes, and 15 from other universities: Birmingham (4) Exeter, Hull, Leeds, Liverpool (2) London (4), St Andrews and South Wales.

Keynes also promoted 'wise spending' in a letter to a conference on unemployment and the means test organised by the Manchester and Salford Trades Council for 23 July. The purpose of the conference was to urge that work needed in the two areas be put in hand for the unemployed. Keynes, who expressed his regret at being unable to attend the conference, continued.

From the Manchester Guardian, *20 July 1932*

It is of the utmost importance that public authorities should revive their programmes of capital expenditure on all useful objects as soon as possible, and on as large a scale as possible.

Until the Government conversion scheme was out of the way there was, I am ready to concede, some argument for restriction, but if we continue to restrict after the successful launching of the conversion scheme we shall be wasting some part of the benefit which it is the object of that scheme to confer. It is often said by wiseacres that we cannot spend more than we earn. That is, of course, true enough of the individual, but it is exceedingly misleading if it is applied to the community as a whole.

For the community as a whole it would be much truer to say that we cannot earn more than we spend. Prices cannot rise, output and employment cannot increase, unless the first stimulant comes from the side of increased spending, though in this context I include, of course, under 'spending,' capital expenditure on housing and the like.

Let our slogan, then, be: 'We cannot as a community earn more than we spend, and let us consider it our civic duty to stimulate and promote every form of wise spending.'

On 29 August Harold Macmillan sent Keynes a memorandum proposing that informed individuals come together to form a public organisation to provide impartial expert advice and urge its implementation. On reading it, Keynes replied.

To HAROLD MACMILLAN, *7 September 1932*

My dear Harold,

I have read the enclosure to your letter of August 29 with much sympathy, but without much hope. You speak the truth at the top of page 4,[3] but whether what you propose would secure more influence for expert recommendations, I do not know.

The main point in my opinion is that we are now in the grip of reactionary forces, and however fair-spoken those in authority may be, they fully intend to take advantage of present circumstances to reverse a great deal of what they regard as semi-socialistic policy. They also conscientiously disbelieve in the kind of schemes for planning, etc., which you and I favour. There is probably no practical good sense in any efforts except those deliberately aimed at ousting them.

Yours sincerely,
[copy initialled] J.M.K.

[3] The passage in question ran: 'Governments have been accustomed in recent times to busy the experts and economists in a variety of Committees and Commissions, and more or less ignore their recommendations.'

Late in the summer, the Labour Party published a policy pamphlet entitled *The Labour Party Policy Report No. 1*, *Currency*, *Banking and Finance*. Keynes reviewed the pamphlet in a two-part article for *The New Statesman*.

From The New Statesman and Nation, *17 and 24 September 1932*

THE MONETARY POLICY OF THE LABOUR PARTY

I

There has recently appeared a convincing and acceptable proof of the continued vitality of the Labour Party—a penny pamphlet, the first of four, entitled, *The Labour Party Policy Report No. 1*, *Currency*, *Banking and Finance*. It contains the text of four resolutions for the forthcoming Annual Conference at Leicester, with a short supporting brief. The fourth resolution is a vague one asking for undefined emergency powers 'to deal with any attempt by private financial institutions to obstruct a Labour Government, damage national credit, or create a financial panic'. The other three deserve more attention than they have yet received. For they set forth a moderate and quite practicable monetary policy for adoption by the political party which represents the only organised body of opinion outside the National Government, and which will therefore be called on some day, presumably, to form an alternative government.

The first resolution plumps in favour of a sterling currency which would aim primarily at stability of value in terms of wholesale prices, and, only secondarily and to the extent that it is compatible with the first aim, at stability of value in terms of an international standard such as gold. I believe that this is a right decision. The true character of the choice before us is somewhat obscured if we express it as being for or against a gold standard. The real alternatives are a managed sterling currency (though there would be nothing to prevent other countries within or without the Empire from linking up with sterling), and a managed, or more probably half-managed, international currency which in practice would certainly turn out to be based on gold (or just possibly on gold and silver). A properly managed international standard would, however, seem to be quite outside practical politics for many years ahead. Perhaps it will never come, unless we first of all institute a managed sterling standard to show the world—which in these matters is still a generation behind even our own Bank of England—how the thing works. Moreover, a national sterling currency might be so managed as to secure the best of both worlds, except at times of great instability in the value of the international currency; and at such times we should be glad enough to be rid of the tie with gold. For I conceive that the Bank of England would continue to maintain gold reserves against emergencies and for the settlement of temporary adverse balances with the rest of the world, and would also have at all times definite buying and selling prices for gold (though with wider gold points than at present), the gold value of sterling being, however, not irrevocably fixed but subject to alteration in accordance with circumstances. Thus in practice the sterling standard would work out differently from a gold standard only on the occasions when gold was misbehaving itself.

Our own authorities, as typified by Mr Neville Chamberlain and Mr Montagu Norman, are not won over in their hearts from an ultimate return to gold as their goal and their ideal; though they will be much more careful this time than they were last time. For they conscientiously disbelieve in the whole order of ideas for which the alternative policy stands. It is, therefore, a matter of first-class importance that the progressive, experimental policy should be expressly endorsed by the second party in the state. Fortunately events are trending this way; and it will, in fact, be the doubting Mr Norman (doubting, not prejudiced, for he is an empiricist with whose scepticism dogma would be incompatible) who will have the first shot at trying to carry out the policy which is not his own choice.

At the same time, in endorsing the Labour Party's recommendation one must emphasise the great difficulties in the way of a successful management of sterling. It is not so easy as some of its advocates would, under the influence of a crude interpretation of the quantity theory, ask us to believe; and we must be content at first with something far short of perfection. It will, I think, require the exercise of a new technique, including, especially, a large measure of control over the volume of new investment.

The Labour Party's second resolution relates to the nationalisation of the Bank of England. This time they have left in abeyance their former proposal to nationalise the joint stock banks. Wisely and prudently in my opinion. For, in the first place, the control of the Big Five, otherwise than through the Bank of England, is not necessary for the purpose of handling the vital controls, whilst as a piece of socialism it belongs to a late stage of socialisation and is not one of the indispensable first measures. In the second place, I would lay ten to one that, were it a plank of the Labour platform, it would nevertheless be dropped as soon as the party assumed office, because of the obviously great difficulties of executing it relatively to the results to be achieved; and it is most important that this time the Labour programme should include some measures which there is a chance of their attempting to carry out in office. The proposal to nationalise the Big Five is first-class if conceived as a piece of irritation policy, but it is not at this stage serious business.

As regards the Bank of England the second resolution provides:

> That the Bank of England should be brought under public ownership and control; and that the Governor of the Bank should be appointed by the Government and be subject to the general direction of a Minister of Cabinet rank, who should in turn be responsible to the House of Commons for banking policy; the day-to-day business of the Bank being carried on by the Governor and his subordinates.

It is not unnatural, after what has occurred, that this resolution should have been so drafted. But we should, I think, consider carefully exactly what we want. I would lay down five propositions as embodying the essentials:

(1) The interest of private shareholders in the profits of the Bank, nominal though it now is, should altogether cease.

(2) The Bank should be expressly recognised as a national institution from which private profits and private interests are entirely excluded. The directorate should be selected on public grounds and should not stand for the interests of the City any more than for other national interests.

(3) The management of the Bank should be ultimately subject to the Government of the day and the higher appointments should require the approval of the Chancellor of the Exchequer.

(4) The principles of the currency system, e.g., whether or not the standard should be gold, or whether stability of wholesale prices or of the cost of living or of some other index, is to be its norm, should be determined by Parliament.

(5) The day-to-day policy of the Bank, its statistics, its technique and its immediate aims and objects should be as public as possible, and should be deliberately exposed to outside criticism.

But if these propositions are accepted I should complete them with a sixth, namely:

(6) The less direct the democratic control and the more remote the opportunities for parliamentary interference with banking policy the better it will be.

If the Bank of England is to carry out the monetary policy which is proposed in this pamphlet, it will be engaged in the practice of a very difficult technique, of which Parliament will understand less than nothing. A planned economy will be impracticable unless there is the utmost decentralisation in the handling of the expert controls. I would suggest to the Labour Party that the demand for democratic interference is not socialism but an echo of nineteenth-century Liberalism. Perhaps, however, I am interpreting the term 'banking policy' in the resolution in a more particular sense than is intended.

Moreover, it has been the recent policy of the Bank of England, rather than its powers or structure, which has been at fault. Its independence and its prestige are assets. Nor, in spite of its origins and the opportunity for interested motives on the part of the directorate, can its public spirit over the last decade be called in question. The demand for its subjection to the democracy largely arises, I think, out of peculiarities of recent years which will not characterise a normal regime. More often than not since the War the country has possessed no defined standard and not even a defined monetary policy laid down by Parliament; with the consequence that the Bank of England has been left free to exercise, though it has not been loth to exercise, a wider discretion than it ought to have or has had in the past or will have in the future, on matters which go far beyond the practice of a technique for the attainment of a purpose, the general character of which has been laid down by higher authority. The widespread feeling that the Bank of England is an irresponsible body exercising arbitrary power without marked success, has also been much accentuated by the mixed autocracy and mystery, as it appears to the outside world, of Mr Montagu Norman. But I am not sure that the blame here, too, is not laid at the wrong door. Mr Norman has often, in my opinion, been ill-judging, not in the details of his technique, of which he has shown himself a great master, nor in his disinterestedness or chivalry or devotion to the public interest, for he is a great public servant, but in his advice as to the main lines of policy, the choice of which, as distinct from the execution, was not properly his affair at all but that of the Government of the day. But Mr Norman is not an autocrat. It has been by his influence with successive Chancellors of the Exchequer and with his own colleagues, by his charm and by his powers of persuasion—gifts which in a social democracy are not yet forbidden (are they forbidden in the Union of Soviet Republics?

Perhaps they are)—that he has attained his ends. A man who can successively induce Mr Winston Churchill, Mr Philip Snowden, and Mr Neville Chamberlain to feed out of his hand, unfortified by success, preaching unpopular and austere courses, would be important under any form of government. With the personalities the same and knowledge no greater, it might not have made much difference if the machinery which the Labour Party desires had been in operation during the last ten years.

II

The third resolution for submission to the forthcoming Annual Conference of the Labour Party is of great importance and runs as follows:

That a National Investment Board, appointed by the Government on suitable grounds of ability, should be set up under the general direction of the appropriate Minister and working in close co-operation with the publicly owned Bank of England. That with the object of preventing waste and mis-direction in the use of long-term capital, the Board should exercise control over all new public issues on the capital market, and its permission should be required before any such new issue could be made. That the Board should be able to refuse 'leave to deal' on the Stock Exchange in any issue which, having been rejected as a public issue, had then been placed privately; and that it might be found necessary to give a Government guarantee, on the lines of the Trade Facilities Acts, in order to secure priority for approved schemes of industrial re-organisation, subject, however, to the acceptance of public control by the industries concerned.

I welcome warmly the acceptance of the principle of setting up a National Investment Board. But the above resolution does not go nearly far enough for me. For, apart from the qualified suggestion in the last clause, the duties of the Board would be mainly negative, and would have the object, apparently, of protecting the private investor from the abuses of private capitalism. There may be a good case for the control of new issues in the manner proposed, but it is difficult to draw the line between a mere permission and an approval which conveys some sort of implied recommendation. It might be difficult to avoid confusion between investments made by the investor entirely at his own risk with no one but himself to blame and investments which were subject to some sort of public guarantee.

But, apart from this, I doubt if the resolution envisages the essential problems in the right way. The real problems, as I see them, are concerned with the quantitative, rather than with the qualitative, control of new investment, partly with securing the right aggregate of new investment, and partly with securing that the amount of *foreign* lending should be appropriate to the circumstances. The resolution also seems to overlook the smallness of the part which purely private enterprise now plays, and is likely to play in future, in the direction of home investment. Moreover, home investment by private enterprise is not only on a comparatively small scale, but proceeds to a very great extent independently of the new issue market out of profits made by industry and retained within the business. Apart from a small volume of industrial debentures, the new issue market is mainly concerned within this field with the marketing to the public of investments made some time previously. Certainly it would be useful to protect the individual investor from loss if an effective means for doing so could be devised. But the amounts involved are relatively small, and there is a good deal to be said for leaving entirely to private choice and initiative the field which still belongs to private enterprise.

In any case this is not the main issue. Apart from the control of overseas loans, which certainly should not be left in future to *laissez-faire*, but which raise special problems of their own lying beyond the scope of this article, the main issue is concerned with the regulation of the pace of that predominant proportion of new investment at home which has already passed irrevocably out of the control of private enterprise and into the control of public and semi-public bodies.

Consider the two sets of statistics following:

	1914	1928	1929	1930	1931
			(£ million)		
Capital expenditure by local authorities	21·1	120·0	90·5	108·9	?
Building financed by building societies	8·8	58·7	74·7	88·8	90·2
Total	29·9	178·7	165·2	197·7	?

Thus £200,000,000 was invested through these two channels in 1930 compared with £30,000,000 in 1914. The above omits capital expenditure by the central Government (including the Post Office) or by public boards such as the Central Electricity Board, the Port of London, the Metropolitan Water Board, the Agricultural Mortgage Corporation, and the component parts of what will be the London Traffic Authority, or by universities and hospitals and the like. For comparison we may quote the aggregate of new issues of all kinds of capital purposes within the United Kingdom:

1928	£177,000,000	1930	£122,000,000
1929	£137,000,000	1931	£40,000,000

These figures include all borrowing through new issues by local authorities and public boards as well as by private enterprise.

Thus in the two years 1930 and 1931 the aggregate finance provided by building societies was appreciably greater than the above aggregate of new capital issues for all purposes within the United Kingdom. In short, considered quantitatively, private industrial investment is very far from being of the first importance. What we need is a co-ordinated policy to determine the rate of aggregate investment by public and semi-public bodies, in which case we could safely leave industry to raise what funds it needs as and when it chooses. Here is a task of vast importance lying ready to our hand. Here also is the instrument without command over which the business of controlling the value of sterling, envisaged by the Labour Party's first resolution, is likely to prove beyond our powers. I would urge that it is this which should be the main preoccupation of the proposed National Investment Board.

Moreover, apart from the proceeds of new capital issues, increasingly large sums are now accumulating in the hands of public and semi-public bodies and available for new investment, out of sinking funds, depreciation funds, and repayments and so forth. For the central Government the figure is, I think, in the neighbourhood of £50,000,000 per annum; for local government some £60,000,000 per annum; for building societies about £50,000,000 per annum. This does not include additional deposits in the Post Office Savings Bank or otherwise accruing in the hands of Government Departments through the National Health Insurance Fund, etc., etc., or additional loan and share capital raised by the building societies (which amounted to £45,000,000 in 1931). Nor does it include the sinking funds and depreciation funds of public boards. If to the total given by the above we add new developments financed out of profits and depreciation funds, retained within the business by private industrial enterprises, we see how small a thing it would be to control new public issues of capital for privately owned domestic enterprises.

The task of the National Investment Board, as I conceive it, is, therefore, first, the maintenance of equilibrium between the total flow of new investment on the one hand, and on the other hand the total resources available for investment at the price-level which we are endeavouring to maintain, i.e., so as to avoid both inflation and deflation; and secondly a division of the aggregate of new lending between foreign and domestic borrowers which is appropriate to the foreign exchange level best suited to the stability of domestic prices. I see no likelihood of our being able to maintain a stable value for sterling unless this task is attacked with knowledge and authority. For the desired equilibrium is most unlikely to come about of itself; and, failing it, nothing can prevent an instability of the price level. The Board's main instrument would have to consist, I think, in some method of pooling a considerable proportion of the funds accruing for investment and then ensuring an adequate demand for them, partly by making them available at a rate of interest which would attract a sufficient demand, and partly by stimulating the undertaking of particular investment propositions.

Occasionally it would be the duty of the Board to damp down the rate of investment. But, as a rule, I should expect that its chief problem would be to maintain the level of investment at a high enough rate to ensure the optimum level of employment. Without such an instrumentality we may be sure that the disastrous fluctuations in the volume of employment will continue in the future as severely as in the past, and perhaps more severely.

I consider, therefore, that this part of the Labour programme should be more ambitious. But this need not diminish satisfaction that the Party is moving in this direction. The grappling with these central controls is the rightly conceived socialism of the future.

On 11 October 1932 (not 10 October as suggested in the letter that follows), *The Times* gave prominence in its letters page to a communication from C. H. St J. Hornby commenting on a letter from a previous correspondent who had urged a programme of 'wise spending'. Hornby concluded his letter as follows

> I write this letter only because I feel that the subject is of such importance that it ought to be widely ventilated, and in the hope that economists will enter the field either to support him [the earlier correspondent] or to blow his possibly erroneous theory sky-high...In any case I am sure that it would interest many of your readers to hear what they have to say on the subject.

One result of this letter was that A. C. Pigou drafted a reply, which he hoped might be signed by a small sample of economists. Keynes was to collect the signatures. All of those approached agreed to sign Pigou's draft, except Sir William Beveridge and Edwin Cannan.

To the Editor of The Times, *17 October 1932*

Sir,

On October 10 you gave prominence in your columns to a letter inviting the opinion of economists on the problem of private spending. There are a large number of economists in this country, and nobody can claim to speak for all of them. The signatories of this letter have, however, in various capacities, devoted many years to the consideration of economic problems. We do not think that many of our colleagues would disagree with what we are about to say.

In the period of the War it was a patriotic duty for private citizens to cut their expenditure on the purchase of consumable goods and services to the limit of their power. Some sorts of private economy were, indeed, more in the national interest than others. But, in some degree, all sorts of economy set free resources—man-power, machine-power, shipping-power—for use by the Government directly or indirectly in the conduct of the War. Private economy implied the handing over of these resources for a vital national purpose. At the present time, the conditions are entirely different. If a person with an income of £1,000, the whole of which he would normally spend, decides instead to save £500 of it, the labour and capital that he sets free are not passed over to an insatiable war machine. Nor is there any assurance that they will find their way into investment in new capital construction by public or private concerns. In certain cases, of course, they will do this. A landowner who spends £500 less than usual in festivities and devotes the £500 to building a barn or a cottage, or a business man who stints himself of luxuries so that he can put new machinery into his mill, is simply transferring productive resources from one use to another. But, when a man economises in consumption, and lets the fruit of his economy pile up in bank balances or even in the purchase of existing securities, the released real resources do not find a new home waiting for them. In present conditions their entry into investment is blocked by lack of confidence. Moreover, private economy intensifies the block. For it further discourages all those forms of investment—factories, machinery, and so on—whose ultimate purpose is to make consumption goods. Consequently, in present conditions, private economy does not transfer from consumption to investment part of an unchanged national real income. On the contrary, it cuts down the national income by nearly as much as it cuts down consumption. Instead of enabling labour-power, machine-power and shipping-power to be turned to a different and more important use, it throws them into idleness.

Conduct in the matter of economy, as of most other things, is governed by a complex of motives. Some people, no doubt, are stinting their consumption because their incomes have diminished and they cannot spend so much as usual; others because their incomes are expected to diminish, and they dare not do so. What it is in any individual's private interest to do and what weight he ought to assign to that private interest as against the public interest, when the two conflict, it is not for us to judge. But one thing is, in our opinion, clear. The public interest in present conditions does not point towards private economy; to spend less money than we should like to do is not patriotic.

Moreover, what is true of individuals acting singly is equally true of groups of individuals acting through local authorities. If the citizens of a town wish to build a swimming bath, or a library, or a museum, they will not, by refraining from doing this, promote a wider national interest. They will be 'martyrs by mistake', and, in their martyrdom, will be injuring others as well as themselves. Through their misdirected good will the mounting wave of unemployment will be lifted still higher.

We are your obedient servants,

D. H. MACGREGOR (Professor of Political Economy in the University of Oxford)

A. C. PIGOU (Professor of Political Economy in the University of Cambridge)

J. M. KEYNES

WALTER LAYTON

ARTHUR SALTER

J. C. STAMP

The result was a series of critical letters from laymen and economists, notably a joint letter from Professors T. E. Gregory, F. A. von Hayek, Arnold Plant and Lionel Robbins of the L.S.E., opposing public expenditure. On 21 October the original six economists replied.

To the Editor of The Times, *21 October 1932*

Sir,

It is not possible for six people in their collective capacity to carry on a continuing correspondence. We wrote to you in reply to a letter to which prominence was given in your columns categorically inviting the opinion of economists in the matter of private spending, and we had no intention of carrying the matter farther. In certain comments, however, that have been made upon our letter there is revealed, as it seems to us, a fundamental confusion which, unless it can be dissipated, must render discussion futile and paralyse remedial action.

We are told that the vital thing to do at the present time is to 'concentrate such resources as we have upon works that are absolutely necessary, or which, when completed, will give the maximum of employment'; while expenditure now upon libraries, museums, and so on 'must inevitably reduce the funds available when confidence returns'. What are these 'resources' and 'funds'? It seems to be thought that there exists a stock of stored-up wealth the amount of which is fixed independently of our action and which we can only employ in setting people to work now, on pain of having less of it available to set them to work later on. This conception, though since its burial by Adam Smith it has enjoyed many resurrections, is an illusion. The resources out of which workpeople and all other persons are paid in any year consist almost entirely of what is produced—either directly or through purchase abroad—by the brains, hands, and capital equipment of the country. In so far as this labour and capital are idle, the resources available for paying income to their owners are not conserved; they simply do not come into existence.

The purpose of our letter to you was to urge that, while in normal conditions money economy of individuals and groups of individuals means that labour and capital are set to producing capital goods instead of consumption goods, in present conditions it often means that they are reduced to idleness. A reply which, ignoring the conclusive evidence of unemployment statistics, tacitly assumes that this reduction to idleness is impossible, misses the whole point of our contention.

We are your obedient servants,

D. H. MACGREGOR (Professor of Political Economy
in the University of Oxford)

A. C. PIGOU (Professor of Political Economy
in the University of Cambridge)

J. M. KEYNES

WALTER LAYTON

ARTHUR SALTER

J. C. STAMP

During the rest of the year, Keynes's journalism concentrated on international problems (see below, ch. 3).[4] However, with the turn of the year came a renewed interest in domestic affairs.

[4] The exception came in his evidence to the Royal Commission on Lotteries and Betting on 15 December. This evidence, and the ensuing letters to the press, appears in Volume XXVIII.

CHEAP MONEY, WISE SPENDING

From The Daily Mail, *1 January 1933*

SOME HOPEFUL PORTENTS FOR 1933

It is dangerous to prophesy about this slump. For one wonders if the economic system may not have lost its resiliency. Yet to judge from previous cases, we moved past the lowest point in the second half of 1932. And it is not safe to ignore the precedents.

In the early days of a slump we are too optimistic; but later on we are too easily discouraged. In 1929 some Americans persuaded themselves that the boom was permanent. Today they are beginning to believe the same thing about the slump.

But slumps, like booms, do come to an end; at least, they always have. It is true that this slump has been more violent than usual, but it has not yet been more prolonged. Slumps carry within themselves the seeds of a reaction—just as booms do.

I believe, therefore, that the wisest course today is to watch through a microscope for the slightest signs of recovery, and to be ready to regard as true portents any faint indications we can discern.

In this spirit I will throw academic caution away and scan the economic scene for what I can discover.

The last eighteen months have not been wasted, and several indispensable preliminaries to the recovery of health have been achieved. This country, and most of the world with it, has escaped from the impediments of a moribund gold system, without disaster and without discredit. As a direct consequence of this, we are no longer afraid to encourage enterprise with cheap money, and we have carried through triumphantly the absolutely vital task of reducing long-term rates of interest towards pre-war standards.

I attach first-class importance to this. Not enough time has yet elapsed for us to gain the full benefit, especially as the Treasury and the Bank of England are at present, for no known reason, prohibiting industry from taking advantage of conversion schemes. But the benefit will surely accrue in the course of 1933.

Scarcely less important, the Lausanne Conference has successfully settled reparations, and recent events have shown that the reopening of this problem is now most unlikely. The War debts are, I venture to believe, settling themselves—in the negative.

India, by exporting £80,000,000 of gold, has rehabilitated her finances and her purchasing power and is politically easier in her mind. Invulnerable China is stirring hopefully. Australia, accepting the advice of her economists, has almost solved a problem which looked, not long ago, insoluble. Germany, by the exercise of inhuman patience, shows an economic stability and even faint signs of improvement which it would have been rash to forecast a year ago.

If only one could forget about the United States! Yet even in that helpless conglomeration the indications suggest that the tide has fitfully turned and that the low points of last summer will not be repeated. America is not built to turn easily in traffic; but she is a new model (in parts) and does not lack horse-power or petrol.

What is the position here at home? If, viewing the prospect at large, I look at the unemployment figures or at the railway traffics, the indications are gloomy. But these things register what is, not what is coming. If I take the microscope, and, using the licence of New Year's Day, shut my eyes to what is unfavourable, I can see quite a few things to be pleased about; some of them, indeed, visible to the naked eye.

Let me make a short list—biassed and partial, I admit—of the favourable signs.

England is the only country in the world where the motor industry is prosperous (though the heavy side is under a cloud). We are not so poor that we cannot motor more; the consumption of petrol is up 5 per cent over 1931. We are buying new cars, as the recent registrations show. We are making remarkable progress towards capturing the export trade of the world, which by hereditary right should surely be ours.

The steel industry is stirring in its sleep. If we consider the effects of the cessation of shipbuilding and the state of the industry elsewhere in the world, the position here is satisfactory. Relatively we have much more than held our own. In 1931 France and Germany each had an output more than 50 per cent higher than ours; in 1932 we have been within striking distance of equality. In 1931 the steel output of the United States was five and a half times ours; in 1932 it has been about two and a half times. Here the tariff can claim a success, since, with the help of the departure from gold, our export trade has held its own; and there are some definite indications of further improvement in the near future.

The building and contracting industries have been hard hit by the cessation of municipal activity. But in the last quarter of 1932 the estimated cost of building plans approved (not very reliable, because the statistics omit London) has recovered to a higher level than for some little time.

The grid progresses gradually. The consumption of electric current is, I think, greater than ever.

The production of artificial silk is at a high figure reckoned on any previous standard. Some branches of woollen textiles are doing well. Even the Lancashire cotton industry seems in recent weeks to have been in a fair way towards settling its domestic quarrels.

The state of British agriculture has been the blackest spot of 1932, and it would be the height of unwisdom not to strain every orthodoxy to protect the farmer from another year like that. I wish all success to the courage and energy of Major Walter Elliot at the Ministry of Agriculture. Perhaps he can claim already to have turned in recent weeks the disastrous course of meat prices. At any rate, his attitude leads one to hope that he will do whatever proves necessary to raise prices to a reasonable figure. For my part, I favour direct action, and I would have the

Ministry, if necessary, enter the markets themselves and bid up prices to whatever they may deem a proper level.

I offer these good tidings for what they are worth. But I must not be misunderstood. I am not alleging that a recovery is in being either here or elsewhere. The improvements to which I point are partial and precarious, relative and not absolute. I am arguing no more than that there exists a possible background for recovery which was not in sight a year ago. The actual outcome of 1933 will depend upon ourselves and our neighbours. I see no cause to be fatalistic. It is our business to make sure that no opportunities are missed. May I offer three suggestions?

During the scare, a year ago, the Ministry of Health instituted a policy of vetoing almost all borrowing by local authorities to finance building or contracting or other enterprises. Since schemes of this kind are planned some time ahead, many months had to elapse before this policy could produce its full effect. But it was certain to increase unemployment in due course, especially as there was already a shortage of work in the industries most affected. It has, in fact, increased unemployment seriously.

My reading of the unemployment statistics for 1932 yields the conclusion that the additional employment created by tariffs and the departure from gold has been approximately balanced by the additional unemployment created by the Ministry of Health. The total unemployment thus caused is much greater than the direct unemployment, since each man whose purchasing power is curtailed by his being put out of work diminishes the employment he can give to others, and so on in a vicious circle.

The increased cost to the Treasury of unemployment relief must have been much greater than the saving to the rates. Initially, it is true, the policy had two excuses. It was started in a panic atmosphere, and it may have slightly helped the Treasury's conversion schemes, just as the general depression of industry has, by diminishing the competitive demand for loans. But today it is absolutely indefensible. It is no longer in key with the public mood. In itself it is silly beyond words.

In the second place, I believe that 1933 will be a better year and yield more taxation if the Chancellor of the Exchequer rides the country lightly in his next Budget. Aggressive taxation may defeat its own ends by diminishing the income to be taxed. It would be a long-sighted policy to grant a greater relief of taxation than is strictly justified by the evidence in hand.

Finally—though this, I suppose, is a remote hope—there is the opportunity for our Government to make bold proposals to the World Economic Conference. Ways exist, I am convinced, for relaxing by sound and healthy means the financial tension between countries which is strangling international trade.

So 1933 will be what we choose to make it.

On 4 January, Keynes discussed the issue of saving and spending on the BBC with Sir Josiah Stamp. The discussion appeared in print a week later.

From The Listener, *11 January 1933*

SPENDING AND SAVING

A discussion between Sir Josiah Stamp and J. M. Keynes

STAMP: *It is a long time, Keynes, since we have had such a chance for a really confidential chat about things, and many a day since I taught you anything. Now, we've been reading all this in the papers about spending and saving, getting mixed up in it ourselves, I suppose. Where do you think the public have got to on the subject? Has all this discussion really brought out any special points and made them clear, or is it all just as confused as when it first began?*

KEYNES: It's my impression that the public mood is changing. There was a good deal of panic about a year ago, but today isn't it getting realised pretty generally that one man's expenditure is another man's income? At any rate, that seems to me to be the central truth, never to be forgotten. Whenever anyone cuts down expenditure, whether as an individual or a town council or a Government Department, next morning someone for sure finds that his income has been cut off, and that is not the end of the story. The fellow who wakes up to find that his income is reduced or that he is thrown out of work by that particular piece of economy, is compelled in his turn to cut down his expenditure, whether he wants to or not.

STAMP: *That means he is cutting down the second man's income, and that is another man out of work.*

KEYNES: Yes, that is the mischief. Once the rot has started, it is most difficult to stop.

STAMP: *Just a minute. Let us first look at the Department or individual economising, and consider the result of the action. A country or a town, just like an individual, must live within its resources, and it will get into grave difficulties if it tries to go beyond them, for very soon it will be living on its capital.*

KEYNES: There can only be one object in economy, namely, to substitute some other better and wiser piece of expenditure for it.

STAMP: *Substitute! Yes, that brings me to my point. For example, what if the Government or the local authority economised in order to relieve taxation or rates, and allowed the individuals to spend more; or if the individuals spent less on consumption, in order that they or other people to whom they lent their money might build houses or factories. Wouldn't that get things right?*

KEYNES: But, my dear Stamp, is that what's happening? I suspect that the authorities are often economising without reducing rates or taxes and passing the extra spending power to the individual, and even when the individual has been given the extra spending power he is often playing for safety, or at least he thinks it virtuous to save and not to spend. But, as a matter of fact, it is not really these economies which will relieve the rates or taxes that I am making trouble about. It is that form of economy which means cutting off expenditure, which would naturally be met by borrowing. For in that case there is no advantage in the taxpayer having more, to compensate the loss of income for the fellow who has been retrenched.

STAMP: *Then what we really mean is that unless the public expenditure which is cut off is balanced by additional personal expenditure, there will be too much saving. After all, normal saving is only a different kind of expenditure, passed on to some public authority or business for producing bricks and machinery. Saving means more bricks; and spending means more boots.*

KEYNES: Yes, that's the whole point. Unless someone is using capital in bricks or the like, the country's productive resources are wasted, and saving is no longer another kind of spending. That's why I say that the deliberate curtailment of normal useful developments, which would ordinarily be met out of borrowing, seems to me to be, in present circumstances, a crazy as well as an injurious policy.

STAMP: *The difficulty is to find what you call 'normal useful developments'.*

KEYNES: On the contrary. The Ministry of Health, if I am rightly informed, is turning down practically all the normal applications of local authorities to borrow. I read, for instance, in a paper—I cannot vouch for the figures myself—that a questionnaire issued to the Building Industry National Council shows that something like £30,000,000 worth of public works have been held up as a result of the national economy campaign. National campaign for the intensification of unemployment is what I should call it!

STAMP: *Why on earth have they carried it to those limits? Why are they doing it?*

KEYNES: I cannot imagine. It's probably a legacy of some panic decision made many months ago, which someone has forgotten to reverse. Think what it would mean to the spirit of the nation, and in human terms, if we had even another quarter of a million employed. And I wouldn't be at all sure that the repercussions would stop there.

STAMP: *I am rather tender about Government Departments. Anyway, ragging a Government Department, whether it deserves it or not, is quite a different thing from urging individuals to spend more. Surely that might be both rather foolish and rather dangerous:*

foolish because of the reduction in their incomes, spending more than they can really afford; and dangerous because if you once encourage people to be reckless and to break down habits of thrift, you don't know where it will end.

KEYNES: I quite agree. It is not the individual who is the sinner, and therefore it is not reasonable to expect that it is from individual action that the remedy can come. That is why I stress so much the policy of public authorities. It is they who must start the ball rolling. You cannot expect individuals to spend much more when they are already, some of them, getting into debt. You cannot expect business men to launch out into extensions while they are making losses. It is the organised community which must find wise ways of spending to start the ball rolling.

STAMP: *I will put my point the other way round. Isn't the importance of keeping up habits of thrift in the individual an extra reason why public authorities should feel their responsibilities in this respect? If these habits and methods of thrift and saving, which are so useful in individual life, are to be made beneficial to the community, then it is absolutely essential to find useful ways of using the money which they are saving.*

KEYNES: Yes, that is my point. Besides, isn't curtailment of activities, and therefore of the national income, an incredibly short-sighted way of trying to balance the Budget?

STAMP: *Well, apart from any far-reaching questions of national credit, it would seem to me that all of it hits the Chancellor of the Exchequer in two ways. First of all, he has to meet the unemployment benefit for the men thrown out of work, and then, again, the yield of his taxes falls away, because he has to depend either on a man's income or on his expenditure, in two kinds of taxes. So that anything which reduces both the income and the expenditure of the individual must diminish the yield of the taxes. And, of course, if you are going to have losses on the receipt side and more on the payment side of the Budget, how would you remedy it, because an unbalanced*

Budget destroys our credit? Of course, I know there is a difference between the normal and the abnormal period.

KEYNES: But, Stamp, you will never balance the Budget through measures which reduce the national income. The Chancellor would simply be chasing his own tail—or cloven hoof! The only chance of balancing the Budget in the long run is to bring things back to normal, and so avoid the enormous Budget charges arising out of unemployment. So I contend that, even if you take the Budget as your test, the criterion of whether the economy would be useful or not is the state of employment. In a war, for example, everyone is busy, and it is difficult to get important and necessary jobs carried out, which is an obvious indication that if one kind of expenditure is reduced, an alternative and wiser expenditure will take its place.

STAMP: *The same would apply if the Government has a great housing scheme or a slum clearance scheme.*

KEYNES: Yes, or additional railways. Or new land which might be drained, or industries expanded rapidly owing to some new invention, or any such reason as that.

STAMP: *But if, as today, a half of the labour and plant of the country are idle, that is an indication that if one kind of expenditure is reduced it will not be replaced by an alternative and wiser expenditure. It means that nothing will take its place: no one will be richer, and everyone will be poorer.*

KEYNES: I find we agree more than we thought, but many a man considers even plausible expenditure today as truly daft. When the county council builds houses, the country will be richer [even] if the houses yield no rent at all. If it does not build houses, we shall just have nothing to show for it except more men on the dole.

STAMP: *Always provided that you pay a reasonable regard to people's ideas about public credit. It is not going to do any government or other authority any good if it is supposed to be heading for bankruptcy.*

KEYNES: I do not believe that measures which truly enrich the country will injure the public credit. You have forgotten my point that it is the burden of unemployment and the decline in the national income which are upsetting the Budget. Look after the unemployment, and the Budget will look after itself.

STAMP: *So much for the public expenditure side of the case. What about developing the outlets for individual saving? These savings have to go on if each man is to be reasonably prudent in his own way of living. What outlets do you approve of yourself, and what new ways can you suggest?*

KEYNES: Let me give you an example of the sort of thing which seems to me to be wholly admirable. The building societies have done splendid work since the War, because they have organised saving on the one hand, and have at the same time organised ways of using the thrift on building houses on the other hand. To them the two complementary activities have gone hand in hand. Are they not even in danger of attracting more funds than they can use?

STAMP: *I won't comment on that, except to say you make me feel virtuous. But I hope you won't draw from their case the conclusion that a movement, say, like the National Savings Certificate movement, ought to be discarded.*

KEYNES: Stamp, you are thinking of our broadcast a year or so ago [*JMK*, vol. xx, pp. 315–25]. I have been much misunderstood about that. Diminished saving for the class of people who buy savings certificates I reckon a very second-rate remedy. My argument was that if public works are stopped, particularly at a time when private enterprise is stopping from temporary overcapacity and is therefore not in a position to expand, then private saving can do any amount of harm. You remember what I said—every pound saved puts a man out of work. I still maintain that, and I doubt if you will deny it.

STAMP: *No, certainly, if nothing is going to be done with the resources which are released, people will have stinted themselves of something useful or pleasant with no other result than that of putting out of work the man who would have worked to provide for them. You mustn't conclude from this that private spending is the remedy that I prefer.*

KEYNES: On the contrary. I only put forward private spending as a way in which well-disposed individuals could undo a little of the harm which the Government is doing by curtailing the work which we ought to set going as an organised community. In my opinion, it isn't really the business of private individuals to spend more than they naturally would, any more than it is their business to provide for the unemployed by private charity. These things should be done by the organised community as a whole—that is to say, by public authorities.

STAMP: *I am very glad that I have got you to clear that up, because I don't think many people have really understood that this is the line you intended to take. I am glad you don't take an objection to private thrift, for whatever benefits you might get today along that line, you would be doing vastly more mischief in the long run, I feel.*

KEYNES: Certainly, I even save myself at times, I am its friend by demanding a policy which would allow thrift to be useful and productive to the community. The enemies of thrift are those who, by cutting off the outlets for it, deprive it of its purpose, and turn what should be a public benefit into an instrument for the aggravation of unemployment. That, I repeat, is what it is in this sort of circumstances. If you cut off the demand from the county council and public authorities, there isn't slightest chance that a private domestic business alone will be able to use anything approaching the amount which a healthy and well employed community of England would save, believing in the principle of thrift.

STAMP: *Aren't you being rather pessimistic about the amount of unemployment which expanding private enterprise might absorb, and have you looked at the thing from the point of view of statistics of saving in the past? Don't you think that with a real revival of business there might be a more remarkable absorption of these savings than we are at present inclined to think?*

KEYNES: I doubt it. You must take into account the embargo which is now in force against a great deal of the foreign lending, which used to get a big proportion of our savings. We have got to replace all that, you know. I doubt if private enterprise at home, even in its palmiest days, ever absorbed half the national savings, and considering the extent to which public utilities are in public hands today, I am sure that they never will in the future. I am all for giving private enterprise a run, and using all the capital it can, but I believe one is living in a false paradise if one supposes that in any foreseeable future it will be able to take up the amount which this country could save when it was prosperous and everybody properly employed.

STAMP: *I believe that that way of looking at it hasn't been faced up to by many people. What about the statistical attitude to it? Savings come to a certain figure. They are bound to, with all the different opportunities for saving—insurance and the like—that ought to go on, and if any individual, being reasonably prudent in his own living, raises the figure, it must be properly used by business expansion or public expenditure, or the two put together, and if these two don't do the trick then there is serious trouble with employment. If there is a gap, then the best thing is for business to expand to fill it up. Failing this, then the next best thing is for public expenditure to increase and fill it up. If both of these fail, or for any good reason the public expenditure cannot be increased enough, then the final device or makeshift to get the two sides to balance is for the savings themselves to be decreased until the excess above the two uses has disappeared, but somehow or other the difference must be used or made to disappear.*

KEYNES: Yes, and I repeat that it won't be by business. In the near future you won't find business expansion in this country anything like enough to absorb the savings. Expenditure from various public authorities and public boards and so on must be increased, or if people won't have that, then the alternative has to be adopted of reducing savings. You can't have it both ways.

STAMP: *I go a long way with you in this direction, but I beg you not to treat too lightly the principle of unwise and unbalanced public budgets. That kind of principle must still be respected. I believe that the true nature of our dilemma is the fact that one principle cannot always walk alone in life, and two principles, each one excellent in itself, may sometimes conflict. We are forced to prefer one to the other at any given time. We know the virtuous person says two things. First, thrift is a fine thing; save all you can. He also says, to reduce public expenditure is bad, cut it out. He doesn't realise that if each of these highly virtuous principles is carried to an extreme, there must be a serious alteration to the equilibrium of savings, so that they are used as a kind of mechanical necessity or virtue in our modern economical scheme, while the views about balanced budgets are a kind of psychological necessity.*

KEYNES: You are always going back to this question of the Budget. So far as that is concerned, I should say that things like the sinking fund aren't so important in these days as they would be in more prosperous times, and I think that the Chancellor of the Exchequer would be long-sighted if he were to take rather an optimistic view, and give us perhaps in his next Budget rather more relief than is strictly justified by the facts actually in sight. If he does, he will help to bring the facts in sight, which would justify the optimism that he has adopted. But that is not really what I want. It is loan expenditure I am wanting. It is all those capital developments of varying utility. I agree that traditionally we think it quite proper to finance all the means by loans, and that expenditure of that kind is carried out by local authorities or by the central government. And I believe that in the long run a policy of that kind would really help the Budget, more than will the other policy, of trying to cut things down and down.

STAMP: *What you are saying really is that at times when business expansion is at a low point people are not launching out, but it is rather at these times that public expansion ought to be at its height. No mention of banks or rate of interest or monetary value! Marvellous! I think we will agree that it is no easy thing to find an outlet for our savings at the present time, and therefore I am with you that we should not neglect any opportunity which offers itself. There are a thousand things which need doing if we are to be a community equipped in proportion to our opportunities, taking advantage of all modern scientific developments. We get rich by doing things, and not by cutting off activities. So up, and be busy.*

KEYNES: Yes, the fact is that spending and saving are in very truth complementary activities. The object of saving is to spend the proceeds on useful and necessary equipment. We must save in order that spending may be healthy, and equally we must spend if saving is to be healthy.

STAMP: *In short, this saving and spending of ours are really, or ought to be, sort of sister shows.*

On 31 January, Keynes took part in a conference at the offices of the Royal Institute of British Architects to consider a proposal to establish a national public utility housing board. Before the meeting Keynes had prepared an article on housing for the next issue of *The New Statesman*, as part of a series on housing and employment. This article reflected his remarks at the meeting.

From The New Statesman and Nation, *4 February 1933*

A PROGRAMME FOR UNEMPLOYMENT

In last week's *New Statesman and Nation* Sir Ernest Simon made out an overwhelming case against the Government's housing policy. It is a posthumous child, I suppose, of the panic of eighteen months ago. With the national mood as it was then, this policy might have found supporters. Today few could be found to defend it. It will show a sad inertia on the part of the House of Commons if the changes in the Bill for which Sir Ernest Simon asks are not made. There are today 400,000 operatives out of work in the building and construction industries, costing the dole some £20,000,000 a year. There are tens of thousands of slum dwellers living, for reasons beyond their own control, in conditions which disgrace the community. The fall in the rate of interest and the fall in building costs have combined in recent months to render it possible for the first time to make a real inroad on the slum problem on the basis of existing legislation. To choose this moment to introduce what Sir Ernest truthfully calls an anti-Housing Bill is to close one's mind to generosity, to good sense, and even to the breath of the popular mood.

The Ministry of Health is indeed in danger of earning a most unenviable reputation. Along with the Foreign Office, it is the outstanding failure of the National Government—the subject of half-hearted and unconvinced apology by other members and supporters of the Government. For whilst the Anti-Housing Bill is, as yet, only a project, the famous Anti-Employment Memorandum to local authorities[5] is nearly eighteen months old. The amount of potential employment which it has nipped in the bud cannot, of course, be accurately computed. The Ministry of Health themselves may not appreciate the amount of devastation they have caused, since they know only the amount of border-line cases reaching them in spite of the circular, which they have turned down. But the most thorough investigation which has been made, namely by the Building Industries National Council, suggests that the curtailment by local authorities has been of the order of £30,000,000. If so, then, reckoning that every man put directly into employment leads to the secondary employment of at least another man (and there is strong evidence that this calculation is not far out), the Ministry of Health have put some 250,000 men out of work, and have thus offset a good proportion of the benefits to employment resulting from the tariffs and the departure from gold. Incidentally, they have made a substantial contribution towards

[5] Circular No. 1222 to Local Authorities of 11 September 1931.

unbalancing the Budget, through the increased cost of the dole and the loss of taxable income and profits throughout industry. And they have done this, so to speak, on purpose. For the bulk of the works with which they have interfered have been the normal developments of English local government, usually and properly financed by loans, and capable, moreover, of being financed in considerable part by current sinking funds on past improvements without increasing net indebtedness. Indeed, what is happening is scarcely credible. For local authorities have been ordered to postpone capital works, which are admitted to be necessary sooner or later, if they are not urgent in the sense that they are reasonably capable of postponement; and there are even cases of roads urgently required, which have been abandoned half-finished—though here it is the decision to suspend loans by the Road Fund which is to blame. What is Sir Hilton Young waiting for? When employment is back to normal and the building trades are busy, is that the moment he will choose for letting local authorities off the leash?

Now it may be that there are those in Whitehall who genuinely believe that 'in these hard times' the country is too poor to afford employment—forgetting that our income is only another name for what we produce when we are employed. It may be that they believe that we can save up our economies against a later day, and that the surplus plant and unemployed men, which are simply the other facet of 'economy', are storing up reserves of energy and enthusiasm which will enable them to work treble time 'when finance permits'. Yet savings are, of course, the one thing which will not 'keep'. If they are not used in capital developments *pari passu*, they disappear forever in doles, deficits and business losses.

But let us take the other hypothesis, which I am sure holds true of most of the members of the Government, of most of Whitehall, of most of the members of Parliament, as it does of most thinking and feeling men. Let us suppose that the authorities are passionately anxious to reduce unemployment and ready to run risks in supporting any plausible measures. Let us suppose, further, that they are large-minded, imaginative, bold, enthusiastic, constructive, energetic. Is it absurd to suppose such things? Why should it be? At any rate, let us suppose them. What then could we do?

In *The New Statesman and Nation* of December 24th I discussed the international field of action, with particular reference to the possibilities of the World Economic Conference.[6] But limiting ourselves to the domestic field, to what is immediately possible independently of improvements outside, and to proposals which probably raise the minimum of controversy, there seem to me to be four matters lying directly to our hands.

The first is to adopt with energy Sir Ernest Simon's proposals for dealing with the slums.

The second is for the Ministry of Health to withdraw their notorious memorandum, and, in place of it, to inform local authorities that now is the time, having regard to low rates of interest and to low building costs, for them to press on with their normal programmes of development, particularly those which it would be usual and proper to finance out of loans, such as municipal buildings, housing and town planning, schools, sewerage, gas, water, electricity, and transport; and that the Ministry is prepared to work overtime giving prompt approval to loans for all useful and desirable things.

The third is to organise public opinion in favour of individual spending of a capital or semi-capital character, such as repairs and improvements to our houses and to their furnishing and equipment, supplying ourselves, to the extent of our means, with the conveniences and amenities which the modern world offers and which once enjoyed are never willingly relinquished. Why does not the Post Office offer to install telephones, free of rent for one quarter 'on approval', in all houses of more than a given rateable value? Why do not the gas and electricity authorities

[6] Below, pp. 210–16.

pipe and wire every house in return for a small annual rental and lend heating apparatus for a three months' trial? Why should not the Inland Revenue allow temporarily an extra depreciation allowance in respect of repairs and renewals, whether private or industrial, undertaken in excess of the normal allowance within the next twelve months? These are samples of many suggestions which could be made. If we seriously desire to break the vicious circle and to start the ball of progress rolling again, why do we not do something? I understand that the Rotarian Societies throughout the country are initiating widespread propaganda for private effort along these lines.[7] As an inhabitant of Bloomsbury, for example, I have received a circular from the Mayor of St Pancras urging a united effort to expand private expenditure. These are right ideas, and those who are advocating them are showing a rightly directed public spirit.

Nevertheless, private efforts of this kind will not prove adequate by themselves. Individual incomes are so contracted today that many individuals, however great their good will, cannot do much. We must first increase individual incomes by setting on foot large-scale capital developments which are capable of causing the stagnant savings of the community to circulate again. I come, therefore, to the fourth expedient, which might, if it were added to the other three, restore to us a large measure of prosperity.

If we look round to discover the outstanding capital requirements of today, it is obvious, beyond controversy, what it is—the provision of houses available *to be let* at modest rentals. Sir Enoch Hill, who is in an excellent position to judge, declared a short time ago that there is today a deficiency of at least 1,000,000 houses. The great work done by the building societies in recent years is meeting the demand for houses *to be owned* by the occupiers. There is no means as yet of dealing with the problem of the slums except along the lines urged by Sir Ernest

[7] See below, p. 190.

Simon. Between these two extremes there lies an urgent and unsatisfied demand which is not being adequately met by the existing instrumentalities.

Yet time and opportunity have at last joined hands to make this possible. Building costs have fallen from 20 to 30 per cent in the last five years. The following figures, which I have extracted from the remarkable issue of *The Architect's Journal* for January 11th, 1933, may be interesting even to the layman:

		1932		1927	
		s	d	s	d
Mechanics' wages	per hour	1	7½	1	9½
Labourers' wages	per hour	1	2¾	1	4½
Hire of three-ton lorry and driver	per hour	4	6	6	6
Blue lias lime	ton	36	6	56	0
Portland cement	ton	46	0	58	6
Building sand	ton	8	6	13	0
Bricks					
flettons	1,000	58	0	63	6
Stocks first quality	1,000	91	0	107	0
Stocks second quality	1,000	82	6	101	0
Red brick facings	1,000	147	6	190	0
Welsh slates	1,000	375	0	540	0
Roofing tiles, machine made	1,000	90	0	130	0
Carcassing timber	F.C.	2	2	2	9
1 in. deal flooring	—	22	0	29	0
Rolled steel joists	cwt	10	9	12	6
4 in. rain-water pipes	F.R.		10	1	3
21 oz. sheet glass	F.S.		3⅜		5
Linseed oil	gall.	2	2	3	7

At the same time the rate of interest has also fallen by a third. The total result is that, if full advantage is taken of the gilt-edged rate of interest, houses can now be built to let at about two-thirds of the rental which it would have been necessary to charge previously. Thus, according to expert calculations, houses can be built today, provided the finance is available at present gilt-edged rates for the period during which the cost is being amortised, to let at 8/- to 9/- a week (including repairs and amortisation, but excluding rates), at which figure there is an unsatiable demand.

A practical scheme might take some such form as the following. There might be set up a National Housing Board on lines already proposed by Sir Raymond Unwin, authorised to borrow, under Treasury guarantee, up to, say, £100,000,000 in the first instance, though a considerable proportion of this could probably be handled (e.g., through the municipalities and the building societies) without a public issue. This Board would enter into arrangements with the operatives and with the building industry for the stabilisation of prices over a period covering the initial programme. It would then proceed to make its funds available for the building of dwelling houses both directly and through all suitable existing organisations. In particular, it should work in close co-operation with the building societies, they providing in the main the bridge between the Board and private individuals, the guarantee of the Board making possible the provision through building societies of houses *to be let*. It should also function through the Housing Committees of Municipal Corporations and other local authorities, providing the means of carrying through the planned developments of these bodies. It would aid the finance of existing town-planning organisations, such as Welwyn. It should also finance and supervise new local housing corporations for the large-scale development of new town-planned areas. In particular, it might make a beginning with the organised rebuilding of London on the south side of the river. The project of a Board of this character is already receiving authoritative support, and was unanimously approved by a largely attended meeting of housing authorities last Tuesday summoned by the Royal Institute of British Architects under the Chairmanship of Sir Austen Chamberlain.

Would such a body need a subsidy, beyond the Treasury guarantee for its loans? I do not see why it should. But it would be advisable that a reserve fund should be established against contingencies as a protection against the Treasury guarantee becoming actually operative. For this purpose a small contribution from the Unemployment Insurance Fund, on the lines proposed by Mr Brebner in his letter to *The New Statesman and Nation* last week, deserves consideration. That is to say, the Unemployment Insurance Fund would make a small overall percentage contribution to the expenditure of the National Housing Board, calculated to represent a proportion of the dole which would have been payable otherwise to the men brought *directly* into employment by the Housing Board's activities.

Keynes sent copies of this article to Sir Hilton Young, the Minister of Health, and to Sir Arthur Robinson, his permanent secretary. His covering letter, which was broadly the same for both men, is of some interest, as are the replies he received.

To SIR HILTON YOUNG, *4 February 1933*

Dear Hilton,

I enclose a copy of an article which I have written for this week's *New Statesman and Nation*. I hope that you won't take these criticisms personally, for that is certainly not what I intend. But I do feel very strongly the points which I have expressed in the article, as do many others; for example, Pigou, as you will have seen from his article in *The Times*, is wholeheartedly on the side of a programme of activity.[8] I wish you would have a talk with him—or with anyone else whose opinion you would respect.

Forgive me, therefore, for the violence of my attack. It would be such a splendid thing if the Ministry could join in an effort for something large and constructive, instead of, as it seems to me, pursuing a policy which cannot have any other effect in present circumstances but to aggravate unemployment and to impoverish the country.

[8] 6 January 1933.

I am also sending a copy of this article to Sir Arthur Robinson.

Yours,
[copy initialled] J.M.K.

From SIR HILTON YOUNG, *6 February 1933*

Private

My dear Maynard,

I am obliged to you for your letter enclosing a copy of your article in *The New Statesman.*

Clearly you are in radical disagreement with the policy of the Government in this matter. If I do not answer your criticisms of our policy in this letter it is because I hope to have an early opportunity of dealing with the matter in the House.

As to practical administration, you are barking up the wrong tree. In general, it is the local authorities that are economising, not the Minister of Health who is enforcing economies upon them.

I read with pleasure what you write about your criticisms not being intended personally; the more so, because I should not have understood that intention from your article.

Yours sincerely,
E. HILTON YOUNG

From SIR ARTHUR ROBINSON, *6 February 1933*

Dear Mr Keynes,

Many thanks for your letter of the 4th and enclosed proof of article.

If you substituted the Government for the Ministry of Health, the result would be more accurate and more fair to the Ministry. That being so, you will not expect a Civil Servant to say anything, the role of a whipping post being familiar to us! I should, of course, be very glad to see you at any time on this or any matter.

Yours very truly,
ARTHUR ROBINSON

On 9 February, the Committee on Economic Information, as a result of a request from the Prime Minister at a meeting on 31 January, sent him a letter on financial policy advocating increased development policy by the Government rather than the retrenchment implied by the economy policy imposed to meet the 1931 crisis. It echoed earlier recommendations of the Committee to end the discouragement of local authority expenditure and complete public works such as by-passes left unfinished during the crisis, if necessary by borrowing.

Keynes also touched on the same themes when he spoke at a dinner which the Cambridge Chamber of Commerce gave in his honour on 17 February.

In late February, Keynes went further.

To GEOFFREY DAWSON, *22 February 1933*

Dear Dawson,

I have felt very strongly moved in the last day or two to write two or three articles on the present situation, which I would offer you for *The Times* and then perhaps expand shortly afterwards into a pamphlet.

The articles would cover two topics. The first would be the question of evaluating the real advantage to the Budget of schemes of home expansion. The second would concern itself with a programme of an international fiduciary gold currency to be adopted by the World Economic Conference as a means of easing the international tension. On each of these topics I feel that I have something substantial to say.

As regards the first, I enclose herewith a first draft, so as to show you the sort of stuff it is. The second would consist in explaining a plan, which is not really my own, but has been evolved by a group which, for your private information, includes H. D. Henderson of the Economic Advisory Council, Stamp, Layton, Salter, Blackett and Sir Alfred Lewis of the National Provincial Bank.[9]

If you were to take the articles, I think they should appear fairly soon. I mean, no later than, say, a fortnight hence; of course the exact date is immaterial.

I would be very grateful if you would let me know if you are attracted by the idea of taking them.

Yours sincerely,
[copy initialled] J.M.K.

[9] On this, see below, pp. 203–4.

Dawson accepted Keynes's proposal on 24 February and Keynes set to work to prepare the series which, owing to the length of the first article, they agreed should run to four articles on consecutive days. Originally the articles were to run from 6 to 9 March, but events in Germany, notably Hitler's accession to power, caused them to be delayed until 13–16 March when 'The Means to Prosperity' (*JMK*, vol. IX, pp. 335–66) appeared.

Before publication, Keynes sent copies to Hubert Henderson. His comments are of some interest.

From H. D. HENDERSON, *28 February 1933*

My dear Maynard,

Many thanks for sending me your article on Internal Expansion. I've no criticisms of a type representing practical emendations, except that I think it would be well, if it is not too late, to modify your reference to Rowe, who didn't really 'propose' to spend £100 millions on the slums. That was a purely hypothetical figure to indicate the limits of the possible burden on the Exchequer of what he was proposing. He implied that he only seriously contemplated an expenditure of 'far less than the amount named'.

But I'd like to convey my general reactions to your article. Of course I'm entirely in favour of reversing the engines in regard to public works programmes; and I think that the beneficial repercussions of doing so in present circumstances would probably be fully as great as you claim. None the less, I don't like the approach of the Kahn calculations; and, what is more important from the practical standpoint, I dislike the implication that something very large-scale might easily be done in the way of public works.

My objection to the calculations is that while they deal with great minuteness with certain qualifications to the repercussion argument, and by so doing create an impression of almost excessive carefulness and moderation, they take no account of the qualifications which are, or may be, of crucial importance. In the first place, there is the point that the subsidised public work may in some degree take the place of work which would otherwise have been done without subsidy. This point has no substance when we are dealing with such questions as whether some needed employment exchanges should be built; and it would have no substance if you were proposing a large expenditure on armaments. But it becomes very important indeed in connection with most of the things which you and others do in fact propose. Take, for example, your £100 millions 'to be spent under the auspices of a National Housing Board'. Obviously to a considerable extent your Board would build houses which private enterprise would build otherwise. To what extent it's quite impossible to say. Some argue, and *a priori* it's quite conceivable, that the reduction in the number of houses built by private enterprise will be more than 100 per cent of the houses your corporation will build in practice. One can't make any general 'allowance' for this factor, which will apply to public works no matter what they are, and no matter upon what scale they are attempted.

At this stage let me appeal to you not to brush aside, as I think you're rather disposed to do, the essential administrative fact that the only kinds of public works which come under the direct control of the central Government are the following:— (1) armaments; (2) Government offices (including employment exchanges); (3) the Post Office (including telephones). Almost everything else, including roads, must be undertaken by a local authority; and all that the Government can do is to bribe and to harry. Now, so long as that is so, it is quite an unreal approach to say—'A capital expenditure of £3 millions will help the Exchequer to the extent of £2 millions. Therefore let us subsidise everything two-thirds.' You have an immense range of different sorts of local authority work, some of which they undertake without any grants from the Exchequer, for some of which they get moderate grants, and for some, like trunk roads, high grants. The main practical question, therefore, for a Government which wishes to press forward with public works, is whether it will increase the various rates of grant, and if so by how much in each case; and it must do so, knowing that it will be paying the higher rate of grant for all the work that would have been done anyway at the lower rate, and without knowing how much additional work will be done. You may say that doesn't matter; you don't care what happens as between rates and taxes. That may suffice as an answer so far as your financial calculations are concerned, but it's no answer to the point that the extent to which any Government can get local authorities to go ahead with schemes of work is necessarily very limited. So long as we retain a system of local government at all, the way in which the cost of local schemes is defrayed as between the local authorities and the Exchequer must be determined by reasonable and defensible principles; and from that standpoint there are grave objections to going so far as the Labour Government did in the direction of increasing the scales of grant, and thereby queering the pitch of normal financial standards in these matters, for the sake of immediate unemployment policy. It adds immensely to a public impression that your policy is irresponsibly profligate, and is thus highly relevant to the questions of confidence and so forth that I shall come to presently, if you are bribing local authorities with grants in excess of what could be justified on normal administrative principle.

For this reason, it is, I am convinced, an illusion to suppose that public works represent something that can be turned on at will by the Government on a large scale. The difficulty of doing so is further increased by the long time period requisite for most public works schemes.

This brings me to my second main qualification of the calculations. This is the familiar one that the public works schemes may in various ways, e.g. by raising rates of interest, disturbing confidence, etc., diminish the volume of general industrial activity. In present conditions I don't think this point has any force as regards a moderate unostentatious programme: but it seems to me to have real force if it were a question of a splash grandiose programme, and in that connection the points I have made in the preceding two paragraphs are highly pertinent. You often say—'It's nonsense to talk about confidence; confidence depends on orders.' Very likely. But I maintain that if you were to announce that you were going in for a large £200 million programme, you would not get a single order under that programme for at least a year, whereas the effects on the gilt-edged market and the like of the announcement of your intention would be immediate. You might thus easily get a vicious circle wound up before your virtuous circle had begun to operate at all. Speaking generally, therefore, I am very much off the idea of public works as a major constructive remedy for our present troubles. My mind is moving just now much more in the direction of, let me say, a minimum Communism. What would you say to a proposal that coupons should be given in respect of every child between nine months and five years of age, entitling it to a pint of milk a day free of charge, the cost to be defrayed until trade revives by frankly inflationary means?

Yours ever,

H.D.H.

From H. D. HENDERSON, *8 March 1933*

Dear Maynard,

Many thanks for sending me copies of your *Times* articles. It seems to me that a more logical order would be to reverse the first two articles. The one on the raising of prices is the true introductory article, surveying the problem as a whole in its national and international aspects, and this article could be placed first without the alteration of a single word other than the subsequent references back. But, of course, this doesn't matter.

Article II: I don't like the reference to the remonetisation of silver at the top of page 5. This is not something which is happening, like the increased gold output, which we 'all welcome'. I suggest a full-stop after 'hoards', and then—'the remonetisation of silver would tend in the same direction, though it has not in my opinion the quantitative importance that some attach to it'.[10] Earlier in this article, at the top of page 3, I don't like your definition

[10] Keynes removed the reference.

of increasing loan expenditure. The reference to relieving taxation gives this too much a public finance flavour at the outset, which is emphasised when you proceed immediately to say that the Labour Government attempted this method. Your fundamental proposition is surely that aggregate spending power can only be raised by increasing the loan expenditure of the community as a whole, not necessarily of the Government. The subsequent development of your argument leads you to your conclusion that in view of the severity of the slump, 'the first step has to be taken on the initiative of public authority'. The reference to taxation is not formally necessary here, since a Budget deficit implies an increase of loan expenditure. I suggest therefore that your definition in paragraph 4 (i) should be simply—'by increasing the loan expenditure of the community',[11] and that the reference to the Labour Government should begin 'By means of public works the Labour Government etc.'[12]

I think your third and fourth articles are admirable and I have no suggestions to make except that it is perhaps worth considering whether you might suggest, in view of the American banking debacle, that a beginning with the international gold note plan might usefully be made by the joint action of Great Britain, the United States and France as a means of safeguarding against violent transfers of funds (more probably, I think, to America than away from it) in the present emergency.

I think the articles as a whole make a very effective series.

Yours ever,
H.D.H.

Keynes also heard from Viscount Astor, the proprietor of *The Times*.

From VISCOUNT ASTOR, *9 March 1933*

Dear Keynes,

After hearing from you the other day that you were proposing to publish your scheme in *The Times* I asked the editor of that paper if I could have two advance copies to send to the U.S.A. I am sending these with covering letters to Franklin Roosevelt and Mr Douglas (who I think is Director of the Bureau of the Budget). I know both of them and it occurred to me that they might consider your suggestions more impartially if they were sent unofficially by me than if your suggestions were in any way connected with our Government policy.

Yours,
ASTOR

[11] Keynes adopted this suggestion.

[12] Keynes adopted this suggestion.

After the final article appeared the Chancellor of the Exchequer wrote to Keynes.

From NEVILLE CHAMBERLAIN, *16 March 1933*

Dear Mr Keynes,

I have been reading your articles in *The Times* and I should be very glad to have an opportunity of a talk with you about them. Unfortunately I shall be engaged tomorrow morning and the earlier part of the afternoon in conversations with Monsieur Bonnet, the French Finance Minister, but I wonder whether you could come and see me at the Treasury at 6 o'clock.

Yours sincerely,
N. CHAMBERLAIN

Keynes was intrigued by the proposal. As he put it to R. F. Kahn on 16 March, 'Could it be that the Walls of Jericho are flickering?' After he saw the Chancellor he reported:

From a letter to R. F. KAHN, *20 March 1933*

I had a very satisfactory talk with the Chancellor of the Exchequer on Friday. He seemed to be pretty virgin soil and to hear everything with an open mind and an apparently sympathetic spirit, but quite for the first time.

By 23 March he began to think of replying to critics.

To GEOFFREY DAWSON, *23 March 1933*

Dear Dawson,

I am now beginning to think seriously as to what form my further contribution to *The Times* should take.

It appears to me that there are three topics which may require further handling.

1. The first one relates to the train of reasoning by which I arrive at the multiplier relating secondary employment to primary employment, and the general question whether or not my estimates as to the employment which would be incurred are unduly optimistic. There is an important criticism along

these lines in the issue of *The New Statesman and Nation* which will be published tomorrow. In any case I have not attempted to show, so far, just how I reached my results, and perhaps have asked people too much to take it on trust.

2. The second question is that of the scale on which I should consider action to be necessary if it were to be effective, with a few details as to the sort of way in which the programme could be carried out in concrete terms. I think a good many critics have a false idea as to the magnitude of the effort which would be necessary to produce valuable results.

3. The third question relates to the international issue and various comments which have been made about that.

Of these three questions, the first is rather technical, though I think I have found a way of expressing the argument in a popular form. Moreover as the main criticism on these lines has appeared in *The New Statesman and Nation*, it would be very suitable if I were to develop this part of my argument there. I know the Editor of that paper would like me to do so. If, however, you would definitely like me to do it in *The Times*, I should be ready to do so. Perhaps the best way would be for me to write out at once what I should say under this head, and let you see it. I could then deal with the criticism in *The New Statesman and Nation* by writing a letter to the Editor of that paper dealing with such points as I was not treating in my article, and referring my critic to *The Times* for the complete story.

Will you let me know what you would like in general; in particular, how much and at what sort of date?

Yours sincerely,
[copy initialled] J.M.K.

To GEOFFREY DAWSON, *27 March 1933*

Dear Dawson,

You will have had my letter of a few days ago. Now that I have actually got down to writing my supplementary articles, my mind is much clearer as to what is most advisable. It seems to me that I require two articles. The first would elaborate and explain in greater detail the character of my basic argument, the second would be of a concrete character and would try to go a little further in the direction of interpreting general principles into terms of concrete policy.

My aim would be to deal with all the main doubts which have been raised, but not to refer to individual critics by name or to write in a debating manner. I could of course easily debate as briskly as could be desired. But it seems to me much sounder and in every way psychologically better not to debate, but to go plodding away with the articles in the light of the criticisms which have been made.

This may make the articles a bit duller than they would otherwise be. But I am inclined to believe that interest in the matter is now of the kind which positively prefers a rather plodding article, the aim of which is to introduce the reader into the real heart of the subject.

I enclose herewith the manuscript of the first and dullest of the two articles. I am afraid that it runs fully into two columns. But I do not see how to do it in less. It is probably the kind of article which has never appeared yet in the daily press, but all the same I hope you will agree that its tone and style and method are what are required.

If you approve the article, could it be set up into proof immediately. I can probably let you have my second article tomorrow.

Yours sincerely,

[copy not initialled or signed]

P.S. I am enclosing for your convenience two copies of the article.

In the end Keynes placed one article in *The Times* and one in *The New Statesman.*

From THE NEW STATESMAN AND NATION,[13] *1 April 1933*

THE MULTIPLIER

What is the relation between a given amount of loan-expenditure, the number of men to whose employment it will lead, and the relief to the Budget?

In my recent articles in *The Times* and in my pamphlet *The Means to Prosperity*,* I started off, on the authority of others, with £500 as the expenditure on typical works required to give one man-year of employment on the spot, and £200, or thereabouts, as the amount required, including employment on the materials used and on transport and other incidentals. These are, of course, average estimates of figures which would vary according to the particular nature of the works. No grounds have been given for questioning their reasonable accuracy as rough guides to the magnitudes involved, and I have allowed a margin to satisfy those who would cut them down moderately. The employment thus created by the expenditure on the capital works themselves, including transport and materials, it is convenient to call the 'primary employment'. Similarly employment, given by the increased expenditure of taxpayers who have been relieved as a result of increased Government borrowing, can be also reckoned as 'primary employment'.

I then proceeded to argue that this primary employment sets up a series of repercussions leading to what it is convenient to call 'secondary employment'. I stated that in my own judgement the secondary employment would be *equal* to the primary employment, i.e., that the multiplier of primary employment to give *total* employment was 2; but, to be on the safe side, I took it as being a half, i.e., a multiplier of $1\frac{1}{2}$, and then, as a further

[13] The substance of this article appeared in the American version of *The Means to Prosperity.*
* [*JMK*, vol. IX, pp. 335–66] Macmillan, 1*s*

precaution against various contingencies reduced it to a third, i.e., a multiplier of $1\frac{1}{3}$.

In two interesting letters, published in last week's *New Statesman and Nation*, these calculations have been seriously called in question. Mr Ronald C. Davison thinks that I have exaggerated my case, inasmuch as 'the indirect effects of the expenditure disperse themselves in so many ways—in thrift, in imports from abroad, in rent, in the employment of women and juveniles, in supplies from accumulated stocks, and, most of all, in the slightly increased employment of men and machines whose previous under-employment was in no way reflected in the unemployment register'. Another correspondent, signing himself 'D', makes much the same objections—'Materials, land, legal costs, compensation, all take their toll. But if we grant him the figure, what is his next assumption? That all the men employed by the new expenditure will come off the dole. How can he believe this? Does he regard production as manned by a minimum *personnel*, incapable of executing a new order except by taking on a new man?' These points are, in principle, perfectly sound. But, if it were not for these deductions, my estimate of the primary expenditure needed to lead to one man-year of employment would, as we shall see, be much less than £150. The question to be considered is whether I have made adequate allowance for them.

The passages quoted above involve two distinct objections. In the first place my critics point out that not all the additional employment will occupy men now supported by the dole. This objection does not, of course, affect my estimates of the additional employment and the additional income. But it is obvious that allowance must be made for it in calculating the relief to the Unemployment Fund. I took £50 as the gain to the Exchequer for each man-year of diminished dole, which already left some margin if we are calculating in terms of male adult workers, upon which my starting points of £500 and £200 were based. For, if we take a complete average, including juveniles and women, the figure would, on the basis of the 1932 figures, be £48·3 (namely £44·2 as the average annual cost of an unemployed person *plus* £4·1 as the average annual employer's and employee's contribution in respect of an employed person). I am not competent to estimate precisely, nor do my critics suggest a figure, as to what adjustment should be made in respect of extra employment which would not relieve the Unemployment Fund. But we have to remember that much part-time [work] is now arranged so as to obtain the benefit of the dole, and that primary employment would largely occupy men who are not now employed at all. It will be easy, however, when I have given below the general basis of my calculation, for anyone to make such adjustment as he may think prudent, and to judge whether, as I believe, I have reserved a sufficient margin to cover this contingency.

The second, and more fundamental, objection relates to the magnitude of the multiplier. I cannot complain of this objection since I did not attempt in the space at my disposal to develop my argument in detail. But since I believe that it can be stated in simple terms, I will now attempt to do so.

The primary expenditure of an additional £100, provided by borrowing, can be divided into two parts. The first part is the money which, for one reason or another, does not become additional income in the hands of an Englishman. This is mainly made up of (i) the cost of imported materials, (ii) the cost of goods, which are not newly produced but merely transferred, such as land or goods taken out of stocks which are not replenished, (iii) the cost of productive resources of men and plant which are not additionally employed but are merely drawn away from other jobs, (iv) the cost of wages which take the place of income previously provided out of funds borrowed for the dole. The second part, which is the money which does become additional income in the hands of an Englishman, has again to be divided into two portions, according as it is saved or spent (spending in this context including all the direct additional expenditure of the recipient, including expenditure on the production of durable objects). To obtain the multiplier we simply have to estimate these two proportions, namely, what proportion of typical expenditure becomes someone's income and what proportion of this income is spent. For these two proportions, multiplied together, give us the ratio of the first repercussion to the primary effect, since they give us the ratio of the second flow of expenditure to the initial flow of expenditure. We can then sum the whole series of repercussions, since the second repercussion can be expected to bear the same ratio to the first repercussion, as the first bore to the primary effect; and so on.

The abstract argument can be illustrated as follows. Two years ago, when the dole was being financed out of borrowed money, this fact required a substantial deduction, which is no longer necessary, in calculating the proportion of expenditure which becomes additional income. Two years hence, if employment is much better than it is now, it may be necessary to make a substantial deduction in respect of resources which are merely drawn away from other jobs; for the smaller the pool of unemployed resources, the more likely is this result from increased expenditure. I am not disposed to make much deduction at any time for goods taken out of stock, since stocks are seldom really large and the sight of depletion soon stimulates replenishment. *In existing conditions*, therefore, I should say that a deduction of 30 per cent for expenditure which for one reason or another does not increase incomes, leaving 70 per cent accruing to one person or another as current income, would be a reasonable supposition.

What proportion of this additional income will be disbursed as additional expenditure? In so far as it accrues to the wage-earning classes, one can safely assume that most of it will be spent; in so far as it increases profits and salaries and professional earnings, the proportion saved will be larger. We have to strike a rough average. In present circumstances we can surely assume that at least 70 per cent of the increased income will be spent and not more than 30 per cent saved.

On these assumptions the first repercussion will be 49 per cent (since $7 \times 7 = 49$) of the primary effect, or (say) one half; the second repercussion will be one half of the first repercussion, i.e., one quarter of the primary effect, and so on. Thus the multiplier is 2, since, if I may take the reader back to his schooldays, he will remember that $1 + \frac{1}{2} + \frac{1}{4} +$ etc. $= 2$. This was the sort of reasoning which lay behind my estimate of the multiplier. The amount of time which it takes for current income to be spent will separate each repercussion from the next one. But it will be seen that seven-eighths of the total effects come from the primary expenditure and the first two repercussions, so than the time lags involved are not unduly serious.

It is to be noticed that no additional allowance has to be made for any rise of prices which the increased demand may bring with it. The effect of higher prices will be gradually to diminish the proportion which becomes new income, since it will probably be a symptom that the surplus resources are no longer so adequate in certain directions, with the result that a larger proportion of the new expenditure is merely diverted from other jobs. It is also probable that higher prices will mean higher profits, with the result that, more of the increased income being profit and less of it being wages, more of it will be saved. Thus, as men are gradually brought back into employment and as prices gradually rise, the multiplier will gradually diminish. Moreover, in so far as wages rise it is obvious that the amount of employment corresponding to a given expenditure on wages will also gradually diminish. These modifications, however, would only become relevant as and when our remedy was becoming very successful. A given dose of expenditure at the present stage will, for several reasons, produce a much larger effect on employment than it will be prudent to expect later on when the margin of unused resources is reduced.

The actual calculations of my first article were based,

however, on a multiplier, not of 2, but of $1\frac{1}{2}$ or $1\frac{1}{3}$. In existing circumstances, therefore, I left myself a very wide margin for various contingencies. To illustrate this, let us consider the effect on the multiplier of certain other assumptions. If we were to assume that each of the two proportions is 60 per cent, the multiplier works out at about the figure of $1\frac{1}{2}$, which I actually took as my working estimate; yet it would seem very improbable that either proportion can be so low as this today. If, on the contrary, we were to expect that the proportion of the primary expenditure which becomes income and the proportion of the income which is spent are each 80 per cent, the multiplier becomes nearly 3 (as those readers who can still do arithmetic will easily verify), in which case the total benefit to the Exchequer might be greater than the *total* primary expenditure. I believe myself that it is chiefly in estimating the proportion of expenditure which becomes additional income that we have to be cautious; and the estimates, which I should feel happiest in making, would be based on some such assumption as that not less than 66 per cent of additional expenditure (whether on new capital works or on additional consumption) would become additional income in the hands of an Englishman, and that not less than 75 per cent of this additional income would be spent; whilst I would more readily increase the latter proportion to 80 than the former proportion to 70.

Let us now return to our opening figures and do the sum again on the basis of proportions of 66 per cent and 75 per cent respectively, allocating our various margins to specific contingencies instead of leaving them in an unallocated pool. On this hypothesis, British incomes will be increased by at least two-thirds of a primary expenditure of £100, i.e., by £66. Let us suppose that two-thirds of this increased income, i.e., £44, will accrue to men previously supported by the dole, which means about one-third of a man-year of increased employment taking the average wage at 50s a week. (This is the point at which those who lay stress on the importance of increased employment which does not relieve the dole must substitute a smaller figure. But on present evidence I believe that the figure I have taken is quite low enough.) If 75 per cent of the increased income of £66 is spent and if 66 per cent of this secondary expenditure again serves to increase incomes, and so on, then the total employment created by our primary expenditure of £100 will be two-thirds of a man-year; from which it follows that £150 primary expenditure will provide one man-year of additional employment for men now supported by the dole, which is the figure I previously adopted. The careful reader will perceive, however, that the total increase in the national income, resulting from £150 additional primary expenditure, will, on the above assumptions, be £300, which is more than I assumed previously and therefore gives an additional margin in calculating the total relief to the Budget sufficient to allow us to reduce to £40 the above figure of £44 out of each £100 expenditure accruing to men previously supported by the dole, if we feel that we need some further provision against the proportion of the new employment which will fall to men who, for one reason or another, are not now drawing the dole. In any case, if the reader considers some other set of figures more probable, I have here provided him with an apparatus which will enable him to work out the answer on his own assumptions.

The argument applies, of course, both ways equally. Just as the effect of increased primary expenditure on employment, on the national income and on the Budget is multiplied in the manner described, so also is the effect of decreased primary expenditure. Indeed, if it were not so it would be difficult to explain the violence of the recession both here and, even more, in the United States. Just as an initial impulse of modest dimensions has been capable of producing such devastating repercussions, so also a moderate impulse in the opposite direction will effect a surprising recovery. There is no magic here, no mystery; but a reliable scientific prediction.

Why should this method of approach appear to so many

people to be novel and odd and paradoxical? I can only find the answer in the fact that all our ideas about economics, instilled into us by education and atmosphere and tradition, are, whether we are conscious of it or not, soaked with theoretical pre-suppositions which are only properly applicable to a society which is in equilibrium, with all its productive resources already employed. Many people are trying to solve the problem of unemployment with a theory which is based on the assumption that there is no unemployment. Obviously if the productive resources of the nation were already fully occupied, none of the advantages could be expected which, in present circumstances, I predict from an increase of loan expenditure. For in that case increased loan expenditure would merely exhaust itself in raising prices and wages and diverting resources from other jobs. In other words, it would be purely inflationary. But these ideas, perfectly valid in their proper setting, are inapplicable to present circumstances, which can only be handled by the less familiar method which I have endeavoured to explain.

Keynes's reply in *The Times* appeared on 5 April.

From The Times, *5 April 1933*

THE MEANS TO PROSPERITY: MR KEYNES'S REPLY TO CRITICISM

The voluminous discussion on *The Means to Prosperity*, to which prominence has been given in *The Times*, in the House of Commons, and elsewhere, has shown a large preponderance of agreement in very various quarters—among members of all political parties, throughout the press of the country, and in the commentaries of those whose opinion commands special respect, such as Sir Arthur Salter, Sir Josiah Stamp, Sir Basil Blackett, Sir William Dampier, the Editor of *The Economist*, and many others. Turning to the criticisms, the doubts which I have to meet are mainly, I think, these three:—

(i) That I have exaggerated the amount of employment provided by a given expenditure.

(ii) That recent experience of the effect of capital works on the volume of employment serves to confute the *a priori* calculation.

(iii) That, even granted the principle, the wise and reasonably productive works, which it is practicable for the Government to set going within a moderate time, are so limited in volume that they cannot help us much.

The topic in its entirety is a large one. I have dealt with the first objection in an article published in *The New Statesman and Nation* for April 1. I attempt below to meet the other two.

It is often said that the policy of spending borrowed money as a remedy for unemployment was tried by the Labour Government and conspicuously failed. Doubts in the public mind thus arising are, perhaps, the chief obstacle which advocates of an expansionist policy have to overcome.

The origin of this misunderstanding is due, I am sure, to a failure to recognise that an increase or decrease in our net foreign balance has exactly the same effects and repercussions as an increase or decrease in loan expenditure at home; which is only another way of saying that the effects of net foreign investment are the same as those of home investment.

Now the Labour Government was fighting the effects on employment of an unprecedented decline in our foreign balance—due in part to the terms of our return to the gold standard and, later on, to the American and international crisis—by means of an increase in loan expenditure which was on a much smaller scale than the decline in the foreign balance. Compared with 1929, which for us was already an unsatisfactory year, the foreign balance declined by £75,000,000 in 1930 and by no less than £207,000,000 in 1931. But the Labour Government's loan expenditure was inevitably on a much smaller scale than this, so that of course unemployment increased—though not by as much as it would have done if there had been no loan expenditure. By 1931 it had become obvious to anyone who was not blinded by mistaken theories that without some improvement in the foreign balance the task had become hopeless. When the Labour Government refused both a tariff and a departure from gold its fate was sealed.

By its tariff policy and its exchange policy the National Government improved our foreign balance in 1932 by £74,000,000 compared with 1931; and the balance looks like being still better in 1933. Moreover, confidence has been restored and cheap money established, both on long and on short term. Yet unemployment has not declined. Where are we to look for the explanation? Not in the international sphere; for our net foreign trade position, though still bad, is much improved. We can find it nowhere, I suggest, except in the decline in our loan expenditure, as the result of our no longer borrowing for the dole and of our restraining the capital expenditure of all public authorities.

Thus the course of events, so far from confuting the means to prosperity which I recommend, has throughout the last four years served to confirm the theory that changes in the national income and the volume of employment depend, in present conditions, on the combined total of the foreign balance and of the volume of loan expenditure at home, public and private, added together.

I come, finally, to the question whether—granted the theoretical soundness of the principles set forth in these articles—it is practicable for official action to do much for us.

It is a question of pace and of degree. I am not unmindful of the delays and disappointments which await those who take the responsibility for an active policy. It will be extraordinarily difficult to contrive a judicious programme; and difficult above all to combine a judicious choice of schemes with speed of execution.

But precisely for these reasons we need to begin quickly and to plan boldly—fully conscious that there will be so many delays and so many projects, apparently excellent, which will not survive scrutiny, that the risk of our over-doing it is nil. We can proceed, moreover, with the better heart because this is not a case where anything short of complete success will be failure. Granted energy in contrivance and execution, we need not relax the spirit of criticism; or spoil the job by too much haste; or aim too high.

It is a mistake, moreover, to assume that we require projects on a gigantic scale, if we are to achieve substantial results. If we could increase investment by £100,000,000 a year I should welcome it. But I should be surprised if it could be accomplished. At any rate I am not reckoning on so much. I consider that an increase of £60,000,000 a year would be satisfactory, and—while no one can tell for certain until the attempt has been made—I see no sufficient reason for supposing this to be impracticable. If my calculations are correct this would put 400,000 men to work for a year.

In what ways could we attain such a total? I will endeavour to make some suggestions. But first, there are certain general considerations which are relevant.

When projects were under consideration three or four years ago, the prevailing rate of interest was 5 to 6 per cent. There has been no intensive study of the problem of what is practicable on the basis of 3½ per cent. Yet the fall in the rate of interest has worked a prodigious change. In the field of building, for example, the combined effect of the fall in interest and of the fall in building costs is to reduce the level of remunerative rent by 30 to 40 per cent compared with a few years ago. Or again, in the field of railway electrification the basic rate of interest assumed is vital to the question of what projects are profitable. I do not believe that we have as yet even begun to exploit the possibilities of 3½ per cent long-term money.

In the second place we should not refrain from good schemes because they will take some time to mature or because the expenditure they involve will be spread over several years. I advocate this, not only because slow maturity is a characteristic of many of the best proposals, but because I agree with the view expressed by the Chancellor of the Exchequer in his much-abused speech that abnormal unemployment, though not on the present scale, may be a chronic problem with us for several years to come. I do not believe that we shall regret five years hence that works started today will be still, in some instances, uncompleted.

There remains the question of the best instrumentality for carrying out a policy of expansion. In the details of execution we require the greatest possible decentralisation. But there should be, I suggest, some central authority under the Chancellor of the Exchequer, charged with the initial selection of schemes and, where necessary, with the provision of finance. Local authorities would continue to borrow through their usual channels as at present. For the rest, it would be of great assistance if a central fund were to be established, with a credit of, say, £50,000,000 in the first instance, which would be lent out for approved projects at 2½ to 4 per cent interest, averaging, say, 3¼ per cent, plus an appropriate sinking fund. In the first instance at any rate it would be advisable to see what could be accomplished with no further subsidies of any kind beyond what is involved in this provision of cheap finance.

It hardly falls within my province to make detailed proposals. But these would probably fall under three main heads: (i) the normal activities of local authorities, (ii) a special housing effort through the agency of a National Housing Board or otherwise, (iii) the mass of miscellaneous projects, not of the first magnitude individually, upon the particular merits of each of which it is impossible for the layman to pass judgement.

In the case of the first, the results might be substantial if the Ministry of Health, reversing their present policy, were to encourage local authorities to press on with their normal programmes. Nearly half the local authorities of the country (920) have recently replied in detail to a *questionnaire* sent them by the Building Industries National Council. These returns show that works to a total volume of £17,168,501 are being held up, of which £9,465,655 are in response to the Ministry of Health's Circulars 1222 or 1413.

Those responsible for the project of a National Housing Board believe that an additional programme of £100,000,000 could be handled over a period of three years.

The large class of miscellaneous schemes includes, among the multitudinous projects of enthusiasts, railway electrification, water and gas grids, rural water supply, land drainage, port and dock works, Atlantic liners, Post Office and telephone development, household electrification, and much else to examine and sometimes, one would hope, to approve.

There remains the second branch of loan expenditure—the relief of taxation out of borrowed money. The greater the prospective delay and the more modest our hopes concerning capital works, the more important is it to press for a relief of taxation. A relief of taxation will operate quickly. Its effects will be widely spread throughout the community. It has the great advantage that it will energise expenditure through numberless normal channels, stimulating into greater activity the whole machine by which our usual needs are satisfied.

On what scale is it reasonable in all the circumstances to ask for relief? Using my judgement to the best of my ability with no more facts at my disposal than others have, I believe that the Chancellor of the Exchequer would find himself well justified on a long view if he were to base his taxation for the coming year on (i) a suspension of the sinking fund and no specific provision for the American debt; (ii) estimates of revenue and expenditure which assume a substantial reduction of unemployment below its present figure by such means as those which are here proposed; and (iii) a loan on suspense account in aid of revenue of £50,000,000, which it would be our duty to repay out of the revenue of later years, when the charge for unemployment has fallen to a more normal figure and the receipts of direct taxation are benefiting from an increased national income. Can anyone doubt that a reasoned Budget on these lines would do more for confidence than a repetition of last year's sacrifices? Unfortunately the more pessimistic the Chancellor's policy, the more likely it is that pessimistic anticipations will be realised and *vice versa*. Whatever the Chancellor dreams, will come true! We must begin by resuscitating the national income and the national output; and, if we succeed in this, we can be sure that, over a period of time, the yield of the taxes will respond. The national income, which is the taxable *corpus*, should be our chief concern today. We must not destroy the body by putting burdens upon its strength which it cannot support until we have given it time to recover.

I should be hopeful that this relief would increase employment, after a certain interval, by 300,000 to 400,000 men, making a total improvement of (say) 750,000 from the two branches of the programme taken together. Nor would there be cause for blame even if time and disappointment were to reduce our hopes by a half. It is not a conclusive argument against a policy, which aims at increasing employment by 750,000 men, that cautious people expect only half this improvement; or that those who are conversant with the administrative difficulties believe that six months or a year may elapse before we enjoy the full results.

I have left myself but little space to mention the proposal for an international gold note issue, which occupied a half of my original articles and to which I attach no less importance than to the domestic programme. In response to Sir Basil Blackett's question, let me say that, while my domestic and international proposals assist and supplement one another, they do not compose an indivisible whole to be adopted or rejected in their entirety. I have, however, little to add. The principles of this proposal have not received much criticism. That foreign countries are not yet ready to accept it seems to be the worst that can be said. But that is no reason why this country should not advocate it and make its ideas familiar. For opinion moves rapidly. If matters do not mend, the world will accept with eagerness next autumn what it might reject today.

Keynes's attitude to international monetary matters brought him charges of inconsistency in the columns of both *The Financial Times* and *The Economist*. In both cases Keynes hastened to reply.

To the Editor of The Financial Times, *17 March 1933*

Sir,

I have always reckoned Mr Hobson a diligent reader of my works. But I fear from the article which you publish today that he does not remember what he reads. 'The sinner has repented', he writes, 'The prodigal son has returned.' Yet the proposal which I made in the last of my *Times* articles is substantially the same as that which I published in 1923 in Chapter 5 of my *Tract on Monetary Reform* [*JMK*, vol. IV], before we returned to gold, and again in 1930 in chapters 36 and 38 of my *Treatise on Money* [*JMK*, vol. VI], after we returned to gold. My present proposal, made after our second departure from gold, only differs from my previous proposals in that it is somewhat more cautious in establishing a link with gold.

I must not, however, complain of Mr Hobson's article, since the leader which you print beside it, offers a valuable corrective to his fanaticism. I should accept your criterion that budget subsidies, direct or indirect, should in no case exceed 50 per cent of the new capital expenditure. Indeed I should think it practicable, as a general rule, to apply a much stricter test. I also agree that, whilst 'profitable objects for public outlay are not to be found on every bush', 'It would, of course, be absurd to presume that there are not substantial opportunities which would satisfy such a test.'

Yours etc.,

J. M. KEYNES

To the Editor of The Economist, *20 March 1933*

Dear Sir,

I do not know that what you call 'the evolution of my ideas' is particularly important. But for the sake of accuracy I should like, in thanking you for your leading article of March 18, to remind you that my recent advocacy of gold as an international standard is nothing new.

At all stages of the post-war developments the concrete proposals which I have brought forward from time to time have been based on the use of gold as an international standard, whilst discarding it is a rigid national standard. The qualifications which I have added to this have been always the same, though the precise details have varied; namely (1) that the parities between national standards and gold should not be rigid, (2) that there should be a wider margin than in the past between the gold points, and (3) that if possible some international control should be formed with a view to regulating the commodity value of gold within certain limits.

You will find that this was my opinion in 1923 when I published my *Tract on Monetary Reform* (see Chapter 5) and again in 1930 when I published my *Treatise on Money* (see chapters 36 and 38); just as it is today, as set forth in my articles in *The Times* and in my pamphlet *The Means to Prosperity*.

I apologise for occupying your space. But since there are people who deem it creditable if one does not change one's mind, I should like to get what *kudos* I can from not having done so on this occasion!

Yours etc.,

J. M. KEYNES

At the end of his *Times* article of 5 April (above p. 184), Keynes remarked that his proposals for an international gold note issue had not received much criticism. Two days later *The Times* published a long article by R. H. Brand filling that gap. Brand criticised Keynes's proposals on three basic grounds—

that the degree of international monetary control proposed would involve too large limits on national sovereignty to be acceptable; that the proposals would work in only one direction, as it would be easier to get the notes into circulation than to redeem them; and that the international authority would have to control the manner in which debtors used the new credits. He also questioned Keynes's diagnosis of the causes of the slump and suggested that the real constraint was the American internal situation, which Keynes's proposals could do nothing to solve.

Naturally Keynes replied.

To the Editor of The Times, *7 April 1933*

Sir,

I am grateful to Mr Brand for at last making vocal a weighty comment on my proposal for international reflation, of a type which I have felt to be present in the background and likely to play a large part in the final decision, but to which it was difficult to reply so long as it was unexpressed. May I, to save space, forbear from mentioning two or three questions of detail which, if Mr Brand will look at my articles again, he will see that I have already answered, and pass to the main substance of his criticisms?

My answer to them is best summed up by saying that my proposal is an attempt to make the best of a bad job. I believe, that is to say, that Mr Brand would have no difficulty in raising equal or graver objections to any other course of action or inaction. The risks to which he calls attention, even rated at his own valuation, are surely nothing at all compared with what may happen if we drift along. Why should a new policy be expected to attain an impossibly high standard compared with old ones, before we adopt it?

The plan which I set forth can be defended on many grounds. But, having been allowed much space already, I must limit myself to repeating what is, I think, its central advantage. There is no possibility of setting the stage for a recovery of world prices and world trade unless we can relieve the tension between debtor and creditor countries and also the potential tension between the countries which hold short-term foreign balances and those which may seek to withdraw them. Apart from the special means proposed, this tension can only be relieved (1) by a renewal of international lending on the old lines, (2) by a widespread, perhaps almost universal, repudiation of international debts, or (3) by an increase of domestic loan expenditure in the creditor countries on so large a scale as to cause them to increase their imports considerably, thus increasing in turn the purchasing power of the weaker countries, and so on. If Mr Brand knows a fourth way, I hope that he will add it to my list.

Now he and I agree, I think, that the first expedient is impracticable, and indeed undesirable, except on a small scale for some time to come. He probably wishes, as I do, to keep the second within as narrow limits as possible, though the War debts present a special case. I hope I may presume that he favours increased loan expenditure in this country; but I doubt whether he would advocate it on the very large scale which would be necessary if it is to have a considerable effect on our balance of trade. So he ends up, very lamely, by hoping that the stimulus will come from the United States.

We can all agree with him that the situation would be eased enormously if America were to recover her former measure of activity. But does he see any reason for expecting this in the near future? Last autumn I was prepared to be moderately cheerful about the American prospects. Today I am much more pessimistic. I think it possible that they will suffer another almighty smash. They are months, and perhaps years, behind us in the calendar of recovery. They have no clear objective and no real convictions. I doubt, therefore, if they are capable of pursuing a difficult policy with persistent and single-minded determination. Inflation will temporarily upset confidence; and further deflation will destroy the very foundations of their economic life. They look like oscillating between the two, offsetting each of the other, until disappointment and suffering provoke a new outbreak of nation-wide hysteria. Let us sincerely co-operate with them, whenever they will let us, and hope for the best; for our interests and objects are the same. But it will not be prudent to rely upon American prosperity to lift the rest of us out of the bog.

I hesitate, therefore, to depend on (3) alone. And that is why I recommend what Mr Brand justly describes as a kind of international borrowing and lending. But it is as limited and cautious as such an operation can be, if it is to be effective. It is, in substance, an undertaking in advance by the creditor countries towards the debtor countries, without its being necessary to decide beforehand which country falls into which group, that, in the event of there being an unbalanced international position, the creditors as a body will, within defined limits, make an advance to the debtors as a body, on the joint guarantee of all the participants. The object is to give a sense of security, so that every country can abate its fears of purchasing abroad, removing the special hindrances which fear has interposed and releasing its domestic credit.

I wish I could move Mr Brand out of his passivity. Though he himself realises the magnitude of the world's present catastrophe, his article shows no signs of it. There may be a gloomy satisfaction in going to perdition according to the rules. But I hate to sit back, hoping for something to turn up in America, whilst abject poverty consumes the possibilities of life and civilisation crumbles.

Yours &c.,

J. M. KEYNES

On 7 April *The Spectator* published a defence of the Government's policy by Ian Horobin, a Conservative M.P. Keynes felt his views were misrepresented and replied.

To the Editor of The Spectator, *21 April 1933*

In your issue of April 7th you published an article by Mr Ian Horobin, purporting to be serious, in which he wrote:

In the summer of 1932 tin stocks in this country were approximately 60,000 tons...Between June 3rd and June 7th the price of this fell nearly £5 per ton. Many of Mr Keynes's camp-followers argue that in so far as this loss was realised, British investment fell short between these dates by no less a sum than £300,000. Upon this premise they demand money with menaces from the Government in order to spend the said sum of £300,000 on new schools and lunatic asylums in order to 'keep savings and investment equal'.

I can't help suspecting that Mr Horobin is himself the camp-follower who has so grossly misunderstood my argument. But if not, perhaps he will kindly give particulars as to where and by whom the above alleged argument was used. I am,

Sir, &c.,
J. M. KEYNES

Rotary International, which had previously sponsored a 'spend for employment' campaign, decided in the spring of 1933 to sponsor a campaign for slum clearance and rehousing. For the campaign they planned a pamphlet and asked Keynes to provide a statement of support.

To W. W. BLAIR-FISH, *11 April 1933*

Dear Sir,

In response to your letter of April 7, I offer you the following paragraph for your pamphlet:

'I can imagine nothing more useful or better conceived than the campaign for slum clearance for which the Ministry of Health has now given the word. It will at the same time remedy a great social evil, find employment for thousands of men who are wasting their lives in uselessness, increase incomes throughout the community by setting in motion the revolving ball of expenditure, and measurably improve the budgetary position of the Chancellor of the Exchequer, by reducing the cost of the dole and improving the yield of taxation.'

Yours faithfully,
[copy initialled] J.M.K.

On 9 April Keynes went to the Ministry of Health to discuss local authority expenditures. Afterwards the Permanent Secretary wrote to him with additional information.

From SIR ARTHUR ROBINSON, *10 April 1933*

Personal

Dear Keynes,

It occurred to me after I saw you yesterday that it may be useful for you to have a summary statement of the local loans actually sanctioned by us over a period of years. I enclose a schedule of the figures from 1922–3 to 1931–2 inclusive. Under 'other services', the main items are sewerage and sewage disposal, roads, and educational buildings.

The figures for 1932–33 are not yet completely available. I should put the total at about forty millions, of which say eighteen millions would be housing.

25/6 and 26/7 were bumper years for housing because of certain factors about the subsidy which will not occur again. 29/30 — 31/2 were the years when, under pressure of the Labour Government, aided by unemployment grants, the figures for 'other services' rose to the peak of nearly forty-two millions in one year and the trading services also went up materially. Naturally local authorities put forward their programmes since rate services could be done partly at Exchequer cost. Once done of course, the things cannot be done again, and the results of those three years would have meant a drop in following years, whether there was or was not an economy circular.

It looks as if the norm for trading and other services would be somewhere about 26–30 millions a year + an uncertain but not a large amount resulting from private Bills sanctioned in the House. I should myself very much doubt the possibility of adding anything like fifteen millions to this now—in the biggest year '30–31, the total figure was, it is true, about forty-seven millions, but there are clear signs of saturation in this sphere.

I meant to add one observation as to housing. You liked our slum circular, and expenditure in that way meets all the conditions I should myself lay down. But when I read that vast sums are to be put at the disposal of a national housing board, I wonder if it is realised that the expenditure by such a board, if and when it can actually be got under way, would by no means be additional expenditure. If e.g. a national housing board proposed to put down x houses in Leeds or Manchester or Bristol I should apprehend that the practical result under the conditions of local government would be that rate expenditure on new housing or slum clearance or reconditioning would come to an end. For good or evil, the local method of housing was adopted years ago, and the central method cannot be put in harness with it, without in effect replacing it.

If I may say so, I found the talk most stimulating and needing to be thought over very carefully. I am afraid I am still old-fashioned enough to look with dread at an annual expenditure out of rates and taxes of the order of nine hundred and fifty millions and to be very nervous indeed about anything which will or may still further increase that Gargantuan total.

Yours sincerely,
ARTHUR ROBINSON

You referred also (1) to proposals for a public utility society at Cambridge to be financed by the Corporation; (2) to proposals for new office accommodation for the Corporation. As to (1) my people here understood that, after a discussion here, it was up to the Corporation to submit a scheme and Mr Raynes was so informed on 6 February. As to (2) the last we heard of this was in October 1922 and if it is now desired to go on, the Town Clerk knows what has to be done—we understood then that local opinion was deeply divided on the scheme and thought that the delay was probably due to that factor, as it so often is.

Year	Trading services (£000)	Housing (£000)	Other services (£000)	Total (£000)
1922–3	5,595	6,501	18,710	30,806
1923–4	3,024	14,911	21,129	39,064
1924–5	3,357	27,682	25,157	56,196
1925–6	5,038	59,481	25,524	90,043
1926–7	4,293	67,418	24,125	95,836
1927–8	3,817	47,852	24,531	76,200
1928–9	3,409	33,130	24,379	60,918
1929–30	4,536	36,000	31,822	72,358
1930–1	5,580	32,281	41,786	79,647
1931–2	4,070	22,738	30,306	57,114

To SIR ARTHUR ROBINSON, *25 April 1933*

Dear Robinson,

The Easter holidays and a visit to Dublin[14] have prevented me from acknowledging sooner the letter of April 10 which you very kindly sent me. I have found it most interesting.

[14] See below, p. 233.

Perhaps the feature which strikes me most strongly is the relationship between the new capital expenditure and the sinking funds on previous expenditure. I think I remember that the latter now comes to something of the order of £60,000,000 a year; and since the annual expenditure in the earlier years, covered by current sinking funds, was much lower than the present figure, this £60,000,000 will tend to increase rather than diminish in the years immediately ahead.

Now according to your figures, even in 1929–30 and 1930–31 new expenditure barely averaged 75 million, whilst in 1931–32 and 1932–33 the average will not reach 50 million. I gather, moreover, that in your opinion it would represent a considerable effort to raise the annual figure under all headings as high as 60 million and keep it there.

Thus, unless there is a very big housing effort, quite outside your figures, it would appear that local authorities will not be borrowers of new money on balance on any appreciable scale. Indeed, there is a risk that as last year they will be repaying a good deal more than they are borrowing. Who on earth is going to absorb the resources thus set free, in addition to current savings, I cannot imagine. It indicates to me that unless we could engineer a considerable further fall in the rate of interest, and at the same time organise every possible form of capital expenditure, we shall be totally unable to replace the gap left by the cessation of foreign investment; and activity in this is unlikely to be resumed on anything like its former scale, if ever, simply because we shall not have a favourable foreign balance to finance it.

If this line of thought is correct, the problem of today will be chronic for some time to come, and we cannot afford to neglect any even plausible outlet for funds.

That is the principle of policy which I should like to see established. When it comes to putting it into practice, I am only too well aware of the practical difficulties. My anxiety is mainly due to the fact that to find outlets on an adequate scale and to keep it up will be so difficult. But I conclude from this that one ought never to miss a favourable chance when it presents itself, and that we ought to have some re-organised machinery expressly designed for handling this problem.

My own pet plan, as perhaps you know, would be some central Government body which would co-ordinate the investment plans of the different departments and form a considered judgement as to the aggregate scale on which operations would be advisable year by year.

As for the burden on the rates, my own policy would of course be to revert to the former policy of putting as much as possible on the central Budget and relieving the local budgets, since beyond a certain point I do not consider rates to be a good way of raising revenue. On the other hand if we pursue the right policy with regard to the long-term rate of interest, the relief to local authorities in the rate on what they borrow might go a long way, perhaps the whole way towards providing for the interest on a larger capital sum.

Yours sincerely,
[copy initialled] J.M.K.

On 25 April, the Chancellor presented his Budget. As was becoming a custom, Keynes provided a survey for the popular press.

From The Daily Mail, *26 April 1933*

A BUDGET THAT MARKS TIME

I have heard President Roosevelt criticised for not being 'consecutive'. No such accusation can be made against Mr Neville Chamberlain. Mr Chamberlain is terribly consecutive.

This year's Budget is too plainly the work of the same man as a year ago. I criticise it mainly because its author has failed to recognise that in the long run the revenue must depend upon an increase in the national income, and that budgetary policy may itself be a potent instrument in determining what the national income is going to be.

If we are allowed to spend, our spending will create new incomes, which can in turn be taxed, and will employ new men whose dole is now burdening the Exchequer.

Mr Chamberlain, if he sees these things, takes no account of them. He is true to the Gladstonian ideal of the Chancellor of the Exchequer as a faithful accountant. He rejects the instrument of milder taxation as a means of restoring prosperity, and tells us that relief can only come after prosperity has returned to us by some other means *unspecified*. Mr Chamberlain boasted that he had made no attempt to *present* things as other than they are. He might have also added that he has done nothing to *make* them other than they are.

Most of us have approached this Budget not doubting that there are good reasons for relieving taxation. But strict budgeting was made such a fetish a year ago, though in quite different circumstances, that we all feared that the Chancellor would not feel himself free to obey the dictates of the good reasons, unless he could furnish himself not only with good reasons but also with a good excuse. For some weeks, therefore, everyone has been doing his best to furnish the Chancellor with a fine set of excuses for doing what good sense tells him to do; what we all wanted him to do; what doubtless he would like to do himself—to take off taxes.

It would not be true to say that he has made no response to these suggestions. To the extent that they were necessary to avoid the imposition of new taxation he has accepted them. No provision is made for the American debt; and the whole country will applaud that. No provision is made for the sinking fund; and there are few purists left who will be offended. But to other suggestions he has been deaf. There is no attempt to bring about better times by anticipating them.

The Chancellor thinks that he has no right to anticipate any large improvement even within three years. If he takes that view and acts accordingly he may, alas! be right; just as he would have been right if he had allowed himself to be cheerful.

Many of the details of the Budget are of inconsiderable importance. The restoration of equal half-yearly instalments of income tax is the most substantial change; and this is greatly to be welcomed. For it will at least leave spending power in the pockets of the taxpayers for another six months. But the nest-egg which provides for this concession might equally well have been used for a definitive relief.

The reduction of the beer tax was generally expected, and is justified both on popular and on fiscal grounds. I see little to criticise in the other minor changes. But how starved one is of any large conception, of anything which deserves the name of constructive policy! Mr Chamberlain has obviously been anxious to do as little harm as he could. But how the country would have responded to him if he had made an effort towards positive good!

Apart from the Budget proper, the eyes of the whole world will be turned to the brief passages where the Chancellor touched upon the problem of the foreign exchanges. At the present stage I make no complaint against his extreme discretion. I welcome the enlargement of the Exchange Equalisation Fund as demonstrating that we intend to remain masters of our own situation. It is, however, by no means clear as yet that the recent action of the American President is seriously intended to restrict our freedom of action.[15]

Americans would doubtless welcome a higher value for sterling. But a creditor country in the position of America cannot depreciate its currency merely by wishing to do so. Moreover, it would aggravate the world's troubles if the United States were, by a relative depreciation of its currency, to increase still further the favourable balance which so largely contributed to the depression, inasmuch as it was not offset, and is not likely to be, by comparable lending. I prefer, therefore, to take the view that the President speaks sincerely when he tells us that he is

[15] America left the gold standard on 20 April.

looking primarily to his domestic situation and does not intend his recent change of policy as an instrument of international offence.

The United States is perfectly entitled to reduce the gold content of the dollar. There is much to be said for this policy, not only for America but for the rest of the world as well. But we need to separate this question from that of relative exchange values. I hope that we shall co-operate with President Roosevelt in everything that he has done, or contemplates doing, to raise prices in the United States by means that will raise them in the rest of the world also. But we must be firmly resolved to maintain the relative exchange value of our own currency at a figure adjusted to our own wage levels and competitive position. The decision to enlarge the Exchange Equalisation Fund is, I hope, an earnest of this intention.

The best defence I can discover for Mr Chamberlain's Budget would be to represent it as a deliberate decision to mark time during a phase of affairs in which international questions are likely to be dominant; a policy of maintaining the financial strength and prestige of this country by a rigid adherence to orthodoxy, even at the expense of postponing our material recovery, in the belief that there is a right order of doing things, and that the decisive moment has not yet arrived for a forward movement on the home front.

He also wrote to *The Times* on the Budget.

To the Editor of The Times, *27 April 1933*

Sir,

The Chancellor of the Exchequer has rejected the proposal to reduce taxation by £50,000,000 more than his Estimates would strictly justify on the ground that the hope of making this good within three years would be 'highly optimistic'. For this meant, he continued, that revenue must increase by £100,000,000 in 1935, i.e., that the profits of next year must increase by £500,000,000, 'if those results are to be produced out of income tax alone, as I understand the suggestion is'.

Since the proposal for a loan of £50,000,000 on suspense account in aid of revenue appeared in the article which I contributed to *The Times* of April 5, perhaps I may be allowed to point out that I made no suggestion, and I know no one who has, that the loan would all be recovered out of the income tax on next year's profits. In my earlier articles I had explained that I should expect a relief to the taxpayer on this scale to increase employment and incomes sufficiently to relieve the dole by £16,000,000 and to increase the yield of the revenue as a whole by £7,500,000, which would leave £26,500,000 to be repaid out of a subsequent increase in revenue due to other causes, which is about 3½ per cent of the existing revenue. If it proves 'highly optimistic' to anticipate, on the present basis of taxation, a surplus of 7 per cent three years hence after allowing for any decreased expenditure on the dole, I should expect very unorthodox finance to be finding favour by then!

Unfortunately it seems impossible in the world of today to find anything between a Government which does nothing at all and one which goes right off the deep end!—the former leading, sooner or later, to the latter.

Yours, &c.,
J. M. KEYNES

There matters stood until July. Then, at the World Economic Conference, Walter Runciman delivered what *The Times* was to call 'a blunt and bare denunciation of public works as a cure for unemployment'. Keynes commented on Runciman's remarks.

To the Editor of The Times, *14 July 1933*

Sir,

When Mr Runciman states that for every £1,000,000 expended on public works 2,000 men are employed directly and 2,000 indirectly, he means, presumably, that 2,000 men are directly employed on the spot and a further 2,000 in production necessary for the public works, but taking place elsewhere than on the spot. For example, if the works in question are buildings, the men employed in laying the bricks are included in Mr Runciman's first 2,000 and those employed in manufacturing and transporting them in the second 2,000. Thus he has made no allowance whatever for the men employed as an indirect result of the expenditure on public works. No one has disputed the calculation, which I advanced in *The Times* earlier this year and have since published, that the total increase in employment resulting from public works can be safely estimated at not less than one man per £150 of expenditure.

If, therefore, Mr Runciman, ignoring the indirect employment, is only making the unimportant distinction between (e.g.) bricklaying on the spot and brickmaking on some other spot, his statement is seriously misleading; while, if he means his estimate to cover the total employment resulting, directly and indirectly, from expenditure on public works, it is seriously inaccurate. Perhaps Mr Runciman will tell us which he means.

Mr Runciman's declaration seems to go beyond anything that the Chancellor of the Exchequer has said hitherto. If the tone and substance of his remarks represent the considered decision of the Government it makes nonsense of their alleged intention to raise prices. A strictly balanced Budget, abstention from public works, and a pegged exchange between sterling and the gold bloc currencies would represent one more victory for the deflationary faction—in spite of the overwhelming contrary opinion which is now to be found in every quarter.

Yours, &c.,

J. M. KEYNES

On 27 July, *The Times*, in the course of a leading article on public works, suggested that Keynes and Professor Pigou differed on the financing of such proposals, with Keynes preferring some credit creation.

Keynes replied.

To the Editor of The Times, *27 July 1933*

Sir,

Your leading article today suggests a difference of opinion between myself and Professor Pigou which does not, I think, exist. Like him, I contemplate that public works would be paid for out of loans. How far 'the creation of new money' would be necessary as a complement of this policy depends on the meaning of these words. If they mean an increased circulation of currency notes this will be the probable result of any policy which is successful in increasing employment without reducing wages, since, in modern conditions, the circulation of notes largely depends on the amount of the wages bill. If they mean open-market operations by the Bank of England this might prove advisable, though not on a scale exceeding a small percentage of the public works loans, to prevent the latter from raising the rate of interest to the detriment of other enterprise. Personally I favour such operations, independently of public works programmes—indeed, they will be even more necessary if we are mainly to depend on private enterprise—as a means of further reducing the long-term rate of interest.

The main point, however, is that which has been emphasised by Professor Pigou—namely, whether there are not many enterprises which would pay for themselves if we were to credit to their cost what they would save the Treasury in unemployment relief, and, I should add, what they would earn for the Treasury in the increased yield of taxation. *Prima facie* there are large fields of development, notably housing and perhaps railway electrification, which would pass this test successfully. I suggest that it is the duty of the Government to set up an expert body to settle this question authoritatively. If schemes are forthcoming, then, on the Government's own showing, they should be adopted. If there exist no large-scale enterprises, public or private, which can pass this test, I should conclude that the long-term rate of interest is much too high, and that open-market operations should be undertaken by the Bank of England until the rate of interest has been reduced to a figure which is consistent with profitable enterprise.

Your obedient servant,
J. M. KEYNES

At the end of the year Keynes took another swipe at the Ministry of Health's housing policies in a letter to *The New Statesman.*

To the Editor of The New Statesman and Nation, *19 December 1933*

Sir,

Since the public is finding it difficult to know how seriously to take the alleged enthusiasm of the Ministry of Health for the building of working-class houses, the following example of their policy may be sufficiently interesting to deserve attention.

Some months ago (in May last) the Exeter City Council applied to the Minister of Health for sanction of a scheme for the erection of 106 houses of the parlour and three-bedroom type for sale to owner-occupiers by a system of weekly payments over twenty years covering principal and interest. In reply the Minister refused to agree to the erection of these houses, on the ground that adequate accommodation could be provided in a house of the non-parlour three-bedroom type. The Town Clerk thereupon pointed out to the Minister, by letter and by interview, that the 106 houses in question were not subsidy houses, but were to be erected by the City Council without any assistance from the Exchequer or from the rates, and would involve no cost whatever either to the Government or to the City Council since they would be sold at the price which they cost;

and, moreover, that it would be unwise for the Council to erect non-parlour houses for sale since those prepared to enter into a house-purchase scheme would undoubtedly require a parlour-type house. He also explained to the Minister that the Council intended to invite tenders at the same time not only for these 106 houses, but for a total of 306 to be erected within the same area, thus obtaining a cheaper price for the houses to be erected under the Council's programme of rehousing under its slum clearance scheme, which meanwhile the Minister's objections were holding up. It may be mentioned that the Town Clerk had, without any request for applications, already received 125 inquiries from persons desirous of purchasing the houses under the scheme. In spite of all this, the Minister responded with a further refusal, maintaining obdurately that he could not agree to the erection of houses of the size proposed. On September 26th the Exeter City Council met to record a strong protest against the action of the Minister and asked him to receive a deputation. The deputation was received towards the end of November, and on December 1st the Town Clerk was informed that the Minister would withdraw his objections. Meanwhile the six months' delay had lost the Council the whole of the summer for building purposes.

What is the explanation of this waste of time, tempers and effort? I am not aware that the Ministry produced rational grounds of objection at any stage of the proceedings. Is the Ministry muscle-bound in its own red tape? Or is it overworked? Had it some solid reason not yet publicly disclosed? Or is its enthusiasm for housebuilding more lukewarm than we had been given to understand?

I have been told that there is nothing unusual or remarkable in the above example, and that one need look for no explanation beyond the normal one of obstructive delay born of some red-tape circular. Can any of your readers throw light on the Ministry's motives? It is fast acquiring an unenviable reputation, not least amongst local authorities.

J. M. KEYNES

Chapter 3

THE WORLD ECONOMIC CONFERENCE

In June and July 1932 the representatives of nineteen countries met at Lausanne to discuss the future of reparations and War debts.[1] The upshot of almost a month's discussion was an end to reparations and a decision to ask the League of Nations to call a World Conference the next year 'to decide upon the measures to solve the other economic and financial difficulties which are responsible for, and may prolong, the present world crisis'.

Before the Lausanne Conference H. D. Henderson prepared a memorandum entitled 'A Monetary Proposal for Lausanne'[2] which suggested that the Bank for International Settlements should issue notes to governments, which would be the equivalent of gold, thus increasing international liquidity and allowing countries to repay debts or engage in expansionary domestic policies. With the note issue proposal came several conditions—the adoption of fixed but adjustable parities, the removal of exchange restrictions and the agreement to repay advances as prices rose towards their 1928 level. The total issue suggested was about £1,000 millions.

During the Lausanne Conference Keynes mentioned the plan to the Prime Minister, reporting that he was 'strongly in favour of it' and suggesting that if Lausanne could settle the reparations issue and if the world then proceeded on lines such as Henderson's 'I should begin to believe that our troubles are at an end'.[3]

Henderson's proposals went to the Committee on Economic Information in July 1932 while it was preparing its Fourth Report. The scheme was incorporated into the Fourth Report which was presented on 20 July.

The next month the Prime Minister created another Committee of the Economic Advisory Council 'to consider the programme of subjects to be discussed at the forthcoming international Monetary and Economic Conference and to advise (the Prime Minister) personally as to points to which British policy should be specially directed'. The members of this Committee on International Economic Policy were Sir Charles Addis (Chairman), Lord

[1] For Keynes's views on the Conference, see *JMK*, vol. XVIII, pp. 370–9.

[2] Reprinted in *The Inter-war Years and Other Papers* (ed. H. Clay) (Oxford, 1955).

[3] *JMK*, vol. XVIII, p. 378.

Astor, Basil Blackett, Lord Essendon, Keynes, Walter Layton, Sir Arthur Salter and Sir Josiah Stamp. Hubert Henderson and A. F. Hemming acted as secretaries.

At its first meeting the Committee agreed to look at the proposals contained in the Fourth Report of the Committee on Economic Information and included in its own First Report in November 1932 a revised version of the Henderson Plan drafted by Blackett, Keynes and Henderson.

From November 1932, Keynes turned as well to some of the subjects the Conference might discuss. On 25 November he opened a series of talks on the B.B.C. on free trade and protection. The talk appeared in *The Listener*.

From The Listener, *30 November 1932*

PROS AND CONS OF TARIFFS

I do not know what claim I can have to be considered an impartial introducer to the partisans who are to follow me on this question of tariffs. We shall all three of us be trying to tell the truth.[4] But I *can* claim that I have considerable sympathy with both parties; though, as you will find, I sympathise with both more from the practical than from the theoretical side. For the theoretical arguments which free traders and protectionists have each used are, many of them, as I think, invalid or misapplied. Each, on the other hand, has got hold of an important practical maxim.

The free trade position

Let me begin with the essential truth of the free trade position. It is best illustrated by beginning at home. We all know that, individually or taken by groups, we are much richer if we concentrate on those activities for which we are best fitted, become specialists in the production of certain articles, and live by exchanging our products for the products of other specialists. We do not doubt that we shall be richer if we concentrate

[4] The other two were Sir Henry Page-Croft and C. R. Attlee, both M.P.'s.

industry in the towns. We know that it would be stupid to put a higher licence duty on a motor-car used in a county where it was not manufactured. It never occurs to us to put on special taxes designed to prevent a Lancashire man from using a car made in Birmingham. And all this is just as true between countries, as it is between individuals or between districts. It is a waste and a stupidity for us to make one thing inefficiently when we might be better employed making something else. There is no mysterious quality in a frontier which upsets this obvious conclusion of common sense. Most protectionist arguments to the contrary are sophistries—particularly the one which contends that what I have been saying holds good under universal free trade, and that, if other countries impose tariffs, then it becomes advantageous to us to do the same. The tariffs of the foreigner reduce the opportunities for advantageous trade; but that is no reason why *we* should reduce them still further. Moreover, if we have to pay more than we need for what we use, that will raise our costs even in those branches of production for which we are best suited; so that our efficiency will go downhill all along the line.

All this is, surely, obvious; but that does not make it unimportant. On the contrary, it is frightfully important. The free trader starts with an enormous presumption in his favour. Nine times out of ten he is speaking forth the words of wisdom and simple truth—of peace and of good will also—against some little fellow who is trying by sophistry and sometimes by corruption to sneak an advantage for himself at the expense of his neighbour and his country. The free trader walks erect in the light of day, speaking all passers-by fair and friendly, while the protectionist is snarling in his corner.

Disappointment with Ottawa

Nor does practical experience of tariffs in the least modify this general presumption. Quite the contrary. There is no important country with an old established tariff system which has not committed a hundred stupidities—stupidities difficult to reverse, once done, without doing a further injury—stupidities frankly confessed by all understanding people within the country itself. We ourselves, in my judgment, have just had an example of this in the outcome of the Ottawa Conference. For, in spite of the high hopes and high ideals with which this conference was entered upon, it is difficult to see how the warmest advocates of economic co-operation within the Empire can regard it otherwise than as a disappointment—even apart from the difficulties which it may put in the way of achieving something useful at the World Economic Conference to be held next spring. It is a good example of how the worse elements in tariff bargaining tend to overcome the better elements, when it comes to business. Instead of promoting freer trade by genuine tariff reductions within the Empire, as Mr Baldwin in his opening address hoped that it would, I personally am of the opinion that it has riveted tariffs more firmly than before on all concerned—though some authorities, I know, are prepared to maintain the contrary.

The limitations of free trade

Why, then, did I begin by saying that I sympathised with both sides? I will tell you. In spite of all that I have just said, there are some important respects in which those who are not afraid to use tariffs have a broader conception of the national economic life and a truer feeling for the quality of it. Free traders, fortified into presumption by the essential truths—one might say truisms—of their cause, have greatly overvalued the social advantage of mere market cheapness, and have attributed excellences which do not exist to the mere operation of the methods of *laissez-faire*. The protectionist has often used bad economic arguments, but he has sometimes had a truer sense of the complicated balances and harmonies and qualities of a sound national economic life, and of the wisdom of not unduly sacrificing any part even to the whole. The virtues of variety and universality, the opportunity for the use of every gift and every aptitude, the amenities of life, the old established traditions of a countryside—all those things, of which there are many, even in the material life of a country, which money cannot buy, need to be considered. National protection has its idealistic side, too—a side which a well-balanced national economic policy will try to marry with the peace and truth and international fair-dealing of free trade.

If it were true that we should be a little richer, provided that the whole country and all the workers in it were to specialise on half-a-dozen mass-produced products, each individual doing nothing and having no hopes of doing anything except one minute, unskilled, repetitive act all his life long, should we all cry out for the immediate destruction of the endless variety of trades and crafts and employments which stand in the way of the glorious attainment of this maximum degree of specialised cheapness? Of course we should not—and that is enough to prove that the case for free trade, as I began by stating it, has left something out. Our task is to redress the balance of the argument.

Tariffs and employment

I will give three examples. But before I come to them, there is a further concession to be made to the protectionist case. There was a time when I denied the temporary usefulness of a tariff as a means of combating unemployment. I still think that a world wide system of tariffs will increase unemployment rather than diminish it, in the world as a whole. But I should now admit that if we put on a tariff at a time of severe unemployment it would be likely to shift on to other countries some part of our own burden of unemployment. For the free trade argument against the use of a tariff for drawing workers into an industry for which they are relatively ill-suited fundamentally assumes that, in the absence of a tariff, they will be employed in some other more suitable industry, and does not allow for the contingency that they may not be employed at all.

Protection for motor-cars—

Now for my examples of tariffs which I deem to be justified. First, our motor-car industry. I have always maintained that the protection which we have accorded to this industry every since the War was wise and beneficial. This was a new, progressive, ever-changing industry, of first-class interest and importance in itself, of a kind for which one would expect our national aptitudes to be excellent, offering highly congenial and attractive tasks and problems to one typical kind of Englishman. Indeed, it would be a shocking thing if we were to be without a prosperous and inventive motor industry. But during the War, when we were otherwise occupied, the United States had gained a great start on us both financially and technically; so that it was certain that the English industry would be bankrupt before it could pay, if it were to be exposed to the full force of foreign competition. The results today are a triumphant vindication of the protection we gave to it. Can anyone deny it?

—For iron and steel—

That is a new industry. My next example is an old one—iron and steel. Here is a case of an industry with a great past, languishing to decay—by our own fault, in no small degree. The problem is intricate—I cannot enter upon it here. But I should not discard the assistance of a tariff if it were part of a well-concerted general scheme for the regeneration of the industry. For I am convinced that this is an industry for which, if one thinks in decades and not in single years, we are singularly well adapted. Yet it is obvious that much lasting injury can be done to it in a short time. Its further debilitation will devastate whole neighbourhoods; it will root up tens of thousands of men from their homes and associations to throw them helpless on the world; and it will render valueless miles of houses the financial fortunes of which the steel plants cannot take into account in their calculations of what will or will not pay. I do not consider it important, over against this, that steel today should be as cheap as possible to the consumer. I wish to see the blast furnaces of the north-east coast roar again and ships of British steel sail out of the Clyde. And I am prepared, if necessary, to pay a little for the satisfaction.

—And for agriculture

My last example is the greatest crux of all for the uncompromising free trader—agriculture. Suppose it to be true that the average farmer in this country will be ruined unless the prices of his output are raised by taxes on food or equivalent measures. Is the free trader prepared to say—Well, let farming go? Of course we must not be foolish in our remedies, or attract the farmer into crops for which the country is unsuited compared with other crops. But that is not the dilemma I am putting to the free trader. Suppose that it is not possible for British farming today, so long as it is exposed to the uncertainties of unrestricted competition, to provide for those employed in it the standard of life set by the mass-produced industries of the towns—and this supposition is by no means improbable. Are there any free traders who say—Well, let farming go? I hope there are none such. For, anyone who does not imprison his mind in a strait-jacket, must know, as well as you and I do, that the pursuit of agriculture is part of a complete national life. I said above that a prosperous motor industry was a national necessity, if only to given an opening to one kind of typical Englishman. It is true in the same way that another kind needs as his pursuit in life the care and breeding of domestic animals and contact with the changing seasons and the soil. To say that the country cannot afford agriculture is to delude oneself about the meaning of the word 'afford'. A country which cannot afford art or agriculture, invention or tradition, is a country in which one cannot afford to live.

The path of wisdom in these matters is, then, a narrow one, to be trodden safely only by those who see the pitfalls on both sides. Neither free trade nor protection can present a theoretical case which entitles it to claim supremacy in practice. Protection is a dangerous and expensive method of redressing a want of balance and security in a nation's economic life. But there are times when we cannot safely trust ourselves to the blindness of economic forces; and when no alternative weapon as efficacious as tariffs lies ready to our hand.

The same day as he spoke on the B.B.C. Keynes finished an article on the forthcoming Conference, and sent a copy to the Prime Minister. The article appeared a month later.

From The New Statesman and Nation, *24 December 1932*

THE WORLD ECONOMIC CONFERENCE 1933

It will be a few months yet before the Conference proper meets; a few months more before it reports; probably a further passage of time before the report can lead to any action. The world, therefore, should not base hopes upon it for the spring or summer of 1933. Yet we need not greatly regret the procrastination. For in the first six months of 1933 the world will be wondering between two alternatives; and until the doubt is resolved it would be vain to expect genuine decisions from an international conference. The alternatives are these. Will it be apparent by the middle of 1933 that this slump is the same in kind as past slumps though so violent in degree, and is gradually working itself off by the operation of natural forces and the economic system's own resiliency? Or shall we find ourselves, after a modest upward reaction and dubious hopes of recovery, plunged back again into the slough? So long as there is any prospect of our realising the first alternative—and its realisation is not impossible—we may be certain that an international conference will confine itself to pious words. Only in the other event, with hopes dashed and the oppression of renewed and universal despair terrifying the delegates, will there be any chance of action commensurate with the problem. If, therefore, there is a risk that the second alternative will materialise—which is not so very improbable—I should wish the Conference to be still in session at the moment when the world discovers that its hopes are not being fulfilled.

It is easy to predict the agenda of the Conference. A number of resolutions will be passed declaring that many things ought to be changed, but without a serious intention of changing them. The Conference will agree in its collective capacity that tariffs and quotas have reached a pitch of absurdity and are a menace to international trade, but there will be no offers by individual countries to reduce them. Exchange restrictions will be denounced, but those countries where they exist will regret that they are in no position to abate them. It will be said that debts should be written down when they are beyond the capacity of the borrower, but no individual creditor will offer to write them down. The Conference will declare that there should be a general return to the gold standard as soon as possible, but those countries which have gained their liberty in this respect will not surrender it except on conditions which they do not expect to see satisfied. The Conference may agree, even with French acquiescence, that prices should be raised. But will it offer any plan for raising them?

So long as the Conference deals with symptoms and not with causes the shadow of futility will lie across its path. Its first task, therefore, should be to distinguish the one from the other. If we study the problem in that way, it is apparent that many of the evils, with which the pious resolutions will deal, are symptoms. The latest extravagances of tariffs and quotas, exchange restrictions, the default of debts, the collapse of the gold standard, even the fall of prices itself, are mainly symptoms. No one has desired these things; none of them is the expression of deliberate policy; they have been forced upon us as the expression and the result of more fundamental forces. It is as though a council of doctors, summoned to cure colds in the head, were to pass resolutions that it is desirable to stop snuffling and that a man who coughs is a nuisance to his neighbours.

What, then, is the root of the matter, upon which the Conference, if it were wise, would concentrate? It is not easily expressed in a few words; but I will try to indicate its nature.

The trouble began with something which is best described as 'a state of financial tension'. In the United States the causes of the tension were internal; elsewhere they were in their origins mainly international. These initiating causes are well known—on the one hand a frenzy of speculation in the United States, on the other hand a cessation of the international lending which had been off-setting the disequilibrium of the balances of payment between countries which War debts and tariffs would have already produced otherwise. A state of financial tension means that individuals and communities suddenly find much increased difficulty in putting their hands on money to meet their obligations, with the result that they take various measures to reduce their purchasing. Others, not actually in difficulty, fear that the same thing may overtake them later, and from precaution reduce their purchasing also. The reduced demand, which is the same thing as reduced purchasing, causes prices to fall; the fall of prices diminishes profits; and the entrepreneurs of the world, whether they are in difficulties or not, have a diminished incentive to produce output or to make the purchases and create the incomes which would have accompanied it. Thus the declines in demand, in prices, in profits, in output and in incomes feed on themselves and one another.

When financial tension leads to a diminution in demand, the

decline necessarily feeds on itself, because each step which an individual (or a community) takes to protect himself and to relieve his own tension merely has the effect of transferring the tension to his neighbour and of aggravating his neighbour's distress. The course of exchange, as we all know, moves round a closed circle. When we transmit the tension, which is beyond our own endurance, to our neighbour, it is only a question of a little time before it reaches ourselves again travelling round the circle.

Two spurious remedies are offered us. One is to endeavour to keep pace with the reduction in demand by an equal reduction in supply, i.e. by schemes of organised restriction. The other is to endeavour to keep pace with the fall in prices by an equal cut in wages. Each of these remedies may succour an individual producer if his neighbours refrain from it. But each of them destroys or diminishes someone's income (and therefore his purchasing power), so that, applied as all-round remedies, they aggravate the disease.

There is one, and only one, genuine remedy; namely, to increase demand—in other words to increase expenditure. As the slump progresses, it becomes more difficult to do this. At first a relief in the financial tension would have been enough by itself. But when the decline of prices and profits has gone beyond a certain point, the incentive to produce, and not merely the financial ability, has disappeared. At this point, the state itself must, in my judgement, start the ball rolling by deliberately organising expenditure. But in any case the relief of the financial tension is the first condition for the success of any other measures. A few of the financially strong countries can help by their domestic financial policy. In recent months the United States has done much, and Great Britain has done something, along these lines. But a great part of the world is helpless until the tension is relieved for them internationally. It is for this reason that an international conference has a significant purpose. It is to this primary object that it should address itself.

The War debts have played an important part in creating the tension. At present they lie outside the scope of the Conference. Perhaps they will be brought within it. Whatever the procedure, their liquidation is necessary to create an environment in which other measures, which would fail by insufficiency otherwise, may be worth while. I assume in what follows that this problem has been dealt with first.

Certainly I wish all success to conversations for the abatement of tariffs and exchange restrictions. But we must remember that these things are measures of self-protection, of which individual countries cannot afford to deprive themselves unless some alternative protection is offered them at the same time. They are not the core and kernel, which the Conference must reach if it is to find nourishment. The essential task is to devise measures for the direct relief of financial tension between nations. Such measures will all fall, I think, into one of four groups of remedies. If anyone knows a fifth, let him declare it.

The first would provide for some consolidation of short-term debts which cannot be met and are now protected by standstills. This is a very technical problem. The solution might be found in separating those debtors who could pay in terms of their national currencies from those who could not, and then providing for the appropriate central banks to take over the liability for the former whilst furnishing the banks with the means to do so—which last requirement causes this group of remedies to be merged in the others.

The second would seek for some writing down of privately owned international debts to correspond with the change in the value of money, so that debtor countries producing raw materials would not be required to devote twice as great a volume of exports to the service of their debts as at the time when they were incurred. This appeals to my feelings of justice, but my practical sense views it more doubtfully. If prices do not rise, the debts are certain to be brought down by their own weight; it will not need an international conference. But if it is our firm purpose to raise prices, the remedy may become unnecessary. Moreover it is not prudent to shake the investor's confidence in bonds at a moment when we are anxious to revive his interest in them.

The third invites the creditor countries of the world to dip their hands into their pockets yet again, to put up a guaranteed loan for the benefit of the others. This will be strongly pressed from several quarters. But I am sure that the British and American Treasuries will fiercely resist it. And they will be right in their resistance. This kind of philanthropy will never be large enough in scale; the division of the burden will never be rightly agreed; nor will the division of the proceeds. For several years we have been trying to buy ourselves out of the mess by such means, and our attempts are a proved failure. One chance there was—at Paris in 1919, when a loan of reconstruction might have been part of a general plan for the world's appeasement; but that we blindly rejected.

I come to the fourth plan—the only safe exit which I can discern. It is on a theme capable of several variations, of which the essence is the same. The following version of it, which is not my own, has impressed favourably some good judges. Our plan must be spectacular, so as to change the grey complexion of men's minds. It must apply to all countries and to all *simultaneously*. Each at the same time must feel able to remove the barriers to trade and to purchase freely. If we *all* begin purchasing again, we shall *all* have the means to do so. The appropriate stimulus to the activity of trade will vary from nation to nation; in some a relief from taxation, in some a programme of public works, in some an expansion of credit, in some a relaxation of exchange and import restrictions, in some a repayment of pressing debts, in some the mere removal of anxieties and fear, in some the mere stimulus to the lords of business to be courageous and active again. What is the charm to awaken the Sleeping Beauty, to scale the mountain of glass without slipping back? If every Treasury were to discover in its vaults a large *cache* of gold proportioned in size to the scale of its economic life, would not that work the charm? Why should not that *cache* be devised? We have long printed gold nationally. Why should we not print it internationally? No reason in the world, unless our hands are palsied and our wits dull.

The plan would be as follows. An international body—the Bank for International Settlements or a new institution created for the purpose—would be instructed by the assembled nations to print gold certificates to the amount of (say) $5,000,000,000. The countries participating would undertake to pass legislation providing that these certificates would be accepted as the lawful equivalent of gold for all contractual and monetary purposes. They would also undertake to provide a lawful ratio of equivalence, though not necessarily an unchangeable one, between gold and their national moneys. The gold certificates would then be distributed to the participants in proportions determined by a formula, based on their economic weight in the world, subject to two conditions. The first would require the payment of a very small rate of interest to provide a guarantee fund against infringement of the second condition, ultimately returnable if not required for this purpose. The second would provide for the gradual withdrawal of this international fiduciary note issue in the event of an index number of the chief articles of international trade recovering to an agreed level. This plan should appeal to those who wish to see the world return as nearly as possible to the gold standard, and also to those who hope for the evolution of an international management of the standard of value. I see no disadvantages in it and no dangers. It requires nothing but that those in authority should wake up one morning a little more elastic than usual.

The delegates to the World Conference should assemble in sackcloth and ashes, with humble and contrite hearts. It is, I suppose, well nigh the fiftieth of post-war conferences. Fear and greed, duplicity and incompetence, but above all conventional thought and feeling, have brought their collective performance far below the level of the participants regarded as human individuals. But here is a last opportunity. *Finis coronat opus.*

At the turn of the year, the Scottish Investment Trust Company asked Keynes to survey the prospects for sterling, as he had a year earlier (above p. 63). He replied on 18 January.

MEMORANDUM ON STERLING EXCHANGE

I would emphasise at the outset that predominant importance should always be attached to the position on income account, owing to the continuous character of income transactions as against the once-for-all character of most capital transactions.

I. *Balance of income account*

A year ago I held the opinion that the real position was probably £20,000,000 to £30,000,000 a year better than the Board of Trade estimate. On this basis I estimated that the adverse balance during 1932 might be quite negligible, and would not at the worst exceed £50,000,000. Last autumn I was again of the belief that the adverse balance looked like being quite negligible, but in deference to other opinions I was ready to admit that it might reach £30,000,000.

We now have the figures for the visible adverse balance of 1932, but not yet the Board of Trade estimate for the net result on income account. The visible trade balance for the last few months of the year was so very favourable, that I have now reverted to the opinion that the adverse balance for the year, if there is an adverse balance, is quite negligible.

The adverse trade balance is approximately £120,000,000 better than in the previous year. Against this there must be set some further deterioration on foreign investment account and from freights. But I should doubt if our total invisible income has shrunk by more than £35,000,000, indeed it may quite well have been better than that. This estimate would be consistent with the view that the total result is a close balance.

It does not follow that the Board of Trade estimate, when it is available, will show such a favourable result, unless they revise their method of compilation. I am assuming that on the old basis of compilation they have, one way and another, underestimated our favourable invisible income by about £25,000,000.

I am confirmed in this view as to the balance on income account by the inferences suggested by the rest of the picture. Indeed, if one takes what one knows of capital movements into account, one is perplexed as to how to explain the actual course of events except on the hypothesis that we have had a favourable balance on income account. In any case I am sure that the story, which was current even quite recently, that we are still running a large adverse balance on income account, is totally without foundation, and is irreconcilable with the actual course of events.

Looking forward into 1933, it seems to me that some further modest improvement is likely in our visible trade balance, even if world recovery continues to progress very slowly. Our imports are now running at a lower figure than a year ago. Imports in anticipation of tariffs were still going on in the early part of last year, whilst tariffs themselves were not yet in full operation. In addition, the measures of the Ministry of Agriculture for reducing the importation of meat were only in operation for a portion of last year, and are still incomplete. On the other side of the account, there is a reasonable ground for hope of a slight expansion of our exports rather than a contraction. The Australian and Indian markets are better, the rate of exchange is very favourable to exporters, and countries of which we are large customers are more and more believing it to be sound policy to direct their own purchases to our markets as much as they conveniently can.

So far as invisible income is concerned, the shipping position is perhaps a little more likely to improve than to deteriorate, at any rate we may hope that we have now felt the worst of that. As regards defaults on interest, it would be optimistic to hope that that has now reached its maximum; but so long as the

Empire countries and Germany do not default, further losses on this heading are not likely to be very material. Thus it would not need much improvement of the visible balance to give us a modest favourable balance over the coming year.

II. *Transactions on capital account*

The actual course of events shows that our account must have been benefited by very large plus items. The difficulty is to imagine how they can have been sufficient to balance the more or less known minus items.

On the adverse side we have to remember the following:—

(i) The Bank of England, after paying off £30,000,000 (gold) very early in the year, followed this up by repaying a further £80,000,000 (gold). It is also commonly believed that the Exchange Equalisation Fund has accumulated substantial resources in gold and foreign currencies. To give a figure for this is pure guess-work, but one would be surprised if the amount is less than £30,000,000, whilst it might be more. Undoubtedly the Bank has helped in securing so much foreign currency by the closing of the international bear position against sterling which had been built up during the crises of 1931. But even so it would seem probable that there has been a substantial net balance of new resources available for the Bank of England to pick up on the exchange market.

(ii) Private investment has probably been on balance outward rather than inward. In the latter part of the year relative interest rates in London have been low compared with those in other centres. I should suppose that we have increased our American investments on balance rather than diminished them, though perhaps the net figure is not large. The indications are that London has purchased a considerable amount of dollar foreign bonds in New York, German and Australian and other. Indeed the relative prices in London and New York for similar securities would make it almost certain that this has happened.

(iii) The conversion of the War Loan must, one would suppose, have led to some removal of money by foreign holders. Probably this was much less than some people at one time expected. But one would hardly expect holders of £150,000,000 to £200,000,000 worth of loan to accept so great a reduction of interest without a certain proportion of them withdrawing.

(iv) It seems likely that there has been some further fall in French balances in London. Perhaps as much as £20,000,000 to £25,000,000 might have been withdrawn in the year.

It is evident from the above that the exchange position could not have been as good as it has been if there were not large counteracting items on the other side of the account. The difficulty, as I have said, is to imagine a sufficient number of such items. As an inference from the negative items mentioned above one would naturally infer that there must have been positive items of at least £100,000,000, and even perhaps £150,000,000. One has to account for this figure amongst such items as the following:—

(i) The Government of India has certainly greatly strengthened its cash balances in London. Exports of gold from India have fulfilled the highest hopes, averaging a full million pounds a week. I have no direct knowledge of the figures, but would not be surprised if the net increase of Indian resources in London, including the Government and the banks, were as much as £30,000,000. Australia, having gone a long way towards righting its balance, has also remitted to London on capital account. The flight of money from South Africa to London, in anticipation of South Africa's abandoning of the gold standard, could be put at £10,000,000 or even £15,000,000. There must also be many smaller items of the same kind from Empire countries.

(ii) There has been a steady repayment of British acceptances throughout the year, sums outstanding under standstill arrangements have also been materially reduced, the depreciation of sterling leading debtors to pay off their British obligations by preference. Probably the aggregate of such items has been larger than is generally supposed.

(iii) The normal sinking funds in respect of old foreign investments are larger, as Sir Robert Kindersley has shown[5], than one used to think.

(iv) There remains the question whether general foreign balances in London have been substantially increased. Apart from the strengthening of the position of Empire countries, referred to above, I have heard little evidence for believing that this has been, on balance, an important item. Perhaps there has been some return of money to London since the end of 1932. But if one takes the calendar year 1932 it is, I think, most improbable that there was any considerable increase of such balances as at the end of the year over and above the normal figure.

The above summary does perhaps make it just credible that capital movements in and out have approximately balanced at some figure not less than £100,000,000 and not more than £150,000,000. Looking to the future, it is of course of the nature of capital movements not to be recurrent. If, however, there can be degrees in this, the adverse movements as recapitulated above are perhaps of a more non-recurrent character than the credit items. Taking, therefore, the prospects of income and capital movements together, there is no evidence of a seriously unbalanced position either way in the neighbourhood of the present rate of exchange (namely 3.35), indeed, since the exchange has lately been held down to this figure by the policy of the Bank of England, it may be that a natural balance would be maintained at 3.40 or 3.45. My main conclusion is that there is really no foundation whatever for the view that there is something inherently unhealthy or unstable in the position of the British international balance. In these days of violent changes, predictions are dangerous. But there is no warrant for the view that the present position is artificially favourable, and that the mere

[5] In his annual surveys in *The Economic Journal* which began in 1930.

development of existing inherent tendencies will be likely to be disastrously adverse.

III. *The policy of the Bank of England*

The actual exchange rate which will prevail in the ensuing months will of course largely depend on the policy of the Bank of England in its management of the Exchange Equalisation Fund. Past experience suggests that the Bank's policy will be, first of all to take advantage of favourable movements to secure such balances as it genuinely desires, and after that, whilst controlling and restricting upward movements, not to resist too strongly a decided tendency. Similarly in the event of downward movements, it will support the exchange so far as it can do so with reserves which it feels it can genuinely spare, after which it will not resist obstinately too decided a tendency. The fluctuations in 1932 were very wide, and probably unnecessarily so. In the light of the experience gained in 1932, it should be possible to keep the fluctuations within much narrower limits. Apart from quite unexpected developments, I should have thought that it should not be too difficult to hold the exchange within extreme limits for the year of 3.25 and 3.50, or a fluctuation of about 8 per cent.

We have to remember in this connection that there will be an immense pressure on us, both in connection with War debts and in connection with the International Economic Conference, to return to the gold standard in some shape or form. I notice a decided tendency in America to link up the idea of concessions on the War debts with assurances on our part as to our sterling exchange policy. One can be sure that the Treasury and the Bank of England will be reluctant to commit themselves; on the other hand the clamour for a return to gold probably inspires them with some measure of sympathy. If some qualified return to gold or *de facto* stabilisation of the exchange were to occur, it would naturally be based on the *de facto* exchange ruling at the time.

Thus the Bank will be anxious that the *de facto* rate should not be too high, whilst everyone else will be anxious that it should not be too low. I believe that these influences may have a stabilising effect on the prospective fluctuations. One in any case assumes that a qualified return of sterling to gold at a high level of the exchange is unthinkable. A high exchange could only occur in the event of widespread fears that France and the United States were intending to abate in some way the rigour of the gold standard,—a prospect which would certainly not be accompanied by an undertaking on our part to peg sterling in terms of gold.

IV. *The position of the gold countries*

It will be seen that I do not look for any sensational developments in the coming year so far as sterling is concerned. Sensational events, if any, will emanate I should expect from the gold countries. In considering their prospects, there are two main groups of facts to be born in mind.

(i) Perhaps the outstanding event of 1931 and 1932, although it has not yet excited much remark, has been the liquidation of the creditor positions of the leading creditor countries. The Macmillan Committee estimated the aggregate creditor balances of the leading creditor countries before the slump at some £500,000,000 to £600,000,000 a year, so that the position could only be kept balanced by loan transactions to a corresponding amount. It was the cessation of these loan transactions which provoked acute financial confusion internationally. But in the last two years, the debtor countries have managed by one expedient or another—by defaults, by exchange and trade restrictions, etc.,—to square their position with the creditor countries. The result is that Great Britain has little or no creditor balance, that France probably has no creditor balance, and that the creditor balance of the United States is no longer formidable. It is only as regards the last named item that one feels some uncertainty, since there is a risk of underestimating the improvement of the American balance due to reduced immigrant remittances and diminished tourist expenditure. But I should be inclined to say that the Macmillan figure should be reduced today to an amount in the neighbourhood of, say, £100,000,000.

Now the new gold becoming available from India and South Africa and other sources is now probably in excess of £100,000,000. Thus, allowing for this, the creditor countries regarded as a bloc no longer have any material claims on the rest of the world (I am assuming here that no further material sums will be paid to the United States in respect of War debts by purchases over the exchanges). Thus the acuteness of the financial position which has played so great a part in the past may be at an end; whilst the obligation of the few remaining gold countries to purchase all the current supplies of gold will be a strain on their resources. This natural tendency towards depreciation of the exchanges of the gold countries can in present circumstances only exhibit itself in a tendency of sterling to appreciate. This is the counterpart, in a sense, of the strength accruing to sterling out of the improvement of Indian, Australian or South African balances in London.

(ii) We saw last year how easily depositors in gold countries can take fright and endeavour to remove their resources to a country like Great Britain which has 'been through it', rather than to gold countries whose troubles may still be ahead. I am told that the French budgetary difficulties will not be solved before next July at the earliest, and that in the meantime several Cabinets may fall. There may well be a tendency for removal of funds from Paris to London. In the United States it would seem highly probable that there will be recurrent alarms as to the success of so-called inflationary policies. Thus if any sensational events are to occur in 1933, I think they will take the form of a widespread distrust of the countries still remaining on the gold standard rather than of exaggerated fears concerning sterling. If I were trying to take account, not only of the more probable, but also of the less probable, I should be more afraid of an overwhelming pressure towards an upward movement of the sterling exchange, than the opposite.

V. *Conclusions*

My general conclusion would be not to expect large changes in the gold value of sterling during the current year, for any reason primarily connected with the financial position of Great Britain. Even if we are to be visited eventually with widespread defaults of interest within the Empire, which would seriously shake the position of sterling, I should not expect this to happen in 1933. Thus, as I have said, the biggest risk of sensational occurrences is to be looked for in the position of the gold countries, rather than of the sterling countries.

If and when the gold prices of commodities begin to move strongly upwards, one would have to revise some of the above conclusions. But this is still some way off, and scarcely likely to occur on any impressive scale during the first half of 1933.

18 January 1933

In December 1932 South Africa abandoned the gold standard and joined the group of countries whose exchange rates moved with sterling. The resulting devaluation of the South African pound implied a sharp rise in the local currency receipts of the gold mining companies. This led to a boom in South African gold shares, or Kaffirs, on the London market. *The Daily Mail* asked for Keynes's views on the significance of the boom. Below we print Keynes's typescript of the resulting article to which *The Daily Mail* gave the title 'Does the Kaffir Boom Herald World Recovery?'. The typescript follows the published version of 7 February 1933 except for paragraphing.

THE KAFFIR BOOM: WILL HISTORY REPEAT ITSELF?

The slump of the eighteen nineties is the nearest historical parallel to the great slump of the nineteen thirties which we are now suffering. The end of that slump was signalised by the Kaffir boom of 1895, based on the discovery of the Cyanide process and the boundless prospects, since realised, which this opened up for South African gold. Will history repeat itself? Will the Kaffir boom, the roar of which is now deafening London and Johannesburg and will soon reverberate throughout the world, prove to be the spark which will re-ignite the tinder of abundant credit, to use Mr Beaumont Pease's metaphor in his speech at Lloyds Bank last week, 'the outstanding event striking men's imaginations and persuading them that now is the time to extend and that, if they do not buy today, they will have to pay more tomorrow for what they require'. It is not impossible. This Kaffir boom is an event of first class importance. It is worth while to consider carefully its wider economic implications.

The Kaffir boom is more solidly based than such affairs usually are. For it depends on an actually realised event, not on the discounting of problematical hopes. It is true that it is an event in the monetary world, rather than in the physical world. It should, indeed, lead in time to a greater output of gold. But its main immediate importance is independent of that and lies in the inflation which it causes in certain money values. But that is precisely what we need today. Nature's physical yield to our efforts is only too abundant, and it is the distorted monetary valuation of assets which prevents prosperity.

The actually realised event is this. Provided that the South African £ is linked to sterling, which seems highly probable, and that there is no large change in the present gold parity of sterling which it seems to be the present object of the Bank of England to prevent, it is then a matter of calculable certainty that, as a result of South Africa's departure from the gold standard, the output of its mines in 1933 will be worth £20,000,000 more in the South African currency in which its expenses and taxes are reckoned, than in 1932. Such events as the devaluation of the franc or the dollar, i.e. a reduction of the gold content of these currency units—which some, though not I, think probable—would not affect this calculation in any way.

The element of uncertainty is the division of this sum between the three claimants for it—the shareholders, the employees and suppliers of the mines, and the South African Government. The second of those three will doubtless share in the good fortune, but the prevailing rates were fixed when the cost of living was much higher than it is now, and this factor is not expected to be of more than moderate significance. As between the other two, speculative uncertainty will continue until the Transvaal Gold Law Amendment Bill, due shortly, has been published and Mr Havenga has introduced his budget, some two months hence. What follows is based on the assumption—how well founded I do not know—that the South African Government will avoid vindictive legislation towards its most important industry, and will welcome a state of affairs calculated to lengthen greatly—some say to double—the life of the Rand. Moreover on the basis of existing taxation and Government profit-sharing in leased mines, it is calculated that the direct share of the Government in the new profits will be at least £5,000,000, apart from its indirect interest, as tax-gatherer, in the large increase in the South African national income and the greater activity of business which will ensue.

In 1932 the aggregate gross working profit of the Transvaal mines was £18,000,000, out of which dividends of £9,000,000 were declared. This, in conjunction with the figures given above, furnishes sufficient *data* for us to gauge the order of magnitude of what has happened in the Kaffir market. The divisible profits of the mines—to give an illustrative guess, it is no more—might be increased by (say) £10,000,000 or approximately doubled. If this be capitalised at 20 per cent, the mines are worth £50,000,000 more than they were two months ago; if at 10 per cent, then £100,000,000. It may be that £50,000,000 is the reasonable figure; and £100,000,000 what the speculators will temporarily believe. Or, rather—for speculators are so subtle!—what all speculators will believe that other speculators believe. For a speculator is a man who anticipates the behaviour of other speculators, so that if all speculators have the same anticipations, all of them will—temporarily—be right; and only when the music stops—for musical chairs is the game which speculators play with one another—will someone find himself without a seat.

Now this is not a large figure in relation to the world's finance—or even to London's. If it were divided out equally between all the savings depositors in the world, it would be an insignificant trifle per head. I may seem, therefore, to attach an exaggerated importance to it. Perhaps I do. But it is not going to be divided out equally between savings depositors. It will be shared between the feather-brained speculators. And they, at this juncture of affairs, are not unimportant people. For they, in truth, are the gay sparks to whom Mr Beaumont Pease must look to re-ignite his tinder.

To raise the spirits of the speculator and to put him in funds would cause but a flash in the pan, if Mr Pease had no tinder. But at the precise phase of the slump which we have now reached, with credit cheap and abundant, commodity markets on the whole sold out, visible stocks no longer increasing and invisible stocks depleted, the speculator's spark—though no use whatever for driving the power system of the world—may be just what we need. I believe that we might have ended the slump before now if governments had had the wisdom to increase the consumer's purchasing power by encouraging loan expenditure. But if our political and banking technique compel us to allow the slump blindly to run its course, then the order of recovery must be reversed. It must begin with a rise of commodity prices, to be followed later by increased consumption. And if the rise of commodity prices has to *precede* the increase in the purchasing power of the consumer, then this, in its turn, must probably be preceded by a rise of security prices,—which requires the combination of cheap money with some accidental event to put speculators in funds and spirits. For it is the nature of speculators to pass on from one field to the next; and as each successive wave of speculators 'takes its profits' in one market, it is eager to seek another outlet.

It is from this aspect that I am inclined, provisionally at least, to attach importance to the Kaffir boom. The sums involved, though insignificant in relation to world finance, are much larger than in most speculative markets. Take today any Rand mine of secondary importance, and you will find that its market capitalisation is much greater than, for example, that of the total stocks of rubber in Great Britain. Or again, Crown Mines, to name a single security, is valued at double all the tin stocks in the world; and so on. Moreover, the attraction of gold mines is international. They have the best qualifications for a world-wide speculative counter, seeming to combine solid certainty with alluring possibilities.

Auri sacra fames! Gold has its special glamour, its age-long appeal to the grasping palm, to those who would be safe and greedy at the same time. This may be an evil way in which to run our economic life. But seen realistically, it is by such tokens in the world as it is, that prosperity waxes and wanes.

Ten days later Keynes reappeared in the columns of *The Daily Mail* to discuss the future of the gold standard. Before publishing the article, he had consulted Hubert Henderson.

From The Daily Mail, *17 February 1933*

SHOULD BRITAIN COMPROMISE ON THE GOLD STANDARD?

In 1923 I wrote that 'the gold standard is already a barbarous relic' [*JMK*, vol. IV, p. 138]. If this was true ten years ago, can it be possible today to forecast a respectable future for it, when in the meantime it has betrayed all the hopes of all its friends? Yet it does not follow that the monetary system of the future will find no place for gold. A barbarous relic, to which a vast body of tradition and prestige attaches, may have a symbolic or conventional value if it can be fitted into the framework of a managed system of the new pattern. Such transformations are a regular feature of those constitutional changes which are effected without a revolution.

I predict, therefore, that central banks will continue in the future, as in the past, to keep gold reserves for the protection of their exchanges and as an emergency means of settling an adverse international balance.

The existing position, however, is highly paradoxical. It is obvious to everyone that those countries which have abandoned the gold standard are enjoying a great advantage over those which still adhere to it. The countries which are off gold have had more stable prices; their exchanges have settled down at a figure at which their export industries can live in relation to world competition; and their central banks, freed from the task of having to protect their gold reserves can, without any anxiety, maintain low rates of interest and abundant credit suited to their domestic needs. Country after country abandons, or moves farther away from, the gold standard—South Africa, New Zealand, Denmark, Canada within the last few weeks.

Yet, while the pressure of the facts is towards a further progressive abandonment of the gold standard, all the pressure of international diplomacy is towards its restoration. At the preliminary meeting of the World Conference last month the utmost pressure was put on the British representative to agree to put a return to gold in the forefront of the programme. Not long ago, *The Daily Mail* reported, even Mr Walter Lippmann, the American publicist, was representing Great Britain's sterling policy as a sort of reprisal against the War debts and was demanding that 'the American people should reject plans to settle War debts before discussing the British policy for sterling'.

These are only some of many indications that the greatest possible pressure to return to gold will be put upon Great Britain in connection both with the War debts and with the World Economic Conference.

Now we must, I think, recognise that existing arrangements,

however convenient to ourselves, are genuinely upsetting to those of our neighbours who remain tied to gold and have, therefore, to bear the brunt of the adjustments. We must also admit the great practical obstacles in the way of their following our example in Central Europe, because memories of the great inflations cause all currency experiments to be viewed with hysterical timidity; in France, because France is the last home of the bullionist complex and of ultra-conservatism in all matters concerning cash; and in the United States because of legal difficulties concerning gold bonds and overwhelming constitutional obstacles. Moreover, if others were to follow our example, it is possible that no country would derive much benefit, since the competitive advantages which now accrue from exchange depreciation would cancel out.

But, further, a greater *de facto* stability of sterling would be an improvement from all points of view. There are only two good reasons for exchange fluctuations—to compensate wide price changes abroad or to make unprofitable those large but meaningless migrations of international short loan money from one international centre to another which have been the chief curse of the foreign exchanges in recent times—first embarrassing London, then New York, and soon, I suspect, to afflict Paris. But these reasons do not justify such wide fluctuations as occurred last year.

Great Britain has, therefore, to consider whether there is any compromise which she can reasonably offer to meet the pressure and the complaints of her neighbours who believe that the unsteadiness of sterling is an important obstacle in the way of world recovery. The only possible compromise would be an undertaking by Great Britain that the maximum range in the gold value of sterling over the next twelve months should be limited to (say) five per cent—subject always to there being no further serious collapse meanwhile in the gold prices of commodities.

Would it be safe and prudent to give such an undertaking?

Yes, if it were part of a general scheme of financial appeasement. Everyone agrees that a solution of War debts and the ratification of the Lausanne settlement with Germany must come first. But it is generally admitted that a further condition is necessary for even a qualified return to gold. This is usually expressed by saying that there must be a more equal distribution of the world's gold reserves. If this means that the Bank of France and the Federal Reserve System of the United States are to share out their gold reserves with the impecunious countries of the world, it is clearly quite remote from anything which can possibly happen.

But there is, I am convinced, a better and more practical way of satisfying this condition, namely, by creating an international fiduciary note issue, based on and equivalent to gold—thus doing internationally what all countries have long done nationally.

The details of such a scheme would need an article to themselves. But, broadly speaking, I would have the Bank for International Settlements or, perhaps preferably, a new international institution created for the purpose, authorised to issue notes up to (say) $5,000,000,000, which all participating countries would agree to accept as the legal equivalent of gold, these notes to be available as reserve money to the central banks of the world against the gold bonds of their governments carrying a nominal rate of interest, in proportions corresponding to each country's normal requirements for gold reserves. The participating nations, thus safeguarded, could then abolish exchange restrictions and other abnormal impediments on international trade.

With this supplement to the effective gold resources of the world available for currency purposes, a qualified return to the gold standard would be practicable for most countries.

Here is a policy which might really achieve something—a policy for which it would be worth while to mobilise world opinion; a policy to evoke a rational enthusiasm. I see no other way, unless after a long interval of time, of satisfying the conditions as to the distribution of monetary reserves laid down by the Preparatory Committee of the World Economic Conference in their recent report as a prerequisite of a general return to gold.

What is the alternative? The risk of a gradual descent into yet greater chaos. Certainly a further progressive abandonment of the gold standard by one country after another, with an accentuation of the difficulties of those nations still adhering to 'the barbarous relic'.

In March Keynes developed his international currency proposals at greater length in the third and fourth articles of *The Means to Prosperity* (*JMK*, vol. IX, pp. 357–64). He had already pointed out to Geoffrey Dawson on 22 February that these were not his own, but rather the proposals discussed by the Committee on International Economic Policy.

Keynes turned his attention back to international trade when he gave the first Finlay Lecture at University College, Dublin on 19 April. The version he delivered in Dublin, with special references to Irish conditions, appeared in the June 1933 issue of *Studies*. A more general version appeared at the end of the World Economic Conference in *The New Statesman*.[6]

From The New Statesman and Nation, *8 and 15 July 1933*

NATIONAL SELF-SUFFICIENCY

I

I was brought up, like most Englishmen, to respect free trade not only as an economic doctrine which a rational and instructed person could not doubt but almost as a part of the moral law. I regarded departures from it as being at the same time an imbecility and an outrage. I thought England's unshakable free-trade convictions, maintained for nearly a hundred years, to be

[6] It also appeared in *The Yale Review* for Summer 1933.

both the explanation before man and the justification before heaven of her economic supremacy. As lately as 1923 I was writing that free trade was based on fundamental truths 'which, stated with their due qualifications, no one can dispute who is capable of understanding the meaning of the words' [*JMK*, vol. XIX, p. 147].

Looking again today at the statements of these fundamental truths which I then gave, I do not find myself disputing them. Yet the orientation of my mind is changed; and I share this change of mind with many others. Partly, indeed, my background of economic theory is modified. I should not charge Mr Baldwin, as I did then, with being 'a victim of the protectionist fallacy in its crudest form', because he believed that, in the existing conditions, a tariff might do something to diminish British unemployment. But mainly I attribute my change of outlook to something else—to my hopes and fears and preoccupations, along with those of many or most, I believe, of this generation throughout the world, being different from what they were. It is a long business to shuffle out of the mental habits of the pre-war nineteenth-century world. But today, at last, one third of the way through the twentieth century, we are most of us escaping from the nineteenth; and by the time we reach its mid-point it is likely that our habits of mind and what we care about will be as different from nineteenth-century methods and values as each other century's has been from its predecessor's. It may be useful, therefore, to attempt some sort of a stocktaking, of an analysis, of a diagnosis, to discover in what this change of mind essentially consists.

What did the nineteenth-century free traders, who were amongst the most idealistic and disinterested of men, believe that they were accomplishing?

They believed—and perhaps it is fair to put this first—that they were being perfectly sensible, that they alone were clear sighted, and that the policies which sought to interfere with the ideal international division of labour were always the offspring of ignorance out of self-interest.

In the second place, they believed that they were solving the problem of poverty, and solving it for the world as a whole, by putting to their best uses, like a good housekeeper, the world's resources and abilities.

They believed, further, that they were serving not merely the survival of the economically fittest but the great cause of liberty, of freedom for personal initiative and individual gift, the cause of inventive art and the fertility of the untrammelled mind against the forces of privilege and monopoly and obsolescence.

They believed, finally, that they were the friends and assurers of peace and international concord and economic justice between nations, and the diffusers of the benefits of progress.

And if to the poet of that age there sometimes came strange feelings to wander far away where never comes the trader and catch the wild goat by the hair, there came also with full assurance the comfortable reaction:

> I, to herd with narrow foreheads, vacant of our glorious gains,
> Like a beast with lower pleasures, like a beast with lower pains!

II

What fault have we to find with this? Taking it at its surface value—none. Yet we are not, many of us, content with it as a working political theory. What is wrong?

To begin with the question of peace. We are pacifist today with so much strength of conviction that, if the economic internationalist could win this point, he would soon recapture our support. But it does not now seem obvious that a great concentration of national effort on the capture of foreign trade, that the penetration of a country's economic structure by the resources and the influence of foreign capitalists, that a close dependence of our own economic life on the fluctuating economic policies of foreign countries, are safeguards and assurances of international peace. It is easier, in the light of experience and foresight, to argue quite the contrary. The protection of a country's existing foreign interests, the capture of new markets, the progress of economic imperialism—these are a scarcely avoidable part of a scheme of things which aims at the maximum of international specialisation and at the maximum geographical diffusion of capital wherever its seat of ownership. Advisable domestic policies might often be easier to compass, if, for example, the phenomenon known as 'the flight of capital' could be ruled out. The divorce between ownership and the real responsibility of management is serious within a country when, as a result of joint-stock enterprise, ownership is broken up between innumerable individuals who buy their interest today and sell it tomorrow and lack altogether both knowledge and responsibility towards what they momentarily own. But when the same principle is applied internationally, it is, in times of stress, intolerable—I am irresponsible towards what I own and those who operate what I own are irresponsible towards me. There may be some financial calculation which shows it to be advantageous that my savings should be invested in whatever quarter of the habitable globe shows the greatest marginal efficiency of capital or the highest rate of interest. But experience is accumulating that remoteness between ownership and operation is an evil in the relations between men, likely or certain in the long run to set up strains and enmities which will bring to nought the financial calculation.

I sympathise, therefore, with those who would minimise, rather than with those who would maximise, economic entanglement between nations. Ideas, knowledge, art, hospitality, travel—these are the things which should of their nature be international. But let goods be homespun whenever it is reasonably and conveniently possible; and, above all, let finance be primarily national. Yet, at the same time, those who seek to disembarrass a country of its entanglements should be very slow and wary. It should not be a matter of tearing up roots but of slowly training a plant to grow in a different direction.

For these strong reasons, therefore, I am inclined to the belief that, after the transition is accomplished, a greater measure of national self-sufficiency and economic isolation between countries than existed in 1914 may tend to serve the cause of peace, rather than otherwise. At any rate the age of economic internationalism was not particularly successful in avoiding war; and if its friends retort that the imperfection of its success never gave it a fair chance, it is reasonable to point out that a greater success is scarcely probable in the coming years.

Let us turn from these questions of doubtful judgement, where each of us will remain entitled to his own opinion, to a matter more purely economic. In the nineteenth century the economic internationalist could probably claim with justice that his policy was tending to the world's great enrichment, that it was promoting economic progress, and that its reversal would have seriously impoverished both ourselves and our neighbours. This raises a question of balance between economic and non-economic advantage of a kind which is not easily decided. Poverty is a great evil; and economic advantage is a real good, not to be sacrificed to alternative real goods unless it is clearly of an inferior weight. I am ready to believe that in the nineteenth century two sets of conditions existed which caused the advantages of economic internationalism to outweigh disadvantages of a different kind. At a time when wholesale migrations were populating new continents, it was natural that the men should carry with them into the New Worlds the material fruits of the technique of the Old, embodying the savings of those who were sending them. The investment of British savings in rails and rolling stock to be installed by British engineers to carry British emigrants to new fields and pastures, the fruits of which they would return in due proportion to those whose frugality had made these things possible, was not economic internationalism remotely resembling in its essence the part ownership of the A.E.G. of Germany by a speculator in Chicago, or of the municipal improvements of Rio de Janeiro by an English spinster. Yet it was the type of organisation necessary to facilitate the former which has eventually ended up in the latter. In the second place, at a time when there were enormous differences in degree in the industrialisation and opportunities for technical training in different countries, the advantages of a high degree of national specialisation were very considerable.

But I am not persuaded that the economic advantages of the international division of labour today are at all comparable with what they were. I must not be understood to carry my argument beyond a certain point. A considerable degree of international specialisation is necessary in a rational world in all cases where it is dictated by wide differences of climate, natural resources, native aptitudes, level of culture and density of population. But over an increasingly wide range of industrial products, and perhaps of agricultural products also, I become doubtful whether the economic cost of national self-sufficiency is great enough to outweigh the other advantages of gradually bringing the producer and the consumer within the ambit of the same national, economic and financial organisation. Experience accumulates to prove that most modern mass-production processes can be performed in most countries and climates with almost equal efficiency. Moreover, as wealth increases, both primary and manufactured products play a smaller relative part in the national economy compared with houses, personal services and local amenities which are not the subject of international exchange; with the result that a moderate increase in the real cost of the former consequent on greater national self-sufficiency may cease to be of serious consequence when weighed in the balance against advantages of a different kind. National self-sufficiency, in short, though it costs something, may be becoming a luxury which we can afford if we happen to want it. Are there sufficient good reasons why we may happen to want it?

III

The decadent international but individualistic capitalism, in the hands of which we found ourselves after the War, is not a success. It is not intelligent, it is not beautiful, it is not just, it is not virtuous—and it doesn't deliver the goods. In short, we dislike it and we are beginning to despise it. But when we wonder what to put in its place, we are extremely perplexed.

Each year it becomes more obvious that the world is embarking on a variety of politico-economic experiments, and that different types of experiment appeal to different national temperaments and historical environments. The nineteenth century free trader's economic internationalism assumed that the whole world was, or would be, organised on a basis of private competitive capitalism and of the freedom of private contract inviolably protected by the sanctions of law—in various phases, of course, of complexity and development, but conforming to a uniform type which it would be the general object to perfect and certainly not to destroy. Nineteenth-century protectionism was a blot upon the efficiency and good sense of this scheme of things, but it did not modify the general presumption as to the fundamental characteristics of economic society.

But today one country after another abandons these presumptions. Russia is still alone in her particular experiment, but no longer alone in her abandonment of the old presumptions. Italy, Ireland, Germany have cast their eyes, or are casting them, towards new modes of political economy. Many more countries after them will soon be seeking, one by one, after new economic gods. Even countries such as Great Britain and the United States, though conforming in the main to the old model, are striving, under the surface, after a new economic plan. We do not know what will be the outcome. We are—all of us, I expect—about to make many mistakes. No one can tell which of the new systems will prove itself best.

But the point for my present discussion is this. We each have our own fancy. Not believing that we are saved already, we each would like to have a try at working out our own salvation. We do not wish, therefore, to be at the mercy of world forces working out, or trying to work out, some uniform equilibrium according to the ideal principles, if they can be called such, of *laissez-faire* capitalism. There are still those who cling to the old ideas, but in no country of the world today can they be reckoned as a serious force. We wish—for the time at least and so long as the present transitional, experimental phase endures—to be our own masters, and to be as free as we can make ourselves from the interferences of the outside world.

Thus, regarded from this point of view, the policy of an increased national self-sufficiency is to be considered not as an ideal in itself but as directed to the creation of an environment in which other ideals can be safely and conveniently pursued.

Let me give as dry an illustration of this as I can devise, chosen because it is connected with ideas with which recently my own mind has been largely preoccupied. In matters of economic detail, as distinct from the central controls, I am in favour of retaining as much private judgement and initiative and enterprise as possible. But I have become convinced that the retention of the structure of private enterprise is incompatible with that degree of material well-being to which our technical advancement entitles us, unless the rate of interest falls to a much lower figure than is likely to come about by natural forces operating on the old lines. Indeed the transformation of society, which I preferably envisage, may require a reduction in the rate of interest towards vanishing point within the next thirty years. But under a system by which the rate of interest finds, under the operation of normal financial forces, a uniform level throughout the world, after allowing for risk and the like, this is most unlikely to occur. Thus for a complexity of reasons, which I cannot elaborate in this place, economic internationalism embracing the free movement of capital and of loanable funds as well as of traded goods may condemn this country for a generation to come to a much lower degree of material prosperity than could be attained under a different system.

But this is merely an illustration. The point is that there is no prospect for the next generation of a uniformity of economic systems throughout the world, such as existed, broadly speaking, during the nineteenth century; that we all need to be as free as possible of interference from economic changes elsewhere, in order to make our own favourite experiments towards the ideal social republic of the future; and that a deliberate movement towards greater national self-sufficiency and economic isolation will make our task easier, in so far as it can be accomplished without excessive economic cost.

IV

There is one more explanation, I think, of the reorientation of our minds. The nineteenth century carried to extravagant lengths the criterion of what one can call for short the financial results, as a test of the advisability of any course of action sponsored by private or by collective action. The whole conduct of life was made into a sort of parody of an accountant's nightmare. Instead of using their vastly increased material and technical resources to build a wonder-city, they built slums; and they thought it right and advisable to build slums because slums, on the test of private enterprise, 'paid', whereas the wonder-city would, they thought, have been an act of foolish extravagance, which would, in the imbecile idiom of the financial fashion, have 'mortgaged the future'; though how the construction today of great and glorious works can impoverish the future no man can see until his mind is beset by false analogies from an irrelevant accountancy. Even today we spend our time—half vainly, but also, I must admit, half successfully—in trying to persuade our countrymen that the nation as a whole will assuredly be richer if unemployed men and machines are used to build much needed houses than if they are supported in idleness. For the minds of this generation are still so beclouded by bogus calculations that they distrust conclusions which should be obvious, out of a reliance on a system of financial accounting which casts doubt on whether such an operation will 'pay'. We have to remain poor because it does not 'pay' to be rich. We have to live in hovels, not because we cannot build palaces, but because we cannot 'afford' them.

The same rule of self-destructive financial calculation governs every walk of life. We destroy the beauty of the countryside because the unappropriated splendours of nature have no economic value. We are capable of shutting off the sun and the stars because they do not pay a dividend. London is one of the richest cities in the history of civilisation, but it cannot 'afford' the highest standards of achievement of which its own living citizens are capable, because they do not 'pay'.

If I had the power today I should surely set out to endow our capital cities with all the appurtenances of art and civilisation on the highest standards of which the citizens of each were individually capable, convinced that what I could create, I could afford—and believing that money thus spent would not only be better than any dole, but would make unnecessary any dole. For with what we have spent on the dole in England since the War we could have made our cities the greatest works of man in the world.

Or again, we have until recently conceived it a moral duty to ruin the tillers of the soil and destroy the age-long human traditions attendant on husbandry if we could get a loaf of bread thereby a tenth of a penny cheaper. There was nothing which it was not our duty to sacrifice to this Moloch and Mammon in one; for we faithfully believed that the worship of these monsters would overcome the evil of poverty and lead the next generation safely and comfortably, on the back of compound interest, into economic peace.

Today we suffer disillusion, not because we are poorer than we were—on the contrary even today we enjoy, in Great Britain at least, a higher standard of life than at any previous period—but because other values seem to have been sacrificed and because, moreover, they seem to have been sacrificed unnecessarily. For our economic system is not, in fact, enabling us to exploit to the utmost the possibilities for economic wealth afforded by the progress of our technique, but falls far short of this, leading us to feel that we might as well have used up the margin in more satisfying ways.

But once we allow ourselves to be disobedient to the test of an accountant's profit, we have begun to change our civilisation. And we need to do so very warily, cautiously and self-consciously. For there is a wide field of human activity where we shall be wise to retain the usual pecuniary tests. It is the state, rather than the individual, which needs to change its criterion. It is the conception of the Chancellor of the Exchequer as the chairman of a sort of joint-stock company which has to be discarded. Now if the functions and purposes of the state are to be thus enlarged, the decision as to what, broadly speaking, shall be produced within the nation and what shall be exchanged with abroad, must stand high amongst the objects of policy.

V

From these reflections on the proper purposes of the state I return to the world of contemporary politics. Having sought to understand and to do full justice to the ideas which underlie the urge felt by so many countries today towards greater national self-sufficiency, we have to consider with care whether in practice we are not too easily discarding much of value which the nineteenth century achieved. In those countries where the advocates of national self-sufficiency have attained power, it appears to my judgement that, without exception, many foolish things are being done. Mussolini may be acquiring wisdom teeth. But Russia exhibits the worst example which the world, perhaps, has ever seen of administrative incompetence and of the sacrifice of almost everything that makes life worth living to wooden heads. Germany is at the mercy of unchained irresponsibles—though it is too soon to judge her capacity of achievement. The Irish Free State, a unit much too small for a high degree of national insufficiency except at crushing economic cost, is discussing plans which might, if they were carried out, be ruinous.

Meanwhile, those countries which maintain, or are adopting, straightforward protectionism of the old-fashioned type, refurbished with the addition of a few of the new plan quotas, are doing many things incapable of rational defence. Thus, if the Economic Conference were to achieve a mutual reduction of tariffs and prepare the way for regional agreements, it would be matter for sincere applause. For I must not be supposed to be endorsing all those things which are being done in the political world today in the name of economic nationalism. Far from it. But I seek to point out that the world towards which we are uneasily moving is quite different from the ideal economic internationalism of our fathers, and that contemporary policies must not be judged on the maxims of that former faith.

I see three outstanding dangers in economic nationalism and in the movements towards national self-sufficiency.

The first is Silliness—the silliness of the doctrinaire. It is nothing strange to discover this in movements which have passed somewhat suddenly from the phase of midnight high-flown talk into the field of action. We do not distinguish, at first, between the colour of the rhetoric with which we have won a people's assent and the dull substance of the truth of our message. There is nothing insincere in the transition. Words ought to be a little wild, for they are the assault of thoughts upon the unthinking. But when the seats of power and authority have been attained there should be no more poetic licence. On the contrary, we have to count the cost down to the penny which our rhetoric has despised. An experimental society has need to be far more efficient than an old-established one, if it is to survive safely. It will need all its economic margin for its own proper purposes and can afford to give nothing away to softheadedness or doctrinaire folly.

The second danger—and a worse danger than silliness—is Haste. Paul Valéry's aphorism is worth quoting—'Political conflicts distort and disturb the people's sense of distinction between matters of importance and matters of urgency.' The economic transition of a society is a thing to be accomplished slowly. What I have been discussing is not a sudden revolution, but the direction of secular trend. We have a fearful example in Russia today of the evils of insane and unnecessary haste. The sacrifices and losses of transition will be vastly greater if the pace is forced. This is above all true of a transition towards greater national self-sufficiency and a planned domestic economy. For it is of the nature of economic processes to be rooted in time. A rapid transition will involve so much pure destruction of wealth that the new state of affairs will be, at first, far worse than the old, and the grand experiment will be discredited.

The third risk, and the worst risk of all three, is Intolerance and the stifling of instructed criticism. The new movements have usually come into power through a phase of violence or quasi-violence. They have not convinced their opponents; they have downed them. It is the modern method—to depend on propaganda and to seize the organs of opinion; it is thought to be clever and useful to fossilise thought and to use all the forces of authority to paralyse the play of mind on mind. For those who have found it necessary to employ all methods whatever to attain power, it is a serious temptation to continue to use for the task of construction the same dangerous tools which wrought the preliminary house-breaking.

Russia, again, furnishes us with an example of the blunders which a regime makes when it has exempted itself from criticism. The explanation of the incompetence with which wars are always conducted on both sides may be found in the comparative exemption from criticism which the military hierarchy affords to the high command. I have no excessive admiration for politicians, but, brought up as they are in the very breath of criticism, how much superior they are to the soldiers! Revolutions only succeed because they are conducted by politicians against soldiers. Paradox though it be—who ever heard of a successful revolution conducted by soldiers against politicians? But we all hate criticism. Nothing but rooted principle will cause us willingly to expose ourselves to it.

Yet the new economic modes, towards which we are blundering, are, in the essence of their nature, experiments. We have no clear idea laid up in our minds beforehand of exactly what we want. We shall discover it as we move along, and we shall have to mould our material in accordance with our experience. Now for this process bold, free and remorseless criticism is a *sine qua non* of ultimate success. We need the collaboration of all the bright spirits of the age. Stalin has eliminated every independent, critical mind, even when it is sympathetic in general outlook. He has produced an environment in which the processes of mind are atrophied. The soft convolutions of the brain are turned to wood. The multiplied bray of the loud speaker replaces the inflections of the human voice. The bleat of propaganda, as Low has shown us, bores even the birds and the beasts of the field into stupefaction. Let Stalin be a terrifying example to all who seek to make experiments. If not, I, at any rate, will soon be back again in my old nineteenth-century ideals, where the play of mind on mind created for us the inheritance which we are seeking today to divert to our own appropriate purposes.

On 27 April, at the request of the Scottish Investment Trust Company, Keynes prepared an appreciation of the German financial position.

MEMORANDUM ON THE GERMAN FINANCIAL POSITION FROM THE STANDPOINT OF THE FOREIGN INVESTOR

The German prospects today are primarily dominated by political and personal factors; and whilst no doubt the fundamental economic factors will assert themselves in the long run, the treatment of foreign debts over the next twelve months will not, I should expect, depend very closely on purely economic factors.

Amongst the personal factors the personality and prejudices of Dr Schacht must play a large part so long as he remains at the Reichsbank. He is a man of strong will and probably the only member of the new regime who has real experience and knowledge of international finance. At the same time he is a somewhat vain man, with strong prejudices, who may allow himself to be influenced by a desire to justify prophesies and statements of policy which he has made in the past. This will particularly affect the Young Loan, since, it must be remembered, he resigned from office rather than accept the responsibility for the final settlement.

One feature which has been characteristic of German policy for some little time past will, I think, remain for the time being, namely a determination to maintain the mark exchange at its present value. If the dollar, and *a fortiori* other gold currencies, were to be devalued, it may be safely assumed that the mark could be devalued to maintain its previous parity with the dollar, but apart from this contingency great efforts will be made, I should expect, to prevent any decline in the exchange in relation to the dollar. There has in fact in the last week or two been some improvement in the mark in terms of the dollar, the mark having followed the dollar only part way in its recent decline.

This means that the protection of the mark exchange will

take precedence of [over?] foreign debts. If the foreign *valuta* is insufficient to meet the service of the foreign debts at the present rate of exchange, then it will be the foreign debts which will be allowed to go, rather than the exchange.

Next in order of preference will come the standstill credits which, apart from the solvency of individual German debtors, I should reckon a better security than long-term debt. After this come the Dawes Loan and the Young Loan in that order, and then other long-term debt, with municipal debt and mortgages probably in an inferior position to commercial long-term debt.

If, however, Germany should find herself in a position when she was unable or unwilling to meet the full service of the existing debt, I feel some confidence that Schacht's policy would consist in the demand for a reduction in the rate of interest, rather than a default in principal or a total suspension of interest payment. The policy to which I believe him to be wedded is that of demanding a reduction in the rate of interest. Where the debts are expressed in dollars and there is a gold clause, this will be coupled with a demand for the abolition of the gold clause, which will indeed be reasonable enough if the dollar parts company with its present parity on gold.

The demand for a reduction in the rate of interest is just as likely to apply to the Dawes and Young Loans as to other debt. Indeed, from what he says in private, I am convinced that Schacht intends at the appropriate moment to put a demand for a reduction in the rate of interest on these loans in the forefront of his programme. I should not be surprised if he would consider the World Economic Conference to be the occasion for putting forward this demand.

It would be rash, therefore, to assume that these loans will continue to bear their present rate of interest. On the other hand, it would be premature to fear unduly their total repudiation. When the loans are standing at a price which would show a satisfactory yield even in the event of a substantial reduction in the rate of interest, then it might be argued that the immediately prospective dangers are sufficiently discounted. On the other hand, if Schacht actually makes such a demand as I foreshadow at the Economic Conference, it will assuredly have a seriously disturbing effect for the time being on the market for these loans. The demand for a reduction in the rate of interest might well apply also to municipal debt and even perhaps to mortgage indebtedness, held abroad.

When we turn to consider Germany's capacity to meet the present service on her foreign debt, it is impossible to arrive at any clear cut conclusion. For 1932 the trade balance was decidedly satisfactory and the balance seems to show not only that the service of the loans was made comfortably, but that there was a considerable repatriation of German debt previously foreign held, and repurchased by Germans at very low prices. This applies particularly to commercial debt held in [the] U.S.A. Indeed a sort of exchange dumping was in progress, since firms with bonds outstanding in the U.S.A. were allowed to use the exchange resulting from exports sold at special prices to buy up their own bonds on Wall Street. Since these bonds were standing at 30 or 40 per cent of par, the firms in question were able to sell their exports well below the cost of production and still show a profit after allowing for the profit on cancellation of the bonds purchased below par.

This year the trade position is decidedly worse, but the March returns recently to hand show that the deterioration is rather less than seemed to be likely earlier in the year. Broadly speaking of course the progress of German exports must be bound up with world recovery generally. But the point must not be overlooked that in the case of a country such as Germany, which imports raw materials and exports manufactured goods, often on credit, the first effect of a greater volume of trade is to make her balance more, and not less, adverse.

It is also necessary to take some account of the probability of the present German administration combining a domestic inflationary policy and high prices for agricultural products with the maintenance of the present rate of exchange. This must work out in the long run adversely to Germany's competitive power on international markets. There is probably almost no limit to the wildness of the domestic experiments which may be made and there is no likelihood of these experiments being of a character to improve Germany's competitive power.

The recent repayment of the Reichsbank's loan from certain central banks has reduced the remaining resources of gold and foreign currency to a exceedingly low figure. Thus Germany has but little to depend upon except her current trade balance. This also means that in the event of an international agreement for the devaluation of gold, the benefit to Germany will be only proportionate to her gold resources, that is to say very trifling in relation to the scale of her economic life. It is to the countries which already have very large stocks of gold that international gold devaluation will furnish a large bonus available to be taken in aid of Treasury operations.

I have kept until last the intangible factor of the Jewish question. But one would expect this to be of first importance as time goes on. Germany's international financial relations, and indeed the whole of her international trade connections, have been largely Jewish. The destruction of goodwill in these directions consequent on her present policy can hardly be exaggerated. She is engaged in tearing up a vital part of her mercantile organisation. It would seem certain that her faculty for international trade will be disastrously impaired.

There is also the question of the flight of Jewish funds. Doubtless this will be difficult, and every sort of regulation will be invoked to prevent it. But here again one can be practically certain that ways and means will be found in course of time, and that a substantial flight of Jewish wealth will be added to her other difficulties.

My general conclusion is to the effect that the position of the foreign investor in Germany is even worse than is commonly supposed. In the present national mood there will be no inclination to treat the foreign capitalist well. It is quite likely that the resources for meeting foreign obligations will be wholly insufficient. A bold and blustering policy towards the foreign investor will be popular. For every reason, therefore, one would expect him to have a thin time.

J.M.K.

On 8 June, four days before the World Economic Conference opened, Keynes discussed payment of the next instalment of Britain's War debt to America due on 15 June (*JMK*, vol. XVII, pp. 387–90). Three days later, the subject came up again as Keynes held a broadcast transatlantic radio conversation with Walter Lippmann. *The Listener* published the full text.

From The Listener, *14 June 1933*

THE WORLD ECONOMIC CONFERENCE

LIPPMANN: *With what expectations are you in London welcoming the delegates to the great Conference which begins tomorrow?*

KEYNES: With mingled hopes and doubts. Sixty-six nations are assembling: statesmen and financiers arrive by every train. The world's needs are desperate: we have all of us mismanaged our affairs: we live miserably in a world of the greatest potential wealth. And we are wondering, at last, whether anything is to be hoped from collective wisdom. But we are wondering a little dismally. For is there anything in the world to which six nations are likely to agree, let alone sixty-six? We have had experience of conferences since the War, and we know that it will be extraordinarily difficult to avoid a fiasco. Every previous conference of the kind has ended in empty platitudes and ambiguous phrases so boring and vapid that they have expired in a universal yawn. Isn't the present shocking state of the world partly due to the lack of imagination which they have shown, or sincere constructiveness or readiness for that reasonable give and take which is the basis of all decent human relations? Isn't there every reason to fear that this Conference will be just as bad? For my part I put all my hopes on one possibility—that England and America should somehow find a way to get together on an agreed programme—to do, in fact, just what we failed to do in Paris in 1919. For there are few remedies which we could not apply, acting together, even if others were to hold back.

I am sure that we shall want to fall in with your plans to the best of our ability. But so far we really don't know what your policy is. Your President has persuaded Congress to provide him with some lovely blank sheets of writing paper and some beautifully sharp pencils, but what part of his powers he really means to rely on, we, over here, simply don't know. For me, however, the outstanding fact is that President Roosevelt seems more willing than most of those in authority in the world to have some kind of bold and constructive policy commensurate with our necessities. Whether I should think his policy the ideal one if I knew in detail just what it is, I am not certain. But I do feel some confidence that it is of a right tendency. Tell me, along what lines, in your opinion, is a common policy most practicable?

LIPPMANN: *I agree with you that great assemblages of delegates from all parts of the earth don't usually make definite and constructive decisions. And so I agree, too, that we have to approach this Conference differently from the many conferences which have preceded it. Thus, for example, we ought not, I think, to look forward to the writing of an elaborate treaty which has to be agreed upon by some sixty-six national delegations and then ratified or rejected by some sixty*[*-six*] *legislative bodies. This Conference is not like the Disarmament Conference, for example, where no nation can act except in relation to all other nations. Many of us over here believe that the governments, particularly in the large nations, have the power to combat the depression without waiting for universal agreement at London on the measures that they are to take. In fact, we believe that only as the principal countries are prepared to deal as boldly with the depression within their boundaries as the*

Roosevelt Administration is dealing with it inside the United States, is there much likelihood of international agreement on such matters as the reconstruction of the world monetary standard and the reduction of trade barriers. In other words, we believe that before the Conference can hope to make real progress with the problems which it has to discuss, the chief financial and commercial nations—Great Britain, France and the United States—must use their own enormous power to raise prices, to relieve debtors and the unemployed and generally to enhance the capacity of their own people to buy goods. The strongest nations must use the powers under their control to lead the way out of the depression. I gather that that is what you have in mind. If so, I heartily agree with it and I believe it represents the dominant view of the American people. The strong nations must lead. International agreements will follow such action. They can hardly precede it. For most of the subjects which are to be discussed in London—the instability of the exchanges, the super tariffs, the hoarding of gold by central banks and by governments—are consequences of the depression and will not be remedied until the depression itself begins to clear up.

If we take this view of the matter, it would follow that in the first and most important phase of the discussion, the problem as between Great Britain and the United States is not a question of matching divergent national interests and of attempting to strike a bargain. Our task is to persuade and encourage one another to act along parallel lines. Both countries, for example, have been revaluing their currencies in terms of gold—Great Britain since September, 1931, the United States since April, 1933. Both countries have been forced to do this for essentially the same reason, namely, that the exorbitant rise in the value of gold made fixed charges in terms of gold socially and politically intolerable to their own peoples. Now, this process of revaluation in terms of gold is not, or at least ought not to be, in my opinion, a matter of trying to gain temporary advantages in international trade. For the United States, certainly, it is a matter of restoring some kind of workable balance between prices, debts, wages, fixed charges and profits. Therefore, if we are clear about our purposes we shall not be concerned about where the dollar is ultimately stabilised in relation to the pound. Our first concern will be where the dollar is stabilised in relation to commodities in the American market. Our second concern will be whether and where the dollar can also be stabilised in relation to gold. It is, as we see it, a matter for Great Britain to decide without our interference where the pound is to be stabilised in relation to commodities and ultimately in relation to gold. This view would not prevent us, perhaps, from agreeing on a temporary stabilisation of the two currencies as a help to other nations. But it would eliminate from the discussion a dangerous and useless argument about the ratio between the dollar and the pound.

We must avoid, it seems to me, an argument about the currencies similar to the argument about capital ships and cruisers and tanks at the Disarmament Conference. We can, and should, make separate decisions, and there is no need for a complicated negotiation on the subject. If we can remove this question from the realm of bargaining we can proceed further on the same principle. Our policy should be, I believe, to have concurrent and concerted domestic policies rather than to attempt immediate complicated international agreements. Both countries can, and should, make credit abundant and cheap with a view to forcing down long-term interest rates and stimulating capital investment. Both countries can adopt, and the United States has adopted, a programme of public works for the purpose of putting the new credit into use and of priming the economic machine. The United States, moreover, is organising control of agricultural and industrial production which has as its main purpose the prevention of further destructive cutting of prices and wages under the pressure of excess plant and excess labour. These, as I see it, are the main policies which the President is writing on the lovely blank sheets of writing paper with the beautifully sharp pencils that Congress has just provided him with. It is, I think, a fair interpretation of these policies to say that we regard measures for restoring purchasing power to farmers, miners and the unemployed as the greatest immediate contribution we can make to world recovery. Leaving out certain food crops we are normally, I believe, consumers of perhaps 40 per cent of the chief raw materials which enter into international trade. I do not know what the figures are for the British Empire, but they must be very large. So that a really bold concurrent attack upon the depression in Great Britain and America ought to have a decisive influence upon the whole world economy.

Such a course as I have been suggesting seems to me not only the most likely to be effective, but also to be the one way to avoid that long tedious fiasco which you described just a few minutes ago. It is a great advantage that it does not call for a complicated diplomatic negotiation; that it does not raise disturbing or wholly secondary questions of national advantage; that it is a course which the enlightened leaders of both countries would wish to pursue, even if there were no World Economic Conference. And yet it is a course which they can pursue far more effectively if they understand and sympathise with each other while they are pursuing it.

In the event that Great Britain and the United States, by concurrent policies, should try to lead the world out of the depression, we shall be fixing our hopes upon a policy which can be put into effect almost immediately. While these policies are being put into effect, the governments and the central banks can be preparing plans for improving world trade, for reviving international investment, for assisting the weaker nations and for reconstructing a world monetary standard. It is no use pretending, however, that these are not difficult and complicated matters, and the world cannot stand still while experts and statesmen and bankers argue about them. That is why the theory of a concurrent attack on the depression by the leading countries would seem to be the immediate need and also the most profitable subject for discussion at the London Conference. Don't you agree, Keynes?

KEYNES: Yes, Lippmann, I think that the general line of approach to the Conference's problems which you suggest is very likely the most helpful one. If an attempt is made to induce a large number of governments to enter into binding engagements on the spot, we can be quite sure that the wording will become so vague and ambiguous as to mean nothing. But I also see great risks of futility in mere declarations of agreement about the general lines of policy. For these can so easily result in no action whatever. After all, very sensible observations about the necessity of raising prices have been common form amongst governments for many months past. But nothing has been done about it.

You will lead me into such deep waters that some of our audience may drown if I try to follow up what you say about stabilising currencies separately on commodities. But this proposal is too vague as it stands. I am no friend of the gold standard, as you well know. But all the same, I think that gold can still provide a convenient link between English and American money, provided we agree that it is not to be a rigid link. I suggest that we should try to agree on four things. First of all, a fair parity between pounds and dollars on the basis of the existing situation. Next, that we fix approximately and for the time being only, the gold value of each on the basis of this parity. Thirdly, that we hold ourselves free to alter by agreement the gold value of our currencies whilst keeping the relation between them the same. And finally, that each country should retain the right to ask for a change in the relation between the currencies if the future course of prices is different in the two countries. This last provision makes my proposal substantially the same as yours, but the general character of my plan is more definite.

The rest of your policy seems to me absolutely right—cheap money, public works, help for the farmers. If only the Conference could get even two or three of the major countries *committed* to these things, it would have laid the foundations for recovery. But I don't know that it will help much merely to announce that they are desirable.

Then you mustn't forget the desperate needs of the debtor countries. We shall hear much during the Conference of the unsupportable load of international debts and how it is impossible to wait for a problematical rise of prices to ease this burden.

There is, also, the important problem of tariffs. Must we not be ready to allow regional agreements for the reduction of tariffs between neighbours which do not apply universally? For this is the only kind of reduction which is practicable.

These things—and much more—are in the hands of the statesmen and their experts. What can our audience in the two countries do to help in the creation of that unheard, unspoken, but always palpable, force which governs the world—I mean public opinion? I think that the great public can play its part by allowing its feelings and its responses to the news to be governed by the simple virtues. Let us try not to be suspicious. Let us avoid the fear of being outdone in a close bargain. Let us seize every opening to approve positive solutions—not obstinate about our own particular plan if the plan of someone else seems also to end in the right direction.

In point of fact, where our interests are opposed to one another, the national advantage which is at stake will be on a trifling scale compared with what we should all gain if prosperity were to return. For prosperity would restore to us, many times over, the greatest possible sacrifice that any country could be asked to make. If we were creating all the wealth of which we are technically capable, we should have a vast margin in hand over any conceivable concessions. I know how difficult it is for a negotiator to live up to this when it comes down to details. But all the same, isn't this what they all ought to have at the back of their minds? And this, too, should be the governing thought of us members of the public who are outside the details. Public opinion, softly ebbing round the rock of the Conference like the waters of a surrounding ocean, should be consistently murmuring 'Amity, Agreement, Action'. We are all of us greedy, competitive, obstinate and suspicious in international affairs, unless we are on our guard. And, above all, let not public opinion lag behind the delegates in its sensitiveness. When delegates meet face to face and find that the other man is a reasonable human being, friendliness and a spirit of accommodation soon spring up. And then, sometimes, public opinion, knowing nothing but the cold and hostile abstraction of an alien country, damps down these kindly feelings. I plead, therefore, for an atmosphere of compromise and reasonableness. I do not ask for signatures to binding agreements; but I do ask for genuine decisions, which those making them intend to carry out, designed to raise prices and restore employment by increasing the effective purchasing power of all the peoples of the world. For there is no other means whatever of accomplishing our purpose. And this, fortunately, is one of the cases where the success of one country will help all the others to success. I trust you feel as I do, Lippmann.

LIPPMANN: *Well, Keynes, we haven't much time left. So let me say in one sentence that I am in entire agreement with you about the spirit in which statesmen and peoples ought to approach this Conference. In the specific question of the currencies I should go along with you on the desirability of seeing whether we can make such a tentative agreement as you have outlined. What I do think is most important, however, is that our two countries should not become deadlocked in a negotiation about the parity between the dollar and the pound. If they do, I greatly fear that attention will be distracted from the much more promising business of getting two or three of the largest countries committed to a policy of cheap money, public works, and the restoration of purchasing power.*

Finally, speaking as an American, I should not be candid if I failed to mention the payment of War debts due on June 15. My own view has always been that to the American people these debts were not worth the financial dislocation and the political disturbance which they produce. The majority of my countrymen do not take this view, and therefore, it is, I imagine, impossible to hope for a final settlement of this troublesome question within the next few days. But, if a final settlement cannot be arranged, it seems to me imperative that the Governments of Great Britain and the United States should find some way of postponing the issue—that, in other words, there should be neither insistence on payment nor insistence on default. The two Governments simply must find a way to avoid insistence either on payment or on default. If they cannot arrange so simple a matter as that, what right have their statesmen to talk about peace and reconstruction in the world?

During the Conference itself Keynes provided *The Daily Mail* with a series of articles which recorded and evaluated the attempts of statesmen and their advisers to come to grips with the change in the international currency situation resulting from America's departure from the gold standard in April 1933.

From The Daily Mail, *20 June 1933*

THE CHAOS OF THE FOREIGN EXCHANGES

The real business of the Conference is beginning to emerge. It is determined not by the Preliminary Agenda of the Experts but by the pressure of events.

In those matters where action is avoidable, action will be avoided. But there are two fields within which events are taking charge, so that there is an actual necessity to do something—where the morning's news is acting on the delegates as a daily stimulus.

I mean, firstly, the debt question—not War debts (which are not strictly the business of the Conference), but the international debts of all countries who have borrowed heavily; and, secondly, the chaos of the foreign exchanges. These problems are, at the moment, more actual and pressing than, for example, tariffs or the organisation of synchronised programmes of public works, in spite of the more fundamental importance of the latter in the long run.

We must regret that this should be the case. It is the penalty of delay and the symptom of our failure to act in time. For the burden of debts (apart from War debts) and the chaos of the exchanges are the result of the collapse of prices. They ought, therefore, to have been tackled, before they reached this critical point, by a concerted policy to restore prices.

I hope that the Conference will not forget that the restoration of the price level is still its fundamental task. But sound methods of bringing this about must necessarily take time. Meanwhile debtor governments are saying that it is beyond their endurance to wait any longer for a problematical rise of prices; while bankers declare that, unless some sort of agreed policy is reached about the exchanges, we shall soon be launched, with disastrous confusion, on a competitive depreciation of currencies.

Characteristically, the Governor of the Bank of England has summoned, side by side with the conference of the governments, a conference of the dominant central banks, which, he doubtless hopes, will do the real business in appropriate privacy—as far separated from the blare of the Geological Museum as East is from West. There is much wisdom in this course, and I hope that he will be successful. But the obstacles are formidable; not the least of them being the lack of any American spokesman in London who is in a position to put America's cards on the table or to enter into a binding conversation.

It is a Danaid task, though one with which we have been long familiar, to deal with negotiators whose provisional concessions bind no one but who expect to rely definitely on whatever we may say.

Two dangers have to be avoided. No rigid return to gold is reasonably possible at this moment. The terms of the return must be provisional, elastic, and subject to safeguards in changing circumstances. There is no reason to fear any lack of caution in this regard from either the Treasury or the Bank of England, who may, on the contrary, prove more timorous than is really necessary in accepting a gold link between the leading currencies.

The other danger, as Mr Walter Lippmann pointed out in the broadcast in which I participated ten days ago, is lest

England and America should become deadlocked in a futile and irritating controversy concerning the *de facto* ratio between pounds and dollars—futile because the ultimate ratio, in the absence of a rigid gold link, will be settled by the comparative intensity and effectiveness with which the two countries pursue an expansionist policy.

According to common report, the attempts to avoid such a deadlock, though not yet successful, are making tentative progress towards a truce for the duration of the Conference. May I attempt to set forth the general lines which the next stage of the solution must probably follow if it is to be successful in the actual circumstances, having regard to the conflicting interests real and supposed? The essence of this proposal is based on a hint thrown out by Mr Walter Lippmann that it is for each country to raise its domestic prices by its own domestic policy to the extent that it deems practicable and desirable, and that the exchange value of different currencies should not be fixed arbitrarily or so as to interfere with the success of domestic policies, but should correspond to the measure of their success.

We have to begin with a basis and we have to work from this basis in accordance with a formula so that changing circumstances are provided for beforehand. I propose that we should take as our basis of prices in Great Britain and in the United States the average level of the twelve months ending June 1, 1933, as shown by the most comprehensive available index numbers, namely, the index of the Board of Trade in Great Britain and the index of the Bureau of Labour in the United States; and as our basis of the exchange value of the pound and the dollar the monthly average over the same period.

In so far as the present level of prices in America exceeds the average level of the previous year by more than it does in Great Britain, this justifies a proportionately lower exchange-value for the dollar. If in the next two years President Roosevelt proves himself a more devoted, or at least a more successful, price-raiser than Mr Neville Chamberlain, this will justify a still lower exchange value for the dollar. If they are both equally successful, the exchange value of the two currencies will remain, as it should, stable.

For the transitional period, therefore—say over the next two years—during which prices are moving at an unpredictable rate, and unequally perhaps in different countries, to the new level at which we shall desire to stabilise them, I suggest that the Bank of England and the Federal Reserve Bank of the United States should agree to take concerted measures to maintain the exchange value of the pound and the dollar at a level, starting from the basis given by the above formula and keeping step with the relative success of the two countries in raising their domestic prices.

It would be prudent to provide that the accuracy with which the exchanges should correspond to this formula should not be exact but within (say) 5 per cent, and that relative price changes of less than 1 per cent should be disregarded.

This arrangement would overcome the risk of unhealthy competitive exchange depreciation, brought about by speculation or by movements of loan capital or even by the operation of rival exchange equalisation funds, while leaving each country to indulge in a healthy competition to raise domestic price levels, not by exchange manipulation at the expense of other countries, but by a genuine stimulation of domestic demand.

America can fairly claim that, if she takes her price-raising programme more seriously than we do ours, as she seems to be doing at this moment, she is entitled to an international value of the dollar which will not act as a drag on the success of her domestic policies. Great Britain, on the other hand, is entitled to resist changes in the international value of sterling, which are injurious to her export industries because they do not correspond to the actual level of prices and costs at home and abroad but have been caused by speculative movements of liquid funds.

The above formula would protect both countries from these dangers. It would recognise the success of price-raising policies as fundamental and would cause the foreign exchanges to follow price changes, instead of impeding them as they must do if they are fixed irrespective of price changes.

This provisional settlement would leave the further question of the value of pounds and dollars in terms of gold entirely open, to be fixed by a further agreement, either immediately or at a later date. There is nothing in the above to interfere with the devaluation of currencies in terms of gold, and President Roosevelt has taken powers to adopt this policy if he thinks it advisable.

A week later, Keynes followed with another article, which he sent to the Chancellor of the Exchequer and the Governor of the Bank of England beforehand. He also probably discussed it with Raymond Moley and Walter Lippmann when he met them on 28 June.

To NEVILLE CHAMBERLAIN, *26 June 1933*

Dear Chancellor of the Exchequer,

I enclose a copy of an article which I am publishing here and in America on Tuesday, in which I make what seems to me the only concrete proposal which can bring the Americans and ourselves together again in a really concrete and far-reaching plan.

I am doing what I can to bring it to the notice of the Americans, and I hope very much that you will give it some consideration.

Yours very truly,
[copy not signed or initialled]

To MONTAGU NORMAN, *26 June 1933*

Dear Mr Governor,

I enclose a copy of an article which I have written for publication here and in America on Tuesday. I cannot think of any other concrete plan likely to lead to action by which the Americans and ourselves can be brought together again; and I fear the consequences of drift.

Will you give it your consideration?

Yours sincerely,
[copy not initialled or signed]

From MONTAGU NORMAN, *28 June 1933*

Dear Mr Keynes,

I thank you so much for the copy of the article on the Conference which you published yesterday. I will certainly have the proposals in it examined and consider them so far as they affect or are likely to be affected by the policy of the Bank.

But to my eyes this is still a night in which all cows look black!

I am,

Yours sincerely,
M. NORMAN

From The Daily Mail, *27 June 1933*

CAN WE CO-OPERATE WITH AMERICA?

I suggest that there is an aspect of the situation created by the Economic Conference which has been overlooked.

The assembled delegates in London compete with one another in their enthusiasm to raise prices by talk. But not one of them does anything definite, or even makes a concrete proposal how to accomplish the desired object by joint action. On the other hand, there is one man in the world who seems to take seriously the purpose to which the others do no more than pay lip-service—namely, President Roosevelt.

He, not unnaturally, is nervous of seeing his policies inhibited by the gang of verbalists who occupy the Geological Museum, and is reluctant to hitch *his* star to *their* wagon. Yet we are all talking as though that man is defeating the alleged objects of the Conference; who, in fact, is the only one to take definite measures to accomplish them.

This, then, is my answer to the question at the head of this article. If the Conference, or any leading members of it, really intend to adopt effective means to raise prices, there need be no insuperable difficulty in discovering a basis of co-operation with the United States. But if they mean only to talk about it and to conclude the Conference with some more of those pious but empty generalities, which are bringing the name of statesman into contempt, then we may rest thankful that there is at least one nation left in the world prepared to stage a demonstration, by isolated action if necessary, that men need not be the helpless victims of a mysterious decree, but can regain the mastery of their fortunes.

Indeed, if we are to criticise the President, it should be on the ground that he, too, may be open to the charge of letting talk outrun action, and of depending too much on psychological factors as compared with real forces. One doubts how far a boom in consumption goods will carry, and whether the President is as active and forward as he should be in laying the foundations, which will necessarily take many months, of a recovery in construction. If he fails, it will not be because his measures are too drastic, but because he has been too tardy and too timid in his programme of public works and in his efforts, by open-market operations and otherwise, to reduce the long-term rate of interest.

How, then, are the parties to the discussion, who are so quickly drifting apart, to be brought together again? Is there any useful concrete measure which, being proposed to the Conference, would divide those who mean business from those who don't?

There are certain prior presumptions of good will and good faith which we must assume to be fulfilled. On the American side, we must believe that the President does not really intend an internecine strife of competitive currency depreciation, and does not desire a lower exchange value for the dollar than is justified by the rise in costs, actual and prospective, inside the United States, compared with the corresponding movements elsewhere. On our side, we must assume that those governments which are so ardently advocating a rise of prices would like to put more purchasing power into circulation if only they knew how to do it.

On these assumptions, I believe that the key to the situation is to be found in the powers which the President has taken for the devaluation of the dollar in terms of gold. For there are great possibilities of advantage behind the President's project. It offers, indeed, the only opportunity of action by joint agreement on a substantial scale. Put very briefly, the sort of plan which the Conference ought now to discuss is on some such lines as the following:-

(1) The gold values of the national currencies of all those countries adhering to the scheme should be devalued forthwith by some figure between 20 and 33 per cent as compared with their recent *de jure* or *de facto* gold values. It is not necessary that every country should agree to this. The plan could be put into effect if the principal countries, which now belong to the sterling and dollar blocs, were to adopt it.

In practice, however, I should be surprised if the remaining gold standard countries—however vehemently they might oppose the project—would remain for long on their present parities, after it had become clear that the sterling and dollar countries were going forward.

(2) The national currencies, thus devalued in agreed proportions, should be stabilised for the time being in terms of one another, with provision for change during a transitional period, if the operation of exchange equalisation funds or movements of gold were to indicate that a particular country had a seriously unbalanced position. With this proviso, there would be no undue risk in agreeing to a compromise in fixing the initial exchange levels.

(3) The large windfall profit thus accruing through the increase in the nominal value of the stocks of gold held by central banks should be appropriated by the Treasuries of each country.

(4) These Treasuries should undertake to put this sum into circulation as an actual addition to purchasing power, either by an immediate relief of taxation or by public works. No stimulus to production and to prices would operate more certainly, more rapidly, or more universally than an immediate relief of taxation on a substantial scale throughout the world. We could not promise for certain that the relief would be permanent. But if those who expect that such a measure would go far towards terminating the slump are right—and I am convinced that they are—it would not be necessary to withdraw the relief subsequently.

(5) Owing to the increase in the effective gold reserves, exchange and import restrictions, designed to protect central banks from a drain of gold, could be abolished.

(6) I would add a provision by which, say, 5 per cent of the profit thus accruing to those countries which would gain more than their fair share owing to the maldistribution of gold should be put into a pool for the assistance of those countries which would gain relatively little because they have lost their gold reserves, and of silver countries.

As a psychological stimulus, this plan would be more reliable than the precarious support of a competitive currency depreciation, which might end in chaos and could not, in the long run, benefit a creditor country such as the United States without producing a renewed financial crisis elsewhere. It is the President's own plan. It is essentially a sound plan because it would furnish the Treasuries of the world with a non-recurrent windfall which they could use to give immediate relief in unorthodox ways without running the risk of getting into bad habits. Moreover, the repercussions of the relief thus given would assuredly benefit subsequent budgets by setting the ball of prosperity rolling.

Such a plan would, above all, lay a solid foundation for a world-wide rise in the price level. It presents few practical difficulties. I wish that the British delegates would adopt it. What is the use of words about raising prices if we reject an effective means of raising them when it is offered to us?

If, however, Great Britain shrinks from so bold a plan, why should not President Roosevelt, who does not lack boldness, bring the Conference to the test by offering it to them? If they, agree, his own policies will be made vastly easier. If they refuse, we shall know that, under cover of fair phrases, there lies hidden a deep and irreconcilable divergence of policy which justifies him in isolated action along his own lines.

On 28 June, Keynes addressed the London Political Economy Club. His notes for his talk survive.

WHAT SHOULD THE CONFERENCE DO NOW?

Scheme of Conference wrongly conceived.
Should have been to discuss, amend, compromise, agree specific proposals.
No such Conference as this can invent a programme.
Nor is a Preliminary Conference of Experts any better.
True—that the Preliminary Agenda was, by no fault of theirs, thrown out of date by America's action.
But apart from this, the Prelim. Conf. is no better than the substantive Conf. of which it is a mere vision in parts.
It is now certain, or at least very probable, that no power has any definite proposal to bring forward.
Consequently the Conference is stillborn.
And probably, therefore, the right answer to the question of the evening is that the delegates should go home.

Yet, if they do so, it will be damaging to the prestige of

international co-operation, damaging to the prestige of contemporary statesmanship. The progressive loss of prestige is one of the most alarming features of present times. When our rulers make asses of themselves, the public of today makes no effort to throw them out, makes no noisy protest, but just inwardly notes the fact; with the result that when a real testing time comes the powers that be, having no support whatever in the confidence of the great public, just collapse like a pack of cards.

Therefore, partly against one's better judgement, one racks one's brains to discover, even at this late date, some constructive programme which would be of sufficiently solid merit to justify by itself this tragi-comic assemblage and to convert it into something serious.

So I will with your permission interpret my question, henceforward, to mean what could we, the Political Economy Club, do next, if *we* were the Conference. Let me, therefore, run over as briefly as I can the main headings.

First of all, tariffs. On this major issue I would make two observations

(1) It is not within practical politics to make serious progress so long as prices are falling and exchanges strained. Tariffism, as history shows, is an inevitable, and indeed not an entirely unreasonable, concomitant of falling prices. The time to try to reach an agreement to reduce tariffs will come when the price trend has turned and has moved sufficiently upward for the ordinary man to be getting more afraid of dearness than of cheapness.

(2) My second observation is also a reason for postponing the real discussion on this matter until times are more normal. The classical doctrine of free trade concerns the optimum distribution of resources between different resources [?uses] when resources are fully occupied. When resources are not fully occupied, [I am] very doubtful how far the advantages of free trade obtain.

Consequently very difficult for F.T. ideas to make progress when resources are not occupied. I conclude that the moment for effective action in free trade direction cannot come until after the slump is substantially over.

(3) Most favoured nation. A technical matter, fairly general agreement, Intern[l] Conference an excellent opportunity.

Second, restriction. I have been sorry to hear that this is the only dep[t] of this Conf. which has any real kick in it.
Restriction has its place for individual commodities.
Already in operation in most plausible cases. Rubber, wheat perhaps but very doubtful. But general restriction schemes at this stage to be viewed with greatest possible suspicion.
Due to over-insistence on *price* phenomena
No cure for sub-normal activity
On the contrary an aggravation of it.
It would be nothing less than a disaster if the major outcome of this Conference were to be some scheme for still further curtailing the sub-normal activity of the world.

Third, price-raising programmes.
Here also over-insistence on raising prices as such
What we primarily want is more activity, more consumption, more production and more employment.
Broadly speaking it is only in agriculture where debt is a pressing problem (both farmers' debt and the international debt of agricultural producers) that we need a rise of price as such. Elsewhere rising prices will be an inevitable concomitant of rising output but not necessarily rapidly rising prices. Over a wide field of manufactured products and raw materials other than agricultural I should have supposed that we need scarcely any price rise except what reflects higher wages and higher agricultural prices. We do not (e.g.) want to bid up the price of motor cars or radio sets or steel rails or bricks as such.

The emphasis should be that we want to put more purchasing

power into circulation with the hope that this will lead to more output and with the expectation that it will partly expend itself in raising prices. But outside agriculture the more it increases output and the less it raises prices the better pleased we should be.

Putting more purchasing power into circulation should be the central theme of the economist to the statesman.

How to do it? Only 3 ways

(1) Stimulating more activity by private business on borrowed money (a) psychological change, (b) building up working capital, (c) reducing long-term interest by open market operations.

(2) Reducing taxation without reducing Gov^t spending correspondingly

(3) Public works

Within this preamble I can return to the practical problems of the Conference.

The Conference will do nothing unless it reaches agreement calculated to lead to action along these lines. Judging from its achievements so far I sympathise with attitude of President Roosevelt. I think we misjudge him gravely if we suppose his object to be [to] excite Wall St. by the dope of competitive exchange depreciation.

The truth is that he is the only one who is taking seriously the problem of price raising whilst the others are only talking about it.

I say, therefore, that what the Conference should discuss is to take steps to augment purchasing power sufficiently to justify the President in action on the assumption that, broadly speaking, the American policy of action is to be adopted by the rest of the world. In return it would be fair to ask him to agree to some substantial measure of *de facto* exchange stabilisation.

For the bankers are right, in my judgement, to attach real importance to some measure of stability

Menace of devaluation of unknown amount hanging over the market must lead to hoarding and to a flight from gold
International lending impossible
Steady confidence impossible
I feel strongly that such devaluation as is coming should come soon, and that it should be as general as possible and with as much agreement as possible.
Some subsequent adjustments will be necessary, but they will be on a relatively small scale, say 10 per cent, as compared with the present vast uncertainties.

What scheme is there which could be sufficiently convincing to America, economically, politically and psychologically that the rest of the world really means business?
I daresay that more than one could be devised
I should like to put forward a definite scheme which I published in an article yesterday.

I think that we should all come, by a simultaneous and agreed devaluation of the gold value of our currencies as compared with their recent *de facto* or *de jure* levels, to a provisional stabilisation of all our national currencies in terms of gold.
(1) For example I would fix
sterling at £7 per oz
dollar at $28
the gold currencies at 6/7 of their present figure (a very mild devaluation for them) and only if they wish a solution not dependent on it
These would not be rigid figures—certainly not for ten years and then only if an international scheme was adopted for the management of gold.
But central banks would agree to co-operate in maintaining their exchanges within 5 per cent of these parities, unless new facts were to arise justifying a change.
These would be either a decidedly different trend of domestic prices or figures of a seriously unbalanced position
$4 a concession to USA but worth making

(2) Gold stocks of central banks would be written up to the higher figure

(3) The surplus of the new nominal value over the old taken by Treasuries as a windfall profit

(4) Treasuries to undertake to spend this sum—in our case about £150,000,000, perhaps more—by public works or relieving taxation

Here is a modest programme. On this basis I can view the establishment of international economic peace. The rest of the world will share the benefit of measures in USA, will supplement this success by its own efforts and will thus repay USA by making world wide a movement which will remain highly tenuous if it is limited to USA

As Keynes had noted in his articles (above pp. 260 and 264) the British, French and American authorities had been discussing arrangements for stabilising exchange rates. Several alternatives were considered and sent to Washington for comment. Finally on 3 July, President Roosevelt effectively torpedoed these negotiations with a blunt message that rejected a stabilisation agreement and referred to the 'old fetishes of so-called international bankers'. The next day Keynes commented in *The Daily Mail.*

From The Daily Mail, *4 July 1933*

PRESIDENT ROOSEVELT IS MAGNIFICENTLY RIGHT

It is a long time since a statesman has cut through the cob-webs as boldly as the President of the United States cut through them yesterday.

He has told us where he stands, and he invites the Conference to proceed to substantial business. But he is prepared to act alone if necessary; and he is strong enough to do so, provided that he is well served by the experts to whom he entrusts the technique of his policy.

Our own Government cannot be expected to decide in a day how far we will follow him. But we are offered an opportunity.

It is important that the general public should understand the broad outline of what has happened in the last week. The story begins with the European attempt to drive a wedge between ourselves and the United States and to link our fortunes to those of the European gold standard countries, by threats of breaking up the Conference.

If common report is correct, the representatives of the Dominions and of India, fortunately at hand in London, immediately waited on the Chancellor of the Exchequer to warn him of the disastrous consequences, so far as they were concerned, of any such commitment. Doubtless the effect of this visit was decisive; though one can scarcely suppose that our authorities would have been so unwise as to yield to the empty threats of the gold bloc.

The next stage of the discussion attempted to accomplish two different things at the same time—to invent some face-saving sentences and to arrange a practical understanding behind the scenes with a view to limiting violent exchange fluctuations when they are due not to fundamental factors but to waves of speculative sentiment. Mr Roosevelt has rejected the sentences, because he believes that their psychological effect in his own country would be injurious, because the suggestion which they seek to convey would be false, and, especially, because they trifle with the world's problem. There is no reason to infer that he looks unfavourably on a collaboration between the Federal Reserve Bank of New York and the Bank of England with the second aim in view.

But the President's message has an importance which transcends its origins. It is, in substance a challenge to us to decide whether we propose to tread the old, unfortunate ways, or to explore new paths; paths new to statesmen and to bankers, but not new to thought. For they lead to the managed currency of the future, the examination of which has been the prime topic of post-war economics.

Since the days of the Peace Conference every constructive

proposal which might have saved us from our repeated errors has fallen to the ground. The Treasury and the Bank of England have depended on their sense of smell alone. Eyes have been blind and ears have been deaf. But a man should be able to see much farther ahead than he can smell. As one reads President Roosevelt's words on the future of monetary policy it seems possible that at last that noble organ the nose is yielding place to eyes and ears.

But if I interpret the President's object rightly, he must not be too timid in the field of international monetary technique. International exchange management should be an essential part of the policy which he has in view. He would be unwise, therefore, to reject every plan, however elastic, for regulating the dollar-sterling exchange. He would make a mistake, moreover, if he were to appear to confirm the attachment of Wall Street to the foreign exchanges, which will be a minor factor whether for good or for evil in American recovery, as a barometer of the success of his expansionism.

Wall Street and those commodity markets which are organised for free dealings are already dangerously ahead of the rest of the programme; and at the moment it is not prudent to exhilarate them further. Moreover, he will be playing a larger and a finer rôle in the world at large, and will be placing his own domestic policies on a firmer basis, by helping the rest of us to pursue, if we are so disposed, a genuine policy of expansionism.

But on the broad political issue—on the things which it should be the business of Presidents and Prime Ministers to understand—he is magnificently right in forcing a decision between two widely divergent policies. The Economic Conference will be a farce unless it brings this divergence to a head. If the opposed parties are not inclined to join issue in public on the fundamental choice which America has presented to the world in unambiguous form, it is much better that the Conference should adjourn.

On the one side we have a group of European countries of

great political and military importance, but increasingly segregated from the currents of world trade. They disbelieve in official expansionist policies as a means of restoring economic life. They cling fanatically to their gold perches, though most of them are poised there precariously. They see no virtue in a rising price level, putting their faith in a 'revival of confidence', which is to come somehow by itself through business men gradually deciding that the world is safe for them.

On the other side, the United States of America invites us to see whether without uprooting the order of society which we have inherited we cannot, by the employment of common sense in alliance with scientific thought, achieve something better than the miserable confusion and unutterable waste of opportunity in which an obstinate adherence to ancient rules of thumb has engulfed us. Nor is the prescription alarming. We are to put men to work by all the means at our disposal until prices have risen to a level appropriate to the existing debts and other obligations fixed in terms of money; and thereafter we are to see to it that the purchasing power of our money shall be kept stable. We are offered, indeed, the only possible means by which the structure of contract can be preserved and confidence in a monetary economy restored.

The Dominions and India, unanimous and unhesitating, beckon us towards this side. South America must necessarily follow in the North American orbit. How can we hesitate? To suppose that the Europeans are children of ancient wisdom holding up to us a restraining finger to protect us from dangerous innovation would be a ludicrous mistake.

There is much that Mr Roosevelt's statement has left unsaid. He refuses co-operation on temporary stabilisation, but he does not make it clear in what respects he desires joint action. The British Government, however, should act on the belief that we have an opportunity, if we choose to take it, to consolidate a sterling-dollar bloc committed to economic progress and the restoration of economic health, which will comprise virtually the whole world outside Western Europe.

This problem is not like that of disarmament where the agreement of all is necessary before anyone dare move. If the Europeans prefer to follow their own course, it will not embarrass the rest of us in the least. It may even be an advantage. For we shall have divided ourselves into groups of like-minded persons, in place of concocting phrases designed to conceal a fundamental difference of outlook.

I write all this on the assumption that, when the British Government declare loudly for higher prices, they are not opposed to measures likely to lead to this result.

Roosevelt's message caused a storm at the Conference and brought attempts to adjourn it. The Americans on the spot in London tried to keep the Conference going by preparing a suitable explanatory statement. The drafting of this document took all of 4 July and the early hours of 5 July. Keynes, who had lunched alone with the Prime Minister at the Athenaeum on 4 July, was involved in the drafting, as were Walter Lippmann and Raymond Moley. The document succeeded in keeping the Conference alive although the work that continued was desultory and half-hearted.

In response to President Roosevelt's 'bombshell' the representatives of the European gold standard countries subscribed to a statement pledging themselves to the maintenance of the gold standard at existing parities. The central bankers of the countries concerned echoed this declaration on 8 July. These developments gave Keynes a focus for his next article.

From The Daily Mail, *14 July 1933*

SHALL WE FOLLOW THE DOLLAR OR THE FRANC?

The rift which has disclosed itself in the Conference between the Western European countries on the one side and the United States and the British Dominions on the other, with Great Britain perched uneasily on the dividing hedge, is based on a real difference in circumstances which we must clearly understand if we are to pursue different paths without recrimination.

Apart from Holland and Switzerland, which may be making a serious mistake in linking themselves to France, Italy, and

Germany, the members of the so-called gold bloc are countries which have already devalued their currencies in the recent past by a much higher percentage than the maximum contemplated by Mr Roosevelt or by the sterling bloc. These countries have already dealt very drastically—even to the point of virtual annihilation—with the debt structure built up during the War and the post-war boom.

While they desire a return to normal economic activity as intensely as the rest of us, and do not object to such rise of prices as a return of activity will unavoidably bring with it, they resist a repetition of the expedient of devaluation, which they, unlike us, have already carried to great lengths. They are willing—much more willing than Mr Neville Chamberlain—to use the expedient of public works as a means of restoring employment. But they cannot share that enthusiasm for higher prices for their own sake which is natural to those countries which have not yet dealt with their old debt structure.

The position of the United States is totally different from this. Their debt structure is a problem which would remain as a social disease even with employment restored to normal if prices and wages were stabilised at their recent level. The same is true of the British Dominions and India—with the added complication that their external sterling debt requires an adjustment of the value of sterling, as well as of their local currencies, if they are to get through without a breach of faith. It is a necessity for their recovery of economic health that they should pursue the same broad policy as the United States, for their problems are essentially the same.

Where does Great Britain stand? The Chancellor of the Exchequer seems to hesitate. The thoughts and feelings of the Bank of England we have to infer, as we infer those of the animal creation, not by the usual methods of human intercourse but solely from its behaviour. This suggests a sympathy with the gold bloc, as a result, perhaps, of confining the grounds of policy within limits which are too narrow to include many of the considerations which a statesman should have in view.

Yet is it possible for Great Britain to hesitate if we fairly face the facts of the situation? Of all countries in the world we are afflicted by the heaviest burden of public debt, inasmuch as we are carrying the whole burden of our War and post-war debt at almost the pre-war price level. A rise of prices and incomes for their own sake is indispensable for us, precisely because we, alone of the European participants in the War, have not yet devalued our currency in the appropriate degree. For us it would be excessively imprudent to link sterling to currencies already devalued by two-thirds or more. On the other hand, we should feel grateful to Mr Roosevelt for making it easier for us to perform what our vital interests demand.

There is, moreover, a second reason of great weight which should move us in the same direction. By virtue of our trade, our investments and our personal ties, our economic life is more closely linked with that of the other continents, and with our own Dominions in particular, than with the economic autarchies of Europe. London is the financial centre of Asia, Africa, Australia, and South America. Our investments, for example, in Australia alone are more than double our total investments in Europe. It would be a rash and foolish act to force the overseas countries to throw over sterling and their sterling debts.

What are the considerations which weigh upon the other side? In the first place, a tenderness for the interests of the gold bloc countries. If we pursue a policy of devaluation which will lead to a greater rise of prices here than in the European countries which reject this policy, the embarrassments will be entirely on their side and not on ours. Indeed, it will actually assist us in the attainment of our own objects if they remain pegged to their present gold parities. Our action may, indeed, make their situation so difficult and precarious as to become untenable, with the result that they are forced in the end to follow our example. If so, it cannot be helped.

In the second place, timidities are aroused and conservative instincts are strengthened by the somewhat wild policies, as they seem to observers here, of President Roosevelt. We are particularly alarmed by his apparent willingness to encourage irresponsible speculation which goes much beyond what his actual deeds so far justify. The President's recipes sometimes conform as little to the new economics as to the old orthodoxy. They are partly self-contradictory. Yet if there is any cause for anxiety, this would be due not to the wildness of his words, but to the fear lest some of his actions, especially in the field of increasing purchasing power by public and private loan-expenditure, may be belated.

As for his apparent extremism, we should be wise enough to know that this is the only atmosphere in which such drastic changes could be accomplished. If the orthodox school had been more reasonable and less obstinate, the transition to new methods might have been effected in a quieter tone and with urbane observances.

For us the issue ought to be decided on such general considerations of national policy as were the subject of an exceptionally useful debate in the House of Commons last Monday. It raises matters within the competence of statesmen and does not depend, for once, on details of economic theory or of banking technique.

We have to determine, on the above broad principles, whether or not to join the Administration of the United States, in the company of the British Dominions and of India, of South America and of Scandinavia, in a concerted policy of currency devaluation and of organised schemes of increased loan-expenditure, public and private, at home and abroad, in pursuit of the twin purposes of raising prices and of restoring employment.

The weight of opinion in the House of Commons was overwhelmingly in favour of our following the dollar and not the franc. The Chancellor of the Exchequer is entitled to move cautiously, provided we can feel sure that he has accepted this policy as his objective.

On 27 July the Conference met in plenary session to adjourn until an unspecified date. It never met again. Keynes commented on the Conference's demise.

From The Daily Mail, *27 July 1933*

FAREWELL TO THE WORLD CONFERENCE

With what emotions do we view the departure of the great World Conference? Certainly not with surprise.

Men of good will have hoped for the best. Those who had constructive suggestions to make have made them. The wounds dealt to the Conference have been inflicted within the Conference. Outsiders must have hoped, even against the weight of the evidence, that those chiefly responsible for summoning the Conference must have had some plan, some object in their minds, beyond what was apparrent to the public. It is now evident that there was no cat in the bag, no rabbits in the hat—no brains in the head.

The Conference's lamentable end is, therefore, a matter for dismay, though not for surprise. There will be no protest from the public. But the facts are duly noted. The fiasco of the Conference merely increases the general cynicism and the lack of respect towards those in power. This growing lack of respect is, as recent examples elsewhere have shown, one of the most serious things which can befall a democracy. For when a real emergency arises, the responsible authorities, having no firm roots in the confidence of their countrymen, go down like a pack of cards. This is, indeed, an aspect of the decay of traditional party controversy which deserves attention. Formerly when one set of Ministers was losing prestige, another set was gaining it. In the long run it is a dangerous thing that there should be no rotation of Ministers, no alternative Government available to function within the same general order of ideas as its predecessor.

The fluctuating and unhelpful instructions given by Mr Roosevelt to the American delegation have, of course, stood in the way of the Conference's success. But they are to be regarded more as an excuse than as a reason for its collapse. For while Mr Roosevelt's course of action deprived the United States of its power of useful initiative or co-operation, it did not prevent others from making constructive proposals if they had any to make.

I trace the failure of the Conference, therefore, not primarily to Mr Roosevelt's perplexing demeanour, but to two more fundamental causes.

In the first place, it should have been obvious from the outset that neither a conference of 66 powers nor a preliminary pow-wow of the experts of 66 powers, could be capable of evolving a constructive scheme for themselves. Such a scheme could only be devised in the first instance by a single power or by a small group of like-minded powers. The only useful purpose of a general conference is to debate concrete proposals which certain of its members advocate and enthusiastically support, with a view to meet criticisms and overcome objections, to ascertain what measure of support can be obtained, to discover what compromises would gain more adherents, and to work out practical details with the help of all those who will be affected. Unless there is reason to suppose that some delegates or group of delegates are prepared to make themselves responsible for a definite proposition, it is futile to summon a world conference.

In the second place even with the lack of a defined programme, the Conference might have accomplished a little, if it had not suffered from the League of Nations mentality, which supposes that nothing can be accomplished except by universal agreement. It is most unlikely from the outset that any significant plan relating to currency, exchanges, capital development or tariffs will receive universal assent. But it does not follow that no progress can be made. The object of the Conference should be, not to cover up differences of opinion with meaningless formulae, but to bring differences to a head with a view to discovering within what group of countries finding themselves in substantial agreement with one another co-operative action is practicable. Groups of countries in like circumstances and with sympathetic policies should have been encouraged to get together for the construction of a common plan. But to concoct formulae, to which a great number of countries whose interests and policies are divergent can do common lip-service, is a business which statesmen should despise.

In one direction in particular the British Government has, I think, missed a great opportunity. The British Dominions and India have found themselves in a remarkable agreement with one another over a wide field of policy. Their interests in these matters have been our interests, and their programme has not run counter to the professions of the home Government. They have begged the British Ministers to take up the leadership in putting forward an agreed policy for the British Empire as a whole. It has been evident that there were other countries outside the Empire ready to follow the same leadership. It has also seemed probable that the general tendency of the policy required by the interests of the British Empire would follow somewhat the same lines as those of President Roosevelt, without proceeding to extremes or insisting on wild haste, and would, therefore, have allowed of some *modus vivendi* with the American Delegation.

Perhaps even now it is not too late to take advantage of the presence of the Dominion representatives in London to make some declaration of agreed policy.

Does nothing remain? Some mutual profit, one may hope, from the giving and the receiving of a genuine hospitality. Let us think of the Conference as being, like other pretexts for bringing men together, primarily an occasion for new friendships and new contacts; for discovering what others think and why they think it; for exchanging ideas and indicating tendencies which are as yet too indefinite to be the subject of formal agreements.

London has enjoyed the presence of her visitors. She has done her best to entertain them with those characteristic occasions of formal beauty and informal friendliness which her long and orderly traditions can suitably furnish. Even her weather has been tolerable. Our visitors have been here long enough, perhaps, to feel those singular charms in London and her neighbourhood which need for their discovery and appreciation more than the casual glance of the tourist. At any rate, we hope that they have enjoyed themselves and have felt that, as human beings, we have been brought nearer together.

For the paradox is true that our respect and liking for individuals may increase at the very time that we feel most hopeless about any kind of useful co-operation between the organised groups which they represent.

With the Conference over, after a period of rest and work in the country, Keynes concluded his 1933 run of *Daily Mail* articles with an evaluation of Britain's experience during the two years since she had left the gold standard.

From The Daily Mail, *19 September 1933*

TWO YEARS OFF GOLD: HOW FAR ARE WE FROM PROSPERITY NOW?

This week sees the second anniversary of Britain's departure from the gold standard.

Two years ago, on September 21, 1931, the National Government, after having been formed to avert the supposed disaster of this event, chose the financial route which the nation has since followed.

But when we woke next morning the bells were ringing a glad peal; everyone knew instinctively that it was not disaster which had befallen us, but a happy release; that the snapping of our golden fetters restored to us the control over our fortunes.

Nevertheless, the actual results have been seriously disappointing. For three months, indeed, employment increased and the index of production rose sharply—by almost 10 per cent.

But as the policies of the new Government took shape, we slipped back again, until a year later, in September 1932, employment and production had fallen below what they had been at the same date in 1931.

Today, in September 1933, we are climbing up again; but we have still made relatively small progress towards the full level of output and of income to which we are entitled.

Unemployment continues to be double what it was in the last part of 1929—itself a period which seemed far from satisfactory at the time.

To measure what our departure from gold saved us we must look abroad. We at least avoided a further fall into the pit of economic ruin.

In the other leading industrial countries of the world, the United States and Germany, economic decay rapidly proceeded to breaking point and to the dissolution of the normal machinery of economic life. The sufferings of both these countries have been much beyond the worst suffered here.

Both have ended up reacting violently to an unbearable situation, though in opposite directions.

The Germans, broken in body and spirit, seek escape in a return backwards to the modes and manners of the Middle Ages, if not of Odin.

America takes a dangerous leap forward into the future, with about as much idea as a pre-war aviator of where she will land.

In another direction the benefits of what we did two years ago can be clearly discerned. The economic position of the Dominions, which own or mine gold and produce raw materials, some of them burdened with a heavy sterling debt, has been revolutionised for the better in the past two years.

The pacification of India, the boom in South Africa, the remarkable recovery of Australia, could not have occurred but for our devaluation of gold two years ago. If we have saved ourselves at home from an epoch of social disorder and wild experiment, we have escaped abroad what might have proved not much less than the break-up of the Empire.

Yet the fact remains that, however much worse our situation might have been, we still have abundant reason for wishing it to be better. Why, then, have we progressed so slowly and fitfully in the past two years? What is the essential significance of leaving gold—and what would be the implications of returning to it?

Our departure from gold made two things possible. It allowed us a price level at which our costs are in reasonable equilibrium with costs in the outside world, so that our producers are no longer subjected to special disadvantage. Foreign trade plays so great a part in our economy that this is of vast importance to us. Our actual policy in the last two years has been, fortunately, such as to have allowed us, broadly speaking, our due share of what trade was going.

But there is a second benefit in the departure from gold, not less important, of which we have not taken equal advantage. The maintenance of the gold standard keeps a country's investment policy and its current rates of interest somewhat rigidly linked to those prevailing in the other gold standard countries, since any considerable departure from the policies pursued elsewhere will lead to a loss of gold. But in the absence of the gold link, we are free to follow the course which we think best adapted to our own requirements.

In the matter of the rate of interest, the Treasury has taken full advantage of its new freedom. The conversion of the War Loan and the reduction of the rate of interest on Treasury bills to a nominal figure, below a half of 1 per cent, would not have been possible if we had remained on gold. Here again, therefore, we have actually reaped a substantial advantage.

But in the field of expansionist policy—that is to say, the free use of loans to promote employment in increasing the capital assets of the country—we have fallen, in my judgement, far short of our opportunities.

To this, and mainly to this, I attribute the fact that we have made such poor progress.

It is impossible to increase employment without first increasing demand, and, so far as the home market is concerned, there is no conceivable way of putting more purchasing power into use except by increasing loan expenditure.

Other measures merely serve to divert purchasing power from one direction to another, without increasing it.

It is not easy to decide what form of loan expenditure is most useful and productive. But to solve this practical problem cannot be beyond the wits of our engineers and our public utility experts.

Whether it is better to electrify the railways or to rebuild South London, or to supply country districts with water, or to build a Cunarder, or to drain the countryside, or to modernise our ports, or to recast our steel plant, or a bit of each, it is not my function to say.

But unless we do one or another of these or similar things, it is utterly impossible that we can increase our national wealth or employ our population.

Nor do we, in truth, refrain from an expansionist policy because, like Buridan's ass, we do not know which bundle of hay to tackle first. We hold back primarily because those in authority are slow to be convinced that the principle of the thing is right.

We have been suffering, like the greater part of mankind, from a simple and foolish fallacy. An individual who abstains can enrich himself, since he can thus acquire a greater share of the community's wealth, even though he does nothing to increase it.

Most people infer from this that in the same way the

community as a whole can enrich itself by abstention. Just as an individual's refusal to spend increases the individual's wealth, so it is supposed that a national refusal to spend increases the national wealth.

But this is impossible. No negative behaviour can conceivably enrich the nation.

There is, and can be, no way of enrichment or of employment except by actually building houses, electrifying railways, erecting the grid, or whatever the appropriate activity may be.

Our departure from the gold standard, two years ago, meant that we had made ourselves free, without interference from abroad, to do in these respects exactly what we chose, as being most likely to enrich the nation.

When we decide to take full advantage of this freedom, employment will recover, our incomes will increase, the yield of taxation will permit a reduction of the taxes, and we shall all be as happy as the material side of life can make us.

So long as we hesitate we shall continue much as we are—sadly below the parity of our real strength.

Chapter 4

THE NEW DEAL

Keynes's guest for the Founder's Feast at King's College, Cambridge on 6 December 1933 was Felix Frankfurter, then Professor of Administrative Law at Harvard, who was spending the year as a visiting professor at Oxford. During Frankfurter's visit to Cambridge, the two men talked of Keynes's writing a letter of advice to President Roosevelt. Keynes agreed to write an open letter to the President which he would send to him via Frankfurter before publication. Keynes then made arrangements for the letter to appear in *The New York Times* on 31 December. He also offered *The Times* of London a shortened version for publication on 2 January.

From The New York Times, *31 December 1933*

London, December 30

Dear Mr President,

You have made yourself the trustee for those in every country who seek to mend the evils of our condition by reasoned experiment within the framework of the existing social system.

If you fail, rational change will be gravely prejudiced throughout the world, leaving orthodoxy and revolution to fight it out.

But if you succeed, new and bolder methods will be tried everywhere, and we may date the first chapter of a new economic era from your accession to office.

This is a sufficient reason why I should venture to lay my reflections before you, though under the disadvantages of distance and partial knowledge.

Opinion in England

At the moment your sympathisers in England are nervous and sometimes despondent. We wonder whether the order of different urgencies is rightly understood, whether there is a confusion of aims, and whether some of the advice you get is not crack-brained and queer.

If we are disconcerted when we defend you, this is partly due to the influence of our environment in London. For almost every one here has a wildly distorted view of what is happening in the United States.

The average City man believes you are engaged on a hare-brained expedition in face of competent advice, that the best hope lies in your ridding yourself of your present advisers to return to the old ways, and that otherwise the United States is heading for some ghastly breakdown. This is what they say they smell.

There is a recrudescence of wise head-wagging by those who believe the nose is a nobler organ than the brain. London is convinced that we only have to sit back and wait to see what we shall see. May I crave your attention, while I put my own view?

The present task

You are engaged on a double task, recovery and reform—recovery from the slump, and the passage of those business and social reforms which are long overdue. For the first, speed and quick results are essential. The second may be urgent, too; but haste will be injurious, and wisdom of long-range purpose is more necessary than immediate achievement. It will be through raising high the prestige of your Administration by success in short-range recovery that you will have the driving force to accomplish long-range reform.

On the other hand, even wise and necessary reform may, in some respects, impede and complicate recovery. For it will upset the confidence of the business world and weaken its existing motives to action before you have had time to put other motives in their place. It may overtask your bureaucratic machine, which the traditional individualism of the United States and the old 'spoils system' have left none too strong. And it will confuse the thought and aim of yourself and your Administration by giving you too much to think about all at once.

N.R.A. aims and results

Now I am not clear, looking back over the last nine months, that the order of urgency between measures of recovery and measures of reform has been duly observed, or that the latter has not sometimes been mistaken for the former. In particular, though its social gains are considerable, I cannot detect any material aid to recovery in the N[ational] [Industrial] R[ecovery] A[ct]. The driving force which has been put behind the vast administrative task set by this act has seemed to represent a wrong choice in the order of urgencies. The Act is on the statute book; a considerable amount has been done toward implementing it; but it might be better for the present to allow experience to accumulate before trying to force through all its details.

That is my first reflection—that N.R.A., which is essentially reform and probably impedes recovery, has been put across too hastily, in the false guise of being part of the technique of recovery.

My second reflection relates to the technique of recovery itself. The object of recovery is to increase the national output and put more men to work. In the economic system of the modern world, output is primarily produced for sale; and the volume of output depends on the amount of purchasing power, compared with the prime cost of production, which is expected to come on the market.

Broadly speaking, therefore, an increase of output cannot occur unless by the operation of one or other of three factors. Individuals must be induced to spend more out of their existing incomes, or the business world must be induced, either by increased confidence in the prospects or by a lower rate of interest, to create additional current incomes in the hands of their employees, which is what happens when either the working or the fixed capital of the country is being increased; or public authority must be called in aid to create additional current incomes through the expenditure of borrowed or printed money.

In bad times the first factor cannot be expected to work on a sufficient scale. The second factor will only come in as the second wave of attack on the slump, after the tide has been turned by the expenditures of public authority. It is, therefore, only from the third factor that we can expect the initial major impulse.

Now there are indications that two technical fallacies may have affected the policy of your Administration. The first relates to the part played in recovery by rising prices. Rising prices are to be welcomed because they are usually a symptom of rising output and employment. When more purchasing power is spent, one expects rising output at rising prices. Since there cannot be rising output without rising prices, it is essential to insure that the recovery shall not be held back by the insufficiency of the supply of money to support the increased monetary turnover.

The problem of rising prices

But there is much less to be said in favour of rising prices if they are brought about at the expense of rising output. Some debtors may be helped, but the national recovery as a whole will be retarded. Thus rising prices caused by deliberately increasing prime costs or by restricting output have a vastly inferior value to rising prices which are the natural results of an increase in the nation's purchasing power.

I do not mean to impugn the social justice and social expediency of the redistribution of incomes aimed at by the N.R.A. and by the various schemes for agricultural restriction. The latter, in particular, I should strongly support in principle. But too much emphasis on the remedial value of a higher price level as an object in itself may lead to serious misapprehension of the part prices can play in the technique to recovery. The stimulation of output by increasing aggregate purchasing power is the right way to get prices up; and not the other way around.

Thus, as the prime mover in the first stage of the technique of recovery, I lay overwhelming emphasis on the increase of national purchasing power resulting from governmental expenditure which is financed by loans and is not merely a transfer through taxation, from existing incomes. Nothing else counts in comparison with this.

Boom, slump and war

In a boom, inflation can be caused by allowing unlimited credit to support the excited enthusiasm of business speculators. But in a slump governmental loan expenditure is the only sure means of obtaining quickly a rising output at rising prices. That is why a war has always caused intense industrial activity. In the past, orthodox finance has regarded a war as the only legitimate excuse for creating employment by government expenditure. You, Mr President, having cast off such fetters, are free to engage in the interests of peace and prosperity the technique which hitherto has only been allowed to serve the purposes of war and destruction.

The set-back American recovery experienced this past Autumn was the predictable consequence of the failure of your Administration to organize any material increase in new loan expenditure during your first six months of office. The position six months hence will depend entirely on whether you have been laying the foundations for larger expenditures in the near future.

I am not surprised that so little has been spent to date. Our own experience has shown how difficult it is to improvise useful loan expenditures at short notice. There are many obstacles to be patiently overcome, if waste, inefficiency and corruption are to be avoided. There are many factors I need not stop to enumerate which render especially difficult in the United States the rapid improvisation of a vast programme of public works. I do not blame Secretary Ickes for being cautious and careful. But the risks of less speed must be weighed against those of more haste. He must get across the crevasses before it is dark.

The other set of fallacies, of which I fear the influence, arises out of a crude economic doctrine commonly known as the quantity theory of money. Rising output and rising incomes will suffer a setback sooner or later if the quantity of money is rigidly fixed. Some people seem to infer from this that output and income can be raised by increasing the quantity of money. But this is like trying to get fat by buying a larger belt. In the United States today your belt is plenty big enough for your belly. It is a most misleading thing to stress the quantity of money, which is only a limiting factor, rather than the volume of expenditure, which is the operative factor.

It is an even more foolish application of the same ideas to believe that there is a mathematical relation between the price of gold and the prices of other things. It is true that the value of the dollar in terms of foreign currencies will affect the prices of those goods which enter into international trade. In so far as an overvaluation of the dollar was impeding the freedom of domestic price-raising policies or disturbing the balance of payments with foreign countries, it was advisable to depreciate it. But exchange depreciation should follow the success of your domestic price-raising policy as its natural consequence, and should not be allowed to disturb the whole world by preceding its justification at an entirely arbitrary pace. This is another example of trying to put on flesh by letting out the belt.

Currency and exchange

These criticisms do not mean that I have weakened in my advocacy of a managed currency or in preferring stable prices to stable exchanges. The currency and exchange policy of a country should be entirely subservient to the aim of raising output and employment to the right level. But the recent gyrations of the dollar have looked to me more like a gold standard on the booze than the ideal managed currency of my dreams.

You may be feeling by now, Mr President, that my criticism is more obvious than my sympathy. Yet truly that is not so. You remain for me the ruler whose general outlook and attitude to the tasks of government are the most sympathetic in the world. You are the only one who sees the necessity of a profound change of methods and is attempting it without intolerance, tyranny or destruction. You are feeling your way by trial and error, and are felt to be, as you should be, entirely uncommitted in your own person to the details of a particular technique. In my country, as in your own, your position remains singularly untouched by criticism of this or the other detail. Our hope and our faith are based on broader considerations.

If you were to ask me what I would suggest in concrete terms of the immediate future, I would reply thus:

Constructive criticism

In the field of gold devaluation and exchange policy the time has come when uncertainty should be ended. This game of blind man's buff with exchange speculators serves no useful purpose and is extremely undignified. It upsets confidence, hinders business decisions, occupies the public attention in a measure far exceeding its real importance, and is responsible both for the irritation and for a certain lack of respect which exist abroad.

You have three alternatives. You can devalue the dollar in terms of gold, returning to the gold standard at a new fixed ratio. This would be inconsistent with your declarations in favour of a long-range policy of stable prices, and I hope you will reject it.

You can seek some common policy of exchange stabilisation with Great Britain aimed at stable price levels. This would be the best ultimate solution; but it is not practical politics at the moment, unless you are prepared to talk in terms of an initial value of sterling well below $5 pending the realisation of a marked rise in your domestic price level.

Lastly, you can announce that you will control the dollar exchange by buying and selling gold and foreign currencies at a definite figure so as to avoid wide or meaningless fluctuations, with a right to shift the parities at any time, but with a declared intention only so to do either to correct a serious want of balance in America's international receipts and payments or to meet a shift in your domestic price level relative to price levels abroad.

The favoured policy

This appears to me your best policy during the transitional period. You would be waiving your right to make future arbitrary changes which did not correspond to any relevant change in the facts, but in other respects you would retain your liberty to make your exchange policy subservient to the needs of your domestic policy—free to let out your belt in proportion as you put on flesh.

In the field of domestic policy, I put in the forefront, for the reasons given above, a large volume of loan expenditure under government auspices. It is beyond my province to choose particular objects of expenditure. But preference should be given to those which can be made to mature quickly on a large scale, as, for example, the rehabilitation of the physical condition of the railroads. The object is to start the ball rolling.

The United States is ready to roll toward prosperity, if a good hard shove can be given in the next six months. Could not the energy and enthusiasm which launched the N.R.A. in its early days be put behind a campaign for accelerating capital expenditures, as wisely chosen as the pressure of circumstances permits? You can at least feel sure that the country will be better enriched by such projects than by the involuntary idleness of millions.

Plenty of cheap credit

I put in the second place the maintenance of cheap and abundant credit, in particular the reduction of the long-term rate of interest. The turn of the tide in Great Britain is largely attributable to the reduction in the long-term rate of interest which ensued on the success of the conversion of the War Loan. This was deliberately engineered by the open-market policy of the Bank of England.

I see no reason why you should not reduce the rate of interest on your long-term government bonds to $2\frac{1}{2}$ per cent or less, with favourable repercussions on the whole bond market, if only the Federal Reserve System would replace its present holdings of short-dated Treasury issues by purchasing long-dated issues in exchange. Such a policy might become effective in a few months, and I attach great importance to it.

With these adaptations or enlargements of your existing policies, I should expect a successful outcome with great confidence. How much that would mean, not only to the material prosperity of the United States and the whole world, but in comfort to men's minds through a restoration of their faith in the wisdom and the power of government!

With great respect,

Your obedient servant,

J. M. KEYNES

From The Times, *2 January 1934*

MR ROOSEVELT'S EXPERIMENTS

Mr Roosevelt has made himself the trustee for those in every country who seek to mend the evils of our condition by reasoned experiment within the framework of the existing social system. If he fails rational change will be gravely prejudiced throughout the world, leaving orthodoxy and revolution to fight it out. But if he succeeds new and bolder methods will be tried everywhere.

It is for this reason, and not merely because we should all like to escape from the slump, that a more than ordinary importance attaches to the outcome of the President's experiments.

At the moment even his sympathisers in England are somewhat disconcerted. They wonder whether the order of different urgencies is rightly understood, whether there is not a confusion of aim, and whether some of the advice he gets is not crack-brained and queer; while the average City man is convinced that the President is engaged on such a hare-brained expedition that, unless he rids himself of his present advisers, the country is heading for a shocking breakdown. Yet I believe that the prevailing British idea is based on a seriously distorted view of what is happening in the United States. In spite of obvious disappointments, I do not see the prospects in a gloomy light.

The position is much complicated by the fact that Mr Roosevelt has been engaged on a double task, recovery and reform—recovery from the slump and the passage of those business and social reforms which are long overdue. For the first quick results are essential. The second may seem urgent, too, in the eyes of the first liberal Administration in effective power in the United States for many years; but here wisdom of long-range purpose is more necessary than immediate achievement. It will be through raising the prestige of his Administration by success in short-range recovery that the President will gain the driving force to accomplish long-range reform. Moreover, even wise and necessary reform is liable to impede and complicate recovery. For it upsets the confidence of the business world and weakens their motives to action. It may overtask the bureaucratic machine, which the traditional individualism of the United States and the old 'spoils system' have left none too strong. And it will confuse the thought and aim of the Administration by giving them too much to think about all at once.

Some fallacies

Looking back over the last nine months, it seems that the order of urgency between measures of recovery and measures of reform has not been duly observed, and that the latter has sometimes been mistaken for the former. In particular it is hard to detect any material aid to recovery in N[ational] I[ndustrial] R[ecovery] A[ct], though its social gains may be considerable, or in the Securities Act.

Thus too much of the energy of the Administration has been occupied hitherto with reform and too little with recovery. And when we turn to the technique of recovery itself the attainment of the best results has been interfered with by certain fallacies of thought—in particular as to the part played in recovery by rising prices. Rising prices are to be welcomed because they are usually a symptom of rising output and employment. When more purchasing power is spent, one expects rising output at rising prices. Since there cannot be rising output without rising prices, it is essential to ensure that the recovery shall not be held back by the insufficiency of the supply of money to support the increased monetary turnover. But there is much less to be said in favour of rising prices if they are brought about *at the expense* of rising output. Some debtors may be helped, but the national recovery as a whole will be retarded. Thus rising prices caused by deliberately increasing prime costs or by restricting output have a vastly inferior value to rising prices which are the natural result of an increase in the nation's purchasing power. Too much emphasis on the remedial value of a higher price level as an object in itself may lead to serious misapprehension as to the part which prices can play in the technique of recovery.

Increase of output

In the second place, the setback which American recovery experienced this autumn has been the predictable consequence of the failure to organise any material increase in new loan expenditure during the new Administration's first six months of office. Indeed, it seems probable that up to the end of October such expenditure had actually been on a smaller scale than under Mr Hoover. The object of recovery is to increase the national output and put more men to work. In the economic system of the modern world output is primarily produced for sale, and the volume of output depends on the amount of purchasing power compared with the prime cost of production which is expected to come on the market. Broadly speaking, therefore, an increase of output cannot occur unless by the operation of one or other of three factors. Individuals must be induced to spend more out of their existing incomes; or the business world must be induced, either by increased confidence in the prospects or by a lower rate of interest, to create additional current incomes in the hands of their employees, which is what happens when either the working or the fixed capital of the country is being increased; or public authority must be called in aid to create additional current incomes through the expenditure of borrowed or printed money. In bad times not much can be expected from the first factor. The second factor cannot be relied on in the United States today except to supply a second wave of attack on the slump, after the tide has been turned by the expenditure of public authority. Thus I lay overwhelming emphasis as the prime mover in the first stage of the technique of recovery on the increase of national purchasing power resulting from governmental expenditure financed by loans. Nothing else will count in comparison with this. The position six months hence will mainly depend on whether the foundations have been laid for larger loan expenditures in the near future.

I am not surprised that so little has been spent up to date. Our own experience has shown how difficult it is to improvise useful loan expenditure at short notice. There are many obstacles to be patiently overcome if waste, inefficiency, and corruption are to be avoided, and there are special factors which in the United States render the rapid improvisation of a vast programme of public works more than usually difficult. I do not blame Mr Ickes for having been cautious and careful, provided he has made sure that loan expenditure will shortly be incurred on a much larger scale. Everything depends on whether or not this is the case. The latest information suggests that such expenditure is now increasing rapidly. If the substantial increase which first showed itself in November is continued and improved upon in the ensuing months, an unmistakable business improvement will be in full swing before the summer.

A further fallacy of thought, of which one detects the influence, is due to a crude economic doctrine commonly known as the quantity theory of money. Rising output and rising incomes will suffer a setback sooner or later if the quantity of money is rigidly fixed. Some people seem to infer from this that output and income can be raised by increasing the quantity of money. But this is like trying to get fat by buying a larger belt. In the United States today the belt is plenty big enough for the belly. It is a most misleading thing to stress the quantity of money, which is only a limiting factor, rather than the volume of expenditure, which is the operative factor.

It is an even more foolish application of the same ideas to believe that there is a mathematical relation between the price of gold and the prices of other things. It is true that the value of the dollar in terms of foreign currencies will affect the price of those goods which enter into international trade. In so far as an overvaluation of the dollar was impeding the freedom of domestic price-raising policies or disturbing the balance of payments with foreign countries, it was advisable to depreciate it. But exchange depreciation should follow the success of a domestic price-raising policy as its natural consequence, and should not be allowed to disturb the whole world by preceding its justification at an entirely arbitrary pace. To suppose otherwise is another example of trying to put on flesh by letting out the belt. The recent gyrations of the dollar have looked to me more like a gold standard on the booze than the ideal managed currency which I hope for.

Conditions of success

Yet, in spite of these criticisms, the President remains the outstanding statesman who sees the necessity of a profound change of methods and is attempting it without intolerance, tyranny, or destruction. He is feeling his way by trial and error, and is felt to be entirely uncommitted in his own person to the details of a particular technique. Here, as in his own country, his position remains singularly untouched by criticisms of this or the other detail. I have, therefore, some confidence that he will, by trial and error, find his way out. If I were asked to say in concrete terms upon what action in the immediate future his success will chiefly depend, I would reply thus:—

In the field of gold devaluation and exchange policy the time has obviously come when uncertainty should be ended. This game of blind man's buff with exchange speculators serves no useful purpose and is extremely undignified. It upsets confidence, hinders business decisions, occupies the public attention in a measure far exceeding its real importance, and is responsible both for the irritation and for a certain lack of respect which exist outside the United States. The President has three alternative exits. He can devalue the dollar in terms of gold, returning to the gold standard at a new fixed ratio. But that would be seriously inconsistent with his declarations in favour of a long-range policy of stable prices. He might seek a policy of exchange stabilisation in conjunction with Great Britain aimed at stable price levels for the future by concerted management. This would be the best ultimate solution; but it is not practical politics at the moment, unless he is prepared to talk in terms of an initial value of sterling well below $5 pending the realisation of a marked rise in his domestic price level. Lastly, he could announce that he will control the dollar exchange by buying and selling gold and foreign currencies at a definite figure so as to avoid wide or meaningless fluctuations, with a right to shift the parities at any time, but with a declared intention only so to do either to correct a want of balance in America's international receipts and payments or to meet a shift in the domestic price level relatively to price levels abroad. This is probably the best policy open to him during the transitional period. He would be waiving his right to make future arbitrary changes which did not correspond to any relevant change in the facts; but in other respects he would retain his liberty to make his exchange policy subservient to the needs of his domestic policy—free to let out his belt in proportion as he put on flesh.

In the field of domestic policy I put in the forefront, for the reasons given above, a large volume of loan expenditure under government auspices. The object is to start the ball rolling. The United States is ready to roll towards prosperity if a good hard shove can be given in the next six months. The task which the President is attempting is essentially an easy one in the conditions of today.

The interest rate

Finally, there is the maintenance of cheap and abundant credit by the Federal Reserve System, and in particular the reduction of the long-term rate of interest, ready for the expansion of private enterprise as soon as the increase in profits resulting from state expenditure has changed the business atmosphere. The turn of the tide in Great Britain is largely attributable to the reduction in the long-term rate of interest which ensued on the success of the conversion of the War Loan, deliberately engineered by means of the open-market policy of the Bank of England. I see no reason why the American Treasury should not reduce the rate of interest on their long-term Government bonds to $2\frac{1}{2}$ per cent or less, with favourable repercussions on the whole bond market, if only the Federal Reserve System would replace its present holdings of short-dated Treasury issues by purchasing long-dated issues in exchange.

With these adaptations or enlargements of the President's existing policies, I should expect a successful outcome with great confidence. I was brought up to think that it is only too easy for a Government to inflate by its expenditures the incomes of its subjects—so easy as to be dangerous. I am still unable to accept the view that this object is so difficult that even a determined Government, ready to use all instruments within reason, will fail to accomplish it. I believe, therefore, that the President is much more likely to succeed than to fail, and that the gloomy views so prevalent in London are the result of an error in prognosis.

Keynes's article in *The Times* brought a critical letter from Ian Macdonald Horobin, a Conservative M.P., suggesting that Keynes's apologia for Roosevelt included open attacks on the N.R.A. and the Securities Act and that many of his other suggestions merely reflected sensible English policies already adopted. Keynes replied.

To the Editor of The Times, *5 January 1934*

Sir,

Mr I. M. Horobin alleges that in my recent article in your columns I 'openly attack the N.R.A. and the Securities Act'. Actually I described these measures as reform but not recovery, adding 'though their social gains may be considerable'. In Mr Horobin's vocabulary to describe a measure as a reform may be to attack it, but it has not this significance in mine.

I am your obedient servant,

J. M. KEYNES

Keynes's January article did have some impact, as a later letter from Walter Lippmann indicates.

From W. LIPPMANN, *17 April 1934*

My dear Keynes,

I have been on the point of writing you for sometime to urge you to write another article, following up your letter to the President of December last. I don't know whether you realise how great an effect that letter had, but I am told that it was chiefly responsible for the policy which the Treasury is now quietly but effectively pursuing of purchasing long-term Government bonds with a view to making a strong bond market and to reducing the long-term rate of interest.

Our greatest difficulty now lies in the President's emotional and moral commitments to the N.R.A. and to the various other measures which he regards as the framework of a better economic order. As they are being administered, they are a very serious check to our recovery, for the obvious reason that they have raised costs faster than production has increased.

Nobody could make so great an impression upon the President as you could if you undertook to show him the meaning of that part of his policy.

With cordial regards,

Yours sincerely,
WALTER LIPPMANN

On 13 January, Keynes made further comments on the American situation in a broadcast which the B.B.C. subsequently published.

From The Listener, *17 January 1934*

ROOSEVELT'S ECONOMIC EXPERIMENTS

The economic experiments of President Roosevelt may prove, I think, to be of extraordinary importance in economic history, because, for the first time—at least I cannot recall a comparable case—theoretical advice is being taken by one of the rulers of the world as the basis of large-scale action. The possibility of such a remarkable event has arisen out of the utter and complete discredit of every variety of orthodox advice. The state of mind in America which lies behind this willingness to try unorthodox experiments arises out of an economic situation desperate beyond precedent.

Although we here feel ourselves to have suffered a pretty severe slump, it is, all the same, hard for us to conceive the pass that things had reached in America a year ago. Unemployment nearly twice as bad as the worst we ever had; the farmers ruined; the banks insolvent; no hope apparent in any direction; and all this only three years after such a pinnacle of pride and prosperity as no other country in the world had ever reached. Moreover, the culminating point of these economic disasters had been reached after a period during which orthodox financial advice and high financial circles of the United States were believed to be exerting great influence over President Hoover and his advisers. This, then, seemed to be the result of following so-called sound opinion. Then, on the top of this, came the financial scandals, which were taken by the general public to discredit the financial leaders morally as much as the ruinous state of affairs had appeared to discredit them intellectually.

It is impossible to appreciate what is now happening in the United States unless one realises this background for the so-called New Deal, with orthodox advice contemptuously rejected and the head of the government turning right away from the financiers and all the so-called practical men to theorists and idealists with little or no experience of affairs.

It is not surprising that some confusion should result. The President himself is not, and does not pretend to be, an economist. Economics, one must confess, is at the moment a backward science, whatever one's hopes are for the future, in which semi-obsolete ideas are widely influential, hardly less in academic circles than elsewhere. It must have been difficult for the President to know in what direction to turn for the best available advice. In practice he has shown himself extraordinarily accessible to anyone with new ideas to air whom he believed to be independent and disinterested. Naturally he had received a great deal of advice, some of it inconsistent with the rest and not all of it of equal quality. Himself an empiricist, not wedded to any particular doctrine or any one technique, tolerant, optimistic, courageous and patient, he has been happy to provide the political skill and the power of authority to give some sort of a run to all kinds of *ideas*, ready to judge by results, but admittedly experimenting and watching carefully to drop in time schemes, the actual operation of which began to seem dangerous or disappointing.

Thus, the President himself has been content with general notions, a conduit pipe for the more general ideas of others, considering quite rightly that detail is not his business. He has not been solely concerned with lifting the United States out of its disastrous slump. He is just as much interested, perhaps even more, in many liberal reforms, some of them long overdue. Above all, he has been deliberately standing for the small man, the employee, the small investor, the small farmer, the bank depositor, the owner of small savings, against high finance and big business. Everyone has felt that this was his general position. That without doubt is the main explanation of the extraordinary popularity which has made him for the moment as powerful a dictator in the United States as any of the other less constitutional dictators of the contemporary world.

It would be a big jog even to run through the headings of the measures already taken to carry the New Deal into law. I can only mention one or two. The National Industrial Recovery Act, or N.R.A., includes such social legislation as, for example, for the abolition of child labour and the regulation of hours. It also tries to provide for organised planning, industry by industry, whilst avoiding the abuses of the trust or the cartel. Apart from this Act there are the measures to help the farmers—provisions for the reduction of their mortgage interest, funds to buy up and hold surplus crops, and inducements to restrict crops where there has been overproduction. Then there are the President's financial measures to enable depositors in insolvent banks to get their money back and to guarantee them against similar losses in future. Help, too, for small investors through the Securities Act, which is largely based on our own legislation for the protection of investors, though in some respects it goes beyond our own Acts.

Most important of all in the short run, and also most dubious and controversial, are the President's monetary measures; partly designed to help the debtor class by raising prices, and partly aimed at curing unemployment. One half of this programme has consisted in abandoning the gold standard, which was probably wise, and in taking various measures—very technical, but, in my opinion, not very useful—to depreciate the gold value of the dollar below its natural level. It is important that monetary arrangements should not hamper business expansion, but it is not easy to bring about business expansion *merely* by monetary manipulation. The other half of his programme, however, is infinitely more important and offers in my opinion much greater hopes. I mean the attempt to cure unemployment by large-scale expenditure on public works and similar purposes. This part of his programme has been very slow to get moving. As recently as the end of October practically nothing had been spent, and as a result of this, employment and output were again falling away. But recently the expenditure seems to have been more substantial. The President's recent sensational budget statement which was in the papers a fortnight ago means vast expenditure on these heads in the near future—if he is able to live up to his programme. Public works, railway renewals, unemployment relief, subsidies to local authorities, further aid to farmers and so forth make up the enormous so-called deficit—much of which, however, will be covered by valuable assets. I doubt whether it will prove practicable for his Administration to live up to their full programme. It may take more time to put it into effect than is now intended. But, if the President succeeds in carrying out a substantial part of his programme, for my part

I expect a great improvement in American industry and employment within six months.

At any rate those of us—and we are many—who hate the idea of revolution and the uprooting of all those good things which grow slowly, yet are disconcerted at our present failure to seize our opportunity to solve the problem of poverty, will hope to the bottom of our hearts that a man who is thus trying new ways boldly and even gaily with no object but the welfare of his people will manage to succeed.

I believe he will win the first round. The testing time, the more difficult task, will come afterwards—to hold the gains once made and to avoid the fatal relapses which in recent times have always characterised our economic system.

On 15 January President Roosevelt moved to remove one of the sources of uncertainty about which Keynes had complained. He asked Congress for legislation 'to organise a sound and adequate currency system'. Amongst his proposals was that the President should be empowered to fix the gold value of the dollar at between 50 and 60 per cent of its old value. Keynes commented in the next issue of *The New Statesman*.

From The New Statesman and Nation, *20 January 1934*

PRESIDENT ROOSEVELT'S GOLD POLICY

Up to this week President Roosevelt's powers in relation to gold have been permissive only. It has been uncertain how he would exercise them, how far the policy of the moment would be adhered to, and, recently, whether there was any serious intention of making paper declarations effective. The vital importance, therefore, of the measures announced in Washington last Monday is that within certain prescribed limits the gold policy of the United States becomes not merely permissive but mandatory. The dollar is to be definitely devalued down to a level not exceeding 60 per cent of the old parity with permissive powers to fix it from time to time at a discretionary figure between 60 per cent and 50 per cent of the old value. At the moment of writing the *de facto* gold value of the dollar is not yet equal to its *de jure* value under the new legislation. But it is only common sense to assume that the two values must after a short time come together. The definiteness thus introduced into the situation sets our authorities a new problem, but it also represents some progress towards the final solution.

At the present time France is on the gold standard, whilst we are not. The effect of the President's declaration, therefore, is to set a maximum value to the dollar in terms of francs so long as France remains on the gold standard; but it still leaves sterling to find a level somewhere between francs and dollars as determined by the policy of the Exchange Equalisation Fund and the pressure of business and speculative forces. Unless prices in America are to rise far more than seems likely, France is put in a position which is very difficult and probably in the long run untenable. But since the United States has now returned to gold within certain maximum limits of fluctuation, it leaves France free to rectify her position whenever she is prepared to do so by altering her own gold parity. Meanwhile we are in a middle position, free to allow sterling to depreciate on the franc or to appreciate on the dollar or to enjoy and suffer a bit of both.

The provisional position of equilibrium when it is reached will probably leave France and the other gold countries with currencies seriously overvalued in terms of sterling as well as in terms of dollars, and with sterling overvalued in relation to the dollar. The position may be appreciably aggravated compared with what it has been until recently, but not in the short run sensationally worse. The adjustment required between the franc and the dollar as compared with a month ago is of the order of 7 or 8 per cent, of which about half has been accomplished already. Thus the fluctuations involved are not large compared with those to which we have become accustomed. We are faced, therefore, with a situation which is not untenable in the short run, but is likely, nevertheless, to become intolerable in course of time.

This brings us to the second and more important phase introduced by the President's announcement. He has virtually offered this country and France an invitation to a monetary conference. At the same time he has set sufficient limits to the uncertainty of his own future policy to provide a basis for discussion. Apart from the difficulties of the transition, I see nothing in the President's scheme which need upset us and much that we should do well to approve. It is true that the rest of us will not find it easy to come to terms with him unless we substantially accept his view as to the future value of gold in terms of the leading world currencies. But why not? A high value for gold is in fact in our interests as much as in his, since it diminishes the burden of national debts through the profit on central bank reserves, a profit, probably, of more than £200,000,000 in our case, and increases the nominal value of these reserves to an extent which should free central banks of needless anxiety if on other grounds they are moved to adopt expansionist policies. At the same time the permitted variation in the gold value of the dollar will allow sufficient latitude for price changes in the United States on a somewhat larger scale than those elsewhere, the margin of 20 per cent [*sic*] thus provided being sufficient for any probable contingency.

The task of coming to terms with the President sets a more anxious problem for the gold currency countries than it does for us. It is reasonably certain that the existing gold value of the franc and the florin can scarcely be compatible in the long run with the new gold value of the dollar. The gold currency countries have to choose whether they will embark on an expensive campaign probably doomed to ultimate failure, or whether they will eat some of their many unnecessarily brave words about maintaining their existing parities with gold at all costs. If, in the end, the result of the President's action is to knock them off their gold perches, the final result will surely be in the interest of their citizens.

If the President's phrases about his ultimate objective of stabilising the purchasing power of the dollar are meant seriously, the purpose of a monetary conference would not be to return to an old-fashioned gold standard. Initial relative exchange values for the several currencies having been fixed, the conference would presumably aim for the future not at rigid gold parities, but at provisional parities from which the parties to the conference would agree not to depart except for substantial reasons arising out of their balance of trade or the exigencies of domestic price policy.

I cannot doubt but that the President's announcement means real progress. He has adopted a middle course between old-fashioned orthodoxy and the extreme inflationists. I see nothing in his policy which need be disturbing to business confidence. In conjunction with his spending programme, which seems at last to be getting under way, it is likely to succeed in putting the United States on the road to recovery. If America is able to emerge from the trough of the slump, it is probable that the industrial activity of the whole world will move upwards for some months to come. It is the problem of how to avoid falling into another slump after no long interval which will be still unsolved.

The Gold Reserve Act of 1934, which gave the President the powers he sought, passed Congress on 30 January. The next day, the President made the Act effective and fixed a new gold price of $35 per fine ounce.

During the rest of the winter, Keynes remained out of the press, devoting himself instead to the composition of his *General Theory*, and beginning work on his project for a theatre in Cambridge. On one occasion, however, he caused a public stir. It came on 21 February when during his statement to the annual meeting of the National Mutual Life Assurance Society he discussed the rate of interest in such a way that gilt-edged prices rose sharply in ensuing days.

The decline of the net rate of interest which we are able to earn on the investment of new money to a figure not much in excess of 4 per cent raises, however, questions of the greatest possible importance and interest to all investment institutions and not least to insurance offices, and I should like to take this opportunity of considering the general problem which this phenomenon presents in a little more detail.

In 1932 long-term British Government securities moved from a 5 per cent to a 3½ per cent basis. This was largely the result of the steps taken by the Bank of England to facilitate the conversion of the War Loan, including open-market operations on an unprecedentedly large scale, which raised the resources of the London clearing banks by £246,000,000, out of which they invested £176,000,000 in British Government securities.

In 1933 Government securities marked time, improving in price by only some 2 per cent and the year was occupied by other fixed-interest securities rising to their usual parity with Government securities, and in some cases beyond it. This was in spite of a further increase of £93,000,000 in the investments held by the banks—no longer out of additional resources provided by the Bank of England, but through the shrinkage of their other assets. Meanwhile the Treasury bill rate has averaged less than 1 per cent, and for more than a year there has been a spread of 2½ per cent between the yield on long-term Government securities and the rate at which the money market has been able to borrow against them. This abnormal and anomalous relationship indicates a grave doubt in the mind of the market as to whether the existing price of long-term securities will be maintained.

Two views

Two views can be held. Those who are afraid of holding long-term securities point out with truth that the rise in their prices is largely due to the purchases of the banks; and they invoke, again with truth, the evidence of past experience to the effect that, as trade recovers, the banks have been accustomed to sell their investments to provide the means of increased advances to industry. They argue, therefore, believing that history will repeat itself, that long-term Government securities will fall in price as soon as there is a material improvement in the demand for advances. It would be rash to affirm that the course of events will be different this time. But I would like to give some grounds for this conclusion, before passing to what seem to me to be more fundamental reasons for expecting a further fall in the long-term rate of interest.

In pre-war days the resources of the banking system were somewhat rigidly linked to the gold reserves of the Bank of England. Open market operations were unimportant and, broadly speaking, the assets of the clearing banks went up and down according as gold was moving into, or out of, the Bank of England. Now in times of good trade this country tended to expand, and in bad times to contract, its foreign lending more rapidly than its favourable balance; the effect of which on movements of gold was to prevent the assets of the banks from increasing in good times, while sometimes the tendency for these assets to increase was actually stronger in times of depression. It is not to be wondered at, therefore, that with improving trade it was often impracticable for the banks to accommodate industry except by selling their investments. This is the historical origin of the expectation that Consols will fall when trade recovers.

Resources of the banks

Today, however, there is no necessity for events to follow this course. The resources of the banks depend at least as much on changes in the volume of securities purchased by the Bank of England as on changes in the Bank's stock of gold. Thus the technique of management lately evolved by the Bank puts it in its power to adjust the resources of the clearing banks to the needs of trade and employment. We are no longer at the mercy of the blind and perverse forces which ensured in pre-war days that, as soon as we began to move towards prosperity and optimum employment, factors would begin to be generated which would shortly throw us back again into the pit which we had lately climbed out of.

Moreover, in present circumstances the increased basis of credit which the Bank of England would have to provide might prove to be moderate in amount. In the first place, part of the clearing banks' existing advances represents frozen rather than active credit, so that increased demands for current credit will be partly met by the repayment of old advances; while some of the largest concerns in the country are now much less dependent on bank borrowing than was the case with the constituent businesses out of which they have been formed. But, apart from this, an increase of (say) £20,000,000 in the Bank of England's assets would enable the clearing banks to increase their aggregate advances by 25 per cent, which should be fully adequate to all requirements unless there is to be a large rise in wages and other costs.

It is clear, therefore, that there is no necessity for reviving trade to break the gilt-edged market unless the authorities desire this to happen. So I return to the fundamental reasons, as I see them, why the authorities should in fact desire just the contrary.

Return on gilt-edged stocks

There is, surely, overwhelming evidence that even the present reduced rate of 3½ per cent on long-term gilt-edged stocks is far above the equilibrium level—meaning by 'equilibrium' the rate which is compatible with the full employment of our resources of men and of equipment. It is often forgotten that 3½ per cent is much in excess of the average yield on Consols, which ruled over the 40 years previous to the War—namely, just under 3 per cent—or even the average yield which ruled over the 80 years from 1835 to 1914—namely, just over 3 per cent.

The argument that this comparison is vitiated by the income tax which the lender must now pay is quite invalid if we are considering the 'equilibrium' rate, rather than the actual market rate; for the rate which the borrower can afford to pay depends in the long run on the yield of capital assets and is not increased by reason of taxes on the lender. Yet during the nineteenth century the annual amount which the community was disposed to save when it was fully employed was much below what it is today, whereas the outlets for profitable investment were vastly greater on account of the rapid growth of population and the opening up of new worlds overseas.

Curtailment of the investment field

With the opportunities for safe and profitable investment abroad greatly curtailed, as much by the unfortunate results of past investment as by the diminished opportunities for new investment, Great Britain and the United States would, if they were to return to the full employment of their resources, save sums so vast that they could not possibly be invested to yield anything approaching 3½ per cent. No one can foretell at what point the rate of interest will reach its equilibrium level until we actually approach it. But it is highly probable that the equilibrium rate is not above 2½ per cent for long-term gilt-edged investment, and may be appreciably less. In the early days of a recovery, while working capital is being restored and various postponements of renewals and fresh development are being overtaken, it is true that business can temporarily stand a higher rate. But the longer the recovery lasts the further will the appropriate long-term rate of interest have to fall. If when the recovery is well on its way the Bank of England so manages the basis of credit as to force the clearing banks to sell their investments on a substantial scale or otherwise to weaken the long-term loan market, then, indeed, it is as certain that depression will follow recovery as that night follows day.

Downward tendency of interest rates

But why, in making our prognostications, should we attribute such disastrous ideas to our financial authorities? No institution is more interested than the Treasury in a falling rate of interest. The further we move from the abnormal rates of the War period, the clearer, I believe, will it become to every one that our economic health needs a rate of interest appreciably below, and not above, the nineteenth-century level. There is no harm in the fall of the rate of interest being gradual, but it is a necessity for the epoch into which we are now entering that there should be a steady movement in the downward direction. In each of the last three years, I have ventured, in addressing you, to predict a falling rate of interest. I say today with undiminished conviction that we are still some way from the end of the journey, and that the course of events which I forecast three years ago will still continue in the same direction.

However, Keynes maintained a watching brief on events elsewhere, as shown by a letter to his American friend Walter Case.

To WALTER CASE, *1 March 1934*

Dear Walter,

I. Though one never knows, it looks as if the gold bloc countries were definitely not coming off their perch this journey. I am told on fairly good authority that they had a meeting together a few days ago, renewed their oaths and roped themselves together even tighter than before, to give one another mutual support and encouragement to maintain the *status quo*.

As you know, I am not surprised at this. It seemed to me the most probable outcome taking a short view.

I still, however, think that taking a longer view the gold bloc countries are getting themselves into an untenable position. Sooner or later domestic political events in one or other of the countries will force their hands. The recent devaluation in Czecho-Slovakia involved the resignation of Pospiscil, the Governor of the State Bank, and all his board, they having nailed their colours to the gold mast. But that did not prevent political pressure from prevailing. So I feel it is bound to be sooner or later with one or other of Holland, Switzerland, Italy, Belgium or France. Switzerland, Holland and France are, all of them, countries where a far reaching political turnover might take place at quite short notice.

Meanwhile, as it seems to me, sterling has been edging its way rather cleverly between the opposing currents. It would be disastrous for us to appreciate too much in terms of the dollar. On the other hand, if we were to depreciate too much in terms of gold, it would certainly bring the gold bloc countries nearer to the edge—an event which we expect sooner or later, but by no means desire to precipitate, since the existing state of the sterling gold exchanges suits our trade admirably.

If your President goes in for any further devaluation which at this distance I cannot see as likely in the near future, it might precipitate things. Failing that, I should not be surprised if the exchange jogged along for some little time without any wide divergence (meaning by 'wide' more than 5 per cent) from the present figures. On [a] short view sterling might tend to appreciate. But, on a longer view, on the whole I share the opinion that sterling is intrinsically weak. So far as I can make out, this is the conclusion of the Bank of England, and their reason for still maintaining the embargo on foreign loans. The evidence which is available to me is far from conclusive one way or the other. But they have more evidence than I have, and it is not impossible that they are right.

II. I should like to put before you what may be impertinent, namely, an opinion concerning your markets rather than ours. The more I consider the future course of events, the more convinced do I feel that in certain respects developments in America will follow much the same order as they have here. I mean by this that unless the recovery plans break down completely and end in universal disorder and discredit and fear, interest rates in America are almost certain, sooner or later, to take the same course they they have over here. It seems to me that it must be right to back this opinion, since, if this is wrong, all other forms of investment in America, except possibly the flight of capital from the country, are certain to turn out disastrously. It seems to me almost absurd to suppose that an investment either in common stocks or in actual cash can turn out well and that an investment in fixed-interest securities of the second class can turn out badly. If there is a class of securities on which the rate of interest falls from $7\frac{1}{2}$ per cent to 5 per cent there is a 50 per cent capital profit. There are innumerable instances of profits on that scale in this country during the last two years on the most steady going securities. It is obvious, looking back, that opportunities which offered profit out of all proportion to possible loss were missed. My feeling is that this is now the position in the United States. If you have any belief in your own prospects at all, this strikes me as the outstanding certainty.

If you are held back, I cannot but suspect that this may be partly due to the thought of so many people in New York being influenced, as it seems to me, by sheer intellectual error. The opinion seems to prevail that inflation is in its essential nature injurious to fixed-interest securities. If this means that an extreme inflation such as is not at all likely is more advantageous to equities than to fixed charges, that is of course true. But people seem to me to overlook the fundamental point that attempts to bring about recovery through monetary or quasi-monetary methods operate solely or almost solely through the rate of interest and that they only do the trick, if they do it at all, by bringing the rate of interest down. The whole subject has, of course, many more ramifications than can be discussed in a letter, but almost everyone who has any pretensions to being a sound or orthodox thinker on financial problems in New York probably has his brain stuffed with fallacies on this particular matter. So there is an opportunity for anyone, if there is anyone, who can think (or so it seems to me) scientifically straight on this issue.

Yours ever,
[copy not signed or initialled]

The spring brought Keynes an opportunity to examine American conditions at first hand when Columbia University offered him an honorary Doctor of Laws degree. Amongst the others to be honoured were Cordell Hull, the American Secretary of State, J. B. Conant, the President of Harvard and C. B. Hoover, an economist from Duke University whom Keynes had met several years earlier. Working his schedule around the Columbia Convocation on 5 June, Keynes planned a three-week visit to America, spending most of his time in New York and Washington.

Keynes sailed to America on the *Olympic* on 9 May and arrived in New York six days later. Using Case Pomeroy and Company as his base he moved widely in New York financial circles, attending, for example, a dinner in his honour sponsored by the Council on Foreign Relations on 21 May. Among the others present were Frank Altschul, Walter Case, Allen Dulles, John Foster Dulles, Russell Leffingwell, Walter Lippmann, Ogden Mills, Wesley C. Mitchell, Walter Stewart and John Henry Williams.

After his initial stay in New York he went on to Washington for a series of meetings that covered 25–30 May. His schedule was a full one: on 25 May he saw Frances Perkins, the Secretary of Labour, Justice Brandeis and Rexford Tugwell before an evening dinner party at Herbert Feis's home; the next day he saw Kenneth Bewley of the U.K. Embassy and Henry Morgenthau, the Secretary of the Treasury, before having dinner with Calvin Hoover, then 'a minor brain-truster'; on the Sunday he managed four further appointments. The Monday, 28 May, saw him with three meetings before he met the President at 5.15. Keynes's interview lasted an hour. He reported it as 'fascinating' and later made some notes on the President's appearance.[1] The President himself reported he had 'a grand talk with Keynes and liked him immensely'.[2] The following day Keynes addressed a luncheon meeting of Senators on his proposals for internal recovery and a dinner meeting of advisers from the Research and Planning Division of the N.R.A., as well as seeing Lewis Bean of the Agricultural Adjustment Administration. He returned to New York the next day.

The remaining days in New York saw Keynes further involved in affairs. On the weekend of 1–4 June he took part in a National Industrial Conference Board Conference at a farm near New York City, while the next week saw not only the Columbia Convocation, but also a speech to the American Political Economy Club (*JMK*, vol. XIII, p. 456) and a special farewell dinner at Case Pomeroy and Co. Keynes sailed from New York on 8 June.

Reactions to Keynes's many activities were favourable. After lunch with the Senators on 29 May, W. W. Reifler commented

From W. W. RIEFLER, *6 June 1934*

Dear Mr Keynes,

I was under the impression they you were already returning to England, or I would have written before.

Your conversations with the Senators had a most salutary effect and may have constituted the turning point in passing the housing legislation. I can't thank you enough for your help.

Sincerely yours,
W. W. RIEFLER

Similarly, his N.R.A. talk brought the following remark from Victor von Szeliski, the Chief Statistician of the Research Planning Division of N.R.A.

From V. S. VON SZELISKI, *11 June 1934*

Dear Professor Keynes,

Here are the national income figures which I promised you, together with the Department of Commerce study of which they are meant to be a continuation. I also enclose an explanatory memorandum of how the figures were derived.

There is one question I did not think to ask you on the occasion of your visit: How do you reconcile the fact that England has had a fair measure of recovery while making every effort to balance the national budget, with

[1] R. F. Harrod, *The Life of John Maynard Keynes* (London, 1951), p. 20.

[2] Felix Frankfurter to Keynes, 23 June 1934.

your contention that the way to get out of a depression is through government loan expenditures at a brisk rate?

I saw Mr Sachs in New York two days ago and he appeared to think that you had definitely given up your belief in government expenditures as a method of recovery, and now regard them only as a transitional device until private capitalism can resume, the latter bringing about the real recovery from depression, while the former merely holds the lines. Either he or I have misinterpreted your position.

The whole Division felt greatly stimulated by your visit. One man told me afterward: 'That was a fine talk, just what we needed to realise just where our efforts fitted into the whole recovery picture'.

Very truly yours,
VICTOR S. VON SZELISKI

Before leaving the United States, Keynes prepared a sequel to his open letter of 31 December. He sent an advance copy to the White House on 5 June. It appeared in the United States in *The New York Times* of 10 June and in London the next day.

From The Times, *11 June 1934*

AGENDA FOR THE PRESIDENT

These are a few notes on the New Deal by one who has lately visited the United States on a brief visit of pure inquisitiveness—made under the limitations of imperfect knowledge but gaining, perhaps, from the detachment of a bird's-eye view. My purpose is to consider the prospects rather than the past—taking the legislation of this Congress for granted and examining what might be done on the basis thus given. I am in sympathy with most of the social and reforming aims of this legislation; and the principal subject of these notes is the problem of consolidating economic and business recovery.

For this reason I have not much to say about N.R.A. I doubt if this is either such an advantage to recovery or such a handicap as its advocates and its critics suppose. It embodies some important improvements in labour conditions and for securing fair trade practices. But I agree with the widespread opinion that much of it is objectionable because of its restrictionist philosophy (which has a proper place in agricultural adjustment today but not in American industry) and because of its excessive complexity and regimentation. In particular it would be advisable to discard most of the provisions to fix prices and to forbid sales below an alleged but undefinable cost basis. Nevertheless, its net effect on recovery can easily be overestimated either way. I find most Americans divided between those who believe that higher wages are good because they increase purchasing power and those who believe that they are bad because they raise costs. But both are right, and the net result of the two opposing influences is to cancel out. The important question is the proper adjustment of relative wage rates. Absolute wage rates are not of primary importance in a country where their effect on foreign trade has been offset by exchange devaluation.

The case of A.A.A. (Agricultural Adjustment [Administration]), on the other hand, is much stronger. For the farmer has had to shoulder more than his share of the trouble and also has more lasting difficulties ahead of him than industry has. A.A.A. is organising for the farmer the advisable measure of restriction which industry long ago organised for itself. Thus, the task which A.A.A. is attempting is necessary though difficult; whereas some part of what N.R.A. seems to be aiming at is not only impracticable but unnecessary.

Problem of recovery

I see the problem of recovery, accordingly, in the following light. How soon will normal business enterprise come to the rescue? What measures can be taken to hasten the return of normal enterprise? On what scale, by which expedients and for how long is abnormal Government expenditure advisable in the meantime? For this, I think, is how the Administration should view its task. I see no likelihood that business of its own initiative will invest in durable goods of a sufficient scale for many months to come, for the following reasons.

In the first place, the important but intangible state of mind, which we call business confidence, is signally lacking. It would be easy to mention specific causes of this, for some of which the Administration may be to blame. Probably the most important is the menace of possible labour troubles. But the real explanation, in my judgement, lies deeper than the specific causes. It is to be found in the perplexity and discomfort which the business world feels from being driven so far from its accustomed moorings into unknown and uncharted waters. The business man, who may be adaptable and quick on his feet in his own particular field, is usually conservative and conventional in the larger aspects of social and economic policy. At the start he was carried away, like other people, by the prevailing enthusiasm—without being converted at bottom or suffering a sea-change. Thus he has easily reverted to where he was. He is sulky and bothered; and, with the short memory characteristic of contemporary man, even begins to look back with longing to the good old days of 1932. This atmosphere of disappointment, disillusion, and perplexity is not incurable. The mere passage of time for business to work out its new bearings and recover its equanimity should do much. If the President could convince business men that they know the worst, so to speak, that might hasten matters. Above all, experience of improving conditions might work wonders.

Serious obstacles

In the second place there are still serious obstacles in the way of reopening the capital market to large-scale borrowing for new investment; particularly the attitude of the finance houses to the Securities Act and the high cost of borrowing to those who need loans most. Moreover, many types of durable goods are already in sufficient supply and businesses will not be inclined to repair or modernise plant until they are experiencing a stronger demand than they can meet with their existing plant; to which should be added the excessively high cost of building relatively to rents and incomes.

None of these obstacles can be overcome in a day or by a stroke of the pen. The notion that if the Government would retire altogether from the economic field business left to itself would soon work out its own salvation is foolish; and even if it were not, it is certain that public opinion would allow no such thing. This does not mean that the Administration should not be assiduously preparing the way for the return of normal investment enterprise. But this will unavoidably take time. When it comes it will intensify and maintain a recovery initiated by other means. But it belongs to the second chapter of the story.

I conclude, therefore, that for six months at least, and probably for a year, the measure of recovery to be achieved will mainly depend on the degree of the direct stimulus to production deliberately applied by the Administration. Since I have no belief in the efficacy for this purpose of the price and wage raising activities of N.R.A., this must chiefly mean the pace and volume of the Government's emergency expenditure.

Up to last November such expenditure, excluding re-financing and advances to banks, was relatively small—about $90,000,000 a month. For November onwards the figure rose sharply and for the first four months of this year the monthly average exceeded $300,000,000. The effect on business was excellent. But then came what seems to me to have been an unfortunate decision. The expenditure of the Civil Works Administration was checked before the expenditure of the Public Works Administration was ready to take its place. Thus the aggregate emergency expenditure is now declining. If it is going to decline to $200,000,000 monthly, much of the ground already gained will probably be lost. If it were to rise to $400,000,000 monthly I should be quite confident that a strong business revival would set in by the autumn. So little divides a retreat from an advance. Most people greatly underestimate the effect of a given emergency expenditure because they overlook the multiplier—the cumulative effect of increased additional individual incomes (volume of income rather than merely of money) because the expenditure of these incomes improves the incomes of a further set of recipients and so on. $400,000,000 monthly is not much more than 11 per cent of the national income; yet it may, directly and indirectly, increase the national income by at least three or four times this amount. Thus the difference between a monthly emergency expenditure of $400,000,000 (financed out of loans, and not out of taxation, which would represent a mere redistribution of incomes) and a $100,000,000 expenditure may be (other things being equal) to increase the national money income by 25 to 30 per cent.

But the full benefit of a given rate of emergency expenditure may not be obtained until it has been continued for a full year. For there are two dead-points to reach and pass. After a long depression, a man will spend a large proportion of this first increment of income in getting financially straight—in paying back taxes, back rents, back interest, back debts. But eventually he will raise the level of his own standard of life. As he does so, demand will revive to a scale which business cannot easily satisfy without spending money on repairs and renewals of plant—which again will put increased incomes into circulation. Thus it is essential for the scale of the emergency expenditure to be large enough to pass by these two dead-points. The best calculation I can make suggests that a monthly figure of $400,000,000, exclusive of re-financing, should be sufficient. This could be attained without reaching the maximum figure which the President has promised not to exceed. But it will not be attained unless the object is pursued more whole-heartedly than in the past three months.

A suggested agenda

This brings me to my agenda for the President:—

1. A small office should be set up, attached presumably to the Executive Committee, to collate the spending programmes, both realised and prospective, of the various emergency organisations, to compare estimates with results, and to report to the President weekly. If the volume or pace of prospective estimates appears to be deficient, the emergency organisation should be instructed to report urgently on further available projects. Housing and the railroads appear to offer the outstanding opportunities. The new Housing Bill is brilliantly conceived, and may be a measure of the first importance. Drought relief may be an unexpectedly large factor in the coming months.

2. Meanwhile active preparations should be on foot to make sure that normal enterprise will take the place of the emergency programmes as soon as possible. Much progress has already been made with the problem of remedying the widespread and paralysing loss of liquidity. But that task must still be carried on. With the Securities Act and the Stock Exchange Act carried into law, the battle is over and the time has come for sincere efforts on both sides to establish co-operative and friendly relations between the Commission which will work the Acts and the leading financial interests. For it is vital to reopen the capital market.

3. Continuous pressure should be exerted by the Treasury and the Federal Reserve System to bring down the long-term rate of interest. For it assuredly lies in their power, and it is a mistake to suppose that because the Government will be a large borrower interest rates will rise; inasmuch as the Treasury's resources in gold and the Reserve System's excess reserves put the market wholly in their hands. If a year hence the Administration cannot borrow for 20 years below $2\frac{1}{2}$ per cent, the Treasury will have muddled its task, which their performance up to date gives one no reason to expect. Meanwhile, it would

seem advisable to reduce the maximum rate which Member Banks are allowed to pay on savings deposits to $2\frac{1}{2}$ per cent immediately, then to 2 per cent, and ultimately to 1 per cent.

4. To an Englishman the high level of building costs in America appears to be scandalous, both of building materials and of direct labour. They must be nearly double what they are in England. So long as the volume of work remains as low as it is now, these high costs do not mean high incomes to producers. Thus no one benefits. It is of the first importance for the Administration to take whatever steps are in its power to reduce unit costs in these industries against an undertaking to increase the volume of business sufficiently to maintain and probably to increase actual earnings. This might involve a national programme of building working-class houses to rent, in itself beneficial.

5. Either by skill or by good fortune the United States seems to me to have arrived at an excellent currency policy. It was right to devalue. It is right to have a value for the dollar currently fixed in terms of gold. It is prudent to keep a discretionary margin to allow future changes in the gold value of the dollar, if a change in circumstances makes this advisable. But all these measures have been carried fully far enough. Thus there would be no risk, in my judgement, if the President were to make it plain that he has now successfully attained his objects so far as they can be attained by monetary policy, and that henceforth a wise spending policy and a gradual but obstinate attack on high interest rates through the agency of the Federal Reserve System and otherwise will occupy the foreground of the economic programme.

Some five months ago I wrote that the relapse in the latter half of 1933 was the predictable consequence of the failure of the Administration to organise new loan expenditure (as distinct from refinancing) on an adequate scale and that the position six months later would entirely depend on whether the foundation had been laid for larger expenditures in the ensuing week. Fortunately the expenditures did increase, rising from less than

$100,000,000 in the month preceding my letter to an average of $300,000,000 in the next four months. As I predicted, the fruits of this have been enjoyed, and I estimate that there has been an improvement of something like 15 per cent in output, incomes and employment. This is an immense achievement in so short a time. But latterly, the expenditures have been declining and, once more as a predictable result, a recession of 3 per cent and perhaps 5 per cent is impending. The present indications suggest an improvement by August or September. But the position in the latter part of this year will depend on wise decisions as to emergency expenditure which have not yet been taken.

After his return to London, Keynes supplemented his article with a letter.

To the Editor of The Times, *23 June 1934*

THE AMERICAN RECOVERY

Sir,

I should be grateful if you would allow me to supplement briefly my notes on the economic position in the United States which you published on June 11 last. In particular I have now obtained a more exact computation of the rate of the net loan expenditure of the American Treasury.

The United States Budget is by no means so heavily unbalanced as the crude figures suggest, the ordinary Budget being in fact fully balanced including a substantial sinking fund ($600,000,000) for the redemption of debt, while a considerable proportion of the emergency expenditure is represented by more or less valuable capital assets, much of it being merely refinancing and the substitution of one document for another. I believe, however, that the following table gives a fairly accurate impression of the rate of Government expenditure not covered by taxation, which gives rise to new purchasing. These totals are arrived at by taking a three months' moving average (so that the figure against any month is the average for that and the two preceding months) of the expenditures which clearly lead to new incomes, plus the excess of payments to farmers in any month over the corresponding processing taxes (or minus the deficiency), plus a half of the advances which in the first instance increase liquidity rather than new purchasing.

	$1,000,000		$1,000,000
September 1933	102	January 1934	369
October	123	February	422
November	158	March	435
December	231	April	348
		May	311

The statistics for the first half of June indicate that the figure for June calculated on the same basis will be in the neighbourhood of $300,000,000. Nor, on the information available, should I expect the three months' moving average to fall appreciably below $300,000,000 for the present, while there is some hope of an increase by the late summer. To indicate the order of magnitude of these figures, I may mention that $100,000,000 a month is about 3 per cent of the national income.

Admittedly there is at the present time some recession in factory output in the United States, due partly to seasonal influences, partly to the falling away of Government expenditure as shown in the above table, and partly to business optimism in the first quarter of 1934 having encouraged industry, particularly in the case of textiles and automobiles, to provide for a somewhat larger effective demand than is in fact maturing today. But I should doubt if this recession will go very far, since a mere continuance of the present rate of Government loan expenditure should gradually provide more stimulus than has yet been experienced. For Americans have not unnaturally used much of their first increment of income to repay debts of all kinds rather than to keep rolling the ball of new purchasing.

Both here and in the United States I have found a tendency to underestimate the extent of the American recovery up to date as compared with the recovery in this country. One has to remember, of course, that the American recovery started from a much lower point than ours. There is also the difficulty that the only satisfactory American index of employment is confined to industrial employment in factories and does not include building, transportation, or distribution. It is possible, however, to arrive at certain broad conclusions. In both countries a peak of unemployment was reached in January 1933. Since that date the increase in the number of men employed in Great Britain as shown by our own statistics is almost exactly 10 per cent, two-thirds of this improvement having occurred in 1933 and one-third in the first five months of 1934. There can be no doubt that the percentage improvement in the United States greatly exceeds this. Factory employment shows an increase exceeding 40 per cent between January 1933, and May 1934; and it would, I think, be generally agreed that a more comprehensive index would show an improvement in excess of 25 per cent. Even more notable is the increase in the factory pay rolls, which have increased over the same period by fully 70 per cent. I should suppose that the American national income must have increased by at least 12 to 15 per cent in 1933 and probably by a further 12 to 15 per cent in the first half of 1934, which is a colossal achievement in the time.

Different authorities will differ in their estimates of the relations of cause and effect. But the above figures may perhaps help all alike to see the matter in a more accurate perspective. The exaggerated improvement during the first three months of office of the new Administration, based almost entirely on psychological excitement and not on real factors, which was inevitably followed by a steep recession, has tended to obscure the extent of the ground gained over the period up to date, taken as a whole.

If we take the average of the pre-boom years 1923–25 as 100, the schematic picture, which I see in my own mind, of the rate of progress of the American economy towards normal, after smoothing out the excessive rise and subsequent fall in the middle of 1933, is—very broadly—as follows:

	1933	1934
1st quarter	63	79
2nd quarter	67	83
3rd quarter	71	—
4th quarter	75	—

I feel that the maintenance of existing policies might continue this rate of a quarterly rise of four points during the rest of 1934. But I cannot see how 1935 can achieve a figure of 95 and better, unless the United States enjoys the two advantages which mainly explain the measure of improvement achieved in this country—namely, a large reduction in the long-term rate of interest and a high degree of activity in the building industry.

Your obedient servant,

J. M. KEYNES

In the months that followed, Keynes provided two additional comments on American events. In November, he supplied the Committee on Economic Information of the Economic Advisory Council with further details on American emergency expenditures.

ECONOMIC ADVISORY COUNCIL COMMITTEE ON ECONOMIC INFORMATION

EMERGENCY EXPENDITURE OF THE UNITED STATES TREASURY

The emergency expenditure of the United States Treasury financed by loans can be approximately estimated as follows:

1. The normal budget is not far from balancing. Indeed there is some provision for a sinking fund. Thus it is safe to restrict one's calculations to the emergency expenditure.

2. Some of the emergency expenditures, however, are merely re-financing, i.e. the exchange of one document for another. I believe, however, that a fairly good result is obtained by taking first of all the R.F.C. items exclusive of re-financing and then adding to them 50 per cent of the re-financing items which, since many of them serve to make various institutions more liquid, partly lead to new expenditure.

3. The total thus arrived at has to be adjusted by reference to the net A.A.A. expenditure. In the long run it is expected that the subsidies to farmers etc. will be approximately balanced by the processing taxes. Over any given short period, however, there is a wide discrepancy between the two, since the processing taxes have been collected much in advance of the money being expended. Thus to the extent that the processing taxes exceed the subsidies the figure is deducted from the total arrived at as above and contrariwise.

The monthly figures thus calculated work out as follows:—

Date	Total monthly disbursements ($ million)	Three months moving average ($ million)
July 1933	92·1	
Aug.	105·7	
Sept.	107·7	101·8
Oct.	155·7	123·0
Nov.	212·3	158·5
Dec.	325·9	231·3
Jan. 1934	568·7	368·9
Feb.	372·8	422·4
Mar.	363·0	434·8
Apr.	309·7	348·5
May	259·9	310·9
June	335·5	302·0
July	314·0	309·0
Aug.	285·0	311·0
Sept.	308·0	302·0
Oct.	292·0	295·0

The next month, he provided an American popular magazine with a positive answer to the question 'Can America spend its Way into Recovery?'[3] Harold Laski provided the negative answer in the same issue.

From Redbook, *December 1934*

CAN AMERICA SPEND ITS WAY INTO RECOVERY?

Why, obviously!—is my first reflection when I am faced by this question. No one of common sense could doubt it, unless his mind had first been muddled by a 'sound' financier or an 'orthodox' economist. We produce in order to sell. In other words, we produce in response to spending. It is impossible to suppose that we can stimulate production and employment by *refraining* from spending. So, as I have said, the answer is obvious.

But at a second glance, I can see that the question has been so worded as to inspire an insidious doubt. For spending means extravagance. A man who is extravagant soon makes himself poor. How, then, can a nation become rich by doing what must impoverish an individual? By this thought the public is bewildered. Yet a course of behaviour which might make a single individual poor *can* make a nation wealthy.

For when an individual spends, he affects not only himself but others. Spending is a two-sided transaction. If I spend my income on buying something which you can make for me, I have not increased my own income, but I have increased yours. If you respond by buying something which I can make for you, then my income also is increased. Thus, when we are thinking of the nation as a whole, we must take account of the results as a whole. The rest of the community is enriched by an individual's expenditure—for his expenditure is simply an addition to everyone else's income. If everybody spends more

[3] Richard Kahn provided a first draft of this article. However, his draft was extensively rewritten and reshaped by Keynes.

freely, everybody is richer and nobody is poorer. Each man benefits from the expenditure of his neighbour, and incomes are increased by just the amount required to provide the wherewithal for the additional expenditure. There is only one limit to the extent to which a nation's income can be increased in this manner, and that is the limit set by the physical capacity to produce. To refrain from spending at a time of depression, not only fails, from the national point of view, to add to wealth—it is profligate: it means waste of available man-power, and waste of available machine power, quite apart from the human misery for which it is responsible.

The nation is simply a collection of individuals. If for any reason the individuals who comprise the nation are unwilling, each in his private capacity, to spend sufficient to employ the resources with which the nation is endowed, then it is for the government, the collective representative of all the individuals in the nation, to fill the gap. For the effects of government expenditure are precisely the same as the effects of individuals' expenditure, and it is the increase in the income of the public which provides the source of the extra government expenditure.

It may sometimes be advantageous for a government to resort for part of its borrowing to the banking system rather than to the public. That makes no difference of principle to the effects of the expenditure. There are many who will raise the horror-struck cry of 'Inflation!' when borrowing from the banks is suggested. I doubt if any of those who speak in this way have a clear idea what they mean by inflation. Expenditure is either beneficial or it is harmful. I say it is beneficial, but whether I am right or wrong, it is hard to see how the effect can be altered if the money spent by the government comes from the banks rather than from the public.

When the government borrows in order to spend, it undoubtedly gets the nation into debt. But the debt of a nation to its own citizens is a very different thing from the debt of a private individual. The nation *is* the citizens who comprise it—no more and no less—and to owe money to them is not very different from owing money to one's self. Insofar as taxes are necessary to shift the interest payments out of one pocket and into the other, this is certainly a disadvantage; but it is a small matter compared with the importance of restoring normal conditions of prosperity. If private individuals refuse to spend, then the government must do it for them. It might be better if they did it for themselves, but that is no argument for not having it done at all.

It is easy, however, to exaggerate the extent to which the government need get into unproductive debt. Let us take, for purposes of illustration, a government hydro-electric power scheme. The government pays out money, which it borrows, to the men employed on the scheme. But the benefit does not stop there. These men who, previously unemployed, are now drawing wages from the government, spend these wages in providing themselves with the necessaries and comforts of existence—shirts, boots and the like. The makers of these shirts and boots, who were hitherto unemployed, spend their wages in their turn, and so set up a fresh wave of additional employment, of additional production, of additional wages, and of additional purchasing power. And so it goes on, until we find that for each man actually employed on the government scheme, three, or perhaps four, additional men are employed in providing for his needs and for the needs of one another. In this way a given rate of government expenditure will give rise to four or five times as much employment as a crude calculation would suggest. Thus there would be some advantage even if the scheme itself were to yield but little revenue hereafter. If, however, it is even a moderately sound scheme capable of yielding (say) three per cent on its cost, the case for it is overwhelmingly established.

That is not all. Unemployment involves a serious financial strain to the municipal, state, and federal governments. The alleviation of unemployment, as a result of government expenditure, means a considerable reduction in outgoings on the support of the unemployed. At the same time the receipts from taxation mount up as the nation's taxable income increases, and as real property values are re-established. These important factors must be allowed for before it is possible to say how far government expenditure involves additional unproductive government debt. The residue cannot be very large. Depression is itself the cause of government deficits, resulting from increased expenditure on the support of the unemployed and the falling-off in the yield of taxation. Public debt is inevitable at a time when private expenditure is inadequate: it is better to incur it actively in providing employment and promoting industrial activity than to suffer it passively as a consequence of poverty and inactivity.

So far I have been advocating government expenditure without much reference to the purpose to which the money is devoted. The predominant issue, as I look at the matter, is to get the money spent. But productive and socially useful expenditure is naturally to be preferred to unproductive expenditure. The arguments for expenditure are very much strengthened if the government, by spending a small sum of money, can induce private individuals and corporations to spend a much larger sum. Thus a government guarantee to facilitate the building of houses is, perhaps, the best measure of all. The government is here operating under the advantage of very considerable leverage; every dollar which there is any risk of the government having to find under its guarantee means a vastly greater number of dollars spent by private persons. There is no better way by which America can spend itself into prosperity than by spending money on building houses. The need is there waiting to be satisfied; the labour and materials are there waiting to be utilised. It will spread employment through every locality. There is no greater social and economic benefit than good houses. There is probably no greater material contribution to civilisation and a sound and healthy life which it lies within our power to make. The man who regards all this as a senseless extravagance which will impoverish the nation, as compared with doing nothing and leaving millions unemployed, should be recognised for a lunatic.

I stress housing, for this seems to me the happiest of the Administration's schemes. But it is difficult to organise quickly any one type of scheme on a sufficient scale. Meanwhile other forms of government expenditure, not so desirable in themselves, are not to be despised. Even pure relief expenditure is much better than nothing. The object must be to raise the total expenditure to a figure which is high enough to push the vast machine of American industry into renewed motion. If demand can be raised sufficiently by emergency measures, business men will find that they cannot meet it without repairs and renewals to their plant, and they will then once again take heart of grace to recover the care-free optimism without which none of us ever has the courage to live our lives as they should be lived.

Keynes's associations with the New Deal naturally left him open to journalistic attack. Normally Keynes made no reply to such comments but he made an exception on one occasion. The case was an article in *The Independent* of 5 January 1935, in which Sir Ernest Benn, warning Americans about being misled by Keynes, used as evidence of his soundness the results of the Independent Investment Company of which Keynes (together with O. T. Falk) was a director.[4] Keynes replied:

To the Editor of The Independent, *13 January 1935*

Sir,

You have done an unworthy thing in writing without knowledge of the essential facts an article which has just reached me through my press-cutting agency.

You have seen fit to write this article (1) without possessing knowledge as to how far my advice was in fact followed by the Board of the company to which you refer, of which I was not

[4] See *JMK*, vol. XII for much more on Keynes's involvement in this firm.

chairman, and which I did not control; (2) on a matter to which it is impossible for me to reply publicly because matters of no public concern may be involved; and (3) on lines which would be extremely dubious, as a method of controversy, even if you were sure of your facts. These are the methods of the gutter press.

Yours, etc.,
J. M. KEYNES

Chapter 5

THE LULL SURROUNDING THE GENERAL THEORY

Throughout the rest of 1934 and all of 1935 Keynes's activities were centred on two major projects, the completion of his *General Theory*, and the Arts Theatre, Cambridge. Not that he gave up all outside activities, for he was still involved in lecturing, bursaring for King's, his two insurance companies, the Economic Advisory Council and other areas. His published output was small, however, even if it was varied.

On his return from the United States, Keynes found the Committee on Economic Information concerned with 'the co-ordination of different agricultural and industrial considerations in formulating trade policies'. This charge from the Government was a result of the desire of the Minister of Agriculture for an extension to other foodstuffs of the 'levy-subsidy' scheme adopted for wheat in 1932, whereby British growers received a subsidy on output financed out of proceeds of a levy on imports. The Committee asked each member to write a note on the factors that should be borne in mind in writing the report. Keynes replied as follows.

MEMORANDUM

I suggest that the Memorandum for which the Prime Minister has asked should be composed of three parts.

The first part dealing with the general philosophy of long-period developments might, I think, follow the lines of paragraphs 1 to 8 of Mr Henderson's Memorandum. It is useful and important to distinguish, as he does, between the object of protecting our agriculture from disaster and maintaining it at its existing level from the object of a long-period programme of expansion which would represent an important departure from the position which we have occupied hitherto in the world economy.

The second section might deal with the criteria applicable to the immediate economic advantage or disadvantage of our agricultural policy. Here it would be useful to point out that in existing circumstances the interests of agriculture and of industry are not likely to interfere with one another, unless

1. the resources of the country are so fully engaged that an expansion in agriculture would be liable to attract resources which would otherwise be employed, probably to better advantage, in industry, or

2. the encouragement given to agriculture was having the effect of increasing rather than decreasing our adverse balance of visible trade.

There are conceivable circumstances in which one or other of these conditions might be fulfilled, but they seem quite remote at the present time. For there is no risk of industry being deprived of resources which it could otherwise employ; whilst so far most of the steps taken to assist agriculture have been calculated rather to improve than to worsen our balance of trade, thus lending assistance to all types of activity alike through repercussions.

The third section should emphasise the importance of taking care that the means adopted to attain our ends are not disproportionately expensive. This need not be a mere platitude since two cases could be cited open *prima facie* to criticism. This section might follow the lines of paragraphs 9 and 10 of Mr Henderson's memorandum. I agree with him that the technique of the wheat subsidy is much better than that of the bacon scheme. It might be well worth our while to suggest to the Government that they should seriously consider the extension of the wheat technique to beef and bacon. We might also invite them to consider whether the beet sugar subsidy is not outrageously expensive in proportion to the benefits received. Assuming that the Treasury is prepared to allocate for the benefit of agriculture the sum which the beet sugar subsidy now costs, I should have supposed that most agriculturists would agree that the sum in question, which is substantial, could be spent to much better advantage.

3 July 1934 J.M.K.

The Committee followed Keynes's and Henderson's lead in favouring an expansion of levy-subsidy schemes.

On 19 November, Keynes broadcast on the B.B.C. on the subject 'Is the Economic System Self-adjusting?' (*JMK*, vol. XIII, pp. 485–92). On hearing the broadcast and reading it as published in *The Listener* for 21 November, R. H. Brand wrote to Keynes.

From R. H. BRAND, *26 November 1934*

Dear Keynes,

I listened to and also read with very great interest your broadcast address the other night. I hope indeed you are on your way to the discovery you hope for, which will enable us all to see clearer.

If (other than your last book) there exists now any more fuller examination of the problems of demand to which you refer, I wish you would guide me to it, as obviously these are the problems which the world is going to concentrate on in the near future, in respect to which in fact it is going to try for good or ill all sorts of experiments.

I think every one must agree that there is an unsolved problem as regards demand, which has only come into prominence now that the supply problem is supposed to be solved, but which I consider enormously more difficult than the supply problem.

In addition to writing to ask you whether there exists any fuller discussion of it anywhere I would like to make a few random remarks, which occur to me on certain general aspects.

Firstly. As regards the supply problem many people, I feel, exaggerate the extent of the plenty round the corner. Has there been any thorough examination of this? I saw the other day the Brookings Institute in the United States had made some inquiry or other. It is quite clear that in the case of *many articles* an enormously greater production is possible. On the other hand it seems to me production in general must advance more or less like a line of soldiers all in step, and there may be some essential articles, which can't at any rate yet keep up quite the pace. You can't have a sort of cancerous growth of certain articles without poisoning the whole body. From a practical point of view economic advance is so much a question of dovetailing an endless number of things with one another.

Secondly. As regards demand I assume the discussion must proceed in this country on the basis that demand is free, that is that our governors do not decide what we shall consume and arrange production accordingly. Apart from the complete revolution involved by the opposite course, the control of all our foreign trade by the Government would be an enormously greater problem in this country than in Russia. Even in the case of Russia, their problem would, I think, be much more difficult if all other countries followed their example and they had not the free market the rest of the world offers them, but had to conduct their foreign trade on a barter basis between governments instead.

Thirdly. Every consumer being free, it seems to me we must accept in a very great measure the *self-adjusting* process, tempered no doubt by taxation, by whatever measure of 'planning' in various directions may be desirable.

Fourthly. I gather from your address, while you would regard greater equality of income as important, you think much more important a much greater advance in capital construction than now, stimulated by a very low rate of interest. Do you regard it as a fact that what I think the economists call the 'natural' rate of interest is now a very low one and that therefore with proper central management the rate of interest will remain low enough to encourage every form of capital expenditure? Do you think this would only be the case if we make ourselves more or less into a 'closed economy' rather than freely invest our savings anywhere we like in the world? I can see that management would be very much easier, if we were a closed system. But we cannot be and the rate of interest here depends to a very considerable extent on our international relations in general and particularly on our international lending or investment generally.

Fifthly. I presume your solution would require a control of our foreign lending. What about our foreign short borrowing, which in the short run can upset us still more? As regards foreign lending I do not think that until we have an international monetary standard there will be a great deal of it, and at any rate of the fixed-interest form. I must say that on reflection I think it is not a bad thing to force lending more into 'equity' channels. Foreign enterprise, as apart from fixed-interest investments, is very desirable and will certainly continue in moderation. But 'equity' lending may take the form again of a huge gamble in American securities. How are you going to stop that sort of thing?

Sixthly. I presume you would like to see a large amount of capital investment internally as well as externally on an equity basis, and by private investors. You may envisage a much more riskless world than we have now. But the longer I am in business the more I am convinced that much capital must always be lost by bad shots, and that the writing [off] of capital as lost as soon as it is lost is a healthy, in fact an essential, process. The worst of state and municipal capital expenditure is that this doesn't take place, except through sinking funds. Certainly not fast enough, if they take up 'risky' enterprises. The burden no doubt would be less if interest is going to be very low. But the bankruptcy or writing down process of private enterprise does clear the decks (though often not enough).

These are disjointed remarks. It is quite clear to me that enormous improvements in private enterprise are possible and necessary. But I gather your main argument really centres round the rate of interest and it is on this that I should like very much to see your arguments more fully developed.

Yours sincerely,
R. H. BRAND

To R. H. BRAND, *29 November 1934*

Dear Brand,

I am afraid there is nothing which I can yet refer you to which deals with the problem of demand along my lines. I am working hard at my new book, but it may be nearly another twelve months before it comes out. When it appears, it will be on extremely academic lines; since I feel, rather definitely, that my object must first of all be to try and convince my economic colleagues. I have, indeed, succeeded in convincing those at Cambridge whom I have seriously tack[l]ed with them so far. If I prove right, a good many fundamental matters of theory will be seen in rather a new light.

As to your six questions:

1. It is quite possible that many people exaggerate the extent of the plenty round the corner. I know of no thorough examination of the problem. A good deal depends on what period one has in view. From a short-period point of view I should doubt if the real income of the community could be increased by more than, say, 10 per cent. But, if time is given for the diversion of resources and for the rate of accumulation of capital which would take place in optimum conditions, I

should put the figure a good deal higher. Certainly 20 per cent, perhaps 50 per cent, but not 100 per cent. Moreover there would be a great difference between the benefits accruing to those people who were prepared to enjoy their income in the shape of the consumption of material goods and the benefits of those who, as they became richer, would want more services. I should say that there might be a very great increase of the physical income of the former, quite disproportionate to anything to which the latter could look forward. But when one is talking about poverty and plenty one is thinking primarily of the former group of consumers.

2. I agree with you in assuming that demand will be free in the sense that consumers will themselves decide how to spend their incomes. The sort of management I have in view would not interfere with this, nor indeed would it interfere with the great bulk of private enterprise. Apart from taxation, it would interfere very little with the working of the economic system except in so far as it was necessary to control deliberately the volume of investment;—subject to the reserve that the taxation or its equivalent might be deliberately aimed at discouraging saving.

3. It follows that, apart from taxation and the planning of the scale of investment, the self-adjusting process would be left pretty free play, so far as I am concerned.

4. So long as there is serious all-round unemployment I consider this proves that the equilibrium rate of interest is lower than the ruling rate. How low we should have to go to reach equilibrium one cannot tell except by experiment. I should agree that the figure would not be so low if we were not making ourselves into a closed economy. I have no objection to foreign investment in this context, provided it does not have the effect of raising the market rate of interest owing to the difficulties of transfer which it raises. That is to say, I have no objection to the equilibrium rate of interest being raised by foreign investment. But I do object to the possibility of difficulties of transfer

attendant on foreign investment having the effect of raising the market rate of interest above the equilibrium rate.

5. What I have said under 4 really answers this. I should require a control of foreign lending not because I objected to it in itself, but because of the attendant risk of transfer difficulties which would upset our internal equilibrium.

6. There are two kinds of risks, the risk to the private investor and the risk to society as a whole. The world is perhaps becoming one in which the divergence between the two is increasing. Investment which may involve but little risk to the community as a whole may mean considerable risk to the individual who undertakes it. For this reason, without disagreeing much from what you say in 6, I look forward to the likelihood of increased investment through public institutions. I agree as to the importance of writing off losses. But so far as experience goes, I should say that public authorities in this country have tended to set up excessive sinking funds rather than otherwise.

You are quite right in thinking that my main argument centres round the rate of interest. And I cannot help being rather obscure and perplexing until I am in a position to set my views about this clearly before the world,—which, as I have said above, I hope to do at no very distant date.

Ever yours sincerely,
[copy initialled] J.M.K.

Keynes also discussed the notions underlying his approach to economic policy with Susan Lawrence, a former Labour M.P. The discussion began in person, but continued by letter.

From SUSAN LAWRENCE, *January 1935*

Dear Mr Keynes,

I have been thinking over our conversation.

It seems to me to come down to this. Are 'the measures which public opinion is ready for' sufficient to restore prosperity—prosperity that is of a moderate pre-war standard?

If so your policy would seem to be right.

But if not,—if present public opinion is wrong, if 'the Country is not ready' for sufficiently drastic remedies—then is not the intelligent course to go on telling them what they really need, until they are ready to take the medicine?

Now on one thing I am pretty clear. 'Public opinion' now isn't really any guide for a serious politician. It is in a very confused & fluctuating state: it may change very quickly after a little more education by experience: it is in the state which precedes a decision: the ordinary man is waiting to see which way the cat will jump: when it jumps he will jump too.

So that we come back to the tremendous objective question: could you, with a 'liberal' policy deliver the goods?

The risk is truly frightful either way the decision is taken; for if the Labour Party tries a reformist policy again & *fails*—it is dead & damned—& the man of discontent is left without a leader, & without a policy, a mere helpless prey to any adventurer.

Now I have put all this down to explain what I meant—& rather to clear myself from your suggestion that I 'wanted a catastrophe', for to think a catastrophe is possible or even probable is a different thing from 'wanting' it!

Sincerely yours,
SUSAN LAWRENCE

To SUSAN LAWRENCE, *15 January 1935*

Dear Miss Lawrence,

It is very possible that I am biased by my intense desire to gain time. I am convinced that if extreme things are done in the near future, either by the Right or by the Left, they are almost certain to be ill-conceived. I am hopeful that ten years hence there will be a much greater chance of wisdom.

Meanwhile it appears to me that there are many matters of great, though in a sense secondary, importance to occupy us, obviously worth doing for their own sakes and thoroughly acceptable to all that is sound and strong in contemporary opinion.

You may very well be right that these sort of measures will be far from sufficient to maintain steady prosperity. My point is, you see, that those measures which will, in my opinion, restore steady prosperity are measures for which no-one is prepared and which have not been sufficiently thought out.

Thus, in my sense, my 'liberal' policy is a stop-gap policy. I find it hard to judge whether my ultimate policy would strike the ordinary person as violently drastic or evolutionary. For, what I am primarily interested in supplying is a sound and scientific way of thinking about our essential problems. Before this way of thinking can be translated into practice, it has to be mixed with politics and passions just like any other way of thinking, and the nature of the outcome is something which I cannot foresee in detail.

Probably it is best of all that for the next few years the existing Government should gradually drift into a reformist policy. But it would be much better for the Labour Party to try a reformist policy than to try a revolutionary policy which was silly and unpractical and had but little conviction and no real steam behind it.

Yours ever,
[copy initialled] J.M.K.

From SUSAN LAWRENCE, *January 1935*

Dear Mr Keynes,

Thank you for your letter. I too enjoyed the evening more than I can say.

Your first sentences are terribly true—if I were a Christian I should clearly recognise that the Beast had come as prophesied and was in the Saar.[1]

Sincerely yours,
SUSAN LAWRENCE

[1] The results of the Saar Plebiscite were announced on 15 January. Over 90 per cent of those voting had favoured a return of this area to Germany.

On 20 February 1935, at the annual meeting of the National Mutual, Keynes, in the course of his speech, continued the campaign for cheaper money which he had started at the meeting of the year before.

CONFLICTING FORCES

A year ago I gave reasons for expecting a further fall in the long-term rate of interest. Since then Government securities definitely redeemable within 25 years have fallen to a yield well below the level of $2\frac{1}{2}$ per cent, which then seemed to me to be within sight, while the yield on longer-dated securities or securities with no fixed date of redemption is now below 3 per cent. Today, however, the prospects are by no means so clear, for we are now, in my judgement, between two sets of strong conflicting forces.

On the one hand, the evidence indicates that the maintenance of the national prosperity and the improvement of employment still require a lower rate of interest than we have yet enjoyed. So far from falling rates of interest having proved excessively stimulating to new enterprise, it has been disappointing to notice how comparatively few large-scale opportunities for the investment of new savings have as yet disclosed themselves under the influence of the low rate of interest, though we must not underestimate the predominant part which new building and new electrical developments, both of them relatively sensitive to the rate of interest, have had in bringing us such measure of prosperity as we have attained. I am, therefore, confirmed in the opinion that we shall require, for our economic health, a rate of interest gradually falling to levels much lower than we have known in the past, whereas the present reduced rates are even now no lower than those which often prevailed in pre-war days.

But, on the other hand, there are serious obstacles in the way of an immediate further reduction. British rates of interest have already fallen much below those which rule elsewhere. At present our domestic rates are protected by the extreme lack of confidence in the economic position of foreign countries. We must hope that a revival of confidence elsewhere will be accompanied by a fall in their interest rates towards a normal parity with our own levels. But meanwhile the existing disparity of rates may make our own position slightly precarious. Far more important than this, however—for I do not expect an early return to anything which one could call an international rate of interest—is the attitude of British institutional investors to the future of the rate of interest. The current long-term rate of interest is a highly psychological phenomenon which must necessarily depend on what expectations we hold concerning the future rate of interest. In the mind of the typical professional investor today the current return does not offer much of a premium against the possibility of a turn in the tide. Investors are watching more anxiously for a change than they would if the position was considered stable.

A difficult task

Thus the task of maintaining a rate of interest sufficiently low to be compatible with national prosperity and good employment is likely to present increasing difficulty. Indeed, one may feel some doubt whether it is capable of solution by 'normal' traditional methods in an industrially advanced community, which is, for various reasons, no longer in a position to invest large sums abroad and of which the population is no longer advancing rapidly.

I would suggest, however, that, for the moment, the wisest course on the part of those in authority is to consolidate the position which has been won, rather than to aim at an immediate further advance. Fixed-interest securities outside the class of British Government securities and the like have not yet fully adjusted themselves to the price of the latter, as the Institute of Actuaries' Index clearly shows: while there are other important rates of interest, in particular mortgage interest, the terms on which building societies lend and borrow, and the rates charged by the banks, which have lagged much further behind. For the encouragement of enterprise a fall in these rates is more important than a further decline in the yield on Government securities.

Moreover, a rate of interest must persist for some time before it has its full effect on business decisions which involve a new technical programme only made possible by the fall in the rate. I feel not less strongly than before the importance of a declining long-term rate of interest, but a greater degree of confidence than now exists in the maintenance of the rates of interest we already have at a level not above their present figure is our most pressing need.

Suggestion to the Treasury

There is, I suggest, an important contribution to this object which it lies within the power of the Treasury to make—namely, that they should themselves show confidence in the expectation of a declining rate of interest in the future. Advice is often offered them on the lines that the present is a golden opportunity for trapping the investor, so to speak, into lending to them for an indefinite period on terms which he will subsequently regret. This advice seems to be based, like most advice, on the extremely improbable assumption that the future will resemble the past. But in any case it is bad advice, for the major purpose of the Treasury should be to establish stable conditions with a gradually declining rate over a long period of years ahead, a necessary condition of which is the creation of a reasonable expectation that this is, in fact, the probable course of events.

To act along these lines will not only increase confidence, but is likely to be profitable to the Treasury and to the taxpayer. I would urge, therefore, that, in future funding or refunding schemes, securities should be offered having fixed terms of redemption well spread over dates from five to 25 years hence.

Local loans are particularly well suited to this treatment, since the bulk of the money advanced by the Fund will be repaid to it at dates already fixed within this period.

This policy has everything to recommend it. The Treasury will borrow more cheaply; they will help the psychology of the market by themselves showing confidence in the maintenance of low rates of interest, and they will improve the structure and stability of the banking system by supplying a type of security suitable to institutions which are themselves borrowing the bulk of their funds on short terms. The present position, in which the greater part of the available supply of Government securities is in the form either of three month Treasury bills or of securities having no fixed date of redemption within the next 50 years, is technically very defective.

An essential factor

I would emphasise the fact that there is no reliable way of establishing a low long-term rate of interest except by fostering a reasonable expectation that the rate of interest will continue low in the future, and by offering fixed dates of redemption to those who, rightly or wrongly, remain doubtful; but, if the Treasury themselves pursue a policy which implies a belief that the current rates of interest are abnormally low, they cannot expect institutions and the public to feel that degree of confidence which is essential to further progress.

On receiving a copy of *New Frontiers* by Henry Wallace, the American Secretary of Agriculture, he touched on matters similar to those he had raised with Susan Lawrence.

To HENRY A. WALLACE, *28 March 1935*

Dear Mr Wallace,

I have to thank you for sending me late last autumn *New Frontiers*. You must forgive me for not acknowledging it before now. But I wanted first of all to read it, and did not find leisure to do so until the present vacation.

I have found it a delightful and most sympathetic work,—more like good conversation than a book, perhaps, but if a Minister in office had spent the time that is necessary to transform the conversation into a treatise, he would have been badly neglecting the duties which had a prior claim on him! You have succeeded most admirably in conveying to the reader your point of view;—your perplexities as well as your convictions and your general line.

As Secretary for Agriculture, you are naturally primarily concerned with securing a shift out of an industry which has clearly been, from the long period point of view, somewhat overextended. But behind the problem of accomplishing such shifts as this lies the question of demand as a whole. My own view is that we shall have a continued difficulty in a wealthy modern community, such as the United States or Great Britain, in solving the problems which arise out of deficient effective demand as a whole. If and when we can solve this problem, we may find that the shifts will occur much more easily than we now think. Resources tend to remain where they are obviously *not* wanted, because there is no direction in which they obviously *are* wanted. But if demand as a whole is adequate, the shifts may take place with astonishing ease.

The momentary position on your side looks very discouraging. But I am not sufficiently in touch to feel that I understand it. I am not clear how important a part is being played by time lags which time itself will overcome, and how far the explanation is to be found in the failure of the Administration to spend anywhere near up to its programme; or how far the difficulties are more fundamental.

If the difficulties in the way of governmentally inspired investment and other forms of loan expenditure prove insuperable, then it would seem certain that it is only a question of months before the demand for more direct methods of augmenting purchasing power becomes too strong to be resisted. It would seem clear that there is no turning back for your Administration. It would be a ground of grave disappointment and, perhaps, severe criticism if the obstacles in the way of wise capital expenditure do prove insuperable. But if, in fact, they are not overcome, then it would seem to me, observing from a distance, that the more direct methods I have hinted at above will undoubtedly be adopted.

Forgive me for venturing so many remarks on matters where my knowledge is necessarily defective.

Yours very truly,
[copy initialled] J.M.K.

July brought another comment of a similar sort when Sir Arthur Salter asked Keynes whether, on reading the document, he would be prepared to join the approximately 150 signatories from all parties to the preface of *The Next Five Years*,[2] the product of a study group which had met over the previous year. The first part of the book concerned economic policy and recommended more planning, a programme of national development, more public involvement in the affairs of the Bank of England, greater public control and regulation of the financial system, agricultural development and social reform. On reading the report Keynes replied.

To SIR ARTHUR SALTER, *10 July 1935*

My dear Salter,

I have just finished reading *The Next Five Years*. I think it excellently done and I am naturally in sympathy with nearly all of it. Indeed I recognise its origins in a good many cases in previous publications with which I was concerned. I think the practical proposals nearly all excellent and a government or a party which adopted this volume as its programme would have my enthusiastic support.

All the same, I think I would rather not sign the foreword.

[2] (London, 1935.)

I am always a very reluctant signer of collective documents with which I have not been closely concerned. But, apart from that, I feel that my own state of mind at this moment, whatever it may have been three or four years ago, is rather materially different from that of the compilers. My own belief today is that neither the real remedy nor the power of persuading people to adopt it will come except from a more fundamental diagnosis of the underlying situation and a wide-spread understanding of this diagnosis and conviction of its correctness. Now, a fundamental diagnosis is just what this document, perhaps quite wisely, entirely avoids; and where one catches a glimpse, by inference, of what the underlying theory of the authors probably is, I find myself much more conscious of differences of opinion than in the matter of the practical proposals.

Taking a broad and long view of the situation, my present conclusion is: first, that there is no room for a programme intermediate between that of Mr Baldwin and Sir Stafford Cripps, except on the basis of a new underlying economic theory and philosophy of the state; secondly, that such a new outlook is required if we are to avoid extremism during the next slump or two; and, thirdly, that the best way of occupying one's time is to busy oneself with forwarding a new understanding of the problem. Meanwhile I want Mr Baldwin to be as reasonable and progressive as his supporters and his own nature allow. I think your book may be very useful in exerting an influence in the right direction. But, whilst I thought that the proposal and the sort of ideas which your book contains was my job two years ago, and I daresay it was, I now consider my job is rather different. To me, though I daresay not to anyone else, the affixing of my signature to a foreword, would, therefore, be an inner inconsistency and perhaps a justifiable cause of misunderstanding.

Yours ever,
[copy initialled] J.M.K.

In July Keynes was also involved in international affairs, for from 11 to 13 July, accompanied by Lydia, he attended a meeting of economists sponsored by the Antwerp Chamber of Commerce to discuss international monetary matters.

Originally Keynes had thought that he would be unable to attend for, as he put it to Alick Le Jeune, one of the organisers, on 10 January:

> I am sorry to be so tiresome about the matter. The truth is I am bending all my efforts to finish my forthcoming book in time for publication in the autumn, and I am reluctant to engage myself to anything which may interfere with that. When once this monster is out of my way I shall be a reasonable being again.

However, he did join R. F. Harrod, Hubert Henderson, Bertil Ohlin, Bertrand Nogaro and a collection of Belgian and Dutch economists in refining a draft report, prepared by Ohlin, designed to allow the gold bloc countries to follow Belgium's example and devalue successfully, as well as join a world of fixed but adjustable exchange rates.

During the meeting, if we are to believe the published proceedings, Keynes's comments were limited to interventions on detailed technical points of drafting and introducing the reports at the final session. However, some rough notes outlining his views survive.

Belgian example great impression on world
Calmness, moderation and skill of Belgian transition
Not surprising
Currency changes much easier than usually supposed
Indian example
Effect on gold bloc
Stupid and obstinate old gentleman at Banks of Netherlands and France crucifying their countries in a struggle which is certain to prove futile

International currency largely a practical question though certain theoretical conditions must be satisfied
Therefore actual character of opinion important
In view of variety of opinions and of national banking provisions no reason for rigid uniformity
I therefore believe it to be an illusion that the international system of the future must necessarily be a *uniform* one

For example, it is quite likely that it is right for the French franc to be rigidly fixed in terms of gold—though at a devalued level; right for Belgium and U.S.A. to have a value in gold between fairly wide determinate limits and right for the sterling bloc to maintain a relationship to gold less rigidly defined.
I consider that progress lies not in uniformity but in *starting* at right parities and reasonable declarations of policy for future
It is *not* necessary that these declarations should all be in identical terms

Position of U.K.
Remarkable transition in opinion in last year or two towards unanimity—obscured from foreign opinion by lipservice of leading bankers
Refusal to use instrument of Bank rate for external purposes
C[hancellor] of [the] E[xchequer], Treasury, bankers, industry, economists, ?B[ank] of E[ngland]
Bank rate policy on pre-war lines utterly discredited in years before 1931
How it operates
Effect on long-term rate of interest
Lamont's experience
Corollary of this that we must be free from time to time to use foreign exchange fluctuations for purposes of adjustment
Reinforced if scope of international lending to be greatly reduced in future
Thus the international system we envisage
  No rigid uniformity
  Arbitrary changes of parity ruled out
  Changes of parity of competitive exchange depreciation type ruled out
But room left for moderate changes from time to time in *both* directions which are called for to adjust the balance of payments
Such changes of parity will take place of changes in Bank rate
But they will only occur to restore international equilibrium

Questions of doubt
 Should permissible occasions of change be precisely defined (Salter)
 Should there be a maximum limit to permissible changes
 Or should we feel our way without rigid rules from day to day
Last-named policy of B of E and Treasury
Justified in view of risks of Gold Bloc, U.S.A., Germany
What is important for international trade is that every country should be relieved of exchange anxiety
This will allow internal expansion
 moderate tariffs
 abolition of exchange restrictions
 abolition of quotas
Fixed parities *not* the best way of removing anxiety

His closing session speech ran as follows:

From Report of Proceedings of the Meeting of Economists, Antwerp, 11–13 July 1935

Ladies and Gentlemen,

In the first place, it is my honourable duty to thank you, Mr President, and the Antwerp Chamber of Commerce for their happy idea in assembling this conference, for your most kind and abundant hospitality and for the great efficiency and helpfulness of your Secrétariat.

It is an appropriate thing that this conference of Belgian and foreign economists should have been summoned in Antwerp. It is the natural and historic rôle of this ancient merchant city to take the lead in any measures which may serve to rehabilitate the shattered fabric of world trade. But it is also an advantage that Belgium has occupied a middle position in the controversy concerning the foreign exchanges and that although you have recently felt yourselves forced to change your policy, your eminent statesmen and economists are still narrowly divided on the merits of the issue. Thus, there could be no more impartial meeting place than Antwerp for an international debate on these important matters.

We have not succeeded in reaching complete unanimity, but that was scarcely to be expected and we should, I think, have been much less useful in our labours if we had endeavoured to obscure or cover up important differences of opinion sincerely held. Too many international conferences have been rendered futile, in my opinion, by producing colourless or equivocal reports intended to combine essentially divergent views.

We are therefore presenting to you three distinct documents. The first and longest has received the support, subject to certain reserves on detailed points, of the great majority of the members of the conference.

The declaration of Mr Nogaro has also received the general sympathy of the majority though their own recommendations express their exact opinions which go beyond Mr Nogaro's conclusions.

The four economists, whose declaration is headed by Mr Ansiaux, also favour concerted measures towards exchange stabilisation and are in accord with the latter part of our recommendations relating to restrictions to international trade; but they consider that stabilisation of the dollar and the pound sterling is a necessary first step.

As regards the text of the majority, it is already before you. It constitutes a far-reaching proposal for the reform and reorganisation of international economic relations.

We have been at pains to avoid recommendations which would be merely academic and where there can be little hope of applying them in the real world. We believe that our recommendations are capable of being put into force immediately if we could persuade the world's statesmen of their wisdom.

As you have heard, the earlier paragraphs deal with the kind and measure of stabilisation which we favour, the prior conditions of its possibility and the technical means of achieving it;

but we explain in the tenth clause that we regard measures to safeguard exchanges not as an end in themselves, but as a basis for an economic policy, by each country separately, of a kind which can lead to a general world recovery.

In our concluding paragraphs, in respect of which, as you have heard, there is a more complete measure of unanimity obtained than in the case of the earlier paragraphs, we pass to the measures which might be adopted towards creating a greater freedom of trade. Some of the tariffs and other restrictions on trade which now exist are the reflection of deliberate national policies. We have regarded these as outside of our purview; but there also are many restrictions, especially those affecting exchange transactions, which no country favours for their own sake. These are not the expression of deliberate national policies, but merely the reflection of the fears and overwhelming practical difficulties of an abnormal period.

If we contribute in the least degree to the development of a sound public opinion on these vital matters and a better technical understanding of the means to secure an improvement, our labours will not have been wasted.

I thank you once again, Mr President, for your hospitality and your extremely efficient, courteous and conciliatory conduct of our proceedings.

Keynes expanded on his views at Antwerp for Lloyds Bank in the autumn.

From Lloyds Bank Monthly Review, *October 1935*

THE FUTURE OF THE FOREIGN EXCHANGES

The problem of the foreign exchanges has been thoroughly discussed both in the pages of this Review and elsewhere during the last ten years, and the main issues involved are more familiar than they were. In this country, though not abroad, the result has been, I think, to bring about a much greater measure of general agreement than existed in 1925. Opinion is, of course, far from unanimous. But it is true today, as it was not true until recently, that there is a body of tentative conclusions which can be fairly described as the British point of view, a point of view shared by many bankers, businessmen, politicians, civil servants and economists. In what follows I shall probably go, at least in details, beyond what can be claimed as agreed ground. But I believe that the general point of view, from which I endeavour to analyse this problem, is one which in this country today is widely spread.

I

The first condition, which must be satisfied before it is worth while to discuss permanent policy, is that the *de facto* rates of exchange, from which we start out, should be in reasonable equilibrium. It is not necessary to be very precise about this. No one now puts faith in the famous 'purchasing-power-parity' theory of the foreign exchanges, based on index numbers. We have to consider, on the one hand, a country's balance of payments on income account on the basis of the existing natural resources, equipment, technique and costs (especially wage costs) at home and abroad, a normal level of employment, and those tariffs, etc., which are a permanent feature of national policies; and, on the other hand, the probable readiness and ability of the country in question to borrow or lend abroad on long term (or, perhaps, repay or accept repayment of old loans), on the average of the next few years. A set of rates of exchange, which can be established without undue strain on either side and without large movements of gold (on a balance of transactions), will satisfy our condition of equilibrium. This does not mean that a set of rates can be found which can be relied on to persist indefinitely without strain. It will be sufficient if a set can be found which the various central banks can accept without serious anxiety for the time being, provided that there is no substantial change in the underlying conditions. Not only must such a set of rates be discoverable by impartial persons, but they must be acceptable to the central banks. If each central bank insists on being on the safe side, no accommodation is possible; for what is the safe side for one bank is the unsafe side for all the others. It is improbable that the initial set of rates could be settled, right off, at a conference, which in present circumstances would merely offer an exhibition of horse-dealing without any horse changing hands. It will have to be reached, in the first instance, by a process of trial and error, conducted in good faith but without prior undertakings. The test of success will be found in the voluntary removal of all those exchange restrictions, import quotas, exceptional tariffs, etc., which are not desired for their own sake as a permanent feature of national policy, but are acts of desperation and an expression of the extreme anxiety of the authorities, either to make both ends meet, or to alleviate the unemployment inflicted by deflation.

Now the commencement of this experimental period is at present delayed by the policy of the gold bloc taken in conjunction with the policy of the United States. For it is certain that the existing rates of exchange overvalue the gold bloc currencies in relation to the dollar; with the result that there is no conceivable policy on the part of the sterling bloc which will establish equilibrium with both. Thus the experimental period cannot even begin until the gold bloc have either changed the gold value of their currencies or have successfully remedied the disequilibrium by other methods. The latter solution is, I suppose, not inconceivable; for example, a decree effectively reducing all money wages by an appropriate percentage might achieve it. But it is very improbable. Moreover the measures which the gold bloc are now adopting, whilst extremely drastic, are based on a false theory inasmuch as they attack everything except wages. These countries seem to be engaged at present in scourging themselves until their situation has become so obviously intolerable that, when the common-sense remedy of altering the gold value of their currencies is finally adopted, no one can be blamed.

Let us, however, assume that the remedy has been adopted, and that the experimental period has lasted long enough for the exchange rates to shake down to levels which can be maintained for the time being without excessive strain on anyone. The test of this will be found, as I have said, in the voluntary removal of those obstacles to the movement of goods and money which are the expression of extreme anxiety and not of deliberate policy. When this stage has been reached, two problems will still require solution: (1) the method of how best to avoid short-term fluctuations, and (2) the question of how to handle a persistent disequilibrium if and when it occurs.

II

By short-term fluctuations I mean such as are due, for example, to seasonal influences, to foreign lending not synchronising precisely with the balance of trade out of which it will be ultimately financed, or to temporary movements of short-term funds under the influence of divergent discount rates at home and abroad.

The first condition of avoiding fluctuations of the exchange, due to such influences as these, is that each central bank should possess a sufficiency of free gold in relation to its economic importance, which it can release without anxiety. The aggregate stocks of gold today are much more than is required for this purpose. But unfortunately their distribution is more unequal than ever before, the recent report of the Bank for International Settlements having shown that, in spite of the huge increase in the aggregate stocks of gold, the great majority of central banks lost gold on balance even in 1934. Clearly, however, the provision of funds for this limited purpose is a suitable object for international collaboration by central banks acting through the B.I.S. No vast sum would be required, if there was a pooling device by which sums drawn by one bank out of its credit with the B.I.S. Equalisation Fund would not be removable by the recipient bank but would have to remain to the credit of this bank with the B.I.S. Fund; but the initial resources of the B.I.S. Equalisation Fund must, of course, be provided by the central banks which possess the bulk of the world's gold. This device, the general character of which is sufficiently indicated in the preceding sentence, is not intended to deal with the contingency of a steady drain and would be quite inappropriate for such a purpose.

Assuming that every central bank is thus supplied with a suitable initial fund, I suggest that the following technical devices would complete the armoury of control for ironing-out those fluctuations which were not due to a deep-seated disequilibrium:—

(1) A moderately wide gap between the gold points. The technique of the British Equalisation Fund has shown how fluctuations within a moderate range can be employed to engage the forces of the market on the side of stabilisation. The gap must be just sufficient for it to be profitable for those to postpone remittances who are in a position to do so, until the exchange has swung back to a more advantageous figure, and for those who have remittances to make in the opposite direction, to anticipate them.

(2) Dealings by central banks (or their equalisation funds) in the forward as well as in the spot exchanges. The great technical advantage of this device, which was recommended a long time ago by the Genoa Conference, has never been properly realised; perhaps because an instinctive understanding of the forward exchanges is rare even amongst bankers. Fluctuations in the premium (or discount) on forward transactions quoted by the central banks would make it possible to have an effective bank rate for foreign transactions different from the effective rate of domestic transactions. Occasions often arise when the short-term rates of interest appropriate to the domestic position have

become inappropriate to the foreign position, placing the central bank in a dilemma as to what its bank rate policy ought to be. But by offering to sell its currency forward at an appropriate discount of its spot value (or to buy it at a premium over the spot rate), a central bank can make its short-term interest rates to an actual or potential holder of foreign funds exactly what it chooses, without ever changing the rates chargeable to domestic borrowers. This is, moreover, a specially suitable matter for quiet collaboration between the central banks. The reluctance of the central banks to operate on the forward market may be partly due to their habitual exaggeration (sometimes in search of an alibi for responsibility) of the influence of speculation. The fear of facilitating speculation might, indeed, be a sound reason against using this method to resist the effects of a deep-seated disequilibrium. But it is not for the purpose of postponing the inevitable that I am suggesting it.

(3) The adoption of Prof. Sprague's proposal that the holding of stocks of gold should be the monopoly of the central banks, the only permissible transactions in stocks of this metal being from the mines to the central banks and from one central bank to another. This is already the position in the United States, and the existing regulations in Great Britain are halfway towards it.

(4) A strict, though not pedantic, control of the rate of new foreign lending, so as to avoid a strain arising out of a serious disproportion between such lending and the accruing foreign balance on income account. Only by this means can we retain a sufficient autonomy over the domestic rate of interest. I do not support the criticisms of the manner in which the Bank of England and the Treasury have actually conducted this control in recent years, in spite of one or two cases of apparent pedantry. They are developing a method which should be a permanent feature of our economy. Circumstances may well arise in future when that control may have to become stricter, if we accept a very low domestic rate of interest as the only means of preserving full employment in a wealthy community.

The reader should notice that I have expressly excluded from my devices changes in Bank rate and in the volume of domestic credit, which were the main instruments of pre-war policy. It is the outstanding lesson of our post-war experience that these methods must be entirely discarded as a means of regulating the exchanges. They required for their success certain special conditions which no longer obtain, and may have been responsible even in pre-war days for much damage. It is essential that they should be employed in future with exclusive regard to internal conditions and, in particular, the state of employment.

I believe, nevertheless, that the above technique can furnish us with a *de facto* stability of the exchanges within a sufficiently narrow range, which can be maintained in all ordinary circumstances and, perhaps, for many years together. But we are now brought to the crux of our problem. Would it be wise and prudent to enter into a permanent undertaking never to allow the gold value of our money to move outside the narrow range which we have so far contemplated?

III

It is evident that the day may come when there will again arise a disequilibrium of the exchanges too violent or too deep-seated to be handled by the above methods. This might occur for internal reasons which were, in a sense, our own fault; such as a rise of money wages not offset by increased efficiency, or a lack of political confidence on the part of the rich inducing them to remove their wealth abroad, or the fear of war. On the other hand it might be due to some external cause lying outside our control which disturbed seriously, and perhaps permanently, the terms of our trade with the outside world and the general current of our international transactions. Are we prepared to pledge ourselves in such circumstances to use all the other weapons open to us, however economically or politically injurious, rather than modify the gold parity of our currency?

Assuredly we are not. Very few today are prepared to contemplate such a course; and even they might hesitate to urge us to give a pledge which we should probably break when the strain came. When the Council of the B.I.S. contemplate (as in their last report) a return to a régime of fixed gold parities, they are living in an unreal world, a fool's world.

Let us consider the mildest and most likely of the possible contingencies—the gradual development of relative levels of gold costs of production at home and abroad which require for equilibrium a change in the gold value of our money. In such a case, whether it be our own fault or due to the action of some foreign country (or is merely the cumulative result of complex causes), there is no possible remedy except to modify the exchanges or to force a change in the level of wages. Yet it would be the height of political, as well as of economic, unwisdom for a central bank to fight the level of wages by the instrument of bank rate and the curtailment of credit. Perhaps I may recall a short dialogue between myself and Mr Montagu Norman before the Macmillan Committee:

MR J. M. KEYNES: What I thought was the more or less accepted theory of the Bank rate was that it works in two ways. It has the effect on the international situation that has been described today, and its virtue really is in its also having an important effect on the internal situation. The method of its operation on the internal situation is that the higher Bank rate would mean curtailment of credit, that the curtailment of credit would diminish enterprise and cause unemployment, and that unemployment would tend to bring down wages and costs of production generally...

MR MONTAGU NORMAN: *I should imagine that, as you have stated it, that is the orthodox theory, taking a long view, and as such, I should subscribe to it—I could not dispute it with you.*

It is realised today, as it was not realised formerly, that the instrument of Bank rate and credit contraction can only be successful as a means of remedying a fundamental international maladjustment, so far as it diminishes employment and, if the unemployment thus caused is sufficiently intense and prolonged, eventually forces a reduction of money wages. As a result of this better understanding of its *modus operandi*, I do not believe that it will ever be used again for this purpose. Yet, unless wages are to be determined by decree, it is to this that we should commit ourselves in accepting a fixed parity for sterling in terms of gold.

We can, and should, commit ourselves—(i) to maintain short-term stability within a certain range; (ii) not to resort to devaluation merely to obtain competitive advantages in foreign trade in conditions where we are under no special strain; and (iii) to submit to some test as to the severity of the strain we were suffering before departing outside the agreed short-term range (though I am a little distrustful of a cut-and-dried formula). But we must retain an ultimate discretion to do whatever is required to relieve either a sudden and severe or a gradual and continuing strain, without laying ourselves open to any kind of reproach.

With good faith and genuine collaboration between central banks rigidly fixed parities are not necessary for international trade; without such conditions they are not only dangerous, but entirely unreliable. We shall get better collaboration if we do not put too great a strain upon it and allow to the collaborators an ultimate individual discretion.

I have assumed throughout that gold will remain the basis of international exchange, in the sense that central banks will continue to hold their reserves in gold and to settle balances with other central banks by the shipment of gold. The only alternatives would be sterling or some kind of B.I.S. bank money; but neither of these is practicable today as the basis of a world system.

One matter may be mentioned in conclusion. The management of the British Exchange Equalisation Fund has been, by common consent, extremely successful. It has, moreover, constituted an important experiment in exchange management on a fluctuating parity which has added to our knowledge of exchange technique and has greatly increased confidence in the likelihood of exchange management proving successful as a permanent policy. It is open, however, to one important criticism, namely, in regard to the secrecy maintained as to the nature and magnitude of its transactions. I am sure that this secrecy is a grave mistake. It is an extraordinary and unwholesome breach with tradition that this country should conceal the magnitude of its gold reserves and the movement of gold into and out of them. Imagine the results of this practice being generally adopted by central banks, until the location of the world's gold could be only vaguely conjectured. The movements of gold into and out of a country's reserves are an economic indicator of the first importance. We might as well suppress the trade returns or the figures of national income and expenditure. If the gold movements are concealed, the advantages of well-informed discussion are forgone; and even amongst those who are responsible for making decisions all but one or two are deprived of a vitally important *datum*, and are left to depend on guesswork. If speculation is made the excuse, it is upon mysteries and mystifications, half-eludicated by gossip and rumour, that speculation feeds. As the current report of the B.I.S. points out, the secrecy of the British Equalisation Fund makes hay of the international gold and currency statistics. But above all it leads to world-wide suspicion of our methods and motives, which is, I believe, quite unfounded and would be quickly dispelled by publicity. The Equalisation Fund is believed abroad to be our instrument for all kinds of subtle and self-seeking policies. Such suspicions, even though they are unfounded, are well deserved. No sound international exchange policy can be built up on secrecy and the concealment of matters which are of common concern.

In the autumn, with the threat of Italian aggression in Abyssinia, Keynes turned to the question of economic sanctions.

From The New Statesman and Nation, *28 September 1935*

ECONOMIC SANCTIONS

There is a widespread belief, prevailing in quarters otherwise differing in outlook, that any sanctions against Italy, which are capable of producing a significant effect, must be tantamount to war. Mr Garvin wrote in last Sunday's *Observer* that 'European War and World War would both inevitably follow from Britain's active intervention by forcible sanctions against another Great Power'. In the pamphlet *Abyssinia*, published by *The New Statesman and Nation*, it is said that: 'We are almost certainly on the eve of a war in which this country will have to take part.' There is an ambiguity in Mr Garvin's 'forcible' sanctions, which may be intended to exclude 'economic' sanctions. However this may be, I would urge that at the present stage we are, or at least ought to be, a long way off considering any action which could be construed as 'forcible' in the sense of 'partaking of the nature of an act of war'. For I believe that the efficacy of comparatively mild 'economic' sanctions is being greatly underestimated.

If Italy proceeds to an act of aggression, the economic sanctions to be imposed on the authority and the advice of the League should, I suggest, be limited to the two outlined below. Only in the event of Italy proving so insane as to treat these sanctions as if they were an act of war and herself take warlike action against the League powers should we, on our part, contemplate further measures.

In the first place, the League powers should impose what is technically called, I believe, the 'municipal' sanction of prohibiting commercial and financial transactions with Italy on the part of their own nationals. No attempt should be made to blockade Italy or to prevent her trading with the nationals of those powers which do not choose to join in the municipal sanction. Over a period of months, it will, in the special circumstances of Italy, be more injurious for her to be cut off from some of her principal customers than to be deprived of all sources of potential supply.

In the second place, the League powers, or some of them at least, including ourselves, should forthwith ratify the draft Protocol of Financial Assistance, already approved in principle by the Assembly of the League and deposited at Geneva awaiting ratification. This document provides an admirably drafted cut-and-dried scheme for a guaranteed League loan to be offered to the aggrieved party in the dispute. It is not essential that it should be ratified by all the League powers, provided some few of them participate. It is doubtful whether this Protocol would have been effective in the event of a dispute between great powers. But Abyssinia offers an almost ideal opportunity for its application. The loan to Abyssina of such a sum as (say) £10,000,000 in the first instance, coupled, of course, with a removal of embargoes on the export of arms, should be sufficient to put quite a different complexion on the campaign and its probable duration.

Neither of these measures is, in any sense, an act of war. The possibility of Italy deciding, in face of them, to declare war on one or more of the major League powers must not be entirely ruled out, in view of the widespread doubts which exist as to the mental stability of the Duce. But such a step could not be regarded as an act of reasonable calculation, and could have only one result.

Would such comparatively mild measures as the above exert a significant pressure? It is easy to conceive of circumstances in which they would not. But in the present case they are exceptionally appropriate. The financial and economic situation of Italy is already almost desperate. The fear is already acute, lest the campaign may have to be prolonged even in the most favourable circumstances. Above all, Italy will not be waging a campaign in an area contiguous to her frontiers, which can be almost wholly supplied from her own internal resources. She is faced with the appalling strain of a vast expeditionary force operating at a great distance overseas in a country which supplies nothing, not even water. It is a case—one of the rare cases—where a moderate weakening of Italy's economic and financial forces and a moderate strengthening of those of her adversary may come near to being decisive. She is already running an unwise risk—which the action of the League can convert into a insane one.

There remains the question of closing the Suez Canal. Nothing could be more decisive than this, if the League possesses the right to order it. It may be worth while to refer the matter to The Hague for a judicial interpretation. But it seems improbable to a layman that the decision could be favourable. This does not, however, affect the material point, that, in the event of Italy declaring war on the League powers, her access to the Canal can be cut off without a formal closing of the Canal itself—which must offer a powerful, indeed an overwhelming, reason *not* to widen the area of hostilities, if there are any persons of sane judgement capable of surviving in authority under a dictatorship.

On 25 October Baldwin had Parliament dissolved and fixed a general election for 14 November. Just before, on 16 October, Herbert Samuel approached Keynes asking him to provide financial assistance to the Liberal Party to maintain it 'as a necessary element in the state'.

To HERBERT SAMUEL, *23 October 1935*

Dear Sir Herbert Samuel,

Thank you for your letter. But, alas, I scarcely know where I stand. Somewhere, I suppose, between Liberal and Labour, though in some respects to the left of the latter, not feeling that anyone just now really represents my strongest convictions. I should be glad to see a stronger representation of either of the above two parties in the next Parliament. But when you ask me to contribute, which I would gladly do in other circumstances, I am afraid I cannot but feel that it would be throwing money away. Perhaps I feel this because I do not really agree with what you quite properly stress in your letter, namely, the question of maintaining the separate identity of the Liberal Party. I may be proved to be wrong, but I am not convinced of the desirability of this.

Yours sincerely,
[copy initialled] J.M.K.

In fact, the only support Keynes provided during the election was a donation of £25 to the Labour Party in the South Norfolk constituency where Colin Clark was the candidate. He also provided Clark's agent with a letter of support.

To W. B. GOODBODY, *31 October 1935*

Thank you for your letter. If any Liberal in the South Norfolk division is interested in my opinion, I should advise him, without hesitation, to vote for Mr Colin Clark. I consider that Mr Clark would be an exceptionally well-qualified member of parliament. He would have the necessary knowledge to give considerable aid in the carrying into actual operation of many purposes which Labour and Liberals have in common. I would particularly emphasise the background of sound knowledge which he brings to the social and economic problems which should be the subject of early legislation.

Yours faithfully,
[copy initialled] J.M.K.

For the year's end he provided *Cosmopolitan* with a message on world peace.

World peace requires two conditions. Those nations which have a real and abiding will to peace must combine to preserve it; their joint action must be sufficiently imposing to make the risk of war too great to be undertaken except by a gambler or a madman. The League of Nations as constituted heretofore has been based on the false assumption that all nations alike are equally desirous of peace and justice. It has aimed therefore at including all nations and not those only which are genuinely peace-loving. Until recently all nations at least pretended to ensue peace. But there are certain nations today which openly and avowedly ensue war. This is causing a gradual evolution of the League by which it may come to embrace only the genuine peace-lovers. This line of development is to be welcomed and will be a source of increased strength not of weakness. It is useless to discuss disarmament today. On the contrary the League nations must possess greater military and economic strength and if possible much greater strength than the law-breakers. But alas this is a dream. For a new League of peace-loving nations will be powerless if it does not include the United States. Yet we are told that this is an impossibility; that the United States is too fearful of outside entanglements, too aloof from the fate of the rest of the world and even of civilisation itself to make the needful commitment.

During 1936, most of Keynes's activities centred on the publication and discussion of his *General Theory* (*JMK*, vols XIV and XXIX), although he also prepared two substantial articles on W. S. Jevons and H. S. Foxwell (*JMK*, vol. X), made one broadcast on literature and wrote one article on 'Art and the State' (*JMK*, vol. XXVIII) and worked to put the Arts Theatre on its feet.

However, he did have some time for other issues. Thus, as before, he continued to press for cheap money in his remarks to the annual meeting of the National Mutual on 19 February.

LONG-TERM RATES OF INTEREST

Two years ago I gave reasons for expecting a further fall in the long-term rate of interest. Last year I spoke more doubtfully since it seemed to me that we were between two sets of conflicting forces, and I concluded that we most needed a consolidation of the existing position coupled with a greater degree of confidence in the maintenance of the existing rates of interest. What is the prospect of the coming year?

In speaking of future prospects it is often difficult to make the distinction clear between what one considers the most desirable in the public interest and what one reckons to be the most probable in the actual circumstances. For unfortunately the course of events which is the most desirable is not always the most probable! Let me explain, therefore, that on this occasion I am primarily concerned with the question of what policy is most advisable.

If the present relatively (though not absolutely) satisfactory position is to be protected from subsequent reaction, I am sure that a further reduction in the long-term rate of interest—which, it must be remembered, will not produce its full effects for a considerable time—is urgently called for. But it is natural to ask by what means this result can be brought about. In attempting to answer this question there are certain considerations which I should like to call to your attention.

Treasury and short-term rates

Short-term money today is extremely cheap. But it is confidence in the future of short-term rates which is required to bring down long-term rates. Now the policy of the Treasury is not calculated to promote such confidence. They seem reluctant to issue bonds of from five to 10 years' maturity and anxious to reduce the short-term debt, in spite of the extraordinary cheapness with which it can be carried. They starve the banks and the money market of the type of security which the sound conduct of their business admittedly requires, and they pay a higher rate of interest than they need.

Take as an example their latest issue. They simultaneously borrowed at $1\frac{1}{2}$ per cent for five years and at $2\frac{3}{4}$ per cent for 25 years. They used part of the proceeds to repay short-term debt which was costing them about $\frac{1}{2}$ per cent. There can be no rational explanation of the longer-dated issue except that they themselves have no confidence in the short-term rate of interest remaining low. Since they largely control the situation, it is natural that humbler folk should be influenced by what the Treasury seem to expect. I suggest, therefore, that it is at least as important that the Treasury should themselves show confidence in the future of the short-term rate of interest as that they should maintain a low rate for the time being.

The supply of bank money

The other main factor (besides confidence in the future of short-term rates) in bringing down long-term rates of interest is a supply of bank money fully adequate to satisfy the community's demand for liquidity. The following figures are, I think, instructive. In the last quarter of 1932 the Bank of England's open market policy had the effect of increasing the volume of bank deposits to a total 12 per cent higher than in the last quarter of the preceding year. During the same period both the index of production and the index of prices were slightly receding. As a result the price of fixed-interest securities rose during this period by 33 per cent.

Two years later the volume of bank money was practically unchanged, although the index of production had risen appreciably and the index of prices slightly. Nevertheless there was a further rise of some 12 per cent in fixed-interest securities, partly due to the delayed effect of the Bank of England's earlier measures. Last year the Bank of England again increased the volume of bank money by about 6 per cent. This was undoubtedly a move in the right direction; but it was not quite enough even to sustain the level of long-term Government securities, and not nearly enough to continue their upward movement in a year in which the London and Cambridge index of production (the Board of Trade index is not yet available) rose 10 per cent, the index of wholesale prices 4 per cent, and that of the cost of living 3 per cent.

The net result is, comparing the end of 1935 with the end of 1932, that, whereas the index of production has risen 33 per cent, wholesale prices nearly 8 per cent, and the cost of living nearly 4 per cent, the volume of bank money has risen only 6 per cent. There are, of course, many other factors of which account must be taken; and these must have been favourable to long-dated securities in view of the way in which the latter have maintained their prices. But it is evident that the time has come for another increase in the volume of bank money, if we wish long-term rates of interest to fall further. The increase should, of course, be very gradual and almost unnoticeable from week to week, and it should be accompanied by an increase in the supply of Government securities of a maturity suitable for the banks to hold in substantial volume.

Treasury and Bank of England steps

The Treasury and the Bank of England undoubtedly deserve great credit for the large steps which they have already taken in the right direction. That they have not achieved more is mainly due, I think, to their underestimating their own powers to achieve what they recognise as desirable. It is true that there exist certain important limitations on their power to influence the rate of interest. But I doubt if these limitations are yet operative. The two main limitations are, respectively, external and internal. So long as the public is as effectively free to lend abroad as to lend at home it is obvious that domestic rates of interest cannot fall far below their normal parity with foreign rates without seriously upsetting the balance of international payments.

In pre-war days this limitation was of great importance. But with our exchanges no longer tied to gold, with the admirable control over the pace of foreign issues which the Bank of England has established, and with the diminished credit of many former large-scale borrowers, the position is greatly changed. I do not believe that this factor need be regarded today as standing in the way of a further reduction in the rate of interest. If I were told that the resources of the Exchange Equalisation Fund are virtually exhausted, I might change my opinion, at least to the extent of advocating a stricter control of foreign investment, especially in American stocks. But I am hopeful that this is not the case.

The other, internal, limitation will come into operation when we have what is for practical purposes a state of full employment. In such circumstances a further fall in the rate of interest will merely stimulate a competition for current output, which will result in an inflationary rise of prices. Pre-war theory presumed that this was the normal state of affairs. Would that it were! But, in fact, this happy condition is not yet ours. When it is the rate of interest will have fallen far enough for the time being.

Industrial share prices

There is another feature of the financial situation which is not entirely satisfactory—namely, the very high relative level of the prices of British industrial ordinary shares. These prices presume not merely a maintenance of the present industrial activity for an indefinite period to come but a substantial further improvement. Not that many people actually believe this, but each is hopeful of unloading on the other fellow in good time. It is true that prices not much below the present level might be justified if the long-term rate of interest were to fall sufficiently to bring forward new types of capital development. But the present *relative* levels of gilt-edged securities and of industrial ordinary shares are calculated, unless they are revised, to being ultimate disappointment to the holders of the latter.

To argue that, on a long view, first-class fixed-interest securities are cheaper today than the general run of British industrial ordinaries is not in accordance with the popular mood. The prospect of large Government expenditure on armaments is thought to lead to precisely the opposite conclusion. The view that I am indicating may, indeed, be premature. But if it is not true now, it soon may be.

Keynes's remarks were the object of comment in *The Times*'s City Notes, which drew an immediate comment from him. However, owing to a mix-up in the newspaper's offices, Keynes's letter was never published.

To the Editor of The Times, *21 February 1936*

Sir,

The remarks on my speech at the annual meeting of the National Mutual Life Assurance Society, printed in your *City Notes* today, involve such queer conclusions in morals and in arithmetic that they should not pass without comment.

In former days changes in the quantity of bank money mainly depended upon whether gold was flowing into or out of our central reserves. Today these movements, being absorbed by the Exchange Equalisation Fund, have no effect on the quantity of money; neither their magnitude nor even their direction is known. Thus the quantity of bank money solely depends on what your writer calls 'monetary manipulation'. I gave figures showing the broad outlines of this manipulation during the past four years. I argued that the Bank of England and the Treasury deserve much credit for their general handling of it, but I ventured to criticise [it] in detail, especially as regards recent months. Yet the Rip Van Winkle who writes your notes seems to be unaware that this has been our actual monetary system for some years, and regards it as a wicked suggestion of my own,—just as he did ten years ago when perhaps it was. Today the question of the criteria which should determine the Bank's policy in creating credit is no longer academic, but a matter of daily practice.

What follows is even stranger. A proposal, he writes, 'that the Treasury should through the machinery of the Bank of England create credit reveals an indifference to the moral side of the monetary question which is certainly striking'. Is it not rather late in the day to make charges of this kind against the Governor of the Bank and the Chancellor of the Exchequer? And why drag *me* in? I pointed out that in 1932–3 the Bank created a 12 per cent increase of credit and last year a 6 per cent increase, indicating that the former had been fully efficacious but that the latter should, in my judgement, have been slightly greater in view of the increase in output and employment. If he means that the moral issue comes in somewhere between 6 per cent and (say) 9 per cent, he should tell us why. Further on he seems to imply that it may be 'moral' to create credit to raise prices, but not 'moral' if the object is to reduce the rate of interest. This is a subtle distinction. There is also the difficulty that, if the creation of credit has no effect on the rate of interest, it will have no effect on prices. The *object* of credit creation is to increase output and employment to an optimum level. The *consequence* of increasing output is to raise prices; but this consequence, though usually inevitable, is often undesired.

Finally in arguing that, if the Treasury were to issue short-term securities instead of issuing long-term securities, the effect would be to depress the long-term market, he is making an obvious blunder, and in thinking that the advantage between borrowing at $2\frac{3}{4}$ per cent for 25 years or at $1\frac{1}{2}$ per cent for 5 years depends, not on the average rate for 5 year bonds during the 25 year period, but on the average rate for 25 year bonds during that period, he has forgotten his arithmetic.

If we are to retain or to improve our hard-won measure of

prosperity, no question is more important than the principles on which the Bank of England and the Treasury should fix the quantity of bank money. It has not been discussed lately as much as it deserves to be. I tried to make a brief contribution to it in a serious spirit. Are the observations in your *City Notes*, on which I have commented, helpful to a serious discussion of a serious question?

Your obedient servant,
[copy not initialled or signed]

During the rest of 1936, the European situation worsened with Hitler's occupation of the Rhineland in March and Spain's drift towards the Civil War which began on 17 July. In these circumstances Keynes set out his views to his father.

To J. N. KEYNES, *15 July 1936*

Dearest Father,

Mother tells me you are very low about the European situation. I do not know that I can say much to cheer you. But there are a few things which I think from our own point of view ought not to be forgotten.

The real difficulty about our making up our minds about our own foreign policy is that it is almost certain that our immediate interests are not threatened by any early ambitions either of Germany or of Italy. Italy wants to master the Mediterranean and, apart perhaps from Egypt (and even that is 'perhaps') it would not matter truly very much even if she does. In the same way, Germany's ambitions are all to the East, and certainly not towards us. As for Germany wanting anything from the Empire, that is put off I am sure, and, after all, at sea we are much too powerful for them to want to try any conclusions in that way.

The problem of our foreign policy is whether we are prepared to enter into any engagements towards other minor people who, in various other parts of the world, may be attacked. I imagine it is almost certain that anything we do will be guarded and we shall really wait for circumstances.

Thus, I think you can be pretty sure that there is very little likelihood indeed of any direct attack by the brigand powers on our own immediate interests. The question for us will be how far we are prepared to go to the assistance, if at all, of other victims. But this, as you will see, makes it all moderately remote.

I have, as it happens, written a letter on foreign policy to this week's *New Statesman & Nation*,[3] which you will see on Friday.

I have been up here [London] for the last two days, spending many hours in the auction rooms at the disposal of the papers of Sir Isaac Newton, which his relations have kept together until now and have just decided to spout. They went, as it seems to me, extraordinarily reasonably, and I think I have bought almost everything which ought to remain in Cambridge. It was rather peculiar that, so far as I could discover, neither the University Library, nor Trinity, nor the British Museum sent a single representative. Two dealers, with both of whom I was in touch, and myself being almost the only buyers. Amongst other things I bought Sir Isaac Newton's death mask, which is extraordinarily interesting.

Tonight or tomorrow I am off to Cambridge for a few days, and then we go down to Tilton for the rest of the summer. Polly [Hill][4] is coming to us on Saturday.

Your affectionate
[copy not initialled or signed]

Keynes's letter to *The New Statesman* and the controversy that followed are discussed in volume XXVIII in connection with his correspondence with Kingsley Martin.

[3] See *JMK*, vol. XXVIII.

[4] Keynes's niece.

Chapter 6

SLUMP AND REARMAMENT

During 1935 and 1936, in the course of several reports, the Committee on Economic Information had started to consider what would happen once the current recovery had ended, and housebuilding, which had played an important role in the recovery, turned down. During 1936 the issue became clouded by the announcement of a large British rearmament programme spread over five years, the gold bloc countries' devaluations in the context of the Tripartite Agreement in September and the spread of recovery, accompanied by rising prices, throughout the world.

Early in November, in conversation with R. H. Brand, Keynes mentioned the idea of writing a series of articles on preventing another slump. He then developed the idea in a letter.

To R. H. BRAND, *12 November 1936*

Dear Brand,

When we met the other day I mentioned to you that I had it in mind to write a couple of short articles on 'The Problem of the Slump', meaning by this some observations on the thought that ought now to be given to the problem of how to prevent or mitigate the next slump, and the policies which are most advisable with this object in view. My own feeling is that we are now approaching the phase when it is much more important to think about how to prevent the slump than about how to stimulate the boom any further than it has already gone.

Do you think that Geoffrey Dawson would care for these articles for *The Times*? I have not written them yet, and there is no particular urgency as to the date. Possibly the first two days of the New Year might be appropriate. But, of course, the precise date is not essential.

Yours ever,

[copy initialled] J.M.K.

Brand sent Keynes's letter on to Geoffrey Dawson, who accepted Keynes's proposals in a letter dated 20 November. Keynes set to work on the articles, which he finished before 6 January. They appeared between 12 and 14 January 1937.

From The Times, *12–14 January 1937*

HOW TO AVOID A SLUMP

I. THE PROBLEM OF THE STEADY LEVEL

It is clear that by painful degrees we have climbed out of the slump. It is also clear that we are well advanced on the upward slopes of prosperity—I will not say 'of the boom', for 'boom' is an opprobrious term, and what we are enjoying is desirable. But many are already preoccupied with what is to come. It is widely agreed that it is more important to avoid a descent into another slump than to stimulate (subject to an important qualification to be mentioned below) a still greater activity than we have. This means that all of us—politicians, bankers, industrialists, and economists—are faced with a scientific problem which we have never tried to solve before.

I emphasise that point. Not only have we never solved it; we have never tried to. Not once. The booms and slumps of the past have been neither courted nor contrived against. The action of central banks has been hitherto an almost automatic response to the unforeseen and undesigned impact of outside events. But this time it is different. We have entirely freed ourselves—this applies to every party and every quarter—from the philosophy of the *laissez-faire* state. We have new means at our disposal which we intend to use. Perhaps we know more. But chiefly it is a general conviction that the stability of our institutions absolutely requires a resolute attempt to apply what perhaps we know to preventing the recurrence of another steep descent. I should like to try, therefore, to reduce a complicated problem to its essential elements.

The distressed areas

It is natural to interject that it is premature to abate our efforts to increase employment so long as the figures of unemployment remain so large. In a sense this must be true. But I believe that we are approaching, or have reached, the point where there is not much advantage in applying a further general stimulus at the centre. So long as surplus resources were widely diffused between industries and localities it was no great matter at what point in the economic structure the impulse of an increased demand was applied. But the evidence grows that—for several reasons into which there is no space to enter here—the economic structure is unfortunately rigid, and that (for example) building activity in the home counties is less effective than one might have hoped in decreasing unemployment in the distressed areas. It follows that the later stages of recovery require a different technique. To remedy the condition of the distressed areas, *ad hoc* measures are necessary. The Jarrow marchers were, so to speak, theoretically correct. The Government have been wrong in their reluctance to accept the strenuous *ad hoc* measures recommended by those in close touch with the problem. Nevertheless a change of policy in the right direction seems to be imminent. We are in more need today of a rightly distributed demand than of a greater aggregate demand; and the Treasury would be entitled to economise elsewhere to compensate for the cost of special assistance to the distressed areas. If our responsibility in this direction could be thus disposed of we could concentrate with a clear mind on our central problem of how to maintain a fairly steady level of sustained prosperity.

Why is it that good times have been so intermittent? The explanation is not difficult. The public, especially when they are prosperous, do not spend the whole of their incomes on current consumption. It follows that the productive activities, from which their incomes are derived, must not be devoted to preparing for consumption in any greater proportion than that in which the corresponding incomes will be spent on consumption; since, if they are, the resulting goods cannot be sold at a profit and production will have to be curtailed. If when incomes are at a given level the public consume, let us say, nine-tenths of their incomes, the productive efforts devoted to consumption goods cannot be more than nine times the efforts devoted to investment, if the results are to be sold without loss. Thus it is an indispensable condition of a stable increase in incomes that the production of investment goods (which must be interpreted in a wide sense so as to include working capital; and also relief works and armaments if they are paid for by borrowing) should advance *pari passu* and in the right proportion. Otherwise the proportion of income spent on consumption will be less than the proportion of income earned by producing consumption goods, which means that the receipts of the producers of consumption goods will be less than their costs, so that business losses and a curtailment of output will ensue.

Difficulty of 'planning'

Now there are several reasons why the production of investment goods tends to fluctuate widely, and it is these fluctuations which cause the fluctuations, first of profits, then of general business activity, and hence of national and world prosperity. The sustained enjoyment of prosperity requires as its condition that as near as possible the right proportion of the national resources, neither too much nor too little, should be devoted to active investment (interpreted, as I have indicated, in a wide sense). The proportion will be just right if it is the same as the proportion of their incomes which the community is disposed to save when the national resources of equipment and labour are being fully employed.

There is no reason to suppose that there is 'an invisible hand', an automatic control in the economic system which ensures of itself that the amount of active investment shall be continuously of the right proportion. Yet it is also very difficult to ensure it by our own design, by what is now called 'planning.' The best we can hope to achieve is to use those kinds of investment which it is relatively easy to plan as a make-weight, bringing them in so as to preserve as much stability of aggregate investment as we can manage at the right and appropriate level. Three years ago it was important to use public policy to increase investment. It may soon be equally important to retard certain types of investment, so as to keep our most easily available ammunition in hand for when it is more required.

The longer the recovery has lasted, the more difficult does it become to maintain the stability of new investment. Some of the investment which properly occurs during a recovery is, in the nature of things, non-recurrent; for example, the increase in working capital as output increases and the provision of additional equipment to keep pace with the improvement in consumption. Another part becomes less easy to sustain, not because saturation point has been reached, but because with each increase in our stock of wealth the profit to be expected from a further increase declines. And, thirdly, the abnormal profits obtainable, during a too rapid recovery of demand, from equipment which is temporarily in short supply is likely to lead to exaggerated expectations from certain types of new investment, the disappointment of which will bring a subsequent reaction. Experience shows that this is sure to occur if aggregate investment is allowed to rise for a time above the normal proper proportion. We can also add that the rise in stock exchange values consequent on the recovery usually leads to a certain amount of expenditure paid for, not out of current income, but out of stock exchange profits, which will cease when values cease to rise further. It is evident, therefore, what a ticklish business it is to maintain stability. We have to be preparing the way for an increase in sound investments of the second type which have not yet reached saturation point, to take the place in due course of the investment of the first type which is necessarily non-current, while at the same time avoiding a temporary overlap of investments of the first and second types liable to increase aggregate investment to an excessive figure, which by inflating profits will induce unsound investment of the third type based on mistaken expectations.

Having made these general observations, let us examine the opportunities for putting them into practice.

II. 'DEAR' MONEY: THE RIGHT TIME FOR AUSTERITY

In one respect we are better placed than ever before. On previous occasions a shortage of cash has nearly always played a significant part in turning the boom into the slump. Prices and wages are sure to rise somewhat with an increase in output. Nor is there anything wrong in that; for it is to be sharply distinguished from the so-called 'vicious spiral' which attended the post-war currency inflations. But the higher incomes resulting from increased output at a higher level of costs naturally require more cash. Formerly there was seldom a sufficient margin of cash which could be made available to finance the higher incomes. Thus the resulting shortage of cash led to a rise in the rate of interest, which, developing at a time when the maintenance of investment was already becoming difficult for other reasons, had a fatal influence on confidence and credit, and decisively established the slump.

But this time there is no risk of a cash shortage in those countries which still maintain a free economic system and are enjoying a normal recovery. The currency devaluations, the huge output of gold, and the newly-won elasticity of the foreign exchanges have combined to give us the needed freedom of action. We no longer rest under a compulsion to do what is ruinous. Unfortunately there is a widely held belief that dear money is a 'natural' consequence of recovery, and is, in such circumstances, a 'healthy' feature.

Playing with fire

Unquestionably in past experience dear money has accompanied recovery; and has also heralded a slump. If we play with dear money on the ground that it is 'healthy' or 'natural', then, I have no doubt, the inevitable slump will ensue. We must avoid it, therefore, as we would hell-fire. It is true that there is a phase in every recovery when we need to go slow with postponable investment of the recurrent type, lest, in conjunction with the non-recurrent investment which necessarily attends a recovery, it raises aggregate investment too high. But we must find other means of achieving this than a higher rate of interest. For if we allow the rate of interest to be affected, we cannot easily reverse the trend. A low enough long-term rate of interest cannot be achieved if we allow it to be believed that better terms will be obtainable from time to time by those who keep their resources liquid. The long-term rate of interest must be kept *continuously* as near as possible to what we believe to be the long-term optimum. It is not suitable to be used as a short-period weapon.

Moreover, when the recovery is reaching its peak of activity, the phase of non-recurrent investment in increased working capital and the like will be almost over; and we can be practically certain that within a few weeks or months we shall require a lower rate of interest to stimulate increased investment of the recurrent type to fill the gap. Thus it is a fatal mistake to use a high rate of interest as a means of damping down the boom. It has been the occurrence of dear money hitherto which has joined with other forces to make a slump inevitable.

If the stock exchange is unduly excited or if new issues of a doubtful type are becoming too abundant, a higher rate of interest will be useless except in so far as it affects adversely the whole structure of confidence and credit. Moreover, alternative methods are available. A hint to the banks to be cautious in allowing their names to appear on prospectuses, and to the Committee of the Stock Exchange to exercise discrimination in granting permissions to deal would be more efficacious. And if necessary a temporary increase of a substantial amount in the stamp on contract-notes (as distinguished from transfers) in respect of transactions in ordinary shares would help to check an undue speculative activity.

Nevertheless a phase of the recovery may be at hand when it will be desirable to find other methods temporarily to damp down aggregate demand, with a view to stabilising subsequent activity at as high a level as possible. There are three important methods open to our authorities, all of which deserve to be considered in the immediate future.

Boom control

Just as it was advisable for the Government to incur debt during the slump, so for the same reasons it is now advisable that they should incline to the opposite policy. Aggregate demand is increased by loan expenditure and decreased when loans are discharged out of taxation. In view of the high cost of the armaments, which we cannot postpone, it would put too much strain on our fiscal system actually to discharge debt, but the Chancellor of the Exchequer should, I suggest, meet the main part of the cost of armaments out of taxation, raising taxes and withholding all reliefs for the present as something in hand for 1938 or 1939, or whenever there are signs of recession. The boom, not the slump, is the right time for austerity at the Treasury.

Just as it was advisable for local authorities to press on with capital expenditure during the slump, so it is now advisable that they should postpone whatever new enterprises can reasonably be held back. I do not mean that they should abandon their plans of improvement. On the contrary, they should have them fully matured, available for quick release at the right moment. But the boom, not the slump, is the right time for procrastination at the Ministry of Health.

Just as it was advisable (from our own point of view) to check imports and to take measures to improve the balance of trade during the slump, so it is now advisable to shift in the opposite direction and to welcome imports even though they result in an adverse balance of trade. I should like to see a temporary rebate on tariffs wherever this could be done without throwing British resources out of employment. But, above all, it is desirable that we should view with equanimity and without anxiety the prospective worsening of our trade balance which is likely to result from higher prices for raw materials and from our armament expenditure and general trade activity, even though this may put a temporary strain on the Exchange Equalisation Fund. The recent decrease in the Bank of England's fiduciary issue indicates that we have today a plethora of gold. It is desirable, therefore, that the raw material countries should be allowed to replenish their gold and sterling resources by sending their goods to us; especially so in view of the difficulties which would remain in the way of foreign lending on the old scale even if the existing artificial obstacles were to be removed. This policy is doubly desirable. First, because it will help to relieve a temporarily inflated demand in the home market. But, secondly, because a policy of allowing these countries to increase their resources in 1937 provides the best prospect of their using these resources to buy our goods and help our export industries at a later date when an increased demand in our home market is just what we shall be wanting.

These, I urge, are the methods which will best serve to protect us from the excesses of the boom and, at the same time, put us in good trim to ward off the cumulative dangers of the slump when the reaction comes, as come it surely will. But we also need more positive measures to maintain a decent level of continuous prosperity. In a third article we will conclude with suggestions to this end.

III. OPPORTUNITIES OF POLICY

While we shall be prudent to take such steps as I have indicated to prevent the present recovery from developing into a precarious boom, I admit that I do not see much sign of this, except, perhaps, in certain special directions. For the moment we have the rearmament expenditure superimposed on the building activity and on the large non-recurrent investment in working capital and in renewals which are characteristic of a recovery as such; and this is a situation which suggests caution.

But, on the other hand, our export industries remain, on the whole, inactive; the peak of the non-recurrent investment in increased working capital (which in the last two or three years has been much larger per annum than the cost of rearmament now is) may be behind us; sooner or later the building activity will relax; and the cost of rearmament is neither permanent nor large enough while it lasts to sustain prosperity by itself (in 1936 at least seven or eight times as much was spent on new building as on rearmament). Thus our main preoccupation should be concerned not so much with avoiding the perils of a somewhat hypothetical boom as with advance precautions against that sagging away of activity which, if it is allowed to cumulate after the usual fashion, will once again develop into a slump. Too much alarm about a hypothetical boom will be just the way to make a slump inevitable. There is nothing wrong with the very moderate prosperity we now enjoy. Our object must be to stabilise it and to distribute it more widely, not to diminish it.

Positive precautions

Thus we need constructive preparations against the future. Recent experience has shown us how long it takes to prepare for useful investment; and what careful handling is necessary to develop a psychological state in the investment market which will accept a reduction in the long-term rate of interest. Moreover, it will be much easier to check a recession if we intervene at its earliest stages. For, if it is allowed to develop, cumulative forces of decline will be set in motion which it may prove almost impossible to check until they have run their course. If we are to be successful we must intervene with moderate measures of expansion before the decline has become visible to the general public. One factor only shall we have in our favour—namely, the improvement in our export trade with the raw material countries which I now anticipate with confidence at a date not far distant. In other directions we shall be hard put to it, in my opinion, to develop useful activities on an adequate scale. The menace of the next slump, and what that would mean to our institutions and traditions, if it comes, should be at our elbow, urging us to new policies and boldness of mind.

Perhaps it is absurd to expect Englishmen to think things out beforehand. But if it is not, there are various thoughts to think. So far I have stressed the importance of investment. But the maintenance of prosperity and of a stable economic life only depends on increased investment if we take as unalterable the existing distribution of purchasing power and the willingness of those who enjoy purchasing power to use it for consumption. The wealthier we get and the smaller, therefore, the profit to be gained from adding to our capital goods, the more it is incumbent on us to see that those who would benefit from increasing their consumption—which is, after all, the sole ultimate object of economic effort—have the power and the opportunity to do so. Up to a point individual saving can allow an advantageous way of postponing consumption. But beyond that point it is for the community as a whole both an absurdity and a disaster. The natural evolution should be towards a decent level of consumption for every one; and, when that is high enough, towards the occupation of our energies in the non-economic interests of our lives. Thus we need to be slowly reconstructing our social system with these ends in view. This is a large matter, not to be embarked upon here. But, in particular and in detail, the relief of taxation, when the time comes for that, will do most for the general welfare if it is so directed as to increase the purchasing power of those who have most need to consume more.

Planning investment

The capital requirements of home industry and manufacture cannot possibly absorb more than a fraction of what this country, with its present social structure and distribution of wealth, chooses to save in years of general prosperity; while the amount of our net foreign investment is limited by our exports and our trade balance. Building and transport and public utilities, which can use large amounts of capital, lie half way between private and public control. They need, therefore, the combined stimulus of public policy and a low rate of interest. But a wise public policy to promote investment needs, as I have said, long preparation. Now is the time to appoint a board of public investment to prepare sound schemes against the time that they are needed. If we wait until the crisis is upon us we shall, of course, be too late. We ought to set up immediately an authority whose business it is not to launch anything at present, but to make sure that detailed plans are prepared. The railway companies, the port and river authorities, the water, gas, and electricity undertakings, the building contractors, the local authorities, above all, perhaps, the London County Council and the other great Corporations with congested population, should be asked to investigate what projects could be usefully undertaken if capital were available at certain rates of interest—$3\frac{1}{2}$ per cent, 3 per cent, $2\frac{1}{2}$ per cent, 2 per cent. The question of the general advisability of the schemes and their order of preference should be examined next. What is required at once are acts of constructive imagination by our administrators, engineers, and architects, to be followed by financial criticism, sifting, and more detailed designing; so that some large and useful projects, at least, can be launched at a few months' notice.

There can be no justification for a rate of interest which impedes an adequate flow of new projects at a time when the national resources for production are not fully employed. The rate of interest must be reduced to the figure that the new projects can afford. In special cases subsidies may be justified; but in general it is the long-term rate of interest which should come down to the figure which the marginal project can earn. We have the power to achieve this. The Bank of England and the Treasury had a great success at the time of the conversion of the War Loan. But it is possible that they still underrate the extent of their powers. With the existing control over the exchanges which has revolutionised the technical position, and with the vast resources at the disposal of the authorities through the Bank of England, the Exchange Equalisation Fund, and other funds under the control of the Treasury, it lies within their power, by the exercise of the moderation, the gradualness, and the discreet handling of the market of which they have shown themselves to be masters, to make the long-term rate of interest what they choose within reason. If we know what rate of interest is required to make profitable a flow of new projects at the proper pace, we have the power to make that rate prevail in the market. A low rate of interest can only be harmful and liable to cause an inflation if it is so low as to stimulate a flow of new projects more than enough to absorb our available resources.

Is there the slightest chance of a constructive or a forethoughtful policy in contemporary England? Is it conceivable that the Government should do anything in time? Why shouldn't they?

In a leading article, 'The Boom and the Budget', *The Economist* of 23 January used the appearance of Keynes's articles as a basis for discussing monetary policy. In the article it argued not only against credit contraction but also against further expansion, and suggested that the Treasury in such circumstances should finance any additional defence expenditure through taxation. Keynes commented:

To the Editor of The Economist, *26 January 1937*

Sir,

In your leading article this week you argue that further recovery will require a substantial increase in bank advances, but must not be allowed any more cash. You imply that I agree with this. You infer that a substantial increase in bank advances, unaccompanied by any increase in cash, will cause a heavy fall in gilt-edged securities and a rise in the long-term rate of interest; which is not indeed a necessary inference (since buyers for the banks' investments may be as readily forthcoming as they would be for a new issue), but is probable in the actual circumstances. Thus you wind up with the old conclusion, which I was particularly concerned to dispute in my *Times* articles, that, if the principles of 'sound finance' are observed, recovery is bound to raise the rate of interest. May I try to define the issue more precisely?

In the first place, I am not convinced by your forecast that an increase will be required in the amount of bank advances up to the 1929 level. The quantity of *deposits* is considerably above the 1929 level (£2,210 millions, compared with £1,789 millions), and, unless the market, becoming alarmed about the prospects of the gilt-edged market, gets keen on keeping liquid, this quantity of deposits ought to support a larger national income. Thus whilst some further increase in advances is quite likely, I doubt the need for so large an increase as the £137 millions which you forecast. This is borne out by Mr Edwin Fisher's very interesting analysis of bank advances which you publish in the same issue, from which it appears that only about a third of bank advances are taken by productive industry, merchants, etc., or applying his percentages to the banks as a whole, say £305 millions, of which the increase you forecast is about 45 per cent. Moreover, we are probably through the period of recovery at which the demand for bank advances, as distinct from new issues, is keenest, namely, when working capital is being increased and repairs and renewals are being carried through but increased cash profits are not yet to hand.

Nevertheless, since my calculations involve some doubtful factors, I am ready to admit that you may conceivably be right about the demand for advances; or, at any rate sufficiently right for the problem under discussion to reach significant dimensions. But if so, surely it must be advisable to allow some increase in the basis of credit? It cannot be wise to put on the brake at that stage and in that way. Even your extreme hypothesis only requires an increase of £15 millions in bank cash.

For consider the nature of the two alternatives. If you force the banks to sell their investments, your policy is to reduce the price of gilt-edged securities until someone with idle cash is induced to part with it in exchange for them, thus placing cash which was idle at the disposal of the new borrowers. The other alternative is to leave the quantity of idle cash unchanged and to supply new cash to the borrowers. The former increases the velocity, and the latter the quantity, of the circulation. But to suppose that the former course prevents prices from rising is a fallacy. Prices are a function of the degree of activity. They can only be checked by reducing the activity, i.e. by *not making* the new advances; though to make them at the expense of the rate of interest will, of course, impair *future* activity. Thus your policy is the historic one—of not checking the boom, but of making sure that it is followed by a slump. Since you cannot intend this, could not the argument be reconsidered?

Yours etc.
J. M. KEYNES

The Economist commented on Keynes's letter both in its correspondence columns and in its Money and Banking columns. It suggested that Keynes had misinterpreted its views in that it believed that without the problem of defence borrowing the situation might be handled without inflation by a slight expansion of bank cash and bank sales of gilts, but that with a Defence Loan 'would Mr Keynes still be confident of avoiding a dangerous boom without raising interest rates?'.

To the Editor of The Economist, *2 February 1937*

Sir,

I am glad that I misunderstood you in thinking that you were opposed to a further increase in bank deposits, if this were necessary to prevent a rise in interest rates. That is to say, on the assumption that there is no Defence Loan. But what is to happen, you ask me, if there *is* a Defence Loan? I agree with you, as you know, in urging that the Defence Loan, if any, should be kept as small as our reasonable capacity for taxation permits. But if in spite of our arguments, there is a loan of (say) £50 million to £100 million this year, does it follow that we are forced back on reversing the downward trend of the rate of interest?

I do not think so. I still think that there are better expedients available to retard activity in directions other than rearmament, if we wish to retard it, and that these should be used by preference. But, if you will let me, I should like to explore a little further the technical aspects of the position.

In the first place, it does not follow that the Defence Loan cannot be gradually taken up by the public. With increased activity incomes rise and increased savings become available corresponding to the expenditure paid for out of borrowed funds; or if defence replaces other activities, then the savings which would have financed these activities are available to take up the loan. Similarly, if it is convenient for business to finance itself through bank advances rather than through public issues, the savings which would otherwise have taken up the public issues are available to relieve the banks of part of their gilt-edged securities. Thus the need for increased deposits is not measured either by the size of the Defence Loan or by the increase in bank advances. It depends on two other factors; first of all, on activity as measured, roughly speaking, by the national income in money, which governs the demand for active deposits; and secondly on the psychological atmosphere towards gilt-edged and other securities which governs the degree of the desire to hold liquid balances. Unfortunately, though very naturally, the readiness to put savings into gilt-edged securities is largely influenced by the ideas which get about as to whether the gilt-edged market is likely to rise or to fall in the future.

It is the latter factor which needs careful handling. If the public is deprived of its normal supply of idle balances by the demand for active balances, or if it gets nervous about the prospects of the gilt-edged market, then I feel strongly that, unless we deliberately desire to raise the rate of interest, this demand for idle balances should be satisfied for the time being, the extra idle balances being subsequently withdrawn as a change in the atmosphere or in the circumstances permits.

Thus it is not a shortage of savings which will impair the position of gilt-edged securities, but a change in psychological expectations as to their future prospects. I believe that it is most important to prevent such a change by maintaining stability in the gilt-edged market. For, if the change occurs, it will make the task of avoiding the slump more difficult. The weakness in gilt-edged securities during the last week or two is an illustration of how psychological the market is and how easily its nerves are upset. The weakness is partly due to anxiety about the Budget. But I believe that it is also partly due to the discussions which have been going on in various quarters about future policy. For, although almost all the participants in the discussion have deprecated a decline in the market and have taken, on the whole, a cheerful view against its likelihood, the discussion has drawn the attention of the public to the fact that the future of the gilt-edged market is not *certain*; and this has been quite enough to affect prices adversely. The actual movement so far is, of course, trifling. But if it were to be allowed to proceed to any length, the effect on public confidence would greatly aggravate the difficulty of our future task.

Yours, etc.,

J. M. KEYNES

Keynes's letter brought a further comment by *The Economist* which suggested that Keynes was being over-optimistic about the ability of the market to absorb a Defence Loan, without some of the liquid balances spilling over into the equity market in speculation. It also asked Keynes how the extra idle balances would be withdrawn without affecting the boom or the rate of interest. Keynes replied.

To the Editor of The Economist, *10 February 1937*

Sir,

The answer to your question is easy and should be obvious. If, subsequently, the desire of the public to hold idle balances is diminished, the excess can, in such circumstances, be withdrawn without detriment to the rate of interest.

It is not easy to become accustomed to the idea of trying to avoid booms and slumps. But it is a necessary first step in this direction to get accustomed to the notion that the supply of idle balances should not be kept constant irrespective of the fluctuating impulses of the public to hold them.

Yours etc.,

J. M. KEYNES

Keynes's articles also had their echo in official circles, for the Twenty-second Report of the Committee on Economic Information, entitled 'Economic Policy and the Maintenance of Trade Activity', dated 19 February, made the same recommendations as Keynes had about public investment, tariff policy and interest rates. Moreover, as had the correspondence in *The Economist*,[1] the Committee's report carried a note of dissent by D. H. Robertson over the rate of interest. Moreover the Committee's Report was taken seriously in Whitehall.[2]

[1] D. H. Robertson to the Editor of *The Economist*, 13 February 1937.

[2] Howson and Winch, *The Economic Advisory Council*, pp. 141 ff.

On 24 February at the annual meeting of the National Mutual, Keynes turned again to rearmament and the rate of interest. By this time, the Government had announced that over the next five years it would borrow up to £500 million for rearmament.

REARMAMENT AND THE GILT-EDGED MARKET

I said a moment ago that the end of 1936 might prove to have been a specially favourable date for the valuation of our assets. For, on the one hand, industrial securities had probably felt by then the major effects of industrial recovery apart from any temporary top-knots due to actual boom conditions; while, at the same time, gilt-edged securities were still retaining the major part of their large gains. The subsequent disclosure of the Government's rearmament programme certainly seems to postpone for some time the prospect of an industrial recession. But the effect on the gilt-edged market has been severe; and an assurance society is, of course, much more largely interested in fixed-interest securities than in equities. Naturally, therefore, the assurance world is scanning the prospects of Government finance with some anxiety. Are we entitled to take a cheerful view?

Treasury's need of a concerted policy

I feel no doubt that the sums which the Chancellor of the Exchequer proposes to borrow are well within our capacity; particularly if as much of the expenditure as possible is directed to bringing into employment the unused resources of the Special Areas. It is incumbent on the Government to have a concerted policy for retarding other postponable capital expenditure, particularly in the near future, if temporary congestion is to be avoided; and there are other suggestions which could be, and have been, made. But over a period of five years there should be no difficulty in finding the resources required. The sinking funds of public boards and local authorities in respect of past expenditure, the huge repayments which the building societies are now collecting as the new houses of recent years are cleared of indebtedness by their owners, the steady growth of deposits in the Post Office and trustee savings banks in times of good employment, the large sums which industry will be able to put to reserves out of its profits—these alone should amount to something like £400,000,000, not in five years, but in one year. We must not estimate investible funds in a period of such large expenditures as are now contemplated on the basis of what they were in the years of depression.

Possibility of avoiding inflation

Thus it lies within the power of the Chancellor to get his money without producing conditions of inflation. But there remains the further question, what will he have to pay for it? This, to my mind, is entirely a matter of management and how the task is handled. If the Chancellor, weighed down by a sense of guilt, feels that for the sin of borrowing he must chastise himself (and us) by borrowing dear, markets will respond accordingly. But he will not find that this will make it any easier to borrow. On the contrary; it is much easier to borrow on a rising than on a falling market. The calls to be made on the gilt-edged market are a reason for encouraging the supporters of that market. And this, with their past experience to guide them, is what I should expect the Treasury to do.

In considering the terms on which new loans can be issued, it is interesting to compare the techniques of the British and the American Treasuries. In our own case by far the greater part of the debt (apart from Treasury bills) has no fixed date of repayment within the next 25 years—in round numbers £5,000,000,000 is long-dated in this sense and only about £1,000,000,000 of intermediate date. Moreover, nearly half of the securities of intermediate date stand above par, and are, therefore, inconvenient holdings to many investors for tax or other reasons. In the United States, on the other hand, practically the whole of the debt is repayable within 25 years; indeed, there is nothing beyond 30 years. And within the next 25 years there are notes or bonds falling due for repayment in almost every year. Thus every taste is suited, the rate of interest rising slowly as the date of maturity becomes later; for example, the tax-free rates are about $\frac{1}{4}$ per cent for one year, 1 per cent for two years, $1\frac{1}{4}$ per cent for four years, $1\frac{3}{4}$ per cent for six years, 2 per cent for 10 years, rising to $2\frac{1}{2}$ per cent for 15 years.

These rates do not greatly differ from the net redemption yields on British Government securities for comparable periods; but the arrangement of the maturities allows the American Treasury to borrow at a materially lower average rate. It is to be remembered that many holders of gilt-edged securities are primarily interested in security of capital; and whilst there are others who are attracted by security of income over a long period, it is unlikely that these latter are five times as numerous as the former. It is, therefore, expensive for the Treasury to keep the long-dated markets in relative oversupply. They should profit from the anxieties of the public and save interest by supplying them with the potential liquidity which they demand.

Present interest rates not exceptionally low

In any case it is a popular error to suppose that the rate of interest today is exceptionally low. During the half-century preceding the War the average yield on Consols was approximately 3 per cent. Today the yield on War Loan is almost $3\frac{1}{2}$ per cent. There was not a single five-year period between 1837 and 1914 when the average yield on long-term gilt-edged securities was as high as it is today. Yet our capital wealth per head is now half as great again as it was during much of that period; and in those years we were providing for a rapidly increasing population and were investing largely abroad. Even with the Treasury's requirements what we now know them to be I see no justification in the years to come for a long-term rate of interest higher than 3 per cent; and, indeed, it should be lower.

On 3 March, Keynes offered *The Times* a follow-up article to those of January 'to try and make a little more precise the question of what inflation is and whether the Chancellor's plans are free from risk'. The editor accepted Keynes's offer and Keynes submitted his copy on 7 March.[3]

From The Times, *11 March 1937*

BORROWING FOR DEFENCE: IS IT INFLATION? A PLEA FOR ORGANISED POLICY

The Chancellor of the Exchequer having published his prospective borrowing plans for rearmament, the question properly arises whether this programme can be superimposed on the present business situation without risking a state of inflation. The question is hotly debated. The Chancellor declares that a loan of £80,000,000 a year is not excessive in the circumstances. His critics dispute this conclusion. Clearly it is a matter of figures. The Chancellor would agree that £200,000,000 a year would be dangerous; his critics are disposed to accept £40,000,000 a year as safe. What calculations are relevant to the answer? I believe that we can carry the argument a stage further than mere assertions based on vague individual judgements.

To begin with, what do we mean by 'inflation'? If we mean by the term a state of affairs which is dangerous and ought to be avoided—and, since the term carries to most people an opprobrious implication, this is the convenient usage—then we must not mean by it merely that prices and wages are rising. For a rising tendency of prices and wages inevitably, and for

[3] Keynes's own title for the article was 'Is the Rearmament Loan Inflationary? (A Justification of the Chancellor of the Exchequer's Programme)'.

obvious reasons, accompanies any revival of activity. An improvement in demand tends to carry with it an increase in output and employment and, at the same time, a rise in prices and wages. It is when increased demand is no longer capable of materially raising output and employment and mainly spends itself in raising prices that it is properly called inflation. When this point is reached, the new demand merely competes with the existing demand for the use of resources which are already employed to the utmost.

Surplus capacity

The question is, therefore, whether we have enough surplus capacity to meet the increase in demand likely to arise out of an expenditure of £80,000,000 raised by loans and not by diverting incomes through taxation. Now the resulting increase in demand will be greater than £80,000,000; since we have to provide for increased expenditure by the recipients of the £80,000,000, and for further similar reactions. There are reasons, too detailed to repeat here, for supposing that the total effect on demand will, in existing conditions in this country, probably lie between two and three times the primary increase. To be on the safe side, let us take three times as our preliminary estimate, which means that the total increase in the national income resulting from the Chancellor's borrowing will have to be in the neighbourhood of £240,000,000 at present prices—an increase, that is to say, of about $5\frac{1}{2}$ per cent. Have we sufficient surplus capacity to provide such an increase? Or will the Government demand merely serve to raise prices until resources, already in use, are diverted from their present employment? This is certainly not a question to be answered lightly.

The number of insured persons who are still unemployed is, indeed, as high as $12\frac{1}{2}$ per cent. But though the new demand will be widely spread (since it will not be limited to the primary employment for armaments, but will also spread to the secondary employments to meet the increased demand of consumers), we cannot safely regard even half of these unemployed insured persons as being available to satisfy home demand. For we have to subtract the unemployables, those seasonally unemployed, &c., and those who cannot readily be employed except in producing for export. Unless we make a liberal allowance for overtime and more output from those already in employment, it would need more planning and transfer of labour than is practicable in the time to increase the national output in 1937 by $5\frac{1}{2}$ per cent over what it was in 1936; although over (say) a period of three years it might be possible.

Thus it is not plain sailing. If we suppose the full rate of Government spending to begin immediately, without any improvement in the export industries or any reduction in other activities, unsupported by organised overtime, by careful planning and an interval for the planning to take effect, there is a risk of what might fairly be called inflation. Is the Chancellor's claim that he can avoid inflation nevertheless justified? For the following reasons I believe that it is.

Other resources

In the first place, my 'multiplier' of three times may, in present circumstances, exaggerate the scale of the repercussions. As prosperity increases, saving probably increases more than in proportion; particularly when profits are rising. It may well be that the total increase in expenditure, resulting from loans of £80,000,000, will be no more than (say) £170,000,000, or 4 per cent of the national income—an improvement which it would be much easier to accomplish than $5\frac{1}{2}$ per cent.

In the second place, some part of the new demand will be met, not by increasing home output, but by imports (which I have not allowed for in the above calculation). This means either that the imports will be offset by increased exports, or, failing this, that there will be a diminution of net foreign investment.

Probably there will be a bit of both. We can look forward to an increase of 'invisible' exports through the increased earnings of our shipping and our foreign investments and, perhaps, from visitors to the Coronation [of George VI]. But it remains particularly advisable to do anything possible to stimulate our staple exports. For it is there that our reserves of surplus labour are chiefly to be found. It is no paradox to say that the best way of avoiding inflationary results from the Chancellor's loan is to increase both imports and exports. In any case, we can make a deduction of (say) 15 to 20 per cent on account of increased imports, which brings down the increase in the national output (apart from exports) necessary to avoid inflation to a figure between $3\frac{1}{2}$ and $4\frac{1}{2}$ per cent.

Thirdly, measures to ensure that all possible orders are placed in the Special Areas where surplus resources are available will greatly help. It is a mistake to suppose that this is merely a form of charity to a distressed part of the country. On the contrary, it is in the general interest. Whether demand is or is not inflationary depends on whether it is directed towards trades and localities which have no surplus capacity. To organise output in the Special Areas is a means of obtaining rearmament without inflation. I am not sure that this is properly understood. One feels that the War Departments are inclined to regard a Special Areas measure as a form of charity, doubtless praiseworthy, which interferes, however, with their getting on with the job in the most efficient way. On the contrary, it is only by using resources which are now unemployed that the job can be got on with, except at the cost of great waste and disturbance. The Special Areas represent our main reserve of resources available for rearmament without undue interference with the normal course of trade. They are not a charity, but an opportunity.

We are still assuming that new capital investment, apart from rearmament, will continue on the same scale as before. It seems possible, however, that there will be some reduction in new building. By an extraordinary and most blameworthy short-sightedness, our authorities do not think it worth while to collect complete statistics of new building, the figures for the County of London being omitted from the published aggregate. But new building may easily fall short of last year by £20,000,000, which would provide a quarter of the Chancellor's requirements. There remains capital development carried out by the railways, public boards, and local authorities, which should be to some extent controllable by deliberate policy. On the other hand, increased investment may be necessary in some directions, to provide new plant where marked deficiencies exist. Nevertheless a net increase in output of 3 per cent might see us through, after allowing for the other offsets we have mentioned; and that is an improvement we might reasonably hope to accomplish in the near future.

Need for planning

I conclude that the Chancellor's loan expenditure *need* not be inflationary. But, unless care is taken, it may be rather near the limit. This is particularly so in the near future. It is in the next year or eighteen months that congestion is most likely to occur. For ordinary investment is still proceeding under the impetus of the recent years of recovery. In two years' time, or less, rearmament loans may be positively helpful in warding off a depression. On the other hand, the War Departments may not succeed—they seldom do—in spending up to their time-table.

This conclusion is subject, however, to an important qualification. The Government programme will not be carried out with due rapidity, and inflation will not be avoided, by happy-go-lucky methods. The national resources will be strained by what is now proposed. It is most important that we should avoid war-time controls, rationing and the like. But we may get into a frightful muddle if the War Departments merely plunge ahead with their orders, taking no thought for general considerations affecting foreign trade, the Special Areas, and competing forms of investment.

I reiterate, therefore, and with increased emphasis the recommendation with which I concluded my former articles in *The Times*. It is essential to set up at the centre an organisation which has the duty to think about these things, to collect information and to advise as to policy. Such a suggestion is, I know, unpopular. There is nothing a Government hates more than to be well-informed; for it makes the process of arriving at decisions much more complicated and difficult. But, at this juncture, it is a sacrifice which in the public interest they ought to make. It is easy to employ 80 to 90 per cent of the national resources without taking much thought as to how to fit things in. For there is a margin to play with, almost all round. But to employ 95 to 100 per cent of the national resources is a different task altogether. It cannot be done without care and management; and the attempt to do so might lead to an inflation, only avoidable if a recession happens to be impending in other directions. The importance of collecting more facts deserves particular attention. For my estimates, given above, are of course no better than bold guesses based on such figures as are accessible. They are obviously subject to a wide margin of error.

On 20 April Neville Chamberlain introduced his last Budget as Chancellor of the Exchequer. In it he proposed a new tax, a National Defence Contribution, levied on profits on a progressive scale.[4] Keynes commented on the proposal.

To the Editor of The Times, *23 April 1937*

Sir,

Since the Chancellor of the Exchequer has invited comments on the new tax before he crystallises his scheme in the Finance Bill, I suggest that the four points following are those which need most attention:—

[4] Eventually Chamberlain withdrew the proposal in the face of widespread criticism and replaced it with a flat 5 per cent tax.

(1) Those firms whose profits suffered most in the slump will now suffer most from the tax. This cannot be intended. It is a condition of far-sighted enterprise that results can be averaged out. The new tax should only operate, therefore, when the cumulative profits averaged over a period of (say) the last six years exceed the prescribed standard.

(2) The tax will mainly fall on the following classes of enterprise:—

(*a*) Young and growing firms of which the real assets chiefly consist in the skill and character of the managers, in the connexions which they have built up, and in equipment paid for out of loans provided by friends or bankers who felt personal confidence in the enterprise.

(*b*) Firms of which the assets are largely intangible in the shape of goodwill, organisation, and some special expertness of which they are beginning to reap the fruits.

(*c*) Firms which have been recently successful in enterprises which are, in their nature, risky, and in which only a minority succeed.

(*d*) Wasting assets such as mines.

(*e*) The firms already mentioned which suffered exceptionally in the slump.

Before the Chancellor proceeds with the tax, he should make up his mind that these are the people he wants to attack, and should defend his proposals by giving reasons for singling them out for a special imposition. The way to get off the tax will be to have plenty of scrap iron in the backyard which cost a lot when it was new, and managers who have passed their best.

(3) The incidence of the tax may largely depend on the accident of the company's capital structure. A company which has debentures or bank loans may have to pay much more than an exactly similar company which has preference shares instead. This could be remedied by interpreting more literally the Chancellor's phrase that the 'capital' will consist of 'the cost of their assets in the business'. A company which recently bought its goodwill from the pioneer concern will escape; while

a business which has not been rehashed for sale to the public will pay. The liability of concerns which have been reconstructed owing to loss of capital would appear to depend on the precise technique of reconstruction which was adopted. It is not obvious how these anomalies can be overcome.

(4) From the way the Chancellor spoke and from the standards of return he assumed, one would infer that he only had home industry in mind. But unless provision is made to the contrary, his proposals will apply to oversea enterprises if their head organisation is situated in this country. Indeed, I should suppose that a large part of his estimated revenue is expected from mines, rubber plantations, and oil companies operating in the Empire or in foreign countries, which are caught both ways because they had little or no profits in the slump, yet require for a reasonable average return much more than 6 per cent in the boom. Moreover, extraordinary anomalies arise. Exactly similar mines or plantations operating side by side in the same district of Malaya or Australia, both owned by British shareholders, will pay a high proportion of their profits or escape altogether according to the accident of where their head office is situated. South African gold mines will get off because the legal domicile of their management is in Johannesburg, but West African gold mines will pay. Rhodesian copper mines, having committed the indiscretion of establishing headquarters in London, will be among the largest contributors to the new tax, while Canadian copper mines will escape. Liability to the tax will depend neither on the country of the enterprise nor on the country of the shareholder, but on the domicile of the head office. I am aware that some such anomalies already affect foreign holders of certain shares. But the Chancellor runs the risk of making the use of London as headquarters prohibitively expensive. Is this what he desires? The principle of an excess profits tax on concerns operating under the laws of another country seems open to question. There is no remedy for this except to restrict the tax to home industry.

On the other hand, I do not agree with those critics who say that the Chancellor has much underestimated the yield of the tax in a full year. Indeed, if all the concessions are made which justice or expediency requires, the Chancellor will be lucky if half his present estimate remains. The Stock Exchange has, I think, taken the financial results of the tax too tragically, though this is a natural reaction to a proposal which creates so much, and perhaps such an enduring, uncertainty. The average investor will suffer from the tax very little. If a representative list of investments is taken, it appears that at least nine-tenths will pay either nothing at all or nothing material. But that, unfortunately, is one of the evils of the tax. It will fall arbitrarily, heavily, and disproportionately on the ordinary shareholders in a minority of enterprises which happen to suffer from an unlucky conjunction of circumstances—accidents of past history and capital structure, of class of business, of head office address, or merely because they are young and prospering. It is like a tax on twins whose names are in the first volume of the telephone book and happen to have been born in 1900.

I have not mentioned what some consider to be the biggest objection—namely, the administrative and legal problems which will waste the time and energy of businessmen for years to come and involve all new plans in an atmosphere of uncertainty. It is for those who have had practical experience of E.P.D.[5] to be eloquent on this. But there is one important objection of principle which it is proper for an economist to emphasise. Future prosperity requires that the returns on enterprise and risk should be improved relatively to the returns on usury. In other words, the margin between the entrepreneur's profit and the *rentier's* interest must be carefully protected if private enterprise is to solve the problems of the future. This tax aims at narrowing the margin.

It is evident that the Chancellor's object in proposing the tax is just and sincere; and few will dispute that he is well advised to look round for a new source of revenue. But when

[5] The World War I Excess Profits Duty.

he claims that the principle of this tax is approved, what does he mean? What is its principle? He disclaims the idea that it is intended as a profiteering tax. The only principle apparent behind its anomalies and arbitrary incidence is that it is a tax on enterprise, growth, and youth as such. Is this principle generally approved?

Your obedient servant,

J. M. KEYNES

Throughout the winter of 1937 Keynes's health had been unsatisfactory. The problem had started with influenza in January, but afterwards he continued to complain of chest pains and shortness of breath. Over the Easter vacation he made 'slow progress' and had 'to behave as though I were feeble'. Early in the Cambridge Easter Term he suffered a serious heart attack and it was only after some weeks that he was in good enough condition to be moved to Ruthin Castle in Wales on 19 June.

During his slow recovery in Cambridge, Keynes wrote one letter to the press on the 'gold scare' caused by rumours that Britain and America would reduce the price of gold to limit accruals to their reserves.

To the Editor of The Times, *9 June 1937*

Sir,

The gold problem presents two distinct aspects. Should the dehoarding process, which was bound to occur some day, cause the authorities to modify their existing gold policy? Will the present price of gold cause an excessive quantity to be mined over a period of years and in the long run? The statements of Sir John Simon and President Roosevelt answer the first question quite clearly in the negative, and imply that the second question has not yet been considered but that both Governments will keep their hands free to deal with it in the light of future circumstances. This attitude seems sensible. Private dehoarding is a non-recurrent event which has been long foreseen, and the maximum amount is small compared with the stocks already in the hands of governments; while no one can answer the second question until we know how much gold output is going to increase, whether war or the fear of war will curtail the use of substitutes for gold, whether the existing maldistribution of gold stocks is to continue indefinitely, at what level money wages will settle down (particularly in the United States), and whether we are going to find ourselves, say, three years hence with good or bad employment.

Nevertheless, I believe that Sir John Simon could help, if he could be a little more explicit on certain matters. The atmosphere of nervousness at home and suspicion abroad is the nemesis of our policy of excessive secrecy. No one knows how much gold we already have or how far it is required to offset the so-called 'hot money', that is, abnormal foreign balances held precariously in London. It is quite possible that we actually need all the gold we have, if we are to avoid relapsing into the position discovered by the Macmillan Committee of having larger short-term liabilities to foreigners than we know how to meet. Moreover, as a former Treasury official whose duty it was during the late War to find ways of scraping together resources which could be used to make foreign payments, I should feel all the happier if I knew that we had in hand a surplus £1,000,000,000 of 'the ready'. We have to remember that, if there is another emergency, there will be no possibility of our being able to borrow abroad. An impregnably liquid financial position is one of the safeguards against trouble which should not be neglected.

If, on the other hand, the figures indicate (which would be contrary to my present expectation) that we have all the surplus gold we can reasonably require and that additional purchases, though we make them for the common good, are rather a nuisance, then let us modify the details of our policy accordingly. For example, this would clearly indicate that the embargo on foreign lending should be raised at once. It would be crack-brained to complain of a surfeit of gold and at the same time try to increase it by maintaining an embargo which dates from the period when we had a deficiency. There are also other ways in which we could reverse our former efforts to find means of economising the use of gold.

In particular, we could ask the Dominions, India, and the Crown Colonies to reconsider their policy, which was at one time extremely helpful to us, of handing their gold reserves to us in exchange for sterling balances. Australia is the outstanding example of this, but for the whole Empire it amounts to a great deal. Indeed, it would be well for the Imperial Conference, before they disperse, to consider whether they could not help us to carry the weight of gold—and this might be desirable even if the amount of the gold is not redundant from the standpoint of the Empire as a whole—by exchanging their sterling resources for earmarked gold. Since many of them are gold producers, they have much to gain from the restoration of confidence which this would undoubtedly effect.

Sir John Simon is new to what he rightly describes as these 'highly technical' problems. He necessarily needs—as anyone in his position must need—the benefit of collective wisdom. If his advisers become too subterranean, they will lack light. I would urge on him that he should first decide in his own mind whether, having regard to all the circumstances, we have or have not too much gold; and should then speak frankly to the House of Commons. He will find that suspicions will be dispelled and that, for the first time for years, the Chancellor of the Exchequer will have the benefit of well-informed comment.

I am, Sir, your obedient servant,
J. M. KEYNES

At Ruthin, Keynes underwent a complete examination. His treatment involved his remaining motionless for much of the summer. However, Keynes was soon rebelling in part, as he told Lydia on 29 June.

I fancy that the embargo on movements of the mind may be removed before the embargo on movements of the body. At least

I hope so! For my mind is terribly active. They can take away drink from patients who drink too much and food from those who eat too much. But they can't take my thoughts away from me. When the Great White Chief comes round this afternoon, I shall have to confess that I have written a letter this morning to the Chancellor of the Exchequer.

To SIR JOHN SIMON, *29 June 1937*

Dear Chancellor of the Exchequer,

I have a bright idea which I feel moved to pass on to you for what it is worth.

I suggest that you should offer to the new French Minister of Finance a loan of £100,000,000 out of the Exchange Equalisation Fund on the following conditions:-

(1) The loan would carry 3 per cent interest and would be repayable in ten equal annual instalments;

(2) Part of it would be used to fund the existing London bankers' loan which will fall due in the autumn (I forget the amount—about £40,000,000 I think, or a little more), the balance being handed over forthwith in the shape of gold;

(3) The Exchange Equalisation Fund would be free at any time to draw against the Bank of France in respect of any outstanding portion of the loan, in the event of the exchanges moving against this country so as to cause London to lose gold, either directly or indirectly, to Paris. This clause would not be quite easy to draft but it could be done. I remember that the first time I ever set eyes on the present Governor of the Bank of England at the Treasury in 1918—he was arguing (quite rightly as it subsequently turned out) in favour of a similar clause in the loans we were then making to France.

To my mind this is a *very* bright idea:-

(1) It amounts to handing back to France some part of the French hoards which have come here.

(2) From the Foreign Office point of view it is just what is

wanted. A gesture of solidarity at this moment would put matters in the right perspective, and do it in a quiet and sensible way. It is the only *quiet* gesture which it is open to us to make. It would strengthen the hands of moderate diplomatists elsewhere *next time* they are trying to give good advice.

(3) From the French point of view it would be of assistance quite out of proportion to the money involved. It would give them a breathing space; and it might just make the difference to sentiment which would render their hideous problem soluble.

(4) It would protect the Tripartite Agreement.

I am sure everyone will be grateful for your speech yesterday on the Equalisation Fund. In existing circumstances it meets the case completely.

Yours sincerely,
[copy initialled] J.M.K.

From SIR JOHN SIMON, *13 July 1937*

Confidential

My dear Keynes,

I am so sorry to hear that you have been laid up and I hope your letter of June 29th means that you are better.

It had not escaped the attention of the Treasury that a direct gold loan to France would be a method of easing the present situation, but I should find it difficult to believe that such a step could be taken as a *quiet* gesture. Whatever the wording of existing statutes may be, I could not feel that the Exchange Equalisation Account could be used for such a purpose without *express* statutory authority, for such a step would not be taken *merely* for the purpose of preventing undue fluctuations in the exchange value of sterling, and, as a practical matter, would require express Parliamentary direction. I should not feel certain how Parliament would view the matter, even with the safeguards you suggest, and the proposal might be regarded as seriously contentious.

The situation in France is disturbing and I am constantly urging on the French Government that they can only save the position by making such obviously sincere efforts to secure Budget equilibrium as to encourage the panic-stricken capitalist to take his capital back to his own country.

Otherwise I cannot see repatriation going on in sufficient volume, whether the exchange is 110 or 129—or 200!

Thank you for your kind reference to my speech on the Equalisation Fund.

With good wishes,

Yours very sincerely,

JOHN SIMON

To SIR JOHN SIMON, *26 July 1937*

My dear Chancellor of the Exchequer,

Many thanks for taking so much trouble to reply to me, and also for the message you sent me by Foster from your meeting at Chester. I did not really mean that you should take so much trouble in replying.

I quite agree that my suggestion would have required legislation. Also the psychological moment for it has clearly passed by for the moment.

It is all very well to urge the French Government to balance the Budget, and indeed they are making some efforts. But I am convinced that they cannot succeed, whatever they do, unless they abandon rearmament, or convert the debt to a near [?new] rate of interest. The latter can only come about either as a result of repatriation of capital or as a forced conversion. I was anxious that no opportunity should be let slip, either now or in the future, of seizing an opportunity to create a situation in which repatriation could occur. On the other hand, it may well be the case that forced conversion will prove, sooner or later, to be the only way out.

I am making good progress here and am really quite enjoying my leisure. But the process seems to be a slow one.

Yours sincerely,

[copy not initialled or signed]

During the summer and early autumn, Keynes made a few further contributions to discussions of foreign policy, both in *The New Statesman* and *The Times.* These appear in volume XXVIII.

Keynes's illness meant that he missed the meetings of the Committee on Economic Information for a period of eighteen months. However, his absence also meant that more of his views on the development of reports, normally lost in the conversations of meetings, took a written form. His first comments concerned the Committee's Twenty-Third Report which the Committee had decided in July would discuss 'questions connected with the price level, the future of international trade, and the future of gold'.[6] Keynes first commented on it on 20 October.

To SIR JOSIAH STAMP, *20 October 1937*

My dear Stamp,

As I have been, I am glad to see, ruled out by the footnote to the preface in the current report of the E.A.C., I really have no business to comment. I do feel, however, that it is extremely inadvisable to make the proposal for an import duty on new gold in its present half-baked and inconsistent form. At any rate, it should be pointed out that of all the proposals yet made this one contains the greatest potentiality of fluctuations in the exchanges and is diametrically opposed to the ideal advocated elsewhere in the report. Moreover, the question of as to how to distinguish new and old gold, after the first instance, is not in the least faced. Suppose Germany or Czecho-Slovakia purchase new gold from Russia and subsequently one or other of these countries make an export of gold, how is the distinction to be made? Clearly the tax must be imposed on all imported gold, with the result that there is a potential fluctuation of 25 per cent in the exchanges between gold import and gold export point.

Nor does there seem any attempt to face the fact that the greater part of the British Empire would have to be excluded from the Tripartite Agreement.

Apart from this, however, I feel that the whole of the paragraphs 44–89, which were quite apropos when they were

[6] Normally the Committee held a meeting to decide what topics to discuss and then the Secretary (Henderson to 1934, Piers Debenham afterwards) prepared a draft report for discussion. It was agreed throughout that members would not quibble over detailed points of drafting.

first conceived, are now completely out of date and ought to be put into cold storage, at any rate for the time being. In present circumstances, with falling prices and widespread fears of a slump, surely nothing is more unlikely than that any sane person will propose steps to reduce the value of gold. Both the subject matter and the treatment are very much out of touch with current events.

I am making excellent progress, but am still to be kept in seclusion for a bit yet.

Yours ever,
[copy initialled] J.M.K.

From SIR JOSIAH STAMP, *22 October 1937*

My dear Maynard,

It is great to hear from you again. There were many enquiries after you from the Committee. I am glad to know from *you*, yourself, that you are making progress, and that the 'topknot' at any rate, is as active as ever!

There were special reasons before the Committee dealing with the subject of the import duty, but with no desire to advocate it, and every desire to disapprove of it. If this has not been achieved we can, at any rate, secure it, and I will put your points to the Committee next week.

Yours ever,
J. STAMP

To SIR JOSIAH STAMP, *25 October 1937*

My dear Stamp,

I am relieved to hear that the Committee do not favour the proposed import duty. But this being so, I think they could well express themselves more trenchantly. I, not having heard the discussion, read the memorandum as being tepid and unconvinced advocacy, but certainly not as definite disapproval. The points to stress seem to me to be:—

1. that it wholly disrupts the sterling bloc and the currency arrangements of the British Empire, and

2. contains greater potentialities for an instability of the exchanges than any scheme yet mentioned.

Need one say more?

Yours ever,
[copy initialled] J.M.K.

On reading the completed report, he went further.

To SIR JOSIAH STAMP, *7 November 1937*

Dear Stamp,

A perusal of this quarter's report of the Economic Advisory Council has brought me reflections, of which I should like to unburden myself to you.

Resting for once under no compulsion to concentrate conscientiously on reading the text, I have been impressed even more than in previous months with its quite appalling verbosity. I should think that there can be very few people who will persevere with it to the end. Even so, they will not find it too easy to discover what it all amounts to, though, in this particular instance, I doubt if that very much matters;—indeed it may be rather fortunate.

I calculate that the text must be somewhere about 35,000 words of intricate and confused verbosity. Apart from the point of view of the reader, this excessive length has great objections from the point of view of the Committee. In the first place, its composition takes much too long, with the result that it is likely to be out of date before it circulates. This is notably so in the present case, where the whole theme is the last one which would have been selected at the date of its actual issue. In the second place, it means that the Committee never has time for its adequate examination and criticism; in spite of the fact that you have the art of reading out aloud faster than any man alive, it is quite impossible for such a busy Committee to tackle adequately such an enormous document. Partly as a result of this it signally fails, I feel, really to express the mind of the Committee. Although Hubert frequently had decided opinions of his own, he was infinitely more successful in drafting something which represented, not too much his own point of view, but the sense of the Committee as it emerged in the discussion. I feel that today a very large proportion of the memoranda does not really represent the view of any member of the Committee. What largely happens today is that individual members of the Committee try to drop on such passages from which they dissent vehemently and endeavour to get them modified. But it would not be true to say that the documents are really representative of the Committee's collective wisdom.

I feel strongly that something drastic ought to be done in the matter. The current production is a really dreadful document.

I am sending a copy of this letter to Hubert in view of his experience in the matter from the secretary's side of the table as well as from ours.

I shall be interested someday to hear the occult reason which lay behind the studious friendliness of the Committee to the surely ridiculous import tax proposal.

Yours ever,
[copy initialled] J.M.K.

From SIR JOSIAH STAMP, *10 November 1937*

My dear Keynes,

Many thanks for your letter of the 7th unburdening yourself of views—very justly held, I'm afraid.

This report has from the beginning—whether due to your absence or not, I don't know—been particularly intractable. The members took a long time to get their ideas into any kind of shape at all as instructions for D.[7] When he got them he hated them, and has never been happy with the job, I know. Recently we have been endeavouring to accommodate two extremes in Leithers,[8] internationalist, and Phillips, isolationist, without much success, I fear.

[7] Debenham.

[8] Sir F. W. Leith-Ross.

The report is excessively long, but as we haven't produced as much this year it may 'get by'. But it will be an object lesson for our next. As a matter of fact its text has been *more* thoroughly looked at by the Committee than usual, and I *haven't* done much reading!

The introduction of the import tax subject was due to me originally, as I got the project as a very likely one hot from Washington, and we wanted to be ready to meet it by examination if it came over. But if it developed on friendly lines that was never intended!

Yours

J. C. STAMP

To H. D. HENDERSON, *7 November 1937*

Dear Hubert,

I enclose a copy of a letter which I have written to Stamp. It explains itself. For some time past I have been feeling that the composition of the memoranda has been taking a wrong course. But this time, reading it from afar, I felt my objections still more strongly, and I felt it a duty to put them down on paper. What is your opinion?

I listened in at your broadcast[9] the other night and thought it very good indeed. The sort of criticism which any kind of prudence appears to be arousing is most alarming.

I enclose a query on a recent note of your[s] to the E.A.C.[10]

Yours ever,
[copy initialled] J.M.K.

From H. D. HENDERSON, *11 November 1937*

My dear Maynard,

First of all how are you? I gather that though still not allowed to bustle about London you really are decidedly better. Is that right? I hope we shall meet soon.

As regards the latest E.A.C. document I think we are all conscious that it is the most unsatisfactory report we have ever produced, and that is really

[9] 'Stock Exchange Slump and Trade Activity', *The Listener*, 3 November 1937.

[10] Not printed.

why some of us are still causing trouble at an unusually late stage, although in our hearts we never wish to see the report, much less discuss it, again. But the main cause that has led to this result is that the Committee are really hopelessly divided on the merits of the issues that arise. Indeed, this understates the difficulty. A clear cut division of opinion on a single central issue can sometimes be glossed over by the method of expounding the pros and cons, so as to produce a result of at least arguable expository value. But in this case there was not a single issue but a variety of issues which never got sharply defined in discussion, and about three or four distinct points of view. And an important contributing factor to the confusion is that the real protagonists of adverse points of view include Leith-Ross and Phillips, who are obviously in complete disagreement with one another but who, after the manner of officials, do not attempt to expound their position clearly. As soon as the confusion of views became apparent in the first discussion I am sure that it was a mistake to attempt to go on with this subject at all.

On the top of that there are Piers' defects as an expositor. Both in speech and writing he tends to be involved and incoherent and he is further a prey to the economist's occupational disease of translating a good and comparatively simple point, which is actually suggested to him by common-sense considerations, into terms of esoteric abstract analysis, for which he has an affection. In general, however, I think he is tending to improve in these respects and it is the confusion of views on the Committee that explains the abnormal degree of confusion in this report.

His strength is that he really has an ingenius [*sic*] and powerful mind and every now and then puts forward a new way of approaching a question which is of real value. And in this connection I do not agree with you about the import tax proposal, which I think is entirely his invention. I approach the question from the following position: Some form of internationally accepted purchasing power is an important, if not a vital, condition of a satisfactory system of international trade; but it is essential that the volume of this international purchasing power should be neither inadequate nor excessive. In principle it is desirable that it should be controlled, and expanded or contracted in accordance with the needs of the situation, by some international authority, e.g. an international note issue which the different countries would treat as they now treat gold. It was in accordance with that line of thought that we suggested a few years ago our 'reflaters' scheme to supplement the stock of gold when this appeared insufficient. The danger ahead is now the opposite one of a redundant supply of gold, which may conceivably lead in the end to the disuse of gold as a store of international value. If this should ever present itself as an acute danger all sorts of serious practical problems will arise, the vested interests of gold producing countries, the balance sheet positions of central banks, etc. Would not it, therefore, be desirable in principle that the various governments instead of abandoning the use of gold altogether should agree to regard one another's gold stocks as constituting the international purchasing power they will still continue to employ, and should further continue to accept newly mined gold as the basis of such additions to the volume of the international purchasing power as would still be required? This points to the solution of a restriction scheme to regulate the volume of gold production; but it is hard to suppose that a producers' scheme could work. Might it not, therefore, be the best plan that the countries which absorb the new gold should agree with one another to limit the amount of new gold they will take? This too would bristle with practical difficulties; but not necessarily insuperable ones. Might not an import tax on newly mined gold be a feasible first step towards an eventually satisfactory solution?

Personally I think it is useful to get the minds of people like Phillips directed to problems and possibilities of this kind, so I am inclined to regard the inclusion of this proposal as the one useful thing in the report. It is true, of course, that no Cabinet Minister would be expected to make head or tail of it; but I imagine they must have given up reading our documents long ago.

As regards your question on my note, which I return, the point is surely that a purchase of gold yields no interest, while an ordinary foreign investment presumably does. There are limits, it seems to me, to the proportion of the national income we can wisely invest in assets which yield no return, and may go bad as regards their capital value.

Yours ever,
H. D. HENDERSON

To H. D. HENDERSON, *14 November 1937*

Dear Hubert,

In the light of what you say, obviously it would have been much better to have scrapped the memorandum on gold. But I feel strongly that the length of these memoranda in itself is a severe handicap, and a great deal would be gained merely if a rigid word limit could be enforced.

As regards the import duty, it is not the object that I was dissenting from but this particular method; partly because it seemed to me so patently inconsistent with so much else in the memorandum. I thought it ought to have been pointed out that it would lead to greater potential instability of the exchanges than any other proposal, and would disturb the currency arrangements of the British Empire. It would valorise vast stocks of gold in the U.S.A. at the expense of the Empire gold producers. It would require a more rigid agreement amongst those adhering to the fact [?pact] even than other schemes.

I should have had no objection to your note if you had said that 'it represents indeed a contraction of the national income to the full extent of the interest on the value of the redundant gold stocks held'.

I am vastly better and doing a great deal more work than I was. Also I walk as much as a mile. But it seems a dreadfully slow business, and I still spend half the day in bed. They promise me complete recovery within the next six months, but not necessarily before then.

Yours ever,
[copy not signed or initialled]

November also saw Keynes express his views more generally in a letter to W. W. Stewart following the death of Walter Case in October.[11]

To W. W. STEWART, *14 November 1937*

My dear Stewart,

Many thanks for your letter of October 21st. I hope very much that we shall be able to keep in touch. I hear from May that you are quite likely to be over here next month. If I am still kept by my health in the country and am not yet about London, I hope very much that you will come down here for a night.

There are several matters of interest to me where Walter used to keep me pretty well informed from time to time, and I should

[11] See *JMK*, vol. X, pp. 326–7.

be extremely grateful if the same sort of information could be passed on. At the moment I might mention Homestakes and U.S. Smelting and also the Lard and Cotton Oil situations, Ruppert's memoranda about which have always been most interesting. And also, of course, I should be greatly interested in your general view of the present rather odd situation.

My own views are of moderate character. I do not expect a war, and I do not expect a major recession. On the other hand, international politics will interfere with the development of full business confidence, and some sort of recession seems obviously to be in progress on your side.

Our economic troubles here are, I should say, not yet at hand; though I think the Government are wrong in not preparing for a setback, I think they are right in not seeing any significant sign of it at present. The reduction in building is not so great that the increase in armament expenditure cannot keep pace with it; and sooner or later I expect a revival of shipbuilding. If we suffer a setback, the impulse will come from outside, either from U.S.A. or from the impact of falling commodity prices on our overseas markets. If you pull yourselves together in the course of the next six months, it will not be 1938 that will see a material setback in England.

As regards your own conditions in America, my view can be summarised as follows:—

The present recession ought not to have taken us by surprise, though, in the case of most of us, in fact it has. It has been obvious for some time that the Administration's earlier house-building programme was a failure, that the railroads had been made so unremunerative that they could not afford capital expansion, and that the President's attitude to the utilities was preventing normal expansion there, however much needed. This means that the major capital industries were under the weather and the recovery was being carried along mainly on the basis of the automobile industry, increasing consumption as a result of Government expenditure and the momentum which any recovery, once started, carries with it. Thus, it should have been obvious that, as soon as the Government began spending less, and as soon as the pace of improvement was somewhat moderated, a set back was entirely inevitable.

On the other hand it appears to me to be unusually easy to correct. It should not surpass the wit of the Administration to evolve a sufficient change of policy to stimulate the major capital producing industries. Physically there is a need for capital, and financial credit is abundant. In these conditions, it is only by the grossest blundering that the recession can be converted into a major slump.

The question of war is something to which you on your side pay much more attention than we do. We ignore it, perhaps because its chances are so entirely incalculable, much more incalculable, I should say, than your commentators are inclined to suggest. Nevertheless, there are plenty of reasons for not expecting a major disturbance. The dictators are bluffs and bullies. It suits their book far better to attack the helpless sheep rather than the other wolves. The other wolves are making it pretty plain that only in exceptional circumstances will they go to the rescue of the sheep. Why should the brigands attack the strong when there are so many weak ones ready to hand? I expect many shameful events, but they may well be such as not to involve a major war.

There is also one other factor, insufficiently emphasised in most people's mind. At present, perhaps, and in two or three years most certainly, Great Britain will possess a far greater preponderance of sea power in European waters than she has ever possessed in her history. I believe that our navy is not afraid of attacks from the air. Germany has no navy at all, and, practically speaking, Italy has none. I doubt if she has more than one or two modern ships altogether. This is the greatest factor for peace which exists. Also, apart from sea power, recent events have shown the tremendous advantages of the defence. I should expect that Czecho-Slovakia could give a pretty good account of herself, even if she is left entirely unsupported.

My idea is that Italy's ultimate objective is without doubt Egypt, and Germany's, although she says nothing about it, is probably Poland. Germany's chance of attaining her objective is very much greater than Italy's. But Italy's is, of course, far the greater menace to world peace.

Yours sincerely,
[copy not signed or initialled]

The recession led Keynes to defend proposals for counter-cyclical spending, when Sir Charles Mallet wrote to *The Times* suggesting that such works were unlikely to mitigate a slump when it came. Keynes replied, circulating his letter to the Committee on Economic Information for discussion at the same time.

To The Editor of The Times, *22 December 1937*

Sir,

Is it Sir Charles Mallet's point that (e.g.) slum clearance and the improvement of transport facilities do not increase employment? Or that they are of no public benefit when made? Does he believe that the present rearmament expenditure, partly financed out of loans, has no effect on employment? Or is he supposing that there is some special virtue in instruments of destruction, so that expenditure on them helps employment, whereas an equal expenditure on, let us say, objects of public health would be no use?

If he disputes the view that public loan expenditure helps employment he is running counter to the almost unanimous opinion of contemporary economists. He must also believe that the Prime Minister is throwing dust in our eyes in regarding our prospective expenditure on armaments as a reason for business optimism. Public loan expenditure is not, of course, the only way, and not necessarily the best way, to increase employment. Nor is it always sufficiently effective to overcome other adverse influences. The state of confidence and of expectation about what will happen next, the conditions of credit, the rate of interest, the growth of population, the state of foreign trade, and the readiness of the public to spend are scarcely less important. But public loan policy remains vitally significant, partly because it is the most controllable element in the situation, and partly because, in the modern world, a very large proportion of domestic investment necessarily depends on the policy of Government Departments, local authorities, public boards, and semi-public corporations, such as the railways. It is therefore very generally held today that there is a good deal of advantage in retarding expenditure by such bodies when other sources of demand are strong and in accelerating it when other sources are weak. This is probably a reason for not pushing such expenditure at present. But it is also a reason for planning beforehand what to do when the turn of the tide comes, since experience shows that quick improvisation is difficult and likely to be ill-advised, whereas action will be twice as effective if it is prompt.

It is almost as important to know when to act as to know what to do when the time comes. So may I add what is perhaps an even less controversial proposal—namely, an improvement in our sources of knowledge? The statistics of building plans approved, published monthly, to which it is usual to attach great importance, omit all building activities in the County of London and in rural areas or by the Government. Is there any good reason for this, which greatly impairs their value? Would Sir Charles Mallet think it unwholesome for us to know, except inaccurately, what building is in prospect? Moreover, we do not know the time lag between planning and execution, or what proportion of the plans are ultimately abandoned. The time lag must vary greatly according to the scarcity of labour and materials. Why should not contractors be required to notify monthly the amount of actual expenditure in respect of building plans approved? In this case our statistics are ahead of, and may exceed, actual expenditure. In the case of issues from the

Exchequer, on the other hand, actual expenditure by contractors is ahead of the statistics, and where capital expenditure is involved may exceed them. Why should not Sir Thomas Inskip obtain monthly returns from Government contractors of actual expenditure by them, including capital expenditure, in respect of rearmament? If we also had monthly returns from the principal steelworks, shipbuilders, electrical manufacturers and contractors, road contractors, railways, and motor manufacturers of (*a*) actual expenditure and (*b*) unfilled orders, we should know much better where we stand and where we are going. For we should have enough facts to give a reliable indication of the trends both of current expenditure and of decisions to spend not yet fulfilled. The Bank of England's excellent computations of the volume of retail trade and stocks show how much can be done by inquiries restricted to large concerns which do not attempt to be fully comprehensive.

Why should we not have convincing evidence of a satisfactory position and good warning of an unsatisfactory prospect? No delicate problems of bastardy or of contracts outside wedlock would be involved.

Your obedient servant,

J. M. KEYNES

To P. K. DEBENHAM, *22 December 1937*

Dear Debenham,

I enclose a copy of a letter which I have written today to *The Times*. In the second half of this letter I am making some suggestions about a collection of facts which I had previously intended to bring to the notice of the Economic Advisory Council with a proposal that something on these lines might be included in the current report.

I should be grateful if you could have copies of this made and put on the table for tomorrow's meeting. The collection of proper statistics is perhaps more urgent and less controversial than almost anything else.

Yours sincerely,

J. M. KEYNES

Sir Charles Mallet replied to Keynes's letter with the remark that Keynes did not meet his main point 'that experience teaches that attempts to provide such work (by Government) have generally failed'. Naturally, Keynes replied.

To the Editor of The Times, *1 January 1938*

Sir,

Examples abound in all parts of the world where public loan expenditure has improved employment; and I know of no case to the contrary. We have an example here at this moment.

Does anyone doubt that employment would decline if public loan expenditure on armaments were to cease tomorrow? On the other hand, there are examples of unprepared and ill-timed efforts proving insufficient. Indeed a prepared policy ready for application at the right time and on the right scale has never yet been tried. That such a policy has been frequently adopted and never successful, is a figment of Sir Charles Mallet's imagination. President Roosevelt's policy, which was nevertheless very useful so long as it was pursued, and saved the United States from grave disaster, was, of course, not a parallel case. It was largely devoted to improvising a system of relief and preventing a collapse of credit and general insolvency. Plans for increased capital expenditure on housing, the public utility services and the railroads were so completely unprepared that even today they are still in the stage of preparation. And it is this unpreparedness which is the cause of the present setback in the United States.

The weight both of authority and of public opinion in favour of meeting a recession in employment by organised loan expenditure is now so great that this policy is practically certain

"THE FELLER OUGHT TO BE ASHAMED! ENCOURAGING RAIN!"

Cartoon by David Low from *The London Evening Standard* of 5 January 1938, by arrangement with the Trustees and *The London Evening Standard*.

to be adopted when the time comes. The choice lies between preparation which will allow prompt, efficient and perhaps effective action, and a last-moment improvisation which will mean belated, inefficient and perhaps ineffective action.

Let me add that my preliminary questions to Sir Charles Mallet were plain questions meant to be answered. But that he acts prudently in finding an airy excuse to avoid them, I do not doubt.

Your obedient servant,

J. M. KEYNES

With the New Year the deepening recession which had struck Britain from the United States the previous year led Keynes to take another step.

To FRANKLIN DELANO ROOSEVELT, *1 February 1938*

Private and personal

Dear Mr President,

You received me so kindly when I visited you some three years ago that I make bold to send you some bird's eye impressions which I have formed as to the business position in the United States. You will appreciate that I write from a distance, that I have not re-visited the United States since you saw me, and that I have access to few more sources of information than those publicly available. But sometimes in some respects there may be advantages in these limitations! At any rate, those things which I think I see, I see very clearly.

1. I should agree that the present recession is partly due to an 'error of optimism' which led to an overestimation of future demand, when orders were being placed in the first half of this year. If this were all, there would not be too much to worry about. It would only need time to effect a readjustment;—though, even so, the recovery would only be up to the point required to take care of the *revised* estimate of current demand, which might fall appreciably short of the prosperity reached last spring.

2. But I am quite sure that this is not all. There is a much more troublesome underlying influence. The recovery was mainly due to the following factors:—

(i) the solution of the credit and insolvency problems, and the establishment of easy short-term money;

(ii) the creation of an adequate system of relief for the unemployed;

(iii) public works and other investments aided by Government funds or guarantees;

(iv) investment in the instrumental goods required to supply the increased demand for consumption goods;

(v) the momentum of the recovery thus initiated.

Now of these (i) was a prior condition of recovery, since it is no use creating a demand for credit, if there is no supply. But an increased supply will not by itself generate an adequate demand. The influence of (ii) evaporates as employment improves, so that there is a dead point beyond which this factor cannot carry the economic system. Recourse to (iii) has been greatly curtailed in the past year. (iv) and (v) are functions of the forward movement and cease—indeed (v) is reversed—as soon as the position fails to improve further. The benefit from the momentum of recovery as such is at the same time the most important and the most dangerous factor in the upward movement. It requires for its continuance, not merely the maintenance of recovery, but always *further* recovery. Thus it always flatters the early stages and steps from under just when support is most needed. It was largely, I think, a failure to allow for this which caused the 'error of optimism' last year.

Unless, therefore, the above factors were supplemented by others in due course, the present slump could have been predicted with absolute certainty. It is true that the existing policies will prevent the slump from proceeding to such a disastrous degree as last time. But they will not by themselves—at any rate, not without a large-scale recourse to (iii)—maintain prosperity at a reasonable level.

3. Now one had hoped that the needed supplementary factors would be organised in time. It was obvious what these were—namely increased investment in durable goods such as housing, public utilities and transport. One was optimistic about this because in the United States at the present time the opportunities, indeed the necessity, for such developments were unexampled. Can your Administration escape criticism for the failure of these factors to mature?

Take housing. When I was with you three and a half years ago the necessity for effective new measures was evident. I remember vividly my conversations with Riefler at that time. But what happened? Next to nothing. The handling of the housing problem has been really wicked. I hope that the new measures recently taken will be more successful. I have not the knowledge to say. But they will take time, and I would urge the great importance of expediting and yet further aiding them. Housing is by far the best aid to recovery because of the large and continuing scale of potential demand; because of the wide geographical distribution of this demand; and because the sources of its finance are largely independent of the stock exchanges. I should advise putting most of your eggs in this basket, *caring* about this more than about anything, and making absolutely sure that they are being hatched without delay. In this country we partly depended for many years on direct subsidies. There are few more proper objects for such than working-class houses. If a direct subsidy is required to get a move on (we gave our subsidies *through* the local authorities), it should be given without delay or hesitation.

Next utilities. There seems to be a deadlock. Neither your policy nor anyone else's is able to take effect. I think that the litigation by the utilities is senseless and ill-advised. But a great deal of what is alleged against the wickedness of holding companies as such is surely wide of the mark. It does not draw the right line of division between what should be kept and what discarded. It arises too much out of what is dead and gone. The real criminals have cleared out long ago. I should doubt if the controls existing today are of much *personal* value to anyone. No one has suggested a procedure by which the eggs can be unscrambled. Why not tackle the problem by insisting that the *voting power* should belong to the real owners of the equity, and leave the existing *organisations* undisturbed, so long as the voting power is so rearranged (e.g. by bringing in preferred stockholders) that it cannot be controlled by the holders of a minority of the equity?

Is it not for you to decide either to make real peace or to be much more drastic the other way? Personally I think there is a great deal to be said for the ownership of all the utilities by publicly owned boards. But if public opinion is not yet ripe for this, what is the object of chasing the utilities round the lot every other week? If I was in your place, I should buy out the utilities at fair prices in every district where the situation was ripe for doing so, and announce that the ultimate ideal was to make this policy nation-wide. But elsewhere I would make peace on liberal terms, guaranteeing fair earnings on new investments and a fair basis of valuation in the event of the public taking them over hereafter. The process of evolution will take at least a generation. Meanwhile a policy of *competing* plants with losses all round is a ramshackle notion.

Finally the railroads. The position there seems to be exactly what it was three or four years ago. They remain, as they were then, potential sources of substantial demand for new capital expenditure. Whether hereafter they are publicly owned or remain in private hands, it is a matter of national importance that they should be made solvent. Nationalise them if the time is ripe. If not, take pity on the overwhelming problems of the present managements. And here too let the dead bury their dead. (To an Englishman, you Americans, like the Irish, are so terribly historically minded!)

I am afraid I am going beyond my province. But the upshot is this. A convincing policy, whatever its details may be, for promoting large-scale investment under the above heads is an urgent necessity. Those things take time. Far too much precious time has passed.

4. I must not encumber this letter with technical suggestions for reviving the capital market. This is important. But not so important as the revival of sources of demand. If demand and confidence reappear, the problems of the capital market will not seem so difficult as they do today. Moreover it is a highly technical problem.

5. Businessmen have a different set of delusions from politicians; and need, therefore, different handling. They are, however, much milder than politicians, at the same time allured and terrified by the glare of publicity, easily persuaded to be 'patriots', perplexed, bemused, indeed terrified, yet only too anxious to take a cheerful view, vain perhaps but very unsure of themselves, pathetically responsive to a kind word. You could do anything you liked with them, if you would treat them (even the big ones), not as wolves and tigers, but as domestic animals by nature, even though they have been badly brought up and not trained as you would wish. It is a mistake to think that they are more *immoral* than politicians. If you work them into the surly, obstinate, terrified mood, of which domestic animals, wrongly handled, are so capable, the nation's burdens will not get carried to market; and in the end public opinion will veer their way. Perhaps you will rejoin that I have got quite a wrong idea of what all the back-chat amounts to. Nevertheless I record accurately how it strikes observers here.

6. Forgive the candour of these remarks. They come from an enthusiastic well-wisher of you and your policies. I accept the view that durable investment must come increasingly under state direction. I sympathise with Mr Wallace's agricultural policies. I believe that the S[ecurities and] E[xchange] C[ommission] is doing splendid work. I regard the growth of collective bargaining as essential. I approve minimum wage and hours regulation. I was altogether on your side the other day,

when you deprecated a policy of general wage reductions as useless in present circumstances. But I am terrified lest progressive causes in all the democratic countries should suffer injury, because you have taken too lightly the risk to their prestige which would result from a failure measured in terms of immediate prosperity. There *need* be no failure. But the maintenance of prosperity in the modern world is extremely *difficult*; and it is so easy to lose precious time.

I am, Mr President

Yours with great respect and faithfulness,
J. M. KEYNES

The President passed Keynes's letter to his Secretary of the Treasury Henry Morgenthau, asking him to draft a reply. The reply thus drafted went out with the President's signature.

From FRANKLIN DELANO ROOSEVELT, *3 March 1938*

Personal and Private

Dear Mr Keynes,

I am in receipt of your letter of February first, which I enjoyed reading. It was very pleasant and encouraging to know that you are in agreement with so much of the Administration's economic program. This confirmation coming from so eminent an economist is indeed welcome.

Your analysis of the present business situation is very interesting. The emphasis you put upon the need for stimulating housing construction is well placed, and I hope that our efforts will be successful in removing the barriers to the revival of this industry.

The course of democracy and world peace is of deep concern to me. Domestic prosperity, you will agree, is one of the most effective contributions the United States can make to their maintenance. You will likewise appreciate, I am sure, that prosperity in the United States will be more potent in attaining the ends we are all interested in if other democracies strive persistently for similar objectives.

I remember your previous visit very well and I hope we may have the opportunity to meet again.

Very sincerely yours,
FRANKLIN D. ROOSEVELT

When Keynes replied, he shifted the discussion on to another topic.

To FRANKLIN DELANO ROOSEVELT, *25 March 1938*

Dear Mr President,

It is very good of you to have written in acknowledgement of my letter. I do not mean to give you the trouble of doing so again by sending another brief comment. But further experience since I wrote does seem to show that you are treading a very dangerous middle path. You must either give more encouragement to business or take over more of their functions yourself. If public opinion is not ready for the latter, then it is necessary to wait until public opinion is educated. Your present policies seem to presume that you possess more power than you actually have.

Today, however, our thoughts are occupied with other things than economic prosperity. I venture to enclose an article which I have published today.[12] At any rate the poem which serves as its motto is very good. The tragedy is that the right-minded show no indication of supporting one another. You will be reluctant to support us; we are reluctant to support France; France is reluctant to support Spain. At long last we shall get together. But how much harm will have been done by then?

Yours very sincerely,
J. M. KEYNES

On 23 February Keynes made one of his first public appearances since his illness to address the annual meeting of the National Mutual Life Assurance Society. As usual, he touched on official financial policy.

FINANCING OF GOLD PURCHASES

I have mentioned that the year has been remarkable for the similarity of the movement in the gilt-edged and the other

[12] 'A Positive Peace Programme', *The New Statesman and Nation*, 25 March 1938 (*JMK*, vol. XXVIII).

markets. The fall in the gilt-edged market was particularly noticeable in the first three quarters of last year and has been commonly attributed to the Government's rearmament programme taken together with the increased demand for trade advances. I am disposed, however, to explain the decline mainly by reference to another factor which has been almost wholly overlooked.

This unsuspected factor is the particular technique by which last year the gold purchases of the Exchange Equalisation Fund were being financed. Attention has been called to this in the January *Bulletin* of the London and Cambridge Economic Service, and I owe the following figures to Mr F. W. Paish, the Secretary of the Service, who has made a special study of the workings of the Equalisation Fund. In these days of large gold movements the policy of the Bank of England is indeed of small account in its effect on credit and liquidity compared with the policy of the Equalisation Fund, about which we know nothing until some months afterwards. The gist of the matter is as follows:—In the first nine months of 1937 the Equalisation Fund purchased about £190,000,000 of gold. How was this paid for? The sale of Treasury bills to the market might be regarded as the 'normal' method. But that course was not adopted on this occasion. Indeed the bills held by the market actually fell by about £36,000,000 in the first nine months of last year, a repayment which can be accounted for by the Exchequer's revenue surplus, not unusual at that time of year but earned on this occasion after meeting the whole of the rearmament expenditure of the period. Actually this surplus amounted to about £48,000,000, leaving in hand a sum of about £12,000,000 beyond what was employed in withdrawing Treasury bills.

Method of payment

How, then, was the gold paid for? It is not easy to draw up an accurate balance sheet, but, ignoring contra items within the

Treasury accounts, the answer, roughly speaking, appears to be as follows:—£14,000,000 was raised by the resale of gold to the Bank of England; receipts on long-term capital account from the $2\frac{3}{4}$ per cent Funding Loan and National Defence Bonds exceeded capital repayments, &c., by about £104,000,000; there was a revenue surplus as above of £12,000,000 after repaying £36,000,000 Treasury bills previously held by the market; and the balance of about £60,000,000 would appear to have been provided out of the capital resources in the hands of various Government Departments, such as the Health Insurance Fund, the Unemployment Fund, &c., which took over Treasury bills from the Equalisation Fund, paying for them either out of current accruals or by the sale of longer-dated securities to the market.

Thus, one way and another, over and above the £36,000,000 Treasury bills repaid, about £176,000,000 of liquid resources was withdrawn from previous domestic holders and placed at the disposal of the foreigners who were bringing to London their 'hot' money in the shape of gold. Now, in so far as the foreign holders of the 'hot' money were prepared to invest it in National Defence Bonds and other securities purchased on the London Stock Exchange, well and good—the circle was complete. The Treasury would have exchanged the National Defence Bonds for the gold, and the domestic credit situation would have been left unchanged. But it is surely improbable that this was the case.

Liquid 'hot' money

Much of the 'hot' money will have been kept liquid in the shape of bank deposits, Treasury bills, and the like. Now the *total* supply of liquid assets in the shape of bank deposits and Treasury bills held by the market was not increased. Thus the amount of liquid assets acquired by foreigners out of the proceeds of the £190,000,000 in gold which they sold to the Equalisation Fund were almost wholly at the expense of the liquid assets previously held by the domestic market. It would seem reasonable to put the amount by which domestically held liquid assets have been reduced at between £100,000,000 and £150,000,000 at least. Thus the gilt-edged and other markets had to fall sufficiently to induce domestic holders, who had previously preferred to keep liquid, to part with this amount of liquid resources in exchange for less liquid assets. The sums involved were so large that it is a matter for surprise that gilt-edged prices did not fall more. This must have been by far the most important factor in the credit market in the course of the year. To the Treasury it may have merely seemed a highly convenient process of getting the resources of the Government Departments more liquid. The hidden transactions of the Equalisation Fund served to obscure the fact that it was entirely at the expense of the supply of domestic credit; but, in conjunction with the policy of borrowing well before the money was wanted so that resources were being hoarded meanwhile, it produced the inevitable and observed results on the gilt-edged market.

Unwanted gold

I suggest that these facts offer considerable food for thought. The object of the Equalisation Fund should be to 'sterilise' an influx of unwanted gold, so as to avoid the inflationary effect of a credit increase up to as much as 10 times the amount of the gold, which might result if the proceeds of the gold were allowed, as in the pre-war system, to be added to the deposits of the Bank of England. It is clearly advisable in general that the liquid resources in the market should not be raised by a multiple of a large precarious gold influx. But if they are not raised at all, then assuming that the vendors of the gold desire to hold a proportion of the proceeds in a liquid form, the influx of the gold must have a strongly deflationary effect on the domestic credit situation; whilst if the same methods are used when the gold flows out again, the loss of the gold will be the signal for the inflation of domestic credit. This is, indeed, a topsy-turvy business; exactly the opposite of what happened with the pre-war gold standard. If the managers of the Equalisation Fund desire the ebb and flow of 'hot' money to have the least possible effect on domestic credit, they must arrange for the market supply of liquid resources to be increased to the extent of the increased demand from the holders of the 'hot' money—in the shape partly of bank deposits, partly of Treasury bills, in the appropriate proportions. As it is, they have largely depleted the liquid resources of the domestic market at a time when the international situation and the recession in America were disposing the market to become more, rather than less, liquid. And the result is that institutional and other investors, no matter what their policy, have had a dismal, and indeed an insoluble, task to keep their assets intact.

Events since September

What has happened in the five months since September 30, 1937, we have not as yet the data by which to tell. It may be that the recent improvement in the gilt-edged market is due to a cessation, if not a reversal, of the above forces. I do not know. The policy of our financial authorities is not, I am afraid, meant to be understood; and perhaps I should apologise for the impiety of this attempt. But I am convinced that there are several aspects of the flux and reflux of 'hot' money, and the perplexing problem of how best to handle it, which deserve a fuller examination than they have yet received. There is, for example, the question of what rate of interest it is advisable for the banks to allow on foreign deposits, to which Lord Wardington rightly directed attention. We need to segregate these funds from the domestic credit system, so far as is practicable, allowing them neither to flood, nor to steal from, the appropriate level of liquid resources in the hands of domestic holders.

What of the future? In spite of the unemployment figures and the depression on the Stock Exchange, I am prepared, for my part, to accept the repeated assurances of the Government and the bankers that no significant further recession is discernible in the very near future. Indeed, it would be disturbing if it were otherwise during a period before rearmament expenditure has reached its peak and after a period during which we have had no benefit from Government loan expenditure, and have, on the contrary, been forced, as I have just shown, to part with a large volume of liquid resources to the holders of foreign refugee funds. The fact that Stock Exchange prices for industrial securities seem to imply complete disbelief in the official forecasts does not mean that the prices are based on superior information.

The speculative markets

Speculative markets are closely linked and cannot escape American and European influences. Moreover, they are governed by doubt rather than by conviction, by fear more than by forecast, by memories of last time and not by foreknowledge of next time. The level of stock exchange prices does not mean that investors *know*, it means that they do *not* know. Faced with the perplexities and uncertainties of the modern world, market values will fluctuate much more widely than will seem reasonable in the light of after-events; and one would hope that in such circumstances insurance offices will show a good example of steadiness.

The notion of us all selling out to the other fellow in good time is not, of course, a practicable policy for the community as a whole; yet the attempt to do so may deflect prices substantially from a reasonable estimation of their intrinsic value, and become a serious impediment to constructive investment. Those of us who have helped to popularise talk about the trade cycle must bear part of the blame for this. I sympathise with the authorities in their appeal to the business community not to become unduly slump-conscious. What we need is that the roles should be reversed, and that they should become more slump-conscious. We could sleep more easily in our beds if we felt that they were sleeping less easily in theirs.

Appeal to Government

For the difficulty of avoiding disastrous depression in the modern world can scarcely be exaggerated. It will need all our knowledge, all our preparedness, all our precaution, all our skill, all our technical accomplishment, and all our endowment of public spirit. I appeal to the Government in fervour of heart to lose no opportunity of adding to our knowledge of the essential facts and figures which alone can make the working of the economic system intelligible and distinguish true theories from false by the test of results. A great deal is at stake. We are engaged in defending the freedom of economic life in circumstances which are far from favourable. We have to show that a free system can be made to work. To favour what is known as planning and management does not mean a falling away from the moral principles of liberty which could formerly be embodied in a simpler system. On the contrary, we have learnt that freedom of economic life is more bound up than we previously knew with the deeper freedoms—freedom of person, of thought, and of faith.

His remarks were the subject of comment in the following Saturday's issue of *The Economist*, which gave it a generally warm welcome under the heading 'Interest Rates and the Treasury'. In the next issue, Keynes used that weekly's columns for a further comment.

To the Editor of The Economist, *2 March 1938*

Sir,

There are some points in your interesting article under this heading on which it may be used for me to comment.

I ought to have given in the first instance the reference to Mr Paish's estimate of the gold purchases in the first quarter of 1937, which is to be found in the issue of *Economica* for last August.[13] Mr Paish's method yielded an estimate for the gold held on March 31, 1937, made before the official figure was available, which was very nearly right. The excess of gold purchased in the first quarter of 1937, given by his method, over the actual imports of the period might be explained by gold earmarked at the Bank of France and actually imported later on. If, however, he has attributed to the first quarter of 1937 gold purchased at a previous period, an excess of, say, £30 millions in his estimate will not materially affect my argument, since I gave a very cautious and conservative estimate of the depletion of domestic liquid assets, which had a sufficient margin to cover an even larger error. I do not know why the Treasury should not give quarterly figures. Meanwhile, however, Mr Paish is performing a very useful service by employing the best available method of interpolation, particularly if his efforts result in the authorities being persuaded eventually to supply the actual figures.

A number of critics have seemed to think that the force of my argument is impaired by the fact that, whilst the fall in gilt-edged prices was fairly continuous over the nine months, about three-quarters of it occurred in the first three months. But I should not have expected a close correlation over very short periods between gilt-edged prices and the liquid resources of the domestic market. In the early part of the year the announcement of the defence programme, combined with a high level of business activity and some expectations of inflation, led to a rapid discounting of the supposed prospects, which would have proved an over-discounting and have been corrected instead of increased in subsequent months, if it had not been for the

[13] F. W. Paish, 'The British Exchange Equalisation Fund, 1935–37', *Economica*, N.S., August 1937.

further continuous depletion of the liquid resources available to the domestic market.

I do not want to overstate the part played by the Exchange Account. If there had been no influx of hot money and no gold purchases, and the Treasury had nevertheless depleted the liquid resources of the market to the same extent by direct action, the result would have been much the same. But, in view of various declarations by the Chancellor of the Exchequer, I felt it unlikely that the Treasury were depressing the gilt-edged market on purpose, and more probable that they were led to do so imperceptibly by a complicated train of events, including a new loan raised long before it was required, the final consequences of which were not fully realised. Thus it seemed worth while to raise an issue of high general importance which will emerge, independently of other events, whenever there are large operations either way by the Exchange Account. Moreover, if it were not for the hidden operations of this Account, the course of events would not be veiled from us until long afterwards.

The available *data* do not allow an exact quantification of the facts, and the statistical points discussed above are only details compared with what is known and agreed. For I infer from your article that you are in full accord with the main substance of the matter, namely that over the period in question there was a large depletion of the liquid resources of the domestic market, and that this was bound to have a very depressing effect on gilt-edged securities and, to a certain extent, on other securities also, particularly at a time when, as you point out, other influences—which, so far from wishing to neglect, I would wish to emphasise—were increasing the demand for liquidity. Furthermore, as you have previously pointed out, the rather absurd result of a deflation of domestic credit when gold flows in, and a corresponding inflation when it flows out again, will continue to occur, until the technique, apparently pursued at present, is revised. I regard this, the full complications of which

I have not attempted to explore either here or in my address to the National Mutual Life Assurance Society, as being today the major issue of credit policy.

I am,

Your obedient servant,

J. M. KEYNES

Keynes also wrote on the subject to Sir Frederick Phillips, the Treasury member of the Committee on Economic Information.

To SIR FREDERICK PHILLIPS, *25 February 1938*

Dear Phillips,

I enclose a copy of my speech this week to the National Mutual, though you may have seen it in *The Times*. I should like to call your attention to the argument which begins in the last paragraph of page 3 [above p. 441]. Probably my actual figures are inaccurate, though they are, I think, the best an outsider can do. But I feel great confidence in the argument.

Part of the adverse effect on markets is, of course, due to the Treasury having borrowed so long in advance of requirements, and would have occurred irrespective of the operations of the Exchange Account, unless other Government Departments had held the stock meanwhile. But the operations of the Exchange Account obscured what was happening for many months afterwards and, if I am right, very considerably aggravated it. I am convinced it would be an enormous help to the gilt-edged market, if the expenditure occurs a little before the borrowing, or at any rate if the two are done *pari passu*. Do not the funds accruing in the various Government Departments make possible a technique by which funded securities could be put on the market practically *pari passu* with the corresponding expenditure? There are, of course, two separate issues involved: the one which I have just mentioned, and the necessity of increasing the liquid resources of the market when the hot money held in London is increased.

Yours sincerely,
[copy initialled] J.M.K.

On 2 March he also sent Phillips a draft of his letter to *The Economist*. On reading the material Phillips replied.

From SIR FREDERICK PHILLIPS, *2 March 1938*

Dear Keynes,

Thank you for your two letters and enclosures which I have read with great interest.

The first point which strikes me is that the fall in gilt-edged took place mainly in the early months of 1937. The Abdication crisis had taken place in December and a little later defence expenditure was attracting great attention. The announcement on the 11th February 1937 of the necessity to borrow £400 millions for defence must surely have affected gilt-edged sentiment deeply, irrespective of any other happening whatever.

The figures for gold movements which you have taken from another source are, I am afraid, altogether wrong so much so as to destroy your statistical argument.

Your main point is however not based on particular figures, and as I see it it amounts to this. One of the causes which may disturb the credit position is an influx of gold, supposing that some considerable proportion of the persons who acquire sterling here as a result of the sale of gold prefer to hold that sterling in London in the form of bank deposits or other very short securities. This disturbance you hold should be countered by special measures first and only after that has been done should the Bank proceed to settle their credit policy generally. It is not however made clear why this primary importance is attached to the effect of gold movements over all the other important factors which may be affecting the credit situation. If in fact the general credit position is judged accurately all the time and appropriate measures taken by the Bank why should it matter that these measures are not ad hoc directed against the result of a gold influx? This it seems to me is the point which needs further explanation.

Yours sincerely,
F. PHILLIPS

To SIR FREDERICK PHILLIPS, *7 March 1938*

Dear Phillips,

Yes, my argument is meant to be a general one, not dependent on exact statistics. I did not work out the gold purchases myself, and in my final estimate of the depletion of domestic liquid resources, I allowed for an error in excess on Paish's part of £30,000,000, or even more.

On the general issue, I agree that credit policy must be decided by taking into account *all* the relevant factors. Thus, if, in the absence of any gold transactions, there was last year a good reason for a substantial contraction of domestic credit, from the practical point of view, my criticism would fall to the ground. But I was aware of no such reason. Certainly no reason has been given. Indeed, there were declarations both from the Chancellor and the Prime Minister, about the advisability of maintaining easy credit conditions, which implied the opposite.

The whole problem is, of course, a complicated one. But the following is a skeleton outline of what I have in mind. Let us assume for simplicity that it is desired to maintain the price of non-liquid gilt-edged assets in terms of liquid assets at about the existing level (the price of equities in terms of non-liquid gilt-edged assets will mainly depend on a different set of considerations).

Fluctuations in the *demand* for liquid assets by the domestic market at a given price level of non-liquid assets will chiefly depend on the state of confidence and expectation as to the future course of credit (which will tend to reduce the demand for liquid resources when it is favourable) and on the level of business activity (which will tend to raise the demand for liquid resources when it is high). On a balance of considerations I should say that this demand was probably rising in the course of last year, so that an increased, rather than a decreased, supply of liquid assets for the domestic market may have been necessary to maintain a constant price level of non-liquid assets.

Fluctuations in the *supply* of liquid assets available to the domestic market chiefly depend on (1) the supply of liquid assets created on the basis of the deposits at the Bank of England (2) the supply of Treasury bills issued to the market and (3) the amount of the above absorbed by foreign holders.

Last year there was no material change in (1) and (2) though such change as there was seems to have been in the downward direction. But there was a very large change in (3), with the result of a large diminution in the supply available to the domestic market at a time when the demand for liquid assets at a given price level of non-liquid assets was probably increasing. Thus equilibrium could only be brought about by a fall in the gilt-edged (and other) markets sufficient to deter people from getting, or keeping, liquid who otherwise would have preferred to do so.

(3) is not the only factor, but over the period in question it happened to be *much* the largest factor. Indeed my whole point was the advisability of offsetting it by changes in the other factors. If a large-scale contraction of credit in the domestic market was engineered on purpose with the object of bringing down the price level of securities, well and good. But, if so, what was the reason for such a reversal of previous policy?

Under the pre-war system there were two automatic safeguards (though in other respects there were much greater dangers to the steadiness of credit equilibrium). In the first place the amount of Treasury bills was very small and more or less constant, the fluctuating element in the supply of this type of liquid assets being trade bills; and trade bills tended to increase when the activity of trade increased. In the second place there were seldom large or sudden changes in 'hot' money, and, if they were sufficient to cause a movement of gold, there was an automatic (and indeed an exaggerated) change in the same direction in the supply of liquid resources.

Undoubtedly one of the sources of the trouble has been the

rearmament borrowing so long in advance of the corresponding expenditure. As I showed in a recent article in *The Economic Journal*,[14] borrowing in advance of expenditure amounts to a sort of hoarding which may cause a grave credit stringency. But borrowing accompanied by expenditure leaves the *credit* situation (it has other repercussions of course) unaffected. If the Supply Departments are returning the money to the market through their expenditure *pari passu* with the Treasury borrowing, the amount of liquid resources in the hands of the market remains unchanged. To borrow the money appreciably before you need it will increase the cost of the rearmament loans by many millions as compared with borrowing a little later.

For the sake of simplicity of exposition, I have assimilated bank deposits and Treasury bills in the above. But of course they are not interchangeable, and the extent to which each has to be increased or decreased must depend on a judgement as to which type of liquid resources is in relatively short supply.

Yours sincerely,
[copy initialled] J.M.K.

P.S. As you will have seen from the final version of my letter to *The Economist*, I do not attach importance to the precise date when the initial fall took place, since this would not have persisted if credit conditions had been subsequently other than they were. Indeed, it is obvious that the abdication crisis need not have had a lasting effect on the gilt-edged rate of interest after it was all over if it had not accidentally happened that the depletion of domestic credit was backing up the bearish view.

On 9 July *The Economist* printed a letter from R. F. Harrod suggesting that a reflationary banking policy aimed at reducing the long-term rate of

[14] 'The "Ex Ante" Theory of the Rate of Interest', *Economic Journal*, December 1937 (*JMK*, vol. XIV, pp. 215–23).

interest would, with rearmament, help end the recession. On reading this Keynes commented.

To the Editor of The Economist, *16 July 1938*

Sir,

May I endorse Mr Harrod's plea in your correspondence columns for concerted measures to reduce the long-term rate of interest. Most people would agree, presumably, that a reduction would be advantageous in present circumstances both to the Treasury and to business. If, however, there are some who doubt the efficacy of Mr Harrod's proposals, is there any objection to settling so important a matter by making the experiment?

I am, etc.,

J. M. KEYNES

On 28 May Oliver Stanley, the President of the Board of Trade, introduced an Essential Commodities Reserves Bill in the House of Commons to enable the Board of Trade to obtain information as to commodities essential in the event of war and make provision for the maintenance of reserves of such commodities. On examining the Bill Keynes wrote to Sir Arthur Salter.

To SIR ARTHUR SALTER, *6 June 1938*

Dear Salter,

The Essential Commodities Reserves Bill marks such tremendous progress that one wants to make sure that it is carried in the most convenient form, since it is not likely that another opportunity will arise for some time.

Do you think it is clear in Clause I (3) that the Board of Trade is nevertheless authorised to publish *aggregate* figures? They are entitled to collect for their own information what may prove to be vitally important facts for future diagnosis, and it is important that they should be free to publish them, provided of course that no clue is provided to the stocks held by any particular individual. The wording 'no information with respect to any particular undertaking' may be interpreted to allow aggregate information. But it might be important to get either an undertaking from the Minister that this is what it means, or express words.

In any case, however, this will only relate to food materials. Presumably the War Departments are dealing with non-food materials. Have they power to collect information as to stocks? If not should not the power to obtain information cover *every* kind of material, even though the rest of the Bill only relates to food materials? It is at least equally necessary to have information on the other kinds of stocks, and this would provide a convenient opportunity for obtaining statutory authority.

Yours sincerely,
[copy initialled] J.M.K.

From SIR ARTHUR SALTER, *8 June 1938*

Dear Keynes,

(1) I think the wording of 1(3) clearly leaves the B[oard] of T[rade] free to publish aggregate figures. Whether they will do so is quite another matter.

(2) The War Depts. are purchasing and storing certain materials they will need (e.g. oil). But I don't think they have legal powers to require information corresponding to those now being obtained for food etc.

I think myself the schedule should be extended so as to enable non-food commodities to be added. I advocated this in the debate, suggesting a distinction between the present category (where only an order 'to be laid before the House' is required) & the additional category for which orders requiring an affirmative resolution should be prescribed. This would be an intermediate step between inclusion in the single category & the present need of new legislation for non-food commodities.

I found Stanley strongly opposed to any extension not because he fears resistance but because he fears pressure to buy a lot more than he wants to. I expect he would oppose an enlargement of the powers as to information as being the 'thin end of the wedge'.

I will take up both points, however, when Parl. reassembles.

I greatly hope you are now nearing complete recovery.

Yours sincerely,
ARTHUR SALTER

From SIR ARTHUR SALTER, *16 June 1938*

Dear Keynes,

I have been talking to Stanley on the points about which you wrote to me.

(1) He confirms that the Bill gives full power to disclose *aggregate* figures. Indeed I don't think there can be any reasonable doubt about this.

(2) He is not prepared to *undertake* to give aggregate figures: & in this I cannot press him successfully, as he will (& indeed does) contend that in certain cases this might be militarily undesirable. In fact there is no hope of securing a promise while conditions are as at present.

(3) He resists any extension of the category of essential commodities—even as regards information; & while I'm still pressing on this I don't think I'll get anything. He is indeed rather morbidly afraid of having wider powers & then being forced to buy by pressure what he doesn't [want], & he thinks 'information' powers would make it more difficult for him to resist the wider powers.

I have agreed that, if he had a second schedule, requiring an affirmative resolution instead of the mere 'laying before the House' required for the second schedule, he would have a defence against pressure by making this distinction & at the same time escape the necessity of new legislation if, as is likely, he finds that he wants wider powers.

He is now considering this.

Yours sincerely,
ARTHUR SALTER

Keynes himself went further into the subject when preparing an Address for the August meeting, of Section F of the British Association for the Advancement of Science. Although he was unable to be present to read the paper himself, through Gerald Shove who read it and R. F. Harrod, the President of the Section, he learned of some of the comments made in the brief discussion that followed.

From The Economic Journal, *September 1938*

THE POLICY OF GOVERNMENT STORAGE OF FOODSTUFFS AND RAW MATERIALS

I

It is an outstanding fault of the competitive system that there is no sufficient incentive to the individual enterprise to store surplus stocks of materials, so as to maintain continuity of output and to average, as far as possible, periods of high and of low demand. The competitive system abhors the existence of stocks, with as strong a reflex as nature abhors a vacuum, because stocks yield a *negative* return in terms of themselves. It is ready without remorse to tear the structure of output to pieces rather than admit them, and in the effort to rid itself of them. Its smooth and efficient working presumes in practice, as stringently as the static analysis presumes in theory, a steady rate, or a steady growth, of effective demand. If demand fluctuates, a divergence immediately ensues between the general interest and the course of action in respect of stocks which is most advantageous for each competitive enterprise acting independently.

There are several reasons for this. The cost of storage and interest is fairly high, especially in the case of surplus stocks which strain the capacity of the normal accommodation. In the case of many commodities the charges probably approximate to 10 per cent per annum; whilst the length of time for which holding will be necessary and the ultimate normal price are both matters of great uncertainty. There are, however, two other still more dominating factors. Experience teaches those who are able and willing to run the speculative risk that when the market starts to move downward it is safer and more profitable to await a further decline. The primary producer is, as a rule, unable or unwilling to hold, so that, if the speculative purchaser holds back, he will get the commodity still cheaper. Thus, even if it would pay him to buy at the existing price on long-period considerations, it will often pay him better to wait for a still lower price. The other factor arises out of the lack of incentive to the retailer or the manufacturing consumer to purchase in advance. By purchasing in excess of his immediate needs he may make a speculative profit or loss just like any outside speculator, but as a trader or a manufacturer his position will be competitively satisfactory when the time comes to use the materials, provided he is paying the *current* price. Thus a cautious user would rather pay the current price for his raw materials on which his own selling prices are based than run a speculative risk; and this attitude is reinforced by the fact that his interests are already bound up with activity in the demand for the commodity in question, so that he is multiplying unnecessarily the same kind of risk if he buys his material in advance of his needs. On the other hand, the long-term holding power of the outside speculator is limited—most participants in the market being more interested in a rapid turnover—and can only be called into action on a sufficient scale by a drastic fall in price which will curtail current output substantially and appears to be a long way below any probable normal cost of future production.

For these various reasons the fluctuations in the prices of the principal raw materials which are produced and marketed in conditions of unrestricted competition, are quite staggering. This is the case not only during well marked trade cycles, but as a result of all sorts of chance causes which lead to fluctuations in immediate demand. The extent of these is apt to be concealed from those who only watch the movements of index numbers and do not study individual commodities; since index numbers, partly by averaging and partly by including many commodities which are not marketed in fully competitive conditions, mask the short-period price fluctuations of the sensitive commodities. Let me give some illustrations.

Rubber, wheat, lead and cotton will give us a good sample of the class of commodity which I have in mind. Let us examine by what percentage the highest price in each of the last ten years exceeded the lowest price *in that year*:-

Rubber. There has only been one year in the last ten in which the high price of the year has exceeded the low by less than 70 per cent. The average excess of the year's high over the year's low has been 96 per cent. In other words, there is on the average some date in every year in which the price of rubber is approximately double its price at some other date in that year.

Cotton. Since rubber may be regarded as a notoriously fluctuating commodity, in spite of its having been subject to an organised restriction scheme, let us take cotton. Only twice in the last ten years has the high price of the year exceeded the low by less than 33 per cent and the average excess of the year's high over the year's low has been 42 per cent.

Wheat, however, is nearly as fluctuating in price as rubber, which may perhaps surprise you. If we take the Liverpool contract as our standard, there has been only one year in the last ten when the highest price of the year has exceeded the lowest by less than 47 per cent; and the average excess of the year's high over the year's low has been no less than 70 per cent.

Lead is mainly marketed by a small number of powerful producers acting with some measure of consultation. Yet, even so, the annual range of price fluctuations is on much the same scale as with the commodities already examined. Only twice in the ten years has the price range from lowest to highest been less than 35 per cent, and the annual average range has been 61 per cent.

Thus for these four commodities—rubber, cotton, wheat and lead—which are, I think, fairly representative of raw materials marketed in competitive conditions, the average annual price range over the last ten years has been 67 per cent. An orderly programme of output, either of the raw materials themselves or of their manufactured products, is scarcely possible in such conditions.

The ill effect of these truly frightful fluctuations on trade stability is great. But the ultimate results of the obstacles which they offer to the holding [of] stocks may be even more injurious. In spite of the fact that the difficulty of rapidly altering the scale of output, especially where seasonal crops are concerned, leads to what appear to be very large stocks at the bottom of the market, nevertheless when the turn of the tide comes, stocks nearly always turn out to be insufficient, precisely for the reason that it is just as difficult rapidly to increase the scale of delivered output as it had been to diminish it. Prices rush up, uneconomic and excessive output is stimulated and the seeds are sown of a subsequent collapse.

Even though fluctuations in the demand for many finished commodities owing to changes in fashion and in the direction of demand may be unavoidable, and though it is certainly the case that no radical remedy for fluctuations is possible except through measures to stabilise the aggregate of effective demand, nevertheless some modification should be possible in the case of the great staple raw materials, most of which can be readily stored without serious deterioration, by direct measures affecting the individual commodity. Assuredly nothing can be more inefficient than the present system by which the price is always too high or too low and there are frequent meaningless fluctuations in the plant and labour force employed.

For many years the orthodoxy of *laissez-faire* and unregulated competition has stood in the way of effective action to fill this outstanding gap in the organisation of competitive industry. Even now the suspicion with which attempts at the long-period stabilisation of individual prices are rightly viewed is often directed also against measures aimed at short-period stabilisation. Nevertheless there are today many signs of attempts to tackle the problem by various methods and from various motives. It is these, and in particular certain important pioneer proposals by our own Government, which it is the object of this paper briefly to review.

II

There are, first of all, the devices for stabilising the prices of their products adopted by private enterprises without the aid or encouragement of governments. In some cases a single producer is responsible for the major part of the output, or a body of producers accepts a joint marketing policy and is in a position to fix the price with only a limited reference to the state of immediate demand. Nickel and diamonds are good examples of commodities subject to such marketing conditions. A recent small change in the British price of aluminium was the first change of any kind for six years. But in such cases the policy of price stabilisation is merely a part of a general policy of monopoly. An approximation to the same state of affairs arises through cartels, quotas and price agreements, sometimes of an international character, such as govern most types of iron and steel products, cement and many other semi-manufactured articles. Where output is in the hands of a small number of financially strong enterprises there may be looser, but nevertheless effective, arrangements, as in the case of copper and oil.

The multitude of such arrangements, which must cover far more products than anyone could specify in detail, only serves to increase the exposure of the remaining materials which are produced by a great number of independent producers, widely scattered in locality, marketing in conditions approximating to those of full competition. For we have today two contrasted types of marketing policy existing side by side. On the one hand, those enjoying what have been called 'administered' prices*—that is, with prices comparatively stable and fluctuations in demand met by a centralised control of output and by organised arrangements for the withholding of stocks on the part of the producers themselves—and, on the other hand, those with 'competitive' prices, where the producers themselves are not in a position to withhold their stocks and the scale of output is governed by price fluctuations. The former arrangement is apt to be objectionable in general, even when it is highly desirable for the particular purpose of meeting fluctuations, because it may be part and parcel of conditions of almost uncontrolled monopoly; whilst the latter arrangement is hardly less objectionable, in that it so greatly increases the risks and losses of enterprise.

The fact that we have two major groups of commodities which

* The term 'administered prices' is due to Mr E. G. Means of the U.S. Department of Agriculture.

respond quite differently to fluctuations in effective demand is of great importance to the general theory of the short period. In practice, however, it is in the United States that administrators have become most expressly conscious of the contrast, and Mr Roosevelt's Administration is simultaneously engaged in attempting to temper the element of monopolistic marketing in the first group and the element of competitive marketing in the second, twin objectives which are not so inconsistent with one another as they are sometimes represented to be. In all parts of the world, however, governments are now interesting themselves in this problem, and a great variety of schemes, most of them national and a few of them international, have come into being. We have the internationally controlled restriction schemes for sugar, tea, rubber and tin. But it is, at present, only in the case of tin that the restriction scheme is supplemented, as seems only sensible, by concerted arrangements for the withholding of stocks and thus securing a somewhat more continuous rate of output. There are many schemes—indeed, few countries are without them—for the marketing of wheat. Above all, there are the ambitious proposals, only in their initial stages at present, of Mr Wallace, the U.S. Secretary of Agriculture, for the establishment of what he calls an ever-normal granary.

The motives behind these various schemes are not all the same. In the majority of cases the primary object of the Government has been the protection of its small-scale producers from ruinous price fluctuations, of which the holding of stocks has been a subsidiary and undesired by-product. There are, however, certain examples of the withholding of stocks for its own sake, with a view to averaging the irregularities of demand and supply. The buffer pool for tin and Mr Wallace's ever-normal granaries for assisting particular commodities have been already referred to. I have heard mention, but not with details, of an experimental purchase by the Bank of Sweden of certain stocks of commodities as a form of central banking reserves alternative to gold, a policy which could be made a means, if widely pursued, of flattening out the fluctuations of prices. Above all, there is, with the primary object of accumulating stocks for use in time of war, our own extremely important *Essential Commodities Reserves Act* lately passed into law, to the rich possibilities of which I will devote the rest of this paper.

III

If only we could tackle the problems of peace with the same energy and whole-heartedness as we tackle those of war! Defence is old-established as a proper object for the state, whereas economic well-being is still a *parvenu*. Social action which is universally approved for the former purpose is still suspect when it is for the latter. Nevertheless, we are at this moment allowing war expenditure for defence to help solve our problem of unemployment as a by-product of such spending, whereas if disarmament had prevailed we might have allowed a serious recession to have developed by now before introducing loan expenditure on a comparable scale for the productive works of peace. So it may be possible, as I hope to show it is, to combine the primary object of the Government's new Act with purposes useful even in peace.

In the first place, the Board of Trade has taken powers to collect comprehensive statistics which it will be free to publish in terms of aggregates, though it is unfortunate that these powers are limited to the commodities which the Board of Trade will handle and does not cover those, such as the metals, which will be purchased by the War Departments (so departmental-minded is our Administration). This is important because, whilst we already have fairly good statistics of the 'visible' stocks, we have none of the 'invisible' stocks in the hands of manufacturers. Yet fluctuations in the visible stocks are often balanced, in part at least, by opposite fluctuations in the invisible stocks; and if the details of this were known, such extreme fluctuations of price might sometimes be avoided. Complete facts about the fluctuations in total stocks would be of great value in handling the trade cycle.

In the second place, the Board of Trade has, very wisely, taken powers to tackle its new and difficult problem by a wide variety of techniques. Broadly speaking, these fall into two classes—those which involve actual purchase by the Government, and those which aim at increasing the stocks physically held in this country but not owned outright by the authorities. Both classes of technique lend themselves to far reaching collaboration with the raw material producers of the Empire. As regards outright purchases, the defence object is to save time and shipping. But it is not essential that the commodities held should always be the same ones. For example, when the crops of sugar are redundant and the price is low, we might come to the rescue of Empire sugar producers by taking over a part of their output; and in another year when wheat is redundant and cheap, but sugar has recovered, the sugar might be replaced by wheat. But I am chiefly interested today in the possibilities of measures, not of outright purchase, but for increasing the stocks physically held in this country but remaining part of the supplies available to the market in the normal way.

The Act has taken wide powers for the provision or subsidy of storage and finance for the purpose of inducing traders to hold augmented stocks. I suggest that this side of the Act should be systematically employed to make this country much the cheapest place for holders of commodities to keep their stocks in and that this should be done in close collaboration with Empire producers. I have the impression that in former years the world surplus stocks were held in this country to a greater extent than is the case today; though I have not the statistics with which to confirm this impression. But however this may be, a very large volume of surplus stocks is now held overseas in the countries which have produced them. For example, a heavy tonnage of tin and rubber is being retained in the East; when the Canadian Government was holding surplus wheat, it held it in Canada;

and generally speaking it is worth while to save shipping costs for as long as possible by retaining output in the country of origin.

My proposal is, therefore, that the Government should offer storage to all Empire producers of specified raw materials, either free of warehouse charges and interest or for a nominal charge, provided they ship their surplus produce to approved warehouses in this country. The Government would not become the outright owners of the stocks in question, which would remain in the ownership of the depositors, who would run the risk of price changes and would be free to remove and dispose of the stocks at any time or to deal in them against warehouse warrants. So far as finance is concerned, the Government might offer to advance either free of interest or at a rate equal to the rate on Treasury bills up to 90 per cent of the market price at the date of delivery into storage, the margin of 10 per cent of the current market price being subsequently maintained by the owners. It might prove advisable to require a certain notice—say, a month—of delivery and withdrawal and a minimum period of deposit—say, three months—so as not to attract normal trading stocks which would be held here in any case.

Under such an arrangement the volume and character of the goods in store would vary from time to time. But one could feel considerable assurance that at most times the aggregate would materially exceed the stocks which would be held without such an arrangement. Moreover, if at any time the aggregate amount appeared to be falling too low, or if the international prospects appeared to be particularly threatening, the Government could secure the position by purchase and the substitution of outright ownership.

I submit that such a plan would have several advantages, of which the following may be emphasised:—

(1) The cost to the Treasury would be very small in relation to the volume of resources involved. For warehouse costs and interest, provided on the lines suggested above, would cost a

great deal less than the 10 per cent per annum which I have estimated above as a normal expense to the outside holder who has no special facilities. The total cost would vary with the commodity, and I am not in a position to estimate it closely; but it might average, perhaps, at 4 per cent.* If we take this as sufficiently indicative of the order of magnitude of the figures, we could store £500,000,000 of stuff at an annual cost of £20,000,000. It is evident that the provision of stocks on that scale would give us much more security than we have at present, whilst the cost would be easily supportable.

(2) The technique adopted, so far from interfering with the ordinary course of trade, would facilitate it. The provision of additional stocks on the spot would avoid time lags in the response of supply to an improved demand, whether in the home or in the re-export trades. The position of this country for entrepôt business would be ensured. An important cost, which is a potent generator of price fluctuations, would be eliminated, with the result of moderating price fluctuations and allowing, at the same time, a more continuous scale of output in the producing countries. Knowledge and experience would be gained which would be valuable in the future control of the trade cycle.

(3) Far-reaching arrangements would become possible with producers of raw materials within the Empire and with their governments. If, for example, as seems likely, the Canadian Government finds itself faced this year with the necessity of acquiring wheat beyond what the market can currently absorb, an agreement would be made for the physical storage of the wheat in this country, whilst it would remain the property of the Canadian Government. The possible field for the application

* Mr Benjamin Graham in his recent book on *Storage and Stability: A Modern Ever-Normal Granary*, (New York, 1932), (p. 108) estimates the average commercial cost to dealers in the commodity exchanges of storing 23 standard raw materials at 13½ per cent of their value per annum, exclusive of interest, whilst he considers that organised government storage could be provided at a quarter of this cost. His estimate of the commercial cost is considerably higher than mine, which is intended to include interest, but his average is somewhat inflated by the exceptionally high cost of storing maize, oats and petroleum.

of this principle is wide—sugar from the West Indies, jute from India, wool from Australia, vegetable oil products from West Africa, non-ferrous metals, and all the endless variety of Empire products which must be stored somewhere. There is, moreover, an outstanding case of a home product which should not be overlooked, namely pig iron. We have recently had experience of the disturbance caused by a temporary shortage of pig iron. The advantage of substantial stocks of pig iron for munitions does not need emphasising; and the advantage in smoothing the trade cycle is hardly less obvious. In war such reserves held in this country would be better than a gold mine; in peace we might find that we had taken the first step towards making possible a steadier scale of output of the principal raw materials, and thus avoiding extreme fluctuations of demand for our own exports from the raw material countries.

(4) The possible strain on the exchanges needs, however, a careful handling. It is for that reason that I have laid special stress on supplies from the Empire. For an important proportion of these may be financed in London, wherever they are situated, whilst in their case the proceeds of additional financing are more likely to remain here as an accretion to the banking reserves of the sterling area. Nevertheless it is certain that a substantial additional burden would fall on the exchanges during the initial period. In the case of Canadian wheat, for example, the major part of the finance would not normally fall on London, and it might be necessary here to make special arrangements with the Canadian Government. Moreover, there are certain products where it would be particularly useful to accumulate stocks—for example, timber and oil—which might not conveniently come, mainly or exclusively, from Empire sources.

Yet, even in this respect, we might contrive to draw advantage out of the difficulty itself. In so far as we were financing or paying for imports in excess of what we should do otherwise, the effect on our own export trade would be exactly the same as an increase in the scale of our current foreign lending. We might reasonably expect some stimulation to our own exports; and sometimes we might be able to link the agreement to import with express arrangements to aid corresponding exports. It would be a form of foreign investment, the security for which would offer the great advantage of being situated at home! It would, of course, be a once-for-all transaction. That is to say, we should be accumulating stocks up to the value of (say) £500,000,000 within the next two or three years; and thereafter we should have no occasion to increase, on balance, the amount of this particular form of investment. But at this juncture of affairs I can see no form of foreign investment which it would be safer or more advantageous for us to accumulate. It is true, of course, that the income we should derive from it would not be in the shape of money interest or dividends, but in the shape of security and in the facility to avoid paying excessive prices for purchases made subsequently in circumstances of unusual need. But, on the other hand, here is an opportunity for a substantial volume of foreign investment, where the capital involved is absolutely safe. And in these days that is a primary consideration. We should be enabled by this technique to make loans, where for other reasons we might desire to make them—in South-eastern Europe, for example—on the absolute security of commodities physically situated within this country. It would be overwhelmingly worth our while to forego the cash income of £20,000,000 a year in return for the compensating advantages in the shape of security, a stimulus to our export industries, an increased control over the trade cycle, and an insurance against having to pay excessive prices at a subsequent date. The gain to our prestige and to our apparent security of so vast an accumulation of these liquid forms of wealth situated at home, an accumulation which others could not afford to imitate, would be worth in itself the really trifling expense. It would be a demonstration of reserve resources which would catch the imagination of the world. And if it should also serve the causes of peace, and prove to be a new and useful instrument in our armoury for the control (which will need more instruments than one) of the trade cycle, let no one complain.

(5) Even if foreign investment of this type is advantageous, it does not follow that it will not throw a burden on the exchanges which will lead to a loss of gold by the Exchange Equalisation Fund. We must expect that the accumulation, on such a scale as is suggested, of liquid resources in the shape of a mixed bag of commodities will be partly in substitution for our existing liquid resources in the shape of gold. But will there be a disadvantage in this? In time of war goods on the spot will be better worth having than the gold. In time of peace to substitute goods for gold when good are cheap in terms of gold, and gold for goods when goods are dear in terms of gold, will be both socially and financially profitable.

I should be much inclined, therefore, though this is not essential to the scheme, to link up the finance of commodity storage with the finance of the Exchange Equalisation Fund, and to regard the policy of holding liquid stocks of raw materials as a natural evolution of the policy of holding liquid stocks of gold outside the banking system. The finance required by the new policy is of the same character as the finance required by the Exchange Fund, and should be segregated from the normal Budget in the same way and for the same reasons. It also happens that the amounts required will tend to be complementary—the greater the finance required to hold stocks, the smaller is the finance required to hold gold likely to be. Moreover, the object of narrowing the range of movement of international commodity prices is a natural development of the policy of narrowing the range of the foreign exchanges. Investment in stocks will be of the same advantage to our trade as foreign investment would be, without, however, diminishing the strength of our liquid position, a consideration which, obviously, is of great importance in present conditions. Our liquid position, internationally, will be properly measured by adding the value of our liquid stocks of commodities to our stock of gold, which is a further reason for treating the finance of the two as a single problem.

The objects of carrying a steady volume of stocks as a war insurance and of carrying a fluctuating volume so as to damp down the trade cycle are, it is evident, objects which partly conflict. At the present time the former must, presumably, prevail, and the latter must await the arrival of happier days. I must not be supposed to overlook this conflict. But I seek to reinforce the former purpose by pointing out that measures useful for defence may eventually evolve into measures of permanent usefulness in peace. Even in the first instance they do not wholly conflict. As a war insurance it does not greatly matter which particular commodities are stored, so that seasonal, as distinct from cyclical, fluctuations can be averaged out. Moreover, it is of substantial advantage as a war insurance if the average volume of international stocks, physically located in this country, is largely increased, even though this volume fluctuates somewhat widely between a higher and a lower limit; and if the stocks held here are normally larger than they would have been otherwise, our authorities will be able to act with greater rapidity, if circumstances make it advisable to convert privately owned deposits into outright Government ownership.

Keynes sent copies of the paper to Oliver Stanley, President of the Board of Trade and Sir Thomas Inskip, the Minister for the Co-ordination of Defence.

His covering letters are of some interest.

To OLIVER STANLEY, *23 August 1938*

Dear Mr Stanley,

I enclose a copy of the full version of the paper which I recently prepared for the British Association on the policy of Government Storage of Foodstuffs and Raw Materials, of which you may have seen an abbreviated version in the press;

and also a copy of a letter which I have sent to Sir Thomas Inskip, since I am not clear how far this is his business and how far it is yours. I feel that the new Act which you secured last session is of first class importance, and has tremendous possibilities of usefulness. I need not repeat what I have said in the paper and in the letter to Sir Thomas Inskip. There is a good deal of ground to explore and it is impossible for an outsider to select, *a priori*, the most favourable ground within it. But there is an opportunity, I am sure, of serving a number of purposes at once. It is possible to combine objects of defence with the improvement of current employment in this country; we can assist our export industries without diminishing our effective liquid resources; and we can provide occupation to our mercantile marine instead of subsidising them. If a complete calculation of all the indirect advantages could be made, I believe one would find that the scheme would pretty nearly pay for itself.

Yours sincerely,
[copy not signed or initialled]

To SIR THOMAS INSKIP, *23 August 1938*

Dear Sir Thomas Inskip,

I venture to send you a full version of the paper which I gave the British Association on the policy of Government Storage of Foodstuffs and Raw Materials.

The full scheme suggested here is, of course, very ambitious and comprehensive. But it is not of such a character that it has to be undertaken all at once or all together. I have no doubt that, in the case of any particular commodity, there would be many technical difficulties to be overcome, and the right techniques will only be discoverable with experience.

The most obvious case for applying this kind of method at the moment may be that of Canadian wheat. The Dominion Government have lately committed themselves to purchasing this year's crop at a price considerably above the market, so that they are likely to have to accept deliveries on a substantial scale. They have no intention, I think, of holding the whole of this off the market so as to secure the price they are paying, though they are almost certain to be involved in holding substantial stock for some considerable time to come. Why not get into touch with them to discuss the terms on which they would hold the wheat in this country instead of in Canada? This is a case where there might be no need to relieve them of the finance. If we met the cost of storage and possibly gave some assistance towards the cost of transport, it might suit both parties to locate the reserves here. And that would be a splendid accession to our war reserves at a minimum cost. As and when the time came for the Dominion to dispose of this particular stock, it could be replaced either by wheat from some other source or by some other commodity.

Generally speaking I suggest that a wide field for useful action might be found in conferences with each of the Dominion and Colonial authorities, with a view to discovering what surplus stocks are likely to be held in any case in their own territory and the terms on which they could be physically transferred to this country. Probably in all cases the Dominions could themselves find the finance by means of their own Treasury bills, subject, if necessary, to our guarantee. It would be a great advantage to leave them to make their own arrangements with their own producers, and to restrict our bargain so far as possible to bargains with them. The tin and rubber restriction arrangements offer a particular kind of opportunity. The troubles of the West Indies over sugar might afford another.

In any case, of course, there is not the slightest reason why the finance of the purchase of the stocks should fall on the Budget any more than in the case of the gold held by the Exchange Equalisation Fund. But it would be an advantage of arrangements with the Dominions that, with a moderate measure of assistance, finance could probably be found in the main from the same sources as at present. It would merely be the location of the surplus stocks which would be affected, and which would involve charges.

In so far as we had to furnish the finance directly or indirectly, it would be desirable to explore the question how far this could not be linked up with some kind of barter arrangements for increasing our exports. This would be particularly necessary in the case of any arrangements with foreign countries. For example, I believe that timber is an outstanding case for storage. The expenses of storage are small; indeed I think timber improves with keeping. It would occupy in time of war a terrific quantity of shipping space. I have a remembrance of the problem of the importation of pit props during the last War. At present the price of timber is greatly depressed. Russia and Scandinavia might jump at arrangements for the accumulation of surplus stocks here and might be ready to link them with arrangements for taking additional imports from us.

Pig iron falls into rather another class, probably more suited for outright purchase. But this would involve no problem of foreign finance and, in the present condition of the coal and iron trades, would be a great assistance to employment. It might pay for itself through saving on the dole. The advantage of stocks of pig iron for munitions purposes in time of war hardly needs to be pointed out.

It would also emphasise the great advantage of such importation to our shipping in present circumstances. It would be a much better plan to use our tonnage at a time when it is redundant to provide services which might be vitally required later on when tonnage is scarce than to return to the subsidy on tramp tonnage.

I have not mentioned the United States in the enclosed paper. But possibly arrangements with them ought not to be overlooked. I fancy that Mr Wallace, the Secretary of Agriculture, might jump at arrangements for the transfer of surplus stocks of American cotton to this country, and also of wheat, if the Canadian Government were not in a position to meet us with their stocks. This would certainly involve no finance at all. In present circumstances, it would suit Mr Wallace's pocket just as much as it would suit ours. This also might be linked up with arrangements for return cargoes in the shape of our exports.

I have mentioned in the paper the point that this is much the safest form in which we can do what is in effect foreign investment at the present time. The worst feature of the present trade situation is the depression of our exports. This is certainly due in part to the obstacles in the way of new foreign lending on our part. Yet there are obvious objections to increasing our foreign lending, both because of lack of security and the possible weakening of our liquid reserves of gold. But this is a form of foreign investment which is useful from the point of view of our export industries, yet offering undoubted security, and increasing rather than diminishing our liquid resources. We ought to think of our liquid resources not merely in terms of gold, but in terms of liquid stocks of commodities of all kinds. We may be quite sure that in time of stress these commodities will be in fact more valuable in relation to gold than they are now.

This is a big subject, and I must not trouble you with a longer letter. But it seems to me that the important Act obtained last session by the Board of Trade opens up tremendous possibilities. As I am rather in a fog as to the respective spheres of yourself and the President of the Board of Trade, I am sending a copy of this letter to Mr Stanley.

Yours sincerely,
[copy not signed or initialled]

Keynes also sent copies of his letters to Stanley and Inskip to Sir Arthur Salter.

From SIR ARTHUR SALTER, *31 August 1938*

My dear Keynes,

I have been motoring in Wales and missing my correspondence, or I would have written before to thank you for sending me copies of your letters to Inskip and Stanley.

I fully agree with your covering letter, in which you say that the right step is to seek conferences with the Dominion and Colonial authorities.

I have read your address to the British Ass. with the greatest interest. I think that most people, like myself, will have failed to realise the *extent* of the price fluctuations within each single year. I am frankly doubtful about your actual proposals for financing storage on the scale and in the way you suggest. I do not feel confident that you have sufficient precautions against (a) the mere substitution of Govt. financed storage and to a large extent purchase of private stocks for similar stocks as now maintained without very substantial increase in the totals or (b) the accumulation of stocks by certain groups, largely at the public expense, which they would use in such a way as to aggravate rather than remedy the present evils. This involves too complicated arguments to discuss in a short letter.

My own position is roughly as follows:

(a) I want the Govt., as a security measure, to purchase £70–£100 mill. worth of foodstuffs, largely chosen on grounds of storeability—e.g. sugar would have a preference over, though not to the exclusion of wheat.

(b) I think they should finance additional storage of private stocks, e.g. give encouragement to millers to double their normal stocks of flour.
In my own present campaign I am limiting myself to this as distinct from raw material storage or the use of stocks in relation to the trade cycle, so as not to diminish the chances of getting the more limited results.

I am, however, very much in favour of extending action to raw materials, and I agree as to the special importance of pit props and pig iron. In fact, with others working on the same lines, I made an effort for both without success when the Bill was before Parliament.

To use stocks in relation to the trade cycle raises, as you know, very strong resistance 'in principle'. While I don't want to involve my own limited campaign with this, I think it is of the greatest importance. Where I think I shall differ from you is in your belief that stronger assistance would be enough to make ordinary economic forces work beneficially. I am inclined to think that the Govt. would need to have the power to vary the extent of Govt. owned stocks on price fluctuation and trade cycle considerations (as they are prohibited from doing by the present Act) on the advice of a suitably composed advisory body.

I hope we may have the opportunity of discussing this in the early autumn. I was extremely glad to find you so far recovered, and much enjoyed seeing you after so long an interval. I am just off to Geneva for a fortnight or so.

Yours ever,
ARTHUR SALTER

He also sent a copy to Henry Wallace, the American Secretary of Agriculture.

To HENRY A. WALLACE, *30 August 1938*

Dear Mr Wallace,

I venture to send you a copy of a paper prepared by me for the August meeting of the British Association in this country, which has received considerable notice in the British press. I do not know whether any mention of it has been made in America. Since it has some slight bearing on matters of interest to you, it occurs to me that you might like to see it.

There is no doubt, I think, that public opinion in this country is very much in favour of fairly comprehensive measures on these lines. But my impression is that the Government will be reluctant to act. Not because they are particularly opposed to this plan, but from a general reluctance to take any action which can be avoided.

You will see that I have suggested that they should enter into discussions with the Canadian Government for the storage of the Canadian surplus in this country. I notice that you have been doing your best to reach some co-operative arrangements with the Canadian Government, and I only hope you will be successful, though the newspaper rumours up to date suggest rather the contrary. It appears to me that a joint scheme between your Government, the Canadian Government and the British Government for the transfer of an appropriate proportion of the North American surplus of wheat to this country, each Government contributing to the relative expense, would serve the purposes of all of us.

Quite apart from the particular problem of war storage I am a convinced advocate of the general principles underlying your policy of a concerted government policy to average fluctuations by an assisted scheme of storage.

Yours very sincerely,
[copy initialled] J.M.K.

In September, the London and Cambridge Economic Service published a memorandum by G. L. Schwartz and E. C. Rhodes, 'Output, Employment and Wages in the United Kingdom, 1928, 1930 and 1935'. Keynes provided a summary for *The Times*.

From The Times, *13 September 1938*

EFFICIENCY IN INDUSTRY: A MEASURE OF GROWTH—THE MORAL

This memorandum, if the results can be fully trusted, is of high interest and importance in many connexions. The upshot of the investigations, which can be explained quite shortly, is worth summarising. The official censuses of production, of which the most recent took place in 1935, report their results in terms of the money value of the net output of the industries covered. Over the whole period from 1924 to 1935 they showed a money value of net factory output which was stationary between 1924 and 1930, and increased between 1930 and 1935 by only a little more than in proportion to the number of employees engaged; the value falling 1 per cent between 1924 and 1930 and rising 7 per cent between 1930 and 1935, while the number of employees was substantially unchanged during the earlier period and rose by about 3 per cent during the last five years. Expressed in this form the returns take no account of the possibility of there having been a substantial increase in physical productivity which was masked by a more or less corresponding reduction in prices.

Data are available, however, by means of which the change in physical productivity can be approximately calculated; and it is to this task in particular that the memorandum has been devoted. The comparison of physical quantities and prices cannot be precise, partly because the available price data do not cover the whole of the output, but chiefly because the constituents of output change in character, so that the composite unit representative of output as a whole changes its make-up year by year. Thus it makes a large difference whether one calculates the change in prices by reference to the composite commodity representative of output at the earlier date or by reference to one representative of output at the later date. The memorandum has calculated the changes on such bases, and should be consulted for details which cannot be reproduced here. For the sake of brevity, I take in what follows a figure midway between the two standards. This complication does not destroy the significance of the results, which remain sufficiently striking after allowing a wide margin for error.

Striking recent results

During the six years from 1924 to 1930 the progress of factory productivity per employee was increasing at a rate of less than 1 per cent a year, while prices were falling at about the same rate. Productivity rose over the six years by about 5 per cent and prices fell by about 6 per cent, leaving the money value of output very little changed. It is in respect of the more recent period from 1930 to 1935 that striking and significant results have been disclosed by this inquiry. They show that during those five years factory productivity per employee increased by at least 4 per cent a year or 20 per cent in all, the price of the output falling by about 3 per cent a year. An increase in productivity per employee, averaged over the whole of factory industry, of not less than 20 per cent in the five years from 1930 to 1935 (following on a gain of 5 per cent between 1924 and 1930) is sufficiently extraordinary; but the increase in productivity per operative employee was still greater, since the administrative employees increased in number more than in proportion to the operative employees.

We can supplement the above by figures relating to certain other branches of output. Productivity per head in public utilities and Government Departments increased by 27 per cent between 1930 and 1935. In mines and quarries, where the volume of employment fell off by about a third between 1924 and 1935, productivity per head increased by 17 per cent between 1924 and 1930 and by 31 per cent between 1924 and 1935. Finally, the sometimes despised agriculture has done best of all, where the output per head (at the prices of 1930) rose by some 40 per cent between 1924 and 1935 (the greater part occurring in the last five years) and has further increased subsequently. I doubt if many of us were aware that such a revolution in this country's physical productivity had been taking place. It helps to explain, I suggest, some of the problems which have been facing us.

Now in assessing the significance of these huge changes, it is important to realise that, although they cover a wide field of activity, they do not relate to national output as a whole. They cover factory trades, public utilities, mines, and agriculture. But it is quite certain that the capacity of the individual to render service in other directions, particularly in the distributing trades, has not increased to the same extent. Thus, if we assume that the national income is spent on different purposes in much the same proportions as before, it follows that the demand for employment in industry itself will be relatively smaller at the end than at the beginning of the period. We have here, therefore, an explanation both of the increased demand for labour in employments outside factories and mines, and also of the redundancy of labour immobilised within those industries. Apart from anything else, the increase in technical efficiency revealed above has in itself involved a serious problem of displacement. The greater the pace of industrial progress relatively to progress in other directions, the more severe will be the problem of the most progressive industries in absorbing the labour which has become naturally associated with them. It is alas! the exceptional and progressive efficiency in certain of our industries which has been in a sense their undoing. If for technical reasons their effective capacity improves on a scale which is out of proportion to the improvement achieved by the rest of the community, they naturally find their output in surplus supply.

Major industries

If the main industries be considered separately (for this purpose the memorandum uses only the method of measurement which gives the higher limit of increased productivity), it will be found, not unexpectedly, that the engineering industry leads, though there are here special difficulties in the way of a precise comparison on account of qualitative changes. But it is perhaps less expected that among factory industries textiles (which include artificial silk, but are not unduly overweighted by it) come second with an improvement of 37 per cent in the five years; and meagre indeed has been their reward for such an achievement. Of other major employments public utilities and agriculture rank high each with an increase of about 27 per cent in the last five years.

The proportion of the value of net output paid away in wages has remained almost the same throughout the period, being 46 per cent in 1924 and 1930, and perhaps 44½ per cent in 1935. Since the cost of living fell by 18½ per cent, while wages fell by only 5 per cent between 1924 and 1935, the wage earners in these industries gained about half of their increased efficiency in terms of their real earnings; while wage earners in other occupations, and the rest of the community, probably gained in their standard of life appreciably more than was represented by any improvement in their own efficiency. We have, indeed, much reason for satisfaction—except in our failure to expand incomes as a whole to keep pace with our new potentialities of production. If output and incomes generally were growing as they should, there would be an intake in other occupations for the labour which technical efficiency is releasing from factories, mines, and agriculture.

Three years have already passed since the latest date to which these inquiries relate, and it will be a few years yet before we have more up-to-date information. Yet it is evident that such facts as are here disclosed are of vital importance for current economic policy. Why should we have to wait for several years before knowing how we stand? The problem of handling our social problems is made immeasurably more difficult by the inexcusable attitude of the authorities towards the collection of fuller information. How can economists be expected to produce a clear and unanimous diagnosis when the facts they have to go upon are so obscure and imperfectly known? In spite of frequent pressure from representative economists and statisticians, the authorities have rejected proposals for an annual census of production, and they also rejected proposals for an additional census which would have furnished invaluable information.

To take a small detail, it has been pointed out in these columns and recently emphasised again that the Ministry of Health restricts the collection of figures relating to building projects to a sample which may be unrepresentative. In these matters Government Departments seem to have an outlook that belongs to a bygone age. As President Roosevelt has been saying of certain Democratic Senators, 'They think in the past and act accordingly.'

Wasted wealth

If we allow for some further improvement since 1935 and imagine that the whole industrial population is fully employed, it is easy to see what a vast potential capacity to produce exists as compared even with so recent a date as 1924. This helps to explain what may otherwise perplex us in the German economy. If British industry could be fully occupied at modern standards of efficiency, the additional output beyond what was sufficing for our needs a few years ago would be enough to provide a prodigious volume of resources available for purposes of peace—or defence. The resources of the country lie in its physical capacity for current production, and no shortage exists there. On the contrary, we are still allowing a great volume of potential wealth to evaporate unrealised.

In present circumstances it seems hardly less than criminal

to allow so much of our resources to lie idle. How can we hope to keep pace with a form of government which has devised a means of producing and maintaining full employment? This is the critical task before us, if we are to maintain the supremacy of our own notions of what civilisation should mean. It is not the purpose of this particular article to suggest specific remedies. Its object is limited to the use of the valuable researches of the London and Cambridge Economic Service to illuminate the contemporary scene in its possibilities—and its actual waste.

On 5 October he provided a supplementary note.

To the Editor of The Times, *5 October 1938*

Sir,

I recently called attention in your columns to the increase in British industrial efficiency as shown in a memorandum published by the London and Cambridge Economic Service. Since then comparable figures have become available for the United States in the September *Bulletin* of the National Bureau of Economic Research of New York. It is interesting to find that the progress in the two countries has been remarkably similar.

In this country the general increase in productivity per head came out at a rate somewhere between 4 and 5 per cent per annum over the five years 1930 to 1935. In the United States the available statistics relate to the change over the six years 1929 to 1935, and are more exact than those for this country in that they allow for changes in the number of hours worked. The American improvement over this period in estimated output per man hour comes out at 27·2 per cent, or $4\frac{1}{2}$ per cent per annum. The gain in the United States is particularly remarkable because the comparison is between a boom year and one of sub-normal activity, so that no assistance was gained from an increase in the scale of production. On the contrary, physical production in 1935 fell to 87·4 per cent of what it had been in 1929, while the employment of wage earners in man-hours fell by nearly a third to 68·7 per cent of the 1929 figure.

In circumstances of such rapid technical progress accompanied by a demand which is no greater than can be met by an unchanged value of plant, it is probable, both here and in America, that the depreciation allowances currently set aside by manufacturers are sufficient to pay for all, or nearly all, of the cost of new plant without requiring to be supplemented out of current net savings. This factor is a further aggravation of the contemporary problem of finding a volume of profitable new net investment sufficient to maintain equilibrium with the readiness to save. With the rates of interest, with the psychology of business enterprise and of saving, and with the distribution of incomes what they are at present, it becomes increasingly improbable that anything approaching full employment can be maintained without abnormal loan expenditure by the Government on one ticket or another. At any rate, it is certain that in the last quarter of a century such a state of affairs has never existed, apart from very brief periods in abnormal conditions, in any industrial country in the world, except perhaps in the United States in 1928.

The problem thus presented is the outstanding economic problem of today, and cannot be solved by turning a blind eye to it. It has to be attacked on several different fronts, besides that of Government loan expenditure. Mr Harrod has recently indicated one of these. In the circumstances of the moment I suggest that the balance-of-trade position and the net disinvestment in this country's foreign assets which is probably going on (about which we have, as usual, no adequate statistics) also needs particular attention—not, indeed, by an aggravation of tariffs but by a new, and now necessary machinery for linking up exports with imports, so as to make sure that those from whom we buy spend a reasonable proportion of the proceeds in corresponding purchases from us. We can no longer afford to leave the barter aspect of foreign trade to look after itself.

Yours, &c.,

J. M. KEYNES

Chapter 7

TOWARDS WAR

In the course of September 1938 the problem of Czechoslovakia, which had been brewing since the German occupation of Austria in March, exploded into a crisis. During the month Neville Chamberlain made three journeys to meet Hitler before coming to an agreement with him at Munich on 29 September. Keynes, who had watched the evolution of events with a mixture of anxiety and horrified fascination, reacted to the Munich agreement in *The New Statesman.*[1]

In the autumn of 1938, Keynes became somewhat more active. For example, for the Twenty-Sixth Report of the Committee on Economic Information, 'Problems of Rearmament', Keynes attended meetings for the first time in eighteen months and drafted what became paragraphs 21–5 of the final report, dealing with the balance of payments on capital account.

ECONOMIC ADVISORY COUNCIL COMMITTEE ON ECONOMIC INFORMATION

PARAGRAPHS FOR THE DRAFT TWENTY-SIXTH REPORT PREPARED BY MR KEYNES

Note by Joint Secretaries

Mr Keynes has prepared the attached paragraphs which would form the conclusion to the Draft Twenty-Sixth Report. Mr Keynes suggests that, as these paragraphs contain a certain amount of material which has not been fully discussed by the Committee, they should be circulated before the circulation of the revised draft report, so that any alterations required to meet points raised by members of the Committee may be included in that document.

FRANCIS HEMMING

28 November 1938 P. K. DEBENHAM

[1] See *JMK*, vol. XXVIII.

The above suggestions relate to methods for diminishing the burden on the balance of payments brought about by the excess of imports over exports and the aggravation of that excess likely to result from the rearmament programme. Nevertheless we should not feel unduly disturbed at our ability to meet any likely adverse balance on trade account, at any rate for some time to come, without the adoption of special measures such as the above, if it were not for the risk that on this continuing drain from our resources there might be superimposed a large outward movement on capital account.

It is advisable, therefore, also to consider measures for retarding or offsetting such movements on capital account. Indeed, we are of the opinion that some at least of the measures suggested below should have priority over those outlined in the previous paragraph.

The outward movements on capital account can take a variety of forms, and the appropriate remedy depends on which of them we are aiming at. They may be classified as follows:—

(i) New foreign issues on the London market and new placings (such as the recent Woolworth issue) of securities previously in foreign ownership, which are not offered under official or semi-official auspices for trade or political purposes. We consider that the restrictions on such transactions formerly in force should be rigorously reimposed at once. The fact that there may be occasion for loans having specific trade purposes in view, with which we should be most reluctant to interfere, makes it all the more necessary to restrict offerings which do not satisfy this criterion.

(ii) New issues for the Dominions, India and the Colonies. In this case we think that there should be a strict supervision with a view to limitation, and that the authorities concerned should be urged wherever possible to borrow on their home markets and especially in the United States. Indeed in any case where other facilities are available, efforts should be made to redeem loans now outstanding in London and to replace them by loans elsewhere. At a time when the Home Government needs the London market for its own requirements, it is reasonable that Empire borrowers should be asked to do everything in their power to satisfy their own requirements otherwise.

(iii) Direct purchases by British investors in Wall Street. This is a case where requests in the right quarters are likely to be more effective than direct prohibitions. We think that British investors should be invited not to increase, for the time being, their American investments, and that the banks, the Stock Exchange and the chief institutional investors such as the insurance offices and the investment trusts should be invited to co-operate to this end.

The depreciation of the sterling exchange, no doubt, operates to some extent as an automatic check on such purchases; since there is a risk of loss through a subsequent recovery in the exchange. Nevertheless uncertainty as to the prospective value of sterling may also operate the other way.

(iv) The removal from London, or the exchange for gold, of the liquid resources of nervous foreign holders. This is probably a large factor in the situation. But it is doubtful whether there are appropriate financial measures for checking it, short of exchange control. These movements depend primarily on political confidence and secondarily on the expectations held abroad as to the future of the sterling exchange (expectations often more extreme, as a result of recent Continental experience, than those held in London itself). Unless and until we are prepared to impose a general exchange control, we have to let these resources go to the extent they want to,—which is a reason for taking any available action under other heads. Unfortunately almost any measures taken to protect the exchange are liable, by indicating nervousness on our part, to accentuate this drain. On the other hand, the amount of such withdrawals is not unlimited; and there is probably no means, short of exchange control, of retaining them in times of stress. They are a perpetual source of danger which we are perhaps better without.

(v) Outright bear speculation against sterling by purchasing dollars in advance of need or by purchase of dollars, cash or forward, as a pure speculation with a view to a profit from a subsequent depreciation of sterling. We have no evidence that there is any large-scale action of this description. Moderate transactions of this kind remedy themselves in course of time and may even be the source of a subsequent support for the exchange.

(vi) Banking and arbitrage balances which have been held in London hitherto because it has been slightly more profitable to hold them there than elsewhere. A few months ago these probably amounted to a large figure, but it is likely that they have been seeping away. The reason for this is partly to be found in the increase of the premium on the forward dollar which has lately occurred. Up to the summer the return to a foreign banker from liquid resources used in the London market was just sufficiently in excess of the return obtainable on equally good security in New York to pay for the cost of eliminating the exchange risk through hedging them by the purchase of forward dollars. Since August the premium on forward dollars has at least doubled, with the result that transactions of the above type are less profitable than before or even unprofitable. Theoretically there are various ways of putting this right, but practically several of them are objectionable.

In pre-war days the remedy of a higher Bank rate would probably have been applied in such a case. Today the domestic repercussions, especially on the gilt-edged market, and the heavy loss to the Treasury constitute, in our opinion, an overwhelming objection in anything like present circumstances; and it would be opposed to the constantly repeated statements of policy which have been made by the Prime Minister and the Chancellor of the Exchequer. An alternative method would be to encourage the banks to offer special terms for foreign balances with or without the assistance of the Bank of England. This course was adopted for a considerable period after the War, and we think it deserves consideration.

Another method would be for the Exchange Equalisation Fund to bring down the premium on the forward dollar by offering forward exchange themselves on more favourable terms. This is open, however, to the objection that it would facilitate speculation against sterling.

There remains the possibility of replacing the bank money thus withdrawn by direct borrowing on the part of the Treasury in terms of a foreign currency. We believe that this might prove the most economical and advantageous method, and we recommend its consideration. It might conveniently take the form of the issue of British Treasury bills and bonds at a low rate of interest in Canada expressed in terms of Canadian dollars with an option to the holder to be paid his capital and interest in American dollars at a fixed exchange. The purchases of the Air Ministry in Canada and some special arrangements for the purchase of Canadian wheat could furnish a sufficiently [good] pretext for this. But in fact the issues might be largely taken up by American banks and thus furnish a substantial and satisfactory source of funds to the Treasury, at the same time supporting the exchange and providing resources to meet current outgoings.

We should add that it is a further advantage, and one not to be overlooked, that all these measures would operate to conserve British savings for our own Government's new borrowing and would thus facilitate the problem of Treasury financing as a whole. We continue to attach vital importance to the maintenance of the gilt-edged market and a policy of cheap money.

We have felt that we could be most useful in setting forth a list of the various available remedies without advocating any one in particular to the exclusion of others. But we desire to emphasise in conclusion our strongly held opinion that action along one or other of these lines is urgently required and that the present position is very far from comfortable.

A few days earlier he had provided a provincial stockbroker who did some dealing for King's College, Cambridge with his views on the future of the rate of interest.

To W. H. BRETT, *24 November 1938*

Dear Mr Brett,

Thank you for sending me that interesting memorandum on the future of the rate of interest. It is, of course, a subject about which I think a good deal. I jot down for you and your staff the following notes of various miscellaneous points which must not be lost sight of.

(1) In my opinion the Treasury can easily prevent the long-term rate of interest from rising either by the methods proposed in *The Economist* or otherwise. But it is not safe to assume that it will actually do what it has the power to do. I should say that there is still in official circles considerable resistance to these techniques. I should predict that at long last they would do what they should, but it would be rash to suppose that they will necessarily do so in the first instance.

(2) It is possible, I think, to make out a strong case that the rate of interest is by no means low today on the orthodox theory. I think it will be found that the present yield on Consols is some 2/- or 3/- above its average yield throughout the nineteenth century, from (say) 1820 onwards. Yet during that period the demand for capital was extremely high owing to a rapidly increasing population, an abundance of new capital-using investments, and the exploitation of a great part of the world. Today the supply of savings must be far ampler than it was then, and the demand for their absorption very much less indeed. If the average yield on Consols in the nineteenth century was about £3.7.6 (or whatever it was), then surely in present circumstances it should not, on the orthodox theory, be anything like as high as £3.10.0.

(3) The new stock to be created henceforward to meet the Treasury needs is likely to be of the dated variety. That is to

say, it will compete with the existing stocks of this type rather than with the long-dated stocks yielding 3½ per cent or thereabouts.

(4) As regards the existing long-dated stocks, the bulk of them has an option against the lender in the neighbourhood of the present price, e.g., in particular, War Loan. Thus this sort of stock is only valid one way. The holder can lose if the rate of interest rises, but he cannot gain much if it falls. There is, therefore, an advantage, very far from being represented in the relative prices, in favour of such stocks as Consols as against War Loan, because, whilst the risk of a fall is much the same, the possible rise is very much greater. If one buys a long-dated stock, one would surely choose one which has as good a chance of rising as of falling. Now the supply of such stocks is extremely limited; it is being constantly absorbed by various institutional purchasers, and ought to have a scarcity yield in course of time. Generally speaking, there are many investors who are more interested in the 3½ per cent yield than in stability of capital value. The Post Office Savings Bank cannot afford a much lower rate of interest. Charities and colleges, and the like, are interested in income rather than in capital. The life offices cannot possibly afford to switch into the dated stocks without risking a reduction in their present rates of bonus. This argument can be produced to show why such stocks as Consols are relatively cheap as compared with the dated stocks.

(5) Taking a short view, it will make a great difference whether the Treasury conducts its borrowing policy with common sense. So far I doubt if they have. It is obviously immensely easier to borrow *after* the money has been spent than *before*. It is much easier to mop up surplus money than to collect large assets into the Treasury balance when there is no surplus at all. So far, they have spoilt their market by trying to borrow before the money was wanted. If they will reverse this policy, I see no reason whatever why their borrowing should not be carried through at present market levels.

(6) Unfortunately, rather overshadowing all these considerations is the question of confidence. I should feel quite happy with the present position if it were not for that. Indeed, I should feel plenty of confidence in favour of a patient holder. But in present circumstances this note of confidence is, of course, incalculable.

Yours sincerely,
[copy initialled] J.M.K.

In January 1939 Keynes took part in one of a series of conversations published in *The New Statesman*. His was entitled Democracy and Efficiency.

From The New Statesman and Nation, *28 January 1939*

DEMOCRACY AND EFFICIENCY

KINGSLEY MARTIN: *You have held that private capitalism is an out-of-date institution incapable of meeting the requirements of the twentieth century. Its failure at present in England is terrifyingly obvious. A couple of million unemployed is sufficient proof in itself. We have spent hundreds of millions of pounds on rearmament, yet everyone agrees that the results have been ludicrously disproportionate; if another great international crisis arises in the next few months I suppose we shall be told that we are still too weak to stand up for ourselves or for anything we value. In this series of conversations Mr Herbert Morrison, Mr Churchill and Mr Lloyd George have all argued, I think convincingly, that this fantastic inefficiency is not due to any faults inherent in democratic institutions. They have spoken mainly of the lack of leadership, and Mr Morrison, argued, as I should, that it is primarily due to the contradictions of an out-of-date economic system which puts profits before national needs. It is on this last point that I should particularly like your opinion.*

J. M. KEYNES: That the delinquencies of the present

Government are in the interests of profit-making strikes me as an odd idea. Surely that is a parrot-phrase in this context. But that we are suffering from the contractions of an out-of-date economic system I agree entirely. In contemporary conditions we need, if we are to enjoy prosperity and profits, so much more central planning than we have at present that the reform of the economic system needs as much urgent attention if we have war as if we avoid it. The intensification of the trade cycle and the increasingly chronic character of unemployment have shown that private capitalism was already in its decline as a means of solving the economic problem. But the breakdown of international good faith and the constant threats to peace are making it still more obvious that, quite apart from war, we have to move a long distance along that very road which actual war would make it imperative for us to take. Arnold Toynbee pointed out the other day that it is impossible to carry on the sort of organisation, to which we have been accustomed, in an atmosphere of complete uncertainty as to the future when we feel that a knife may at any moment cut every activity. But it is not the threat which the necessary measures might offer to personal liberty and democratic institutions which stands in the way of what wants doing to make us prosperous within and safe without. Any such threat is so remote from the first and the next and the next things that want doing, that it is not now, and is a long way from being, a practical issue.

K.M.: *When the reorganisation we need is so desperately obvious, what is it, in your view, that holds us back? What are the obstacles?*

J.M.K.: Well, first of all, there is a lukewarmness on the part of the public opinion which is organised towards the particular amalgam of private capitalism and state socialism which is the only practicable recipe for present conditions. This recipe is not in tune with the inherited slogans of either side. Most politicians are committed either to the view that private capitalism works very well as it is, or to the view that it should be got rid of altogether. From the days when I served on the Liberal

Industrial Inquiry, I have felt that there was too little organised sympathy for attempts to make the private property system *work better*. Your thinking it necessary just now to make that remark about profit-making is a good example of what I have in mind. Yet I am ever more convinced that there was deep wisdom in those seventeenth and eighteenth century thinkers who discovered and preached a profound connection between personal and political liberty and the rights of private property and private enterprise. The fact that the lawyers of the eighteenth century perniciously twisted this into the sanctity of vested interests and large fortunes should not blind us to the truth which lies behind. As Count Kalergi has recently reminded us, 'in all ages private property has been an essential element in liberalism, a bulwark of personality against the omnipotence of the state and a stimulus to seek comfort and culture,' and it was recognised in the French Revolution by the 17th paragraph of the *Declaration of the Rights of Man* as 'an inviolable and sacred right'. It is because of the dispute over the principle of private property that freedom's front today has broken up. Yet it is only on lines of liberalism that there can be a peaceful, non-violent evolution of social and economic institutions.

K.M.: *The right of private property that was historically associated with liberty in the period before the French Revolution referred to the right of the peasant proprietor to own the fruits of his own labour and of the man who invented a new process or ran a small business to make a profit out of it. But the ghosts of political theories are very erratic in their habits of walking, and I know of no more extraordinary confusion than that which identifies this right to own the fruits of one's own labour in pre-industrial society with the right of Mr Rockefeller or the Duke of Westminster to own the labour and control the conditions of life of thousands of other people. Surely the monopoly ownership of our day is one of the great enemies of liberty. But I agree that the right of personal property is inseparable from the conception of liberty, and that this confusion between personal property, which no intelligent Socialist has ever wished to take away from anyone, and property in the sense of the right to play the money market, and employ, sack or pay what wages one likes, has had very serious results. In any case there is no very early prospect of getting a complete socialism so that an understanding of the 'middle way' you speak of becomes urgently important. You say that there is a lack of organised sympathy for it. Do you mean that Britain is sharply and irrevocably divided between the two extreme views?*

J.M.K.: Quite the contrary. I believe that the real convictions of at least three-quarters of the country today are, in the most fundamental and genuine meaning of the word, *liberal*. Indeed, it is this which explains the unreality of contemporary party politics. Most of the Conservative Party and most of the Labour Party are liberals; yet this is the one shade of opinion which lacks organised expression. Mr Lloyd George is a good enough liberal himself. But of the two dark deeds of his career, the Treaty of Versailles and the slaughter of organised liberalism, we are suffering today as much from the second as from the first. Mr Churchill, Sir Archibald Sinclair, and Mr Herbert Morrison are politicians very representative of popular opinion today. And where could you find a finer trio of typical liberals? The real obstacle lies in our not having a Government of that complexion. Or take some others, not quite so near the centre of gravity—Mr Walter Elliot, Mr Eden, Mr Attlee, Lord Cecil, the Archbishop of York, the Duchess of Atholl, Prof. Laski, Mr Harold Nicolson, Mr H. G. Wells, Sir Arthur Salter, Mr A. P. Herbert, Commander Stephen King-Hall, yourself, Mr G. D. H. Cole, Lord Stamp, Mr Maxton, Mr Bevin, Sir Walter Citrine, Mr Dalton, Mr Noel-Baker, and I could go on until I have mentioned everyone in public life outside G.B.S., a dozen Tories and National Liberals (not all of them in the Cabinet), a dozen leaders of big business and perhaps a dozen agitators (though I cannot remember their names)—what are any of you but excellent liberals? There is no one in politics today worth sixpence outside the ranks of liberals except the post-war generation of intellectual Communists under thirty five. Them, too, I like and respect. Perhaps in their feelings and instincts they are the nearest thing we now have to the typical nervous nonconformist English gentleman who went to the Crusades, made the Reformation, fought the Great Rebellion, won us our civil and religious liberties and humanised the working classes last century.

K.M.: *You have started a very pretty hare there by calling me and all these other people liberals; but if you mean that most people in Britain still maintain a preference for social change with the minimum of violence, that they cling to certain standards of decency and are not always opposed to compromise, you are, of course, perfectly right. But many Communists really agree on these points and some of those whom you call liberals are deeply affected by Marxian philosophy. The greatest practical difference I notice between the generations is that the under thirty fives are uninhibited by experience of the last War and the last peace. In any case the situation is hopeless unless the two elements that you have called liberal and Communist can work together. That is why I find myself so dismayed by the attitude of the official Labour Party today.*

J.M.K.: Yes; the attitude of the official Labour Party towards all this strikes me as one of the silliest things in the history of British politics. Why cannot they face the fact that they are not sectaries of an outworn creed mumbling moss-grown demi-semi-Fabian Marxism, but the heirs of eternal liberalism, whose sincere convictions reflect and should inspire those of the great majority of their countrymen? Mr Herbert Morrison gave out splendid doctrine in his interview with you the other day, and his manifesto in the current number of *The Political Quarterly* is magnificent. But the official utterances which are concocted when he gets together with his friends are pathetic. I sympathise with Mr Bevin in fighting shy of contact with the professional Communists, regarding their body as a Trojan horse and their overtures in doubtful faith. But I should risk the contact all the same, so as not to lose touch with the splendid material of the young amateur Communists. For with them in their ultimate maturity lies the future, and not with the old jossers whose names I have been mentioning. I am all for Sir Stafford Cripps, and I would join his movement if he is successful in getting it launched; but I should like the movement all the better if Mr Herbert Morrison and the others would join it too. How foolish, too, to decry the Left Book Club! It surely is one of the finest and most living movements of our time. If the official Labour Party reject the notion that they are the heirs of eternal liberalism (which, of course, they are, if they are anything at all), that is all the greater reason why they should be something more than an alms-house for retired agitators.

K.M.: *Yes. The regular party leaders seem to regard all vitality as heresy, and, like the Social Democrats in some countries (which now put their Social Democrats into concentration camps), they seem intent rather on fighting their own left than on providing an alternative to the capitalist governments they are supposed to be opposing.*

J.M.K.: You have put your finger on the spot when you compare the official Labour leaders to the defunct Social Democrats of the Continent. That is the path to Hades they are walking unless they pull themselves up. But perhaps we are wandering from our main thread; though not, I think, as far as might seem on the surface. Shall I pass on to the other main obstacle in the way of the necessary action? I find it in the fact that the present heads of our Civil Service were brought up in, and for the most part still adhere to, the *laissez-faire* tradition. For constructive planning the civil servants are, of course, much more important than Ministers; little that is worth doing can be done without their assistance and good will. There has been nothing finer in its way than our nineteenth-century school of Treasury officials. Nothing better has ever been devised, if our object is to limit the functions of government to the least possible and to make sure that expenditure, whether on social or economic or military or general administrative purposes, is the smallest and most economical that public opinion will put up with. But if that is not our object, then nothing can be worse. The Civil Service is ruled today by the Treasury school, trained by tradition and experience and native skill to every form of intelligent obstruction. And there is another reason for the heads of the Service being what they are. We have experienced in the twelve years since the War two occasions of terrific retrenchment and axing of constructive schemes. This has not only been a crushing discouragement for all who are capable of constructive projects, but it has inevitably led to the survival and promotion of those to whom negative measures are natural and sympathetic. It has been a case of the survival of those who are particularly fit for retrenchment and retreat, and who are, therefore, unfit for energetic expansion. Great as is my admiration for many of the qualities of our Civil Service, I am afraid that they are becoming a heavy handicap in our struggle with the totalitarian states and in making ourselves safe from them. They cramp our energy, and spoil or discard our ideas.

K.M.: *Quite so. Our civil servants, like our politicians, have a good tradition and habits of decency, but are at a loss to adjust themselves to the appalling speed of new developments. They just go ca'canny like tortoises and hide under their shells. It is partly, I think, a question of age. One result of losing a war is that you lose the older generation; today in Britain few people in authority are under 60, and in Germany few over 40.*

J.M.K.: Is my line of thought now clearer? The idea that we cannot do what seems necessary without endangering our personal liberties and democratic institutions is a bogey. The obstacle lies not here, but in our rulers—first of all in the personnel of the Cabinet, and secondly in the personnel of the heads of the Civil Service. They spend their time, not in forging chains for us—far from it—but in finding plausible reasons for not doing things which public opinion almost overwhelmingly demands.

K.M.: *Yes, that is quite clear, though I think you attribute too much to the deficiencies of personnel and too little to the 'contradictions' of our economic system. To me the situation is unintelligible except on the basis of a class analysis. Our ruling classes are, above all, afraid of losing power; as long as the Reds are defeated they are content to sell us all into slavery. It is almost incredible, but many of them are still more afraid of Soviet Russia than Nazi Germany. It is not very comforting to think that they will be destroyed in a war, because so much else will be destroyed at the same time.*

J.M.K.: If, indeed, it ever comes to war, this lack of preparation may prove disastrous. Our mere survival will then require that constructive ideas and energetic action shall take charge, even though too late. We shall not pass through the slow evolution of the late War, but shall leap at once to something at least as drastic as the system of 1918. One sometimes forgets how slow the transition was last time from *laissez-faire* to control. I spent part of my time in 1915 on the earliest scheme for the state purchase and importation of wheat. We had no compulsory powers whatever, not even in engaging shipping freight. All we could do was to put on our best manners and engage the good offices and assistance of private trade. For most of that year there was a nearly complete freedom of dealing over the foreign exchanges. The voluntary system in almost every field survived more than a year of warfare. The controls in force in 1918 were built up tentatively and by slow degrees. No such period of gestation and experiment will be allowed us next time. Yet our plans and preparations are ludicrously feeble.

K.M.: *Just so; but how do* you *account for the apparent complacency of our rulers?*

J.M.K.: J. B. Priestley said the other day that 'we have at present a rich-tired-old-man Government, the worst we have had since that of Lord North which lost us the American colonies'. The second part of this is very plausible. But I doubt if being rich and tired and old, though true, is all the explanation.

One underestimates, I think, the extraordinary out-of-dateness of mind of men like the Prime Minister or Sir Thomas Inskip or Sir John Simon. They live faithfully according to their lights, but they are blind to what seem to others the most obvious aspects of the contemporary world. These simply do not reach them. In the case of the Prime Minister this blindness is an essential element in his strength. If he could see even a little, if he became even faintly cognisant of the turmoil of ideas and projects and schemes to save the country which are tormenting the rest of us, his superbly brazen self-confidence would be fatally impaired.

K.M.: *I doubt if anything would impair it, but what puzzles me most of all about him is his complacency as a businessman. If he regards himself rather as the head of a great capitalist state, why doesn't fear of bankruptcy keep him awake at night?*

J.M.K.: And there is one very elementary point, the ignoring of which is the most difficult of all to understand. Something like 10 per cent of our productive resources are at present unused. How can it weaken or impoverish us to employ these resources, even if we fail to do so with full efficiency? To take the simplest illustration—the use of the unemployed miners and others to dig underground shelters and exits. Not to do this and the like appears the very delirium of insanity. Yet to the Chancellor of the Exchequer and to the Treasury, brought up to apply the principles of private housekeeping to the state, this is an extravagance, a costly and perhaps insufficiently considered measure. What *I* think will *employ* our resources, *they* think will *exhaust* them—as though the labour of the unemployed could keep. This puts in two words the different attitudes.

K.M.: *Does it come to this then? Because democracy has failed to do the things that you are wanting our democracy to do, the totalitarian states have found a rough-and-ready way for using their national resources for a national purpose. Unfortunately that purpose is war, and in the process of reorganising capitalism the totalitarian method has wiped out liberty, decency and indeed almost everything that makes life worth living. That they were ever able to do this is due to the failure of democracy to make these absolutely essential economic changes. In other words, we in Britain are doomed unless we can make the essential changes quickly and without these unnecessary and appalling sacrifices.*

J.M.K.: Yes. That is the truth. The totalitarian states have shown us clearly enough that the central mobilisation of resources and the regimentation of the individual can be carried to a point which threatens the elements of personal liberty. I do not deny that. I say that we are so far from such a situation that the risk does not now exist. Nor is the real controversy about this. The question is whether we are prepared to move out of the nineteenth-century *laissez-faire* state into an era of liberal socialism, by which I mean a system where we can act as an organised community for common purposes and to promote social and economic justice, whilst respecting and protecting the individual—his freedom of choice, his faith, his mind and its expression, his enterprise and his property.

Keynes's article brought him into correspondence with Lady Violet Bonham-Carter and with Sir Stafford Cripps, who had been expelled from the Labour Party in January 1939, and was trying to organise a broadly based front to deal with the international situation.

From LADY VIOLET BONHAM-CARTER, *31 January 1939*

My dear Maynard,

I must write a line of congratulation to you on your *brilliant* 'interview' in *The New Statesman* this week. It *cld.* not have been better. Your two points—(one) about the 'sherdigeff' between State Socialism & Free Capitalism—& (2) about the Civil Service—needed saying badly—& *no one* has said them. The state of the C.S. is I think a very real danger today. Fifth-rate Ministers always get fifth-rate Civil Servants—or make them so.

I am having a private meeting with Stafford Cripps on Wed. I wish you were going to be there. I don't know him—but spoke on the same platform last Wed. at the Queens Hall at a rather remarkable meeting on Spain. His move is the first hopeful thing that has happened—& will be a test to the sanity of the Labour rank & file. But time is so short—& every day Fate is gaining on us—the Fate we have made for ourselves—there is the bitterness.

I do hope you are better? I send this to Gordon Square though I expect you are in the country. If you *are* in London & feel up to it do let me come & have a talk with you sometime.

Yours,
VIOLET B. C.

To LADY VIOLET BONHAM-CARTER, *3 February 1939*

My dear Violet,

I am very glad indeed you liked the article. I wonder how you got on with Cripps. I have known him slightly for some time and like him very much. But whether it is possible today to create a new movement as distinct from capturing and old one, I have some scepticism.

I shall be in London in the middle of next week. I wonder if you could look round to tea here on Tuesday, the 7th about 5 o'clock. It would be very nice to meet.

Yours ever,
[copy initialled] J.M.K.

From LADY VIOLET BONHAM-CARTER, *4 February 1939*

My dear Maynard,

Thank you for your letter. Alas! on Tuesday I have to go away for the night to give a lecture. Wld. Wed. (8th) at 5 o'clock (or any other time) suit you? Since writing to you last I have met Cripps & had a talk with him. (He is not a plural! tho' he sounds like one.)[2]

I think our aim shld. be not to create a new Party—but to break the existing Labour *machine* from within so as to make a fusion of the progressive forces possible.

Unfortunately so many Labour people depend on the machine for their very livelihood that it needs a rare degree of courage to 'come out'—& it all depends on how many *do* whether a 'purge' can or cannot be carried out by Transport House. I return tomorrow to 40 Gloucester Square, W.2 (Pad

[2] In the original, 'them' had appeared first and had been crossed out and replaced with 'him'.

1881). Perhaps you wld. send me word there whether Wed. is possible for you or not.

Ever yours,
VIOLET B. C.

From SIR STAFFORD CRIPPS, *2 February 1939*

My dear Keynes,

I was very grateful to you for your remarks in *The New Statesman* as regards the suggestions I have put forward.

We are about to embark on a very large scale effort to get the most widespread popular support for the movement and for this we shall require a great deal of financial support. I wonder if you could get us some substantial financial assistance and whether you could possibly get some of your friends who are sympathetic to the point of view to do the same.

Yours very sincerely,
R. STAFFORD CRIPPS

To SIR STAFFORD CRIPPS, *9 February 1939*

My dear Cripps,

I am in full sympathy with what you are doing. It seems to me very important not to split existing parties, but to capture them. I am entirely sceptical about the possibility of forming a new movement. It is about as difficult as starting a new bank. One can only build on and develop the old ones. But that, I gather, is your own point of view. I fancy that a spontaneous coming together of Liberals and of Left Book Clubbers to make an attempt on [?at] persuading the Labour Party is psychologically the best way the thing could have happened. But, it all depends on the persuasion being successful. That means the holding out of a chronic olive branch and keeping it as easy as possible for the Labour leaders to reconsider their disastrous decisions. My belief is that there is enough steam behind your effort to cause them to reconsider their ideas, *if great care is taken to make it easy for them to do so at every stage.*

I had a talk yesterday with Violet Bonham-Carter, and agreed to sign the petition of which she had a copy, though I made some suggestions about some additional words to it. I can see that the business of collecting names will need a lot of financial support. How much, would depend on how long the effort has to be continued before it produces results. I doubt if there is any source I can tap except myself. For one thing, it is rather difficult to explain exactly to what one is contributing. For myself, I gladly enclose a contribution of £50, and will send more later on if what is happening seems to require and deserve it.

If the Labour leaders are successful in manipulating the machine to maintain and support the attitude they have taken up, even though your movement secures a very large amount of support, it will be difficult to know what to do next. For I would emphasise again my belief that it is hopeless to try to form a new movement as distinct from capturing old ones.

Sincerely yours,
[copy initialled] J.M.K.

From SIR STAFFORD CRIPPS, *10 February 1939*

My dear Keynes,

Very many thanks for your letter and the most kind contribution you have sent to the expenses of the Petition.

I entirely agree with your thesis and shall do everything I can to make it easy for the Labour Party to compromise. There is not the slightest doubt that it would be fatal to do anything towards setting up any fresh political organisation. I have great hopes that the pressure that will be generated through the Petition will bring about some change and some attitude of compromise.

Yours sincerely,
R. STAFFORD CRIPPS

To LADY VIOLET BONHAM-CARTER, *9 February 1939*

My dear Violet,

I enclose for your private information a copy of a letter I have sent today to Cripps. It was very nice having a crack with you yesterday, and made me feel that I was really returning to life.

Yours ever,
[copy initialled] J.M.K.

From LADY VIOLET BONHAM-CARTER, *11 February 1939*

My dear Maynard,

Thank you so much for sending me your letter to Cripps. I am sure your advice of holding out the 'chronic olive branch' is sound—though difficult to translate into concrete form. I will show him your suggested addition to the petition when he dines here on Tuesday to meet Archie [Sinclair]. (Confidential) I am looking forward with some amusement to their confrontation— they have such different minds. *How* I wish you were going to be with us—you could help so much. As it is I have the sole responsibility of acting as 'hyphen' between them.

How *very* generous of you to send Cripps £50. He will be deeply touched & grateful. Gollancz, who rang me up the other night, was stressing the 2 difficulties of (A) Time & (B) Money—& the relationship between the two. To get *millions* of signatures you want 6 months & *many* thousand pounds. Cripps has only till Whitsuntide to create and mobilise his opposition—& I don't know what his funds are.

I can see that Archie is a little nervous about mobilising the Liberal *organisations* for fear of getting a split—(the name of Cripps is anathema to so many people of the stuffy sort). Yet this is the only way we can really contribute—except by the blessing of a few important 'symbolic' figures like your own.

I loved seeing you again & hope that I didn't stay too long & tire you. I will 'report progress' & should love to see you sometime again when you are up here.

My love to Lydia.

Ever yours,
VIOLET B. C.

On 2 February the preparatory committee for an international wheat conference met Keynes to discuss both the effect of changes in stocks of primary commodities on the price level and Keynes's 1938 storage proposals (above pp. 456–70). Before the meeting Keynes prepared a memorandum.

THE WHEAT PROBLEM

It is important to distinguish between the problem of dealing with excessive supply and the problem of dealing with fluctuating supply. In so far as the former problem exists, it may be attributed to:

(1) Excessive subsidies and tariffs.

(2) The stimulus of occasional years of high prices.

In so far as the second cause is operative, the problem of excessive supply is partly a result of fluctuations of supply. If occasional years of high prices could be avoided, the problem of excessive supply might be less intractable.

From statistics supplied the problem of excessive supply does not appear to be above 10 per cent of the total output at the outside, and may be not more than $7\frac{1}{2}$ per cent. The existing forecasts for 1939 acreage perhaps indicate that this acreage is not more than 5 per cent above requirements on the basis of an average crop.

The problem of excessive supply must mainly be dealt with by each country separately, supported perhaps by a quota system. In what follows I concentrate on the problem of fluctuating supply.

I suggest that an important contribution might be made towards mitigating fluctuations and towards reducing fluctuations of price to a moderate amount round a normal figure by improved arrangements for storing and financing stocks of wheat,—some sort of international extension of Mr Wallace's ever-normal granary scheme for the United States. Wheat is not so ideally suited as some other commodities for storage, but I understand that, with the most modern type of elevator, costs and wastage can be reduced to a reasonable figure, assuming, of course, that the stock is kept in motion, deliveries being taken from the older stock and replaced at the other end. I should add that, in proposing a scheme to facilitate the storage of wheat, I have not in mind merely the advantages of greater stability to wheat producers, but am thinking of this as part of a wider scheme which would aim at mitigating economic fluctuations generally by insuring greater stability of supply and prices, and might also serve the special purposes of this country in time of war, on the lines of a paper which I read last August to the British Association and subsequently printed in *The Economic Journal* (September, 1938).

There is one point which needs particular emphasis, if any scheme for storage is considered. Experience shows that, if some central authority undertakes to store stocks of a commodity and combines this with an attempt to limit price fluctuations, that authority must be prepared to store nearly all of the total stock. It is extremely difficult in the present conditions to combine a scheme of storage by public authority with the ordinary operations of private enterprise. Storage by private enterprise not only involves material costs, but also a serious lack of liquidity and the risk of price fluctuations. Even as it is, the incentives to storage are by no means adequate. Indeed, that is part of the explanation of the magnitude of price fluctuations. As it is, the main incentive is to be found in the large profits to be derived occasionally from periods of shortage. Any government scheme of storage will be regarded by the market speculator as much more likely to deprive him of profits than to protect him from losses. The amplitude of price fluctuation which is in the public interest is nothing like enough to attract or compensate the speculative holder of stocks. In particular, as soon as prices appear to approach the figure at which the public authority is expected to unload, speculative holders will take the opportunity of unloading first. The very interesting and important case of the buffer pool in tin is a good example. It may yet prove to be the case that the buffer pool will not be successful unless it is prepared to hold a very large proportion of all the surplus stocks of tin which are not actually in transit. I emphasise this point because half measures are likely to be futile and dangerous. I have the impression that control schemes generally have enjoyed less success than they deserve because they have tended to be half measures.

The actual figures in what follows are purely illustrative. I have not the knowledge or experience to indicate what they ought to be. But a suggested scheme is more intelligible if illustrative figures are introduced.

Let us suppose that the problem of excessive supply has been in some way handled by individual countries, or by means of a quota, and that the problem of fluctuating supply is the only one we have to attend to. Let us suppose that the normal price aimed at is 30/- per quarter for Liverpool contract wheat, with the usual premiums and discounts for wheat of other qualities. The basic price is taken for wheat in store at Liverpool, the price of wheat in other positions to be adjusted accordingly. It is suggested that each exporting country should erect really adequate storage of the most modern description, and that they should be prepared to take in wheat at the equivalent of 27/6 and dispose of it at the equivalent of 32/6. In practice the relation should not be quite so rigid as this, but it might be better if the element of elasticity was brought in by a fluctuating allowance for quality, grade and position, rather than through an elasticity in the basic price. For example, the difference between the price of Argentine wheat and the basic price, and the price of Canadian wheat and the basic price, would be allowed to depend on the comparative demand at any time for the two qualities and on the cost of shipping etc. So that neither country would have to hold out for an absolutely fixed relationship to the basic price. But this raises technical points beyond my competence.

It is suggested further that importing countries might share in the task. It would be very useful for a substantial part of the stock to be held in the countries of consumption rather than in those of production. There are three types of inducement to such participation, which might operate. In the first place, by arrangement between governments the exporting countries might, in certain cases, finance stocks held in the consuming countries; and there might be a division of the expenses; for example, the government of the consuming country providing storage and the government of the exporting country providing finance. In the second place, by arrangement between governments, surplus stocks might be transferred from the exporting government to the consuming government at a price somewhat below the basic price, on the understanding that the consuming government would not dispose of its stock to millers below the basic price;—such a plan might compensate the importing government for the costs and risks involved. In the third place, the governments of the consuming countries might be prepared to go to some definite expenditures in support of the scheme, so as to obtain large stocks on the spot in time of war.

It would be important if the existing surplus could be cared for at the outset of any scheme. I suggest that an important contribution to this might be made by the British Government. I believe it would be to the advantage of this country if the British Government were to erect stores in convenient places all over the country to hold, say, a full year's supply of the wheat requirements of Great Britain. The exporting governments would forthwith supply and ship this quantity to Great Britain at a price equivalent to 25/- (assuming the normal is the equivalent of 30/-), the f.o.b. price to be payable by Great Britain in five annual instalments.

It should, of course, be open to other importing countries to accumulate stocks on the same terms.

In conclusion it is important to emphasise once again that any conceivable scheme would be broken down if a condition of chronic excessive supply is allowed to exist.

J. M. KEYNES

Prior to the Budget, Keynes outlined the authorities' policy options as he saw them.

From The Times, *17 and 18 April 1939*

CRISIS FINANCE: AN OUTLINE OF POLICY

I. EMPLOYMENT AND THE BUDGET

We have experience of peace finance and of war finance. But this is neither. And it needs fresh thinking to know how to act. If there were war, the prices of shares and commodities would be raised, sooner or later, by the great increase in demand; and if peace were secure, by the great increase in confidence. But in this twilight depression is inevitable. Since, therefore, it is impossible for private enterprise to plan confidently for the future, we should feel in any other circumstances great anxiety concerning unemployment. But in the actual conditions of today it is safe to say that no such anxiety is necessary. I doubt if Parliament and the country have as yet fully appreciated the certainty and the magnitude of the impending change. Yet, for the reasons given below, the shift in the prospects is now so assured that the authorities should anticipate it in their plans. There is nothing immoral in foreseeing things before they happen—at any rate for a private citizen, even though a statesman may hesitate.

The Chancellor of the Exchequer should frame his Budget on the assumption that the problem of abnormal unemployment will cease to exist during the financial year 1939–40, and that all plans and special provisions for dealing with this problem should be dropped forthwith as being a waste of time and money. It follows that the budgetary provision for the cost of unemployment can be greatly diminished and that important resources available to take up Government loans will accumulate in the Unemployment Fund. He should also assume that the national income will gradually increase by (say) 8 per cent, which should mean a corresponding increase in the yield of a number of taxes; though, on account of the time lag in tax receipts, appreciably longer than a year must elapse before the full benefit of this will accrue to the Exchequer. One way and another, an important proportion of this year's Government loan expenditure will, sooner or later, pay for itself—in an increased yield from the existing taxes and in the reduced cost of unemployment.

Compared with America

There is nothing bold or rash in this forecast if due weight is given to the following figures. This year's loan expenditure has been estimated at £350,000,000, or (say) £220,000,000 greater than last year's; and it is probable that subsequent developments have substantially increased this figure. Many adjustments have to be made before the net effect of this can be estimated. Private investment for the purpose of carrying out Government orders, as a result of the stimulus to shipbuilding, for A[ir] R[aid] P[recautions], and in the consumption industries, may balance most of any decline in normal enterprise. But there may be an important offset in an increased adverse balance of trade; and the growing surplus in the Unemployment Fund, which lies outside the Budget, has to be deducted to give the net deficit. Taking everything into account, the increase in primary demand may be of the order of £200,000,000, which should mean an increase in total demand of perhaps twice this amount. Now, this is a very big figure. To show how big it is we may compare the present rearmament programme with the public works programme of President Roosevelt. If our own Government's loan expenditure comes to £400,000,000 it will be about 8 per cent of the national income. This is, in proportion, about twice the maximum public works expenditure in America and nearly twice their maximum Treasury deficit incurred in any recent year for all purposes apart from the Veteran's Bonus. I doubt if it is generally recognised that our programme this coming year is about double President Roosevelt's biggest.

The economic consequences of such expenditure will be far-reaching. With an average output of £250 a head, the prospective increase in demand would require the services of about 1,500,000 men. If we allow for overtime and longer hours by those already employed and make other deductions, there should be work for upwards of 1,000,000 men now unemployed. Accurate estimates are impossible in such a case. But it is hard to see how anything except a failure to spend the money can prevent the broad character of the situation from developing along these lines. If we put the number of men whom we can expect to re-employ at no more than 750,000, the nature of the problem facing us is not essentially changed.

It means, to begin with, that the prospects for home industry are better than they have been for years. It does not mean that we have no serious labour problem in front of us. On the contrary. But its character will be exactly reversed. The important thing is that we should not waste several months getting used to this new idea, but should prepare for it immediately. Government priorities, an acute shortage of skilled labour, trade union restrictions, the task of shifting workers to the districts where demand is greatest, the curtailment of unessential services—all the problems of the last War—are round the corner.

I repeat that nothing can prevent this forecast from coming true, except a failure to spend the money. There will, of course, be no sudden change. Experience shows, moreover, that programmes are usually behindhand and that there is a delay in the realisation of the final result. This means, not that no planning is necessary, but that we still have time to undertake it; though shortages of some types of material and skilled labour may be near at hand. Even in March the output of steel was within sight of our capacity. It is full time for a complete readjustment of our mental outlook. We have been so long set in the notion—it is nearly 10 years now—that we have a vast unused surplus capacity that we are being extraordinarily slow in facing the palpable fact that a complete reversal is in sight.

The balance of trade

At a time of rapid increase in domestic expenditure there are two physical obstacles to overcome: and in such circumstances only these physical obstacles are fundamental. The first is the shortage of labour; the second is the shortage of foreign resources. Apart, therefore, from the labour problem, the balance of foreign trade must be our chief preoccupation. Our demand for imports will surely increase, and this may facilitate, at the same time that it makes more necessary, Mr Hudson's excellent efforts to adapt our export methods to the times. But, in addition to our demand for imports, it is clear that we shall need large resources for political loans, while it is important not to impair our ultimate gold reserves more than is unavoidable. The handling of foreign trade cannot safely be left to individual enterprise unaided. For individuals have no machinery for the linking of imports to exports which is now essential for our financial strength. This is an urgent problem of immense difficulty—not less so because the solution is so contrary to our traditions and our preferences.

The time has also come to tighten up to the fullest extent the embargo on sending capital funds overseas by British nationals. Remittances arising out of *bona-fide* trade transactions or on behalf of foreign holders should remain free. Nor is it possible in peace time to close up every loophole. But a definite instruction forbidding fresh transactions on capital account involving remittance of funds abroad, except such as are specifically approved, addressed to all private and institutional investors and to banks and brokers, should prove sufficient. There are already such instructions covering a part of the field and they seem to be effective. But they need to be extended, so as to cover, in particular, the remittance of any further funds to the United States. The whole of our liquid capital resources must be concentrated henceforward to meet the adverse balance of trade and to provide for political loans.

But it is not only for these reasons that British nationals must be asked to keep their capital resources at home. It is essential for the Treasury's loan programme, which we shall discuss in a further article, that the Treasury should be free to pay regard solely to domestic considerations. It is a small measure of sacrifice to ask from owners of capital: that they should refrain from running away.

II. THE SUPPLY OF SAVINGS

It was suggested in the previous article that, in order to meet the requirements of the Treasury during this financial year, the public may have to save some £200,000,000 more than they did last year. This was on the assumption, which may or may not prove to be correct, that the carrying out of the Government's programme is within the physical capacity of the country without deliberately curtailing private investment. Since the net savings of the country have been reckoned recently as being (very roughly) in the neighbourhood of £400,000,000 a year, this task may seem at first sight scarcely practicable. The figure for net savings is, however, misleading. It is after a full allowance for wastage and depreciation of existing plant and buildings, and after offsetting all business losses. Depreciation and maintenance has been estimated at nearly another £400,000,000. I know no reliable estimate of gross business losses, but when times are not good they mount up to a large figure.

There are, therefore, three sources for the additional £200,000,000 likely to be required by the Treasury. There can be some postponement of full maintenance—with which can be included any reduction of stocks below normal—a temporary and dangerous expedient, but one which Germany has certainly exploited on a large scale. In the second place, with industry approaching full capacity, the waste of savings to offset business losses will largely disappear; to which we may add an increased retention of profits within businesses (which is normally the source of about half the savings of the country) as profits increase, especially at a time when there is need for additional working capital and the source of the profits is of a temporary character. Finally, individuals may be expected to increase their personal savings as a result of their enjoying increased incomes. Virtue will come into its own. Recently private saving has been open to the charge that it might aggravate unemployment. But in the new circumstances it will again serve a social purpose, and private prudence will coincide with the public interest. If in these days of uncertainty the ordinary individual is inclined to be more economical than usual, his inclination and his duty will agree.

Two signs to be watched

Taking all these things into account, it is possible that the present Government programme can be carried through without its becoming necessary to take special measures to curtail other forms of current investment, in particular by local authorities, the Road Board, and so forth. But we cannot be sure of this until we try. If, however, there is occasion for a more restrictive policy, it will become physically apparent. If we are pressing too nearly on the limit of our resources, this will be noticeable in an acute labour shortage, so that the Government programme cannot physically be executed without the aid of Government priorities, and in an excessive growth of imports relatively to exports. We need watch nothing else but these two signs.

So long as the Government's programme can be physically carried out and the adverse balance of trade is within our means, the savings to finance it must necessarily be available. What needless anxieties and expensive mistakes will be avoided, if we can only believe this. All experience, notably in the last War and in the recent practices of the totalitarian states, confirms the simple logic on which this elementary conclusion depends. Yet the so-called 'financial' mind is often prone to reject it. Is this the result of a habit of regarding as a postulate the liberty of a rich man to remit his financial resources abroad? For it is—we must not only admit but insist—a condition of maintaining the equilibrium of the national finances that this liberty should be taken away. National service for savings is the first step which the Government should now take, as I pointed out in my former article—as much, perhaps, on moral as on financial grounds. No blame to those who have been strengthening our foreign resources up to now by building up our foreign investments. That a part of our resources should have been used in this way hitherto is an inestimable element in our strength, which we can draw upon when the time comes. But the season for this has come to an end and the moment has arrived for recognising the arrival of a new phase by the issue of overt instructions.

Expenditure and income

Now if we assume that current savings cannot escape abroad, which would mean, if it occurred, that our domestic programme was being partly financed out of our gold reserves, they are necessarily available to the Treasury. If we leave out the adverse balance of foreign trade which is admittedly a separate (and real) problem, the income of the community will be equal to what the Government spends plus what individuals spend. What is one man's expenditure is another man's income. Thus the excess of the community's aggregate income over what individuals spend, which is left over and available to pay taxes and loans to the Government, must be exactly equal to what the Government spends. Perhaps the B.B.C. will set this problem in 'Puzzle Corner' to discover whether the conclusion is beyond our arithmetical powers.

Thus there is nothing for the Treasury to worry about except the physical capacity of the country to carry out the Government's programme, the proper technique for preventing the leakage of resources abroad, and the ever-present anxiety of the adverse balance of foreign trade. Truly these are sufficient troubles without adding to them the wholly spurious one of how to 'finance' the programme. The savings will come into existence *pari passu* with the expenditure. The only question which arises is as to the ultimate form in which they are held—whether as balances at the Bank of England, in Treasury bills and bonds, or in longer-dated Government debt.

It is sometimes believed that the choice between these forms is important because the avoidance of 'inflation' depends on it. But this is not so. Inflation results when the physical capacity of the country is insufficient to provide both for the Government's programme and for the expenditure of the public at the current level of prices, or if the adverse balance of trade becomes more than we can pay for at the current level of the exchanges. The avoidance of inflation is a real and important problem, as (without using the word) we have already emphasised. In Germany it may soon become the outstanding problem. But it is a different problem from the form chosen for the Government debt. Rationing and a compulsory reduction of public consumption will make a difference to it. But if the public have been free to spend what they choose and the Government has incurred a given expenditure not covered by taxation, the particular form of the Government debt makes no difference to the threat of 'inflation'.

Rate of interest

The main principles of loan policy in times of emergency are two. The first might be thought obvious if it were not sometimes overlooked. Loans must be raised after the expenditure has been incurred and not before. The savings come into existence *pari passu* with the expenditure, and owing to various time lags and transferences are not likely to be available for subscription to a loan until some time later. If an attempt is made to borrow them before they exist, as the Treasury have done once or twice lately, a stringency in the money market must result, since, pending the expenditure, the liquid resources acquired by the Treasury, must be at the expense of the normal liquid resources of the banks and of the public.

The second principle of loan policy is that the forms of the loans should be mainly dictated by the preferences of the public. If the public prefer short-dated debt, nothing can be gained and much will be lost in terms of interest and in the disturbance to the financial fabric by attempting to force long-dated loans on them. There is no object in offering higher rates of interest for loans than will be appropriate when the emergency is over and restrictions can be removed. The best interests both of the Treasury and the public will be served if stability and continuity of interest rates is preserved between the emergency and ordinary times. What object is there in offering an exceptionally high rate of interest? If private investment competes for limited physical resources, Government priorities and a control of new issues are the appropriate remedy. On the other hand, the offer of a higher rate will overburden the Exchequer and disturb the national finances for a generation to come; and in the immediate present it will cause a ruinous depreciation to financial institutions.

It would be well for the Chancellor of the Exchequer to announce that in no circumstances will he offer loans carrying a rate of interest in excess of $2\frac{1}{2}$ per cent. In the first instance a large addition to the volume of Treasury bills will be right and probably inevitable. Thereafter loans of varying maturities might be offered with rates of interest rising according to maturity from $\frac{1}{2}$ to $2\frac{1}{2}$ per cent.

Co-ordinated efforts

I began these articles timidly by suggesting that the problem of unemployment might now be disregarded. But, if we are only at the beginning of our effort, so that continual additions to the

Government's programme will be necessary as the months pass by, that is, of course, an absurd understatement. We are faced with the prospect of an acute shortage of manpower and all the difficulties which attend the co-ordination of public and private demands and the right allocation of limited resources between different Government Departments. The Ministry of Supply has been discussed as though it were no more than a piece of inter-departmental machinery which might or might not be useful. Whether we call it by that or another name, we shall save time and wasted effort if we set up a Department of Coordination, with an Economic General Staff attached to it, for the special purposes of dealing with the supply of labour and its mobilisation, with the allocation of limited resources and with the delicate task of preventing an excess of imports over exports which, taken in conjunction with political loans, is more than we can support. There is much to be said for attaching this organ to the Treasury rather than to the spending Departments. For in times of emergency, when physical resources rather than money are the reality, this is the only channel through which Treasury control can be effectively exercised.

I doubt if those of us who were concerned with these tasks in the last War have much to contribute to the present situation in the way of detailed suggestions. Too many circumstances have changed, and, if the crisis comes, we should find ourselves plunged straight into the conditions of 1918 without passing through the gradual experiments and slow evolution of the previous four years. Moreover, the period of the twilight has its special difficulties. But we do know the nature of the problem and have had indelibly impressed on us by experience the importance of a good organisation to solve it.

Keynes's articles brought one letter which was to establish contacts for him that were to prove most useful once war began (*JMK*, vol. XXII, pp. 215, 255, 274–6, 335).

From CHARLES MADGE, *18 April 1939*

Dear Mr Keynes,

We are investigating the social psychology of small savings in this town [Bolton] as part of a survey by Mass Observation of social-economic factors, with help from the Economics Research Department of Manchester University. We were very much struck by a passage in one of your remarkably shrewd articles in *The Times*:

'Individuals may be expected to increase their personal savings as a result of enjoying increased incomes. If in these days of uncertainty the ordinary individual is inclined to be more economical than usual, his inclination and his duty will agree.'

These are important assumptions in social psychology and we should be most grateful if you could tell us:

(a) Whether you regard them as hypothetical or proven?

(b) Whether they are based on statistical or other evidence?

(c) Whether you are including working-class savings in your generalisation about the 'ordinary individual'?

(d) Whether you think that work like ours might help the economist in those of his forecasts which involve psychological assumptions?

We can hardly expect you to answer the last of these queries without knowing what we *are* doing in this field. Dr Loewe, of Manchester University, who is in close touch with our work, thinks it may make a valuable contribution. As we are in the middle of the fieldwork, we can't state any conclusions yet. We are collecting answers to the enclosed questionnaire,[3] on a sample of 1,000. Our approach is as personal as possible, since working-class people react strongly against any 'official' inquiry. Things have not altered much since 1833, when the questionnaire sent out by the Factory Commissioners on working-class savings was such a failure. But our team has been living here for over two years, our contacts are wide and varied and the material we need comes rolling in.

The important question, and our real reason for writing to you, is whether the crisis is likely to have a big effect on savings and if so, for what psychological reasons. Of those questioned if they were worried about the future, so far only 5 per cent have made any reference to the international situation—which confirms the general impression of all our studies in public opinion, that the working-class is relatively indifferent to 'crises' except for 24 hours at a time, e.g. at the climax of the September crisis. Actual outbreak of war would of course be a different matter; when the breadwinners go to the front, the economic realities of the situation can no longer be avoided.

[3] Not printed.

We have also done some work on middle-class saving and investment, but on a smaller scale.

We would gain immensely from having your opinion on these questions. Few of the leading economists have recognised, as you have, the relevance of psychological questions to economics. Possibly, by modifying our research on savings, we might make ourselves useful both during the 'twilight' period and in war time.

Yours truly,
CHARLES MADGE

To CHARLES MADGE, *20 April 1939*

Dear Mr Madge,

The question you raise in your letter of the 18th is an interesting and important one. The worst of it is, however, that it is difficult to deal with it adequately within the compass of a letter. My own attitude to the problem is given much more fully in my book, *The General Theory of Employment*, and I am asking my publishers to send you a copy of this for your acceptance.

In my *Times* article I was not thinking principally of increased savings by the working classes. On the information before me it is difficult to arrive at a clear conclusion about this and, for that reason, I very much welcome the enquiry which you are making.

On general grounds I should expect an improvement in employment to lead to increased working-class savings, but on what scale or through what channels it is difficult to know. I shall be interested to hear, in due course, the results of your questionnaire. But it will not, of course, give much light on the question of the effect of a change in earnings on working-class savings. Possibly you might consider a supplementary enquiry on this. For example, an unemployed man has very likely run into debt with tradespeople, his landlord and his friends. When he regains employment, he will endeavour to pay off these liabilities, and that, from the point of view we are discussing, would mean a corresponding increase in savings. Indeed, one can double the amount, since, whilst he is running into debt, the unemployed man has negative savings to the amount of his debts, and is spending more than his income by that amount, and when negative savings are replaced by positive savings of an equal amount, the effect is doubled.

Again, it would be interesting to know if, when a man's earnings increase from, say, 50/- to 60/- a week, he will save more. For example, will he take out additional insurance policies; will he pay up any instalments which he owes more rapidly; will he put more in his building society, or pay off more rapidly what he owes them?

Very little is known in detail about the habits of [the] working classes in the matter of savings. All we have are certain aggregate figures. And these certainly include large sums which are attributable to the middle classes rather than the working classes. I much hope, therefore, that you will continue actively with your very valuable enquiry. When you have finished your present sample, I would suggest that you should embark on another one, carried out on somewhat different lines, and see how far the results are in comformity. And it will be particularly interesting if you can get a clue as to how far changes in employment and earnings are reflected in changes in working-class savings, through one channel or another.

Yours very truly,
[copy initialled] J.M.K.

From CHARLES MADGE, *21 April 1939*

Dear Mr Keynes,

Thank you so much for your letter which really supplies just the guidance we were hoping for. It is some time since I read your book on the *General Theory of Employment*, and it is very kind of you to have a copy sent to us.

We should certainly add to our questionnaire, as you suggest, a question on the effect which an increase in the family incomes has on the amount set aside for savings. The whole economic life of working-class people is of course on a weekly basis, and savings proper, in the economist's sense, get mixed up with short-term saving for holidays, clothes and heavy bills—the attitude to saving is largely in terms of these rather than of a distant future. Moreover, working-class weekly incomes fluctuate surprisingly.

We should value it very highly if you would read through our first draft report when it is ready in a few months time. We are to produce a book on it by next February.

We had intended to have another large-scale questionnaire on how people spend the margin of their income apart from the relatively fixed spending on food, rent, fuel and weekly contributions. It would be a great help if you would look at this and vet it before it is printed. Some such question as 'If you had 10/- a week more, how much of this would you save, and how would you save it?' would fit into this second questionnaire probably.

With many thanks

Yours sincerely,
CHARLES MADGE

To CHARLES MADGE, *25 April 1939*

Dear Mr Madge,

I will gladly comment on your new questionnaire when the time comes. The question you suggest about what would happen if they had 10/- a week more seems to me a very good one to ask.

If you could find out to what extent the unemployed get into debt, and how far this is a first charge on their increased earnings when they get work again, this would be a matter of extreme interest.

Yours very truly,
[copy initialled] J.M.K.

On 26 April the Prime Minister, in announcing compulsory military service, also said that the Government would take steps to take the profit out of war and limit the profits of armament firms in forthcoming measures. Keynes commented.

To the Editor of The Times, *27 April 1939*

Sir,

The increase in incomes and profits resulting from armament expenditure will spread far beyond the armament firms whose profits the Prime Minister proposes to limit. As he pointed out, part of these increased incomes will be recovered by the Exchequer in the shape of taxes. But it is proposed, wisely, in my opinion, that a substantial part of them shall be provided out of Government loans.

The savings the Treasury is to borrow will be the result of the loan policy, and could not come into existence if the whole of the expenditure was being covered by taxation. It is surely unthinkable that either public opinion or the Chancellor of the Exchequer will allow the cost of loans raised in such circumstances to exceed the rates of interest which were current before the present critical conditions had begun to develop, say, in February, 1938. If the Treasury were to offer loans at higher rates than those then current, this would be a deliberate encouragement to a form of war profiteering as unnecessary as it would be inexcusable. Indeed the sacrifices asked from others make it appropriate that the rates should be lower, and not higher, than those prevailing early last year.

I urge, therefore, that as a necessary complement to the Prime Minister's announcements of yesterday, the Chancellor of the Exchequer should clear the position by saying at once that he will in no circumstances offer any loans at a higher rate of interest than, say, $2\frac{1}{2}$ per cent as a maximum for maturities up to 15 years.

Considerations of justice are here reinforced by those of expediency. The benefit to the Exchequer is obvious. But the security and stability of financial institutions, such as banks and insurance offices, and of the whole financial fabric would be enhanced; while the cost of necessary new investment, likely to increase in most other directions, would be in this respect diminished. The policy of borrowing at a high rate of interest the savings which are only made possible by the Government's decision to borrow rather than to tax would be open to the further objection that it would depreciate the present value of all loans made out of past savings.

Yours, &c.,

J. M. KEYNES

Keynes's letter brought comments from W. J. Borough of the *Investors' Review*, and Messrs C. A. Alington and L. S. Hunter of Tyneside. Mr Borough questioned Keynes as to the implications of his suggestions concerning borrowing policy, given that Government issues had to compete with other new issues on the market and rates of return elsewhere. He suggested that Keynes's interest-rate target might involve dividend restrictions elsewhere. The other two correspondents questioned Keynes's remarks about unemployment policy, quoting Sir Ronald Davison. Keynes replied to both letters on 2 May.

To the Editor of The Times, *2 May 1939*

Sir,

Mr Borough asks me whether a policy of setting a maximum to the rate of interest at which the Treasury will borrow involves controlling the rate paid by other domestic borrowers. I do not think so. For, as will be seen below, I do not propose that the Treasury should borrow otherwise than at the current market rate. What I am advocating involves no technical difficulties. Indeed it follows the line of least resistance. But several comments which have been made indicate that I must explain myself in more detail.

The early stages of the natural sequence of events are, I think, common ground. To begin with, the Treasury will finance itself by Treasury bills taken up to the extent of about 10 per cent by the Bank of England, and for the rest mainly by the joint stock banks. It happens, as a result of the large amount of bills recently taken off the market by the Equalisation Fund, that this process can continue some time before the banks' holdings of Treasury bills are restored to the figure at which they stood not very long ago. Meanwhile the deposits of the public with the banks will be correspondingly increased. These deposits will be accumulated out of unspent income—that is to say, they represent savings and would normally be available to purchase Government stocks or other investments.

It may be, however, that both the public and the banks will prefer in such times as these to keep much more liquid than usual, sacrificing interest income for the sake of security and liquidity of capital. If so, no harm will be done. The savings will be none the less savings because they are lent to the Government through the banking system than if they were lent direct; while the Government will enjoy the advantage of financing its expenditure at a cost of ½ per cent or less. Even if this were to continue until normal conditions are restored it would not greatly matter. Probably, however, a point will come sooner or later when the banks and the public will feel that to keep any more resources in a liquid form yielding a negligible rate of interest would be a waste of income. Two-and-a-half per cent Conversion Loan, repayable at par in 10 years time at latest, will begin to look a great bargain at its present price of 92 and more attractive than deposits or bills at ½ per cent or less. With the approach of this phase the price of this and similar stocks will steadily rise. When, that is to say, the public are ready to invest their savings in a more permanent form their demand will have its natural effect in raising the market price of securities. I am merely recommending that the Treasury should postpone the issue of new loans, other than Treasury bills, until this process is well advanced.

The Treasury have the power to fix the rate of interest at which they will borrow only in the sense that it lies with them to decide when the market rate of interest has fallen low enough to justify a funding operation. But this is a very real power. For the market is bound to come their way in due course. The savings of the public are increasing all the time. If the supply of funded loans is left unchanged the force of demand must raise their price. The notion that it is natural for the price of Consols to fall over the next year neglects this factor. At present the demand for liquidity due to crisis conditions outweighs the growth of savings. But fresh national savings will be forthcoming in the next year exceeding £350,000,000. It is only common sense to suppose that new demand from this source coming on an unchanged supply of funded securities will raise their prices in the market. The Treasury is in a position, therefore, to decide at what level of price it will increase the supply. When the market prices of Government stocks have risen to a fully normal level, thus indicating that the public no longer desire to keep their savings in an ultra-liquid form, the time will have come for the issue of new Government stocks of various types in accordance with what the public wants. The object of this funding, when the time is ripe for it, will be to facilitate the eventual return to the conditions of an economy free from physical restrictions on private investment.

There is only one possible ground for a different policy—namely, a mistaken belief that to persuade the public to put their savings into Treasury bonds instead of Treasury bills is the way to avoid 'inflation'. But it is expenditure, public and private, which raises prices, not the way in which the expenditure is financed. I do not say that the offer of Treasury bonds at 6 per cent instead of at 2½ per cent would have no effect on private expenditure. I agree that it would, for example, interfere with private building. But so long as there is a surplus of building labour this is unnecessary; and when we are pressing against the limit of the available supply of specialised resources there can be no efficient method of control except through a system of priorities for Government and other essential services.

Moreover, a high rate of interest is restrictive in all directions equally; yet it might be the case that there was no reason for a drastic interference with, for example, private building. Free competition for finance is a sequel of free competition for physical resources; and if physical resources are controlled the need for financial restriction disappears. Six per cent Treasury bonds would be an insanely expensive, misdirected, and inefficient method of dealing with a shortage of steel or skilled engineers. No one is proposing that the Army should be recruited by raising Army pay to whatever level is necessary to attract the required number of men out of industry; though this would be more efficient for the purpose and less open to objection on other grounds than six per cent Treasury bonds as a means of reducing the private demand for steel.

Let me take this opportunity of saying that I have expressed no opinion—I am not competent to do so—on the number of the present unemployed who are for practical purposes unemployable. I said that the problem of abnormal unemployment was at an end, and that the carrying out of the Treasury programme would require the labour of 750,000 additional workers as a minimum. So far from expecting that the task of drafting this number of men into the appropriate jobs would be easy, I went on to say that the prospect meant that 'Government priorities, an acute shortage of skilled labour, trade union restrictions, the task of shifting workers to the districts where demand is greatest, the curtailment of unessential services—all the problems of the last War—are round the corner.'

I am inclined to take a more optimistic view than Sir Ronald Davison as to the number of the unemployed whom we can hope to absorb. But he writes on this with more authority than I can. If he is right my plea for a planned mobilisation of labour without any delay is reinforced. The closest collaboration with the T.U.C. will be required.

When a satisfactory agreement with Russia has been reached there will no material difference of opinion about the objectives of our foreign policy; and one must pray that labour leaders may be ready to recognise that those who will the end must will the means.

Yours, &c.,

J. M. KEYNES

On 6 May in an article entitled 'First Line of Defence', *The Statist* in dealing with Keynes's proposals attempted to dismiss them by suggesting that he lacked market experience. In a letter Keynes reproached the editor.

To the Editor of The Statist, *12 May 1939*

Private

Dear Sir,

A letter which I wrote to *The Times* after you had written the article which appeared in *The Statist* of May 6th will have shown you that there is in that article a misunderstanding of what I was proposing. As this letter is not for publication, perhaps I may be justified in reminding you, in relation to your statement that 'Mr Keynes has no experience of the working of the great money markets and still less of the international finance which was involved in the recent War', that I was in fact throughout the recent War head of the department of the Treasury in charge of our international finance, and drafted and assisted to negotiate nearly all the international financial arrangements which we made during that period.

Yours faithfully,
[copy initialled] J.M.K.

On 23 May Keynes spoke on the B.B.C. on the relationship between rearmament and unemployment. The talk was subsequently published.

From The Listener, *1 June 1939*

WILL REARMAMENT CURE UNEMPLOYMENT?

We have suffered so long from severe unemployment that we have come to regard this state of affairs as a chronic malady. Those in authority have refused to believe that it could be cured by large-scale state expenditure on housing and other needed improvements. If this were correct, it would follow that neither can it be cured by large-scale state expenditure on armaments, of all forms of expenditure the most unproductive. But, for reasons beyond our control, the grand experiment is to be made. In rearming this country, shall we, by accident so to speak, cure unemployment? This is a most exciting question for the workers—and also, I may add, for the economists. What are the arguments? They are not very simple. But they are not very difficult either. So I will try to explain them.

The Government is likely to spend this year under all heads

upwards of £250 million above what it spent last year. Obviously more men will be employed making what the Government buys. How far will this be offset by fewer men being employed in other directions? For instance, the taxpayer will pay more and spend less, which means that fewer men will be employed making what the taxpayer would otherwise buy. But the Chancellor of the Exchequer has decided this year that there is to be only a modest increase in taxes. So the deduction to be made on this head is not large. Again, private investment of the ordinary peacetime character may fall off, on new housing for example, either because of a very natural lack of confidence in the prospects, or because it is difficult to get the necessary finance, or because the Government has taken away for its own purposes the specialised labour which alone is able to tackle the job. Moreover, some of the Government expenditure will be spent on imports or will employ labour which would otherwise provide exports. It is difficult to say beforehand how large these offsets will be. Up to date it is not clear that total private investment is falling away very much, though its character may be changing. Private firms and local authorities will be spending a lot of money on A.R.P. beyond what is included in the Government's Budget. Firms with large Government orders are having to extend their permanent plant. A substantial increase in private shipbuilding is in prospect, as a result of Government subsidies. And this is scarcely the time for economising in transport improvements, when smooth and rapid movements of people and of goods may be all important. On the other hand, it is inevitable that there is a good deal of private work which will be postponed for less anxious times. My own guess is that the net decline in other investment will only be large if the Government, on purpose or because they can't help it, put difficulties in the way of people getting hold of finance or of labour. And there will be no occasion to put such difficulties in the way, until we are approaching the full employment of the labour which is both of the required kind and in the right place.

This brings us up to the kernel of our problem and to the question about which there is the most difference of opinion between experts. How many of the men now unemployed are capable of being employed on the particular jobs offering? Even the optimists would not put the proportion higher than two-fifths or perhaps three-fifths of the men now registered as unemployed. And I, who am reckoned an optimist in this matter, agreed that even the lower of these proportions can only be reached as the result of very good organisation by the Government and by industry and of very good will on the part of the trade unions. I know that too often action is not taken until six months or a year too late and then only in response to great pressure from public opinion—a poor substitute for the foresight of true statesmanship; but I expect that the Government will act in the end—they generally do. If any trade unionists and heads of private business who are listening to me show themselves quicker in the uptake than the Government, that will do no harm. For the work can only be done if men are drafted into jobs to which they are not accustomed, and sometimes away from home, and if the skilled men are willing to work in with unskilled men who have to be taught a good deal. Trade unionists have many things of which they can properly complain. But I hope that at this time and in this matter they will be easy and reasonable, for the sake of all of us; and for the sake of themselves, too, because it is only by this means that we can use this opportunity to make a big impression on the curse of continuing unemployment.

The Economist newspaper has given some examples of how acute the problem is likely to be in particular cases. They calculate that if all the unemployed recorded in the aircraft and motor-car industry were to be put to work, they could only supply about a quarter of the Government's increased demand. But perhaps this does not allow nearly enough for the increasing efficiency of production and for overtime by those already in work. If all those concerned behave in a practical way, I see no reason to think that the Government programme cannot be carried through—and without undue interference with other work.

My final guess is that the total national expenditure at home on general investment, public and private, and on armaments not provided out of taxes, may be as much as £200 million more than it was last year. Let us call it £150 million to be on the safe side. How many men will this employ? Somewhere about 600,000, if all the work were to be done by men now unemployed. But this would be a large exaggeration. Men already employed will put in more work and bring home more wages. Perhaps half the extra work may get done this way. If so, the direct effect of the armament expenditure may be to take 300,000 men off the dole. I fancy that even the pessimists would reckon that a fairly conservative figure.

That is the first part of the story. But it is only the first part. As a result of spending £150 million extra, all sorts of people will have bigger incomes. Not all of it will be extra, for those who used to be unemployed will no longer have the dole. But a good proportion will be extra; and those who get it, being ordinary sort of people, will spend most of it. This expenditure of theirs will employ another lot of people, and so on. The money, in the old phrase, will circulate. By how much will this second effect multiply the first effect? It is not easy to say. We have only lately begun to look at the problem just this way, and the statisticians have not yet collected enough material for a safe forecast. I must leave out the details and give you my own estimate for what it is worth, and I will try to be on the safe side. In places where I was more easily open to contradiction than I am on the air, I have given bigger figures all through than I am giving you here. But the figures I am giving are sufficient to establish the argument. Let us put the multiplier effect, as it is called, of the subsequent waves of expenditure, at two-thirds of the initial impulse. Two-thirds of the 300,000 men primarily employed is 200,000, which means that 500,000 men will be taken off the dole altogether. Now this secondary expenditure will be much better spread and easier to meet than the initial expenditure. For the extra wages and incomes will be spent in shops all over the country on all sorts of things. It will not be concentrated on a few special industries.

We reach the conclusion, therefore, that, as compared with last year, the number of the unemployed should fall in the course of the year by 500,000 as a minimum. And some people think that a good case can be made out for putting the estimate half as big again as this, or even double. And this isn't the end. Two hundred thousand young men are going to be called up; and the raising of the school-leaving age this autumn will make a big cut in the numbers of lads coming forward.

What a difference all this makes! It is not an exaggeration to say that the end of abnormal unemployment is in sight. And it isn't only the unemployed who will feel the difference. A great number besides will be taking home better money each week. And with the demand for efficient labour outrunning the supply, how much more comfortable and secure everyone will feel in his job. There will be other reasons for plenty of anxiety. But one of the worst anxieties is anxiety about getting and keeping work. There should be less of that than for years past.

I have a special extra reason for hoping that trade unionists will do what they can to make this big transition to fuller employment work smoothly. I began by saying that the grand experiment has begun. If it works, if expenditure on armaments really does cure unemployment, I predict that we shall never go back all the way to the old state of affairs. If we can cure unemployment for the wasted purposes of armaments, we can cure it for the productive purposes of peace. Good may come out of evil. We may learn a trick or two which will come in useful when the day of peace comes, as in the fullness of time it must.

At the beginning of the next week Keynes sent a memorandum on Government borrowing and the rate of interest to the Chancellor of the

Exchequer and the Governor of the Bank of England. He also sent copies to Ian Macpherson of Buckmaster and Moore, his principal stockbrokers, and R. H. Brand.

To SIR JOHN SIMON, *28 May 1939*

Dear Chancellor of the Exchequer,

You may have seen a couple of articles which I recently contributed to *The Times* in which I discussed the prospects of employment and in particular the borrowing policy which the Treasury might adopt.

In these articles I have but little space at my disposal and was covering a good deal of ground. Correspondence which has reached me since makes it plain that I have not yet done all I could to bring the discussion to a head or make the relevant factors really clear. This has inspired me in the last few days to prepare a further and fuller memorandum on the matter, a copy of which I enclose. I have written this in the first instance primarily for the eye of yourself and other people in the Treasury; and I am also sending a copy to the Governor of the Bank. But later on I may print it somewhere, either in this or in a modified form.

I make no excuse for bothering you with this manuscript, for the problem is obviously of the most tremendous importance. It matters enormously whether or not the right policy is adopted. I feel that the technique of the matter has not been thought through thoroughly enough in the light of modern conditions and modern thinking; and this is an attempt to bring the issue to a head.

Yours sincerely,

J. M. KEYNES

To MONTAGU NORMAN, *28 May 1939*

Dear Mr Governor,

I enclose a copy of a memorandum which I am sending to the Chancellor of the Exchequer. You may have seen articles which I recently contributed to *The Times*, which discussed, amongst other matters, the Treasury's borrowing policy. Various correspondence which has reached me makes me feel that I did not in those articles really make the argument as clear as I might, or bring the issue to a head. In this paper I have given myself rather more room and have tried to analyse the problem as clearly and also as uncontroversially as I can.

It is a long time since you and I have written to one another. A long spell of ill health on my part has until recently seriously interfered with my activity. But I need make no excuse for sending you such a document. It obviously matters enormously that a right policy should be pursued. The issues which I discuss, whether I am right or wrong, are obviously of tremendous importance for the future of public finance in this country.

Yours sincerely,

J. M. KEYNES

GOVERNMENT LOAN POLICY AND THE RATE OF INTEREST

This is a matter of such enormous importance that I need no excuse for a further attempt to analyse the relevant factors.

The traditional reasons for expecting, and even approving, a substantial rise in the rate of interest at a time when heavy loan expenditure is being incurred by the Government (or by other borrowers) are three in number, different in character from one another, which were apt to be inextricably tangled in the old *laissez-faire* world, but must be sharply distinguished, and handled separately, in the modern world.

The first two reasons were reasons for *approving*, and not merely for expecting, a rise in the rate of interest.

I

In the first place, a high rate of interest is likely to deter competitive users of the resources of men and materials which are required by the Government programme. The conclusion that a high rate of interest would have some effect—and, if it were high enough, an important effect—in this direction is undisputed. But this may not be the best way of attaining the desired result, for the following reasons.

(1) The necessity for a deterrent only arises when full employment is in sight. This situation has not yet arisen. On the contrary, in the twilight finance between peace and war, it must be our object to carry out the Government programme with the least possible interference with other useful purposes, the labour for which is still in surplus, e.g. housing schemes.

(2) This form of deterrent is undiscriminating and stops employment just as much in those directions which do not interfere with the Government programme as in those which do interfere.

(3) Other deterrents are available which are both more discriminating and more effective.

Apart from foreign borrowers, the only competitors with the Government who are on a large enough scale to be worth bothering about are

(i) Local authorities
(ii) Building societies
(iii) Public boards and other public utilities
(iv) Transport, both roads and railways
(v) Shipbuilding
(vi) The heavy and engineering industries.

The first four can be tackled by direct representations at the fountain head and through the new issue market; (v) we are deliberately encouraging; (vi) is obviously in the interests of the Government's own programme. They can also be dealt with, if the necessity arises, by Government priorities, thus making it difficult or impossible for these investors to get hold of the actual men and materials for which the Government has a more urgent need.

It is, indeed, very important that there should exist an authority to decide which of these other investment activities can be allowed to go forward unhindered and which not. But when the decisions have been made, their carrying out will not require the clumsy and expensive method of a punitive rate of interest payable by the Government equal with others.

(4) It is argued—this is a modern argument—that a high rate of interest deters not only alternative capital projects but also luxury expenditure. A high rate of interest depreciates the market value of existing investments. This makes the investing class feel very poor and therefore disinclined to incur avoidable expenditure. If War Loan were to fall to 80 and everything else in proportion, one would certainly expect such a result;—and also a corresponding fall in the Exchequer receipts from death duties, stamps and certain classes of profits.

But here again there is a much better way of attaining the same object. At present the Chancellor of the Exchequer is being moderately merciful in the matter of taxation. This is because he thinks it advisable at the present stage—rightly in my opinion—not to discourage private enterprise and expenditure more than is necessary. But if and when the approach of full employment makes it essential to discourage all avoidable expenditure, the existing reasons against heavier taxation are replaced by reasons in favour of it. Taxation is in every way a much better instrument for discouraging private expenditure than a high rate of interest.

It would be a strange policy on the part of the Treasury to keep taxation moderate so as to encourage outside business, and then to pay a high rate of interest on Government borrowing so as to discourage outside business—thus making sure of the worst of both worlds, smaller receipts and larger expenses.

II

The second traditional ground for a high rate of interest is the importance of competing against foreign securities. In the *laissez-faire* investment markets of pre-war days when foreign investments were a half or more of our total current investment, this was undoubtedly of the first importance.

It remains of importance today. Indeed I feel more serious concern about our balance of foreign payments, both on capital and current account, than is at present clearly obvious in the policy of the authorities. I consider that this should be one of our first objects of concern, particularly because it is not so easy to find the best remedy. But it is surely obvious that the authorities now have at their command methods which are much more completely efficacious than a high rate of interest. So far as new foreign issues are concerned, a *laissez-faire* investment market is a thing of the past. The control of purchases in Wall Street may need tightening up. But a depreciating tendency in home markets, due to a rising rate of interest, is not the way to keep money at home. The psychology of the domestic investor is such that the way to retain him is to put domestic markets better, not to put them worse.

And the same is true of the foreign investor. A steadily falling market, as the rate of interest rises, is not the clever way to attract him to London.

III

So far I have been casting no doubts on the theoretical validity of the traditional arguments. I have been arguing only that, in the contemporary environment and in the special and peculiar circumstances of the hour, they are not the best way of attaining the desired object. But it is otherwise with the third compartment of the argument. It is believed by many people—by most people, I suppose—that, however desirable it may be that the Treasury's loans should be placed on the cheapest possible terms, it is utterly impracticable to secure cheap terms when there is a necessity of borrowing an enormous sum. On this matter, however, a shift is discernible in the accepted theory. It would, I think, be fair to say that the traditional arguments, on which most bankers and civil servants have been brought up, are no longer accepted as adequate by many British economists who have specially studied these problems. At the present stage economists are not all expressing themselves in the same way or with the same emphasis. But the variant forms of the modern theory come to much the same thing for the present purpose. The following is an attempt to explain the shift of emphasis in a way which is as uncontroversial as possible.

It is common to the old view and to the new that increased loan expenditure can only be met out of increased saving. According to the old view, the required increase in saving can only be stimulated by a higher rate of interest. According to the new view, this argument would only be correct if it is tacitly assumed that the increased loan expenditure has to be made out of the same total national income as before,—an assumption which would, indeed, be valid if all the available resources of men and materials were already employed, so that no increase in output was physically possible—and that there are no other methods for diverting existing expenditure. If, however, an increase in output and income is physically possible, the stimulus to demand resulting from the increased loan expenditure will bring about an increase of output both directly and indirectly. In such circumstances, it is mainly out of the increased incomes corresponding to the increased output that the increase of saving will occur. Moreover the loan expenditure will only be physically possible if the Government is successful in attracting resources for its own use; which means that a sum equal to the incomes generated by the Government's expenditure is physically withdrawn from consumption and must therefore be saved. Thus the required amount of saving necessarily comes about, irrespective of whether the rate of interest rises or falls. The proportion of the increased incomes which is spent on imported goods raises a dangerous complication. For both directly and indirectly the Government's loan expenditure will worsen the trade balance. But a high rate of interest will be of no assistance in this, or in any other respect, except to the extent that it diminishes current consumption. And here, as we have already seen, there is little or nothing to be hoped from a high rate of interest, which import control and Government priorities cannot do better. The old view was assuming that no weapons except high interest are available.

Thus, the contemporary economist, as a result of living in a world where unemployment has become chronic, puts more stress on our power of drawing on resources which were not fully employed and less stress on the diversion of resources already in use. In so far as diversion becomes necessary he is able to call attention to the efficacy of controls on imports and on foreign investment and through Government priorities; whereas in the *laissez-faire* world, which ruled out these instrumentalities, the offer of a high rate of interest was the only permissible weapon, however expensive and inefficacious it might prove to be. Both would agree as to the effect of high taxation. But, in view of the other controls available today, it is not so necessary in the early stages; and without the other controls, it would at the later stages, be inadequate in any case, as the last War showed.

IV

Let us return to the more practical point of view. There are two distinct reasons why the Treasury might be eager to issue funding loans at the earliest possible date. The first is to 'get hold of the money' with the idea that you cannot spend money until after you have got it. If all transactions were on a cash basis with gold coins the only form of cash, this would be true. The Treasury, like Charles II, would have to borrow gold coins from the goldsmiths in Lombard Street, before it could pay for an order. But with modern representative money and a modern banking system, we know that the necessary 'finance' can be created by a series of 'book' or 'paper' transactions. The Treasury can 'pay' in effect by 'book' entries and the book entries can be transformed into a regular loan at a much later date. Thus this reason no longer exists; though unrecognised remnants of it may still lurk in popular thought.

The second reason is a much more practical one, namely that it is dangerous to allow these 'book' entries to remain on an unlimited scale in a form, such as Treasury bills for example, which can be so easily converted into purchasing power. For this might lead later on to an uncontrolled expansion of private enterprise. Perhaps the risk of this is overestimated. But, nevertheless, it is possible. It would be better not to enter the post-armament period with an enormous and abnormal volume of Treasury bills outstanding, since this might make necessary the continuance of vexatious controls which were no longer required on other grounds.

But this objection misunderstands what is proposed. I am not advocating an unlimited expansion of Treasury bills. On the contrary, I am saying that, if the Treasury is moderately patient, the weight of natural market forces will by themselves render a funding policy possible at a reasonable cost. It is simply a question of waiting and of making it clear that loans will only be available at a modest rate of interest, becoming still more modest as time goes on.

Let us suppose that, in the first instance, the Treasury bill issue is expanded by £200,000,000 with no increase, for the moment, in other types of loans. These bills will all be owned by someone and will represent an increase of private wealth;— there must, that is to say, be a corresponding increase of savings. Now these savings will be owned by all sorts of individuals and institutions up and down the country. Is it to be supposed that all these people will suddenly change their habits, abandon their life-long practices of investing their savings, and decide that they want to keep all their growing resources absolutely liquid earning interest at $\frac{1}{2}$ per cent per annum or less? The money will accrue in the hands of savings banks, insurance offices, building societies and private and business bank balances; and many of the holders will be unwilling, and often unable, to forego a normal rate of interest. Moreover, there can be only one motive in most cases for such hoarding, namely that the Treasury will be offering loans on terms increasingly favourable to the public as time goes on. The only risk, that is to say, would be a widespread belief that the Treasury are likely to mug their business.

I say that it is reasonable to suppose that a fair proportion of this £200,000,000 will seek investment in the market. By this extent demand for investments will be increased, whilst for the time being there will be no increased supply to meet it. What is the floating supply available in the market to meet this demand? Nothing anywhere near adequate, I should suppose. And the floating supply will not be materially increased unless institutional holders strongly believe that, sooner or later, the Treasury will be offering stocks appreciably below the then existing market terms. The Treasury should not squeeze the market. They should have an eye to an eventual smooth transition to normal times. But they should remember that when armament expenditure comes to an end and has to be replaced by a corresponding amount of productive investment, a very low rate of interest will surely be required to attract new investment on the same scale.

V

Since most people prefer a practical example to a difficult argument, it will be useful to quote the recent experience of the United States. In several respects it is not a satisfactory analogy; but it is a fair example of the result of supplying the market with all the liquidity it requires in circumstances otherwise adverse.

President Roosevelt has now been in office for six years. During that period he has nearly doubled the aggregate of the national debt, having borrowed on the average about six thousand million dollars a year. During nearly the whole of this time he has been faced by banking and business hostility. No one believes that his borrowing is at an end. What has happened to the rate of interest on government debt as a result of all this?

Rates of interest on gilt-edged loans of all maturities have steadily fallen, until they have reached the lowest figure ever recorded. On Treasury bills the rate is now described as 'negligible', which is not an exaggeration, since a holder would have to keep them for about 1,000 years before the accumulated simple interest would have added up to as much as 1 per cent of the principal. On Treasury notes having a maturity of 3 to 5 years, the rate is approximately $\frac{1}{2}$ per cent. On Treasury bonds due or callable after 12 years the yield does not exceed $2\frac{1}{4}$ per cent. The highest yield obtainable on any U.S. Government bond is about 2·35 per cent. I see no sufficient reason why the British Treasury should pay rates 50 per cent in excess of these. The reasons for believing that it is unnecessary to do so are at least sufficiently good to deserve a trial.

VI

If these general principles were to be accepted, the right technique for the borrowing programme would be as follows. During the initial period it is necessary that the banks and the public should find themselves becoming a little more liquid than they really wish. This also means, of course, that the bankers' cash at the Bank of England must be allowed to increase by an appropriate proportion, usually taken at about 10 per cent, of the increment of their deposits corresponding to the temporarily uninvested savings of their customers. This task of supplying an amount of liquidity a little above the demand for it involves a quantitative decision, which cannot be settled beforehand and must depend on the touch of the market. But the initial period must also be long enough in point of time for the new savings to reach the ultimate holder, who alone is in a position to embark them in a permanent investment, and to allow him to make an unhurried decision. This is an important point. Current savings are not available for permanent investment immediately that they accrue. This is particularly the case with savings out of dividends or other profits which are only distributed to the proprietors with an average time lag of more than six months. Moreover the primary saver may use his savings to discharge some of his liabilities and pay off debt, e.g. to anticipate instalments on house purchase, so that the new permanent investment will be made not by him but by someone else to whom his liquid resources ultimately pass. It is essential, therefore, that the Treasury's programme should be unhurried and be framed with a view to a continuing policy. Once the initial time lags have been overcome, borrowing can proceed *pari passu* with expenditure, except in so far as loan expenditure is at an *increasing* rate, in which case there will again be a time lag before the *increase* becomes available.

This ability to wait constitutes the signal advantage of the Treasury over private borrowers. So much so, that it is much easier for the Treasury to reduce the rate of interest when they are the main borrowers and therefore in charge of the market, than when the bulk of investment is being made by private borrowers. It is worth while to dwell for a moment on this apparent paradox.

The point is that it is not a *high* rate of borrowing which causes congestion in the market, but an *increasing* rate of borrowing. A private borrower cannot, as a rule, wait and has to arrange his permanent finance preferably before, or at any rate soon after, he enters into his commitments. He has to acquire purchasing power, that is to say, before he makes his expenditure, and therefore before the new saving has come into existence. If investment is proceeding at a steady rate, the finance required during the preliminary period, before the flow of new savings is available in an investible form, becomes a revolving fund. The investible savings available from the previous batch of capital expenditure releases the finance, which the latter had temporarily required, for the next batch of capital expenditure. But if the rate of borrowing *increases*, the amount of the finance thus released is insufficient; and competition between borrowers to acquire a share of an insufficient aggregate of finance raises the rate of interest. Popular opinion about the rate of interest is the result of a confusion between the risk of an insufficiency of finance during the preliminary period before new savings are available in an investible form, and the risk of an eventual insufficiency of the savings themselves. The essential clue to the Treasury's problem depends on understanding that the Treasury can wait, whereas the private borrower cannot, until the new savings have had time to become available in an investible form. To raise the rate of borrowing to a higher level involves the provision of an increased volume of liquid bank money. No further increase is required to avoid a rising rate of interest, when once the required level has been reached. If, however, the Treasury allows itself just a little more rope and waits just long enough for the market to become greedy for stock, the weight of savings seeking investment will force the rate of interest downwards. It is all a question, as I began by saying, of giving the market just a little more liquidity than it wants.

When the time to feed the market is arriving, one would expect it to be ready for 3 to 5 year bonds before loans of longer term. For this involves a smaller sacrifice of liquidity and offers a compromise to those who still hesitate about the longer outlook. Also these bonds will suit the banks, and, perhaps, other institutional investors, who are likely to be ready to make a partial shift out of Treasury bills for the sake of the higher interest before the private investor is in a position to make up his mind.

When the time comes to decide what type of longer maturities should be offered, it is obviously advisable to pay close regard to the preferences of the investor as shown in market prices. It will be the time to begin when market prices represent terms which are low but not too low; for it is important that they should leave room for further improvement so that subsequent offers can be sibylline and on progressively less favourable terms. The terms current on the average of the years 1935 and 1936 might offer a rough and ready rule for determining the suitable starting point. The successful handling by the Bank of England of the conversion of the old War Loan showed how easily the psychology of the investor could be accustomed to a new level. Indeed the problem will solve itself, more quickly perhaps than seems possible today, as soon as it is confidently and generally believed that the policy of the Treasury is on the above lines.

The importance, especially during the initial period, of the funds currently accruing in the hands of the Treasury itself and available for investment should not be overlooked. At the present and prospective level of unemployment, the growing resources of the Post Office and Trustee Savings Banks, of the Unemployment, National Health Insurance and other Departmental Funds and of various sinking funds should allow the Treasury by ordinary routine investment and without the use of any special devices or resources to take existing Government stocks off the market to an amount of between £1,000,000 and £2,000,000 a week; which by itself will exercise a strong stabilising influence and is capable, especially in combination with a favourable market sentiment, of taking up any slack.

VII

It is scarcely necessary to emphasise the extraordinary importance of all this to our future task. But there are two aspects to which I should like to call special attention. If we borrow on the average at a cost of, say, 3 per cent including a sinking fund of

$\frac{3}{4}$ per cent, which should be easily within our power without including an undue proportion of Treasury bills and very short bonds, instead of, say, 4 per cent including a similar sinking fund, we can borrow and spend £2,000,000,000 instead of £1,500,000,000 at the same final cost to the taxpayer. The difference in tactics will have been worth £500,000,000.

The other aspect is this. The armament programme will bring abnormal unemployment to an end. Some day, and the sooner the better, we hope to stop the existing abomination and return to the ways of peace. Is that to mean a return to abnormal unemployment? It will go hard with the fabric of society if it does. To avoid this outcome, it will be necessary for productive investment, public and private, out of borrowed money to continue at a rate at least as high as this year's programme. How is this to be possible if we find ourselves saddled, at the end of the armament period, as we were at the end of the late War, with a highish rate of interest?

J. M. KEYNES

27 May 1939

When Keynes sent a copy of his memorandum to Brand, he raised the issue of publication.

From a letter to R. H. BRAND, *28 May 1939*

I am glad you found my *Times*[4] articles interesting. As a result of a good deal of correspondence which has reached me since, I have felt that I ought to make a further effort to express my arguments and my analysis more clearly. It is all of such gigantic importance. Yet it is difficult to make progress against the weight of tradition or to get people to consider the problem afresh in the light of modern conditions and modern thought. This has inspired me in the last few days to make another attempt, giving myself more space than was possible in the original *Times* articles, and trying to meet objections as well as to give my own

[4] Brand had written to Keynes on 24 May saying he appreciated them.

prescription. I have done this primarily with a view to sending copies to the Chancellor of the Exchequer and the Governor of the Bank.

I am sending off copies to them, but I feel that it might also be useful to give it some general publicity, and have it published somewhere. The worst of it is that I am rather doubtful whether it is quite suitable to *The Times*, or at any rate whether Geoffrey Dawson would think it was. I do not want to persecute him by trying to take up more space than is fair. This would make two substantial articles even with a little curtailment. On the other hand, I do think it is of general public interest, at any rate to bankers and civil servants and politicians. And it all matters so very much that one does not want to lose the best possible form of publicity. I enclose a copy and wish that you would tell me, after you have read it, whether or not you think it very unsuitable for *The Times*, or whether you would encourage me at any rate to let Geoffrey Dawson see it. What makes me hesitate is the fact that it requires so much closer thinking than is usually expected of the reader of a daily newspaper.

From a letter from R. H. BRAND, *31 May 1939*

Now for your memorandum which I have read cursorily today and intend to read more thoroughly. It *is* somewhat highbrow for a daily newspaper, even for *The Times*, but after all the subject is of immense importance and must interest a great number of people, both in the City and in politics. If I were Geoffrey Dawson I would therefore certainly publish it. *The Times* has got to be highbrow and to be so up to the limit of what its readers will read is its lifeblood. I am always urging that it should be rather more than less highbrow, certainly on the economic and financial side. I would therefore certainly recommend that you write and send it to Geoffrey Dawson. If you like you can ask him to speak to me and say that I have seen it. Or if you liked you could send it to me and I could get Greene, the Financial Editor, to request Dawson's approval for its insertion; but perhaps the first is the proper course.

Meanwhile, for what it is worth, I would like to make one remark. It seems to me that your whole argument rests on the supposition that there is not a full employment of labour and capital. If there were such full employment, and capital expenditure privately and by the Government continued to increase, presumably (whatever the mechanism used) savings could not increase at the same rate. But although there is still some unemployment may we not in various directions have already reached full employment, account being taken of the relative immobility of labour? Does not your theory, in order to be absolutely water tight, demand complete mobility of labour? Today, however, labour is, unfortunately, far from being fully mobile and it may be that in a good many trades we have practically reached full employment. If that is the case I suppose in any particular industry of such a kind the disadvantages that arise when you get increased investment in a state of full employment immediately occur. I do not know how far this question of full employment in certain trades coupled with relative immobility is important; but I should have thought that in toto it was quite important. Whether any effort has been made to estimate this importance I do not know.

From a letter to R. H. BRAND, *9 June 1939*

Many thanks for what you say about my MS on the rate of interest. I shall be sending it shortly to Geoffrey Dawson, and will tell him that you have encouraged me to do so. I shall, I think, write to him, without actually sending him the article, suggesting that, if he is inclined *prima facie* to consider it, I might send it along to Greene. I can, of course, make it a good deal less highbrow in appearance, though perhaps not in substance, compared with what it is in the version I sent you. In reply to the point you make on your last page, you are right in supposing that an important part of my argument depends on our having not yet reached a position of full employment. One can get increased saving along the lines I am suggesting so long as it is still possible to obtain a significant increase in the national income, even though there are bottlenecks in particular directions. Even the bottlenecks seem to me to be arriving rather more slowly than one had anticipated. But, even if they do shortly put in an appearance, I still think that there is room for a very substantial increase of the national income, say, by something between 5 and 10 per cent, out of which savings can be secured.

But I would emphasise that this is not by any means the whole of my argument. As soon as full employment is reached, all sorts of special measures have to be taken, if the Government programme is to be carried through without provoking various disagreeable conditions. But my point is that, even so, a high rate of interest is very far from being a serviceable tool. I should expect that the relief that one could get in that way would be almost negligible, whilst the injury in other directions would be severe. An appreciably higher level of taxation, rationing and Government priorities must then be the order of the day.

Of course, when full employment really has arrived, one will have to reconsider the whole position in the light of the then circumstances. At present I feel it is by no means imminent; though I fancy that my views on this matter are nearer yours than those of the Government seem to be, who are, to all appearances, quite remarkably unconcerned.

To GEOFFREY DAWSON, *9 June 1939*

Dear Dawson,

The articles which I recently contributed to *The Times* have brought me more comment and have involved me in more correspondence than anything I have done for a long time past. I get the impression from all this that there is a good deal of sympathy with the views I have been putting forward, and a feeling that, if only what I am recommending is *possible*, how nice that would be. But it is also clear that, so far as the rate of interest is concerned, the argument needs a good deal of development before the points at issue will be fully comprehended by the financial public. The field is really rather a new one and it takes people a little time to get accustomed to the central ideas involved.

Thus, it seemed to me, that it would be useful for me to prepare a more extensive memorandum. I have written something, therefore, primarily for the purpose of sending it in the first instance to the Chancellor of the Exchequer and the Treasury, but with the idea that something on those lines might be published subsequently. The worst of it is that it is somewhat lengthy (it would fill two full articles), and probably needs closer thinking that I have attempted to require in the previous articles which I have contributed to *The Times*. For these reasons, I have hesitated to send it to you. I have also felt that you have been extremely liberal to me in the past and did not want to take advantage of this to press on you something which, even in my own judgement, was doubtfully suitable.

I happened, however, at the time to be in correspondence with Brand over another matter, and sent him a copy of my document. He has so definitely encouraged me to send it to you that I am now writing this letter. He argues that 'after all the subject is of immense importance and must interest a great number of people both in the City and in politics'. Even so, I hesitate to inflict it on you without first of all writing. It could certainly, on a re-draft, be made rather lighter in form, even though the substance remained much the same. If you are at all inclined to consider it, should I perhaps send it in its present form to Mr Greene, and then, if you feel that you are inclined for something on those lines, re-draft it in a form a little more suitable for appearance in a daily newspaper?

Yours sincerely,
[copy initialled] J.M.K.

From GEOFFREY DAWSON, *11 June 1939*

My dear Keynes,

Bob Brand, who was at All Souls last night, led me to hope for this letter from you. Do please go ahead with your project of writing another couple of articles, and let Greene have your memorandum for a start.

Yours sincerely,
GEOFFREY DAWSON

Keynes sent his article to *The Times* on 1 July. However, owing to pressures on space, the articles did not appear until 24 and 25 July.

From The Times, *24 and 25 July 1939*

BORROWING BY THE STATE

I. HIGH INTEREST AND LOW: A RECOMMENDATION

In two articles which appeared in this column three months ago I advanced two conclusions: that the scale of Treasury borrowing in prospect would bring abnormal unemployment to an end, and that this borrowing could, and should, be accomplished at a low rate of interest. The first conclusion is being put to the test of experience. The Chancellor of the Exchequer, by raising the telescope to a closed eye (prudently perhaps), assumed in his Budget only a trifling reduction in the cost of unemployment. But he now agrees that he had thus provided himself with a concealed surplus available to meet subsequent commitments. Indeed, in the light of present figures it would not be too optimistic to expect a budgetary saving of from £10,000,000 to £15,000,000 in the cost of unemployment assistance, and in addition a surplus of more than £20,000,000 in the Unemployment Fund.

The second conclusion remains in the realm of debate. The comment and criticism it has aroused indicates that the public opinion which tries to be well informed on so important a matter of broad public policy demands, what the subject certainly requires, a fuller discussion than could be attempted in the space available in the previous articles. The fresh increase in his borrowing programme which the Chancellor of the Exchequer announced recently is a compelling reason for entering into the problem, which is as fascinating as it is important, somewhat more deeply.

Other borrowers

The traditional argument for expecting a substantial rise in the rate of interest at a time when heavy loan expenditure is being incurred by the Government has two blades. The high rate is thought necessary to deter the competition of other borrowers and also necessary to stimulate the extra saving required. It is only those who deplore any departure from the old *laissez-faire* order who positively approve the policy of a high rate of interest in such conditions; and most people today recognise that, for better or for worse, we have left that easy world behind us. But many are ready to applaud a policy of carrying through with a low rate of interest, if only it were possible, yet remain sufficiently under the influence of the old ideas to doubt the possibility. It is these who ask for further explanations.

That a high rate of interest would have some effect—and, if it were high enough, an important effect—in deterring competitive users of the resources of men and materials required by the Government programme is undisputed. But it does not follow that it is the best way of attaining the desired result. To begin with, the necessity for such a deterrent only arises when full employment has arrived. In the twilight finance between peace and war it must be our object to carry out the Government programme with the least possible interference with other useful purposes, the labour for which is still in surplus; and it is a grave disadvantage of this form of deterrent that it is undiscriminating and stops employment just as much in those directions which do not interfere with the Government programme as in those which do. Nevertheless, it now seems certain that it is only a matter of time, and perhaps of a short time, before we reach the point where there are no longer any surplus resources available, so that it is necessary to limit somehow investment which is competitive with the Government's needs. Even in such circumstances other methods are available which are both more discriminating and more effective. Apart from foreign borrowers, the only competitors with the Government who are on a large enough scale to be worth troubling with are:-

(1) Local authorities.
(2) Building societies.
(3) Public boards and other public utilities.
(4) Transport, both roads and railways.
(5) Shipbuilding.
(6) The heavy and engineering industries.

The first four can be tackled by direct representations at the fountain head and through the new issue market; the fifth we are deliberately encouraging; the sixth is in the interests of the Government's own programme. It is certain that, when the necessity arises, Government priorities will have to be established which will make it difficult or impossible for other investors to get hold of the actual men and materials needed more urgently by the Government.

Foreign payments

It is indeed important that there should exist an authority to decide which of these other investment activities can be allowed to go forward unhindered, and which not. But when the decisions have been made, their carrying out will not require the clumsy and expensive method of a punitive rate of interest payable by the Government equally with others. In semi-war conditions we cannot allow private investment to conflict with Government needs, however high the rate of interest which the former is prepared to pay. It is, therefore, absurd to set up the rate of interest as the criterion whether or not the Government are to be allowed to acquire the physical resources they need.

There remains the justification of a high rate of interest that it is a means of competing against the purchase of foreign securities by British nationals. In the *laissez-faire* investment markets of pre-war days, when foreign investments were a half or more of our total current investment, this problem was of the first importance. It remains of importance today. Indeed, I feel more serious concern about our balance of foreign payments, both on capital and current account, than is at present clearly evident in the policy of the Government. But the authorities now have at their command methods which are much more efficacious. So far as new foreign issues are concerned a *laissez-faire* investment market is a thing of the past. The control of purchases in Wall Street has been tightened up. But, apart from these necessary controls, a depreciating tendency of domestic securities, due to a rising rate of interest, is not the way to keep money at home. The psychology of the domestic investor is such that the way to retain him is to put domestic markets better, not to put them worse. And the same is true of the foreign investor. A steadily falling market, as the rate of interest rises, is not the clever way to attract him to London.

That a high rate of interest deters not only alternative capital projects but also luxury expenditure, is a more modern argument which one sometimes hears. A high rate of interest depreciates the market value of existing investments. This makes the investing class feel very poor and therefore disinclined to incur avoidable expenditure. If War Loan were to fall to 80 and everything else in proportion, one would certainly expect such a result; and also a corresponding fall in the Exchequer receipts from death duties, stamps, and certain classes of profits. But here again there is a much better way of attaining the same object. At present the Chancellor of the Exchequer is being moderately merciful in the matter of taxation. This is because he thinks it advisable at the present stage—rightly in my opinion—not to discourage private enterprise and expenditure more than is necessary. But if and when the approach of full employment makes it essential to discourage all avoidable expenditure, the existing reasons against heavier taxation are replaced by reasons in favour of it. Taxation is in every way a much better instrument for discouraging private expenditure and private enterprise than a high rate of interest.

It would be a strange policy on the part of the Treasury to keep taxation moderate so as to encourage outside business, and then to pay a high rate of interest on Government borrowing so as to discourage outside business; thus making sure of the worst of both worlds, smaller receipts, and larger expenses. Clearly the effect of high taxation in discouraging outlay should be tried before recourse is had to a high rate of interest. (When the time comes for hindering non-armament enterprise, it would seem more practical to tax non-armament profits than to exempt them. The superficial argument for A.P.D. will be overcome in due course by the profounder argument for E.P.D.)[5]

The supply of savings

So far I have been casting no doubts on the theoretical validity of the traditional arguments. I have only pointed out that, in the contemporary environment and in the special and peculiar circumstances of the hour, they do not offer the best way of attaining the desired object. But it is otherwise with the second blade of the argument. Many people—most people, I suppose—believe that, however desirable it may be that Treasury loans should be placed on the cheapest possible terms, it is utterly impracticable to secure cheap terms when we have to borrow such an enormous sum. On this matter, however, a shift is discernible in the accepted theory. It would, I think, be fair to say that the traditional arguments, on which most bankers and civil servants have been brought up, are no longer accepted as adequate by many British economists who have specially studied these problems. At the present stage economists are not all expressing themselves in the same way or with the same emphasis. But the variant forms of modern theory come to much the same thing for the present purpose. The following is an attempt to explain the shift of emphasis in a way which is as uncontroversial as possible.

[5] A.P.D. = Armaments Profits Duty; E.P.D. = Excess Profits Duty.

It is common to the old view and to the new that increased loan expenditure can be met only out of increased saving. According to the old view, the required increase in saving can be stimulated only by a higher rate of interest. According to the new view, this argument is not correct unless it is being tacitly assumed that the increased loan expenditure has to be made out of the same total national income as before; an assumption which is not valid unless all the available resources of men and materials are already employed. For if an increase in output is physically possible, the stimulus to demand resulting from the increased expenditure will lead to increased earnings and profits, and it is largely out of these that the increase of saving will be made. In any case, the loan expenditure will only be physically possible if the Government are successful in attracting resources for their own use; which means that a sum equal to the incomes directly generated by the Government expenditure has been physically withdrawn from consumption and is therefore, of necessity, saved.

A banana example

Thus the required amount of saving necessarily accumulates as an inevitable result of the Government's withdrawing a part of current output from consumption, irrespective of whether the rate of interest rises or falls. The proportion of the increased incomes spent on imported goods raises a dangerous complication. But if higher earnings lead us to import more bananas than we can afford, this cannot be remedied by the Treasury chastising itself with a high rate of interest. The same is true of a general tendency for prices to rise due to consumption out of increased earnings. No one today would expect an appreciable reduction of consumption simply as a result of a rise of 1 or 2 per cent in the rate of interest. If the larger incomes do not yield a sufficient increment of spontaneous savings except at a price level of consumption goods which is rising unduly, then in the last resort the balance must be acquired either by increased taxation or by putting obstacles, such as would certainly be necessary in a war, in the way of the public buying what they want. If the Government has decided to spend the money in any case, the question whether this expenditure is being financed by Treasury bills or by loans funded at a high rate of interest is utterly irrelevant to the threat of inflation.

The contemporary economist, as a result of living in a world where unemployment has been chronic, puts more stress on our power of drawing on resources which were not fully employed and less stress on the diversion of resources already in use. In so far as diversion becomes necessary he is able to call attention to the efficacy of controls on imports and on foreign investment and through Government priorities; which in the *laissez-faire* world were ruled out. When there are no longer surplus resources to draw on, and further restrictions would be clumsy or inefficacious, he points out that a high rate of taxation can do much more than a high rate of interest and without jeopardising the financial future. Thus the special advantages, if any, to be got from a high rate of interest are negligible compared with the cost to the Treasury, the injury to the capital market, and the impairment to normal investment when the crisis is over.

PRACTICAL POINTS

II. A PROGRAMME OF METHOD

How enormously important this question is to the future of our public finance! If we borrow on the average at a cost of, say, 3 per cent including a sinking fund of $\frac{3}{4}$ per cent, which should be within our power without including an undue proportion of Treasury bills and very short bonds, instead of, say, 4 per cent including a similar sinking fund, we can borrow and spend £2,000,000,000 instead of £1,500,000,000 at the same final cost to the taxpayer. The difference in tactics will have been worth £500,000,000. The matter is well worth studying. So let us turn to the practical problem in the light of the general considerations in the previous article.

We will assume that the Government have spent a part of the money and have financed themselves in the first instance by an issue of Treasury bills. Some individual or some institution owns these bills, which means that the necessary amount of savings has been forthcoming from one source or another, either additional savings or savings diverted from some other potential investment. The subsequent problem consists, therefore, not in evoking the necessary savings—that has been done already—but in inducing the holder to lend them to the Government in some more permanent form. This problem has often been made to appear more difficult than it really is by the mistake of confusing the problem of evoking the savings with the problem of inducing their holder to sacrifice his liquidity. The object of offering a given rate of interest on a funded security is to persuade the holder of liquid assets to accept in exchange something less liquid.

Three simple principles

A private borrower has to accept the terms prevailing in the market. But market conditions depend, partly at least, on the policy of the Treasury and the Bank of England. Thus when the Treasury is itself the principal borrower it has the power within certain limits to provide that the terms shall be 'reasonable'. And I suggest that for the present purpose 'reasonable' terms are those which would be compatible with keeping the volume of investment in a free market, in which the prospective return obtainable from an investment was again the criterion, at an optimum level; that is to say, at a level leading to optimum employment. My own belief is that such terms would be lower than any which have recently prevailed. But it is not advisable at the present stage to push things to extremes or to depart too far from preconceived ideas. I suggest, therefore, that we should take as our rough criterion the interest rates which prevailed in the market on the average of the three years 1935 to 1937. We can have some confidence that these rates would not prove to be too low when the present crisis is over, since investment in those years was certainly a long way below the optimum. If we start with this standard we can hope to improve upon it subsequently. The important thing is that the Treasury should not concede a 'fear' premium to holders of savings above the normal return, any more than it concedes a 'fear' premium in the earnings of those liable for war service.

Well and good, the reader may remark; by all means let this be the objective of the Treasury; but is it attainable? I believe that it is attainable by attending to three simple principles: by giving the market the increased amount of liquidity which it demands in present circumstances, by waiting until the market is ready, and by promoting a sense of confidence in what the future borrowing policy of the Treasury is going to be.

Supply of liquidity

The public should not be bribed by being offered a high rate of interest to give up their liquidity. But there is not the same reason against allowing them to retain some measure of increased liquidity to the extent that they themselves are ready to sacrifice the normal rate of interest. Indeed, if we are to preserve the semblance of a free capital market in present circumstances, some increase in the liquidity supplied by the banking system is a necessary condition of maintaining a normal rate of interest. For it is natural that in critical times people should want to keep more liquid, and it would be sheer waste of money for the Treasury to submit to a high rate of interest to deprive the public of a reassurance which it costs the Treasury nothing to provide. Apart from a limited number of institutions, 'liquidity' means as a rule larger bank balances. The first step, therefore, is to increase the bankers' balances at the Bank of England and the supply of Treasury bills held by the banks just sufficiently to provide the banks and, through them, the public with a little more liquidity than they want. I am not advocating an unlimited expansion of Treasury bills. On the contrary, I am saying that, if the Treasury is moderately patient, the weight of natural market forces will by itself render a funding policy possible at a reasonable cost. For, although some additional liquid resources will be in demand, it is most unlikely that the public will want to hold the bulk of their new savings in this form earning a negligible rate of interest, especially if they learn by experience that nothing is to be gained through doing so.

Let us suppose that, in the first instance, the Treasury bill issue held outside Government Departments is expanded by £200,000,000 with no increase, for the moment, in other types of loans. Although these bills will be mainly held by the banks and the money market, the increased bank deposits corresponding to them will be owned by all sorts of individuals and institutions up and down the country. Is it to be supposed that all these people will suddenly change their habits, abandon their life-long practices of investing the bulk of their savings, and decide that they want to keep all their growing resources absolutely liquid, earning interest at ½ per cent a year or less? The money will accrue in the savings banks, insurance offices, building societies, and private and business bank balances; and many of the holders will be unwilling, and often unable, to forego a normal rate of interest.

Moreover, there can be only one motive in most cases for such hoarding—namely, that the Treasury will be offering loans on terms increasingly favourable to the public as time goes on. If the Treasury makes it clear that this will not occur, it would be reasonable to expect a fair proportion of this £200,000,000 to seek investment in the market. By this extent demand for securities will be increased, while for the time being there will be no increased supply to meet it. The floating supply available in the market is nowhere near adequate to meet such a demand. Thus the stage would be set for a steady rise in the price of

Government stocks under the pressure of the additional demand.

Since most people prefer a practical example to a hypothetical argument, it will be useful to quote the recent experience of the United States. In several respects it is not a satisfactory analogy; but it is a fair example in circumstances otherwise adverse of the result of supplying the market with more than the liquidity it requires. President Roosevelt has now been in office for six years. In that period he has nearly doubled the aggregate of the national debt. During nearly the whole of it he has been faced by banking and business hostility. No one believes that this borrowing is at an end. What has happened to the rate of interest on Government debt as a result of all this?

Rates of interest on gilt-edged loans of all maturities have steadily fallen until they have reached the lowest figure ever recorded. On Treasury bills the rate is now described as 'negligible', which is not an exaggeration, since a holder would have to keep them for about 1,000 years before the accumulated simple interest would have added up to as much as 1 per cent of the principal. On Treasury notes having a maturity of three to five years the rate is about $\frac{1}{2}$ per cent. On Treasury bonds due or callable after 12 years the yield does not exceed $2\frac{1}{4}$ per cent. The highest yield obtainable on any United States Government bond is about 2·35 per cent. Is there sufficient reason why the British Treasury should pay rates 50 per cent in excess of these?

Right technique

If this objective is accepted, the right technique for the borrowing programme would be as follows. During the initial period it is necessary that the banks and the public should find themselves becoming a little more liquid than they really wish. In his statement last Thursday the Chancellor of the Exchequer suggested that it would be proper to increase the amount of Treasury bills held outside Government Departments to the figure at which it stood a year or more ago. This is a good argument for a substantial increase above the present amount. But the figures of a year ago can scarcely provide a useful criterion of what will be advisable in the completely changed circumstances of six or nine months hence. The question of how much additional liquidity is required cannot be settled beforehand and must depend on the touch of the market. It will largely depend on the confidence felt in Treasury intentions. Apart from this, the initial period must be long enough for the new savings to reach the ultimate holder, who alone is in a position to embark them in a permanent investment.

This is an important point. Current savings are not available for permanent investment immediately they accrue. Savings out of dividends or other profits are only distributed to the proprietors with an average time lag of more than six months. The primary saver may use his savings to pay off debt, e.g., to anticipate instalments on house purchase, so that the new permanent investment will be made not by him but by someone else to whom his liquid resources ultimately pass.

The ability to wait constitutes the signal advantage of the Treasury over private borrowers. So much so that it is easier for the Treasury to reduce the rate of interest when it is the main borrower and therefore in charge of the market than when the bulk of investment is being made by private borrowers. It is worth while to dwell for a moment on this apparent paradox.

Private borrowing

The point is that it is not a *high* rate of borrowing which causes congestion in the market, but an *increasing* rate of borrowing. A private borrower cannot, as a rule, wait. He has to arrange his permanent finance preferably before, or at any rate soon after, he enters into his commitments; and therefore before the new saving is available. If investment is proceeding at a steady rate, the investable savings available from the previous batch of capital expenditure release the finance, which the latter had temporarily required, for the next batch of capital expenditure. But if the rate of borrowing *increases*, the amount of the finance thus released is insufficient; and competition between borrowers to acquire a share of an insufficient aggregate of finance raises the rate of interest.

Popular opinion about the rate of interest is the result of a confusion between the risk of an insufficiency of finance during the preliminary period before new savings are available in an investable form and the risk of an eventual insufficiency of the savings themselves. The clue to the solution of the Treasury problem lies in the Treasury's ability to wait until the new savings have had time to become available in an investable form. If the Treasury waits just long enough for the market to become greedy for stock the weight of savings seeking investment will force the rate of interest downwards. It is all a question, as I began by saying, of giving the market just a little more liquidity and a little more time than it wants.

Confidence

One would expect the market to be ready for three to five year bonds before loans of longer term, for this involves a small sacrifice of liquidity and offers a compromise to those who still hesitate about the longer outlook. Also these bonds will suit the banks and other institutional investors, who are likely to be ready to make a partial shift out of Treasury bills for the sake of the higher interest before the private investor can make up his mind. The opportunity to offer longer maturities will have arrived when market prices represent terms which are low but not too low; for it is important that they should leave room for further improvement so that subsequent offers can be sibylline and on progressively less favourable terms. I have suggested that the terms current on the average of the years 1935 to 1937 might offer a rough and ready rule for determining the suitable starting point.

Perhaps the most important factor in the whole situation is

the impression which the Treasury itself creates concerning its objective and future policy. If the Treasury gives an impression of defeatism or of asking the market to accept risks it is not prepared to accept itself, the preference for remaining liquid will, of course, be greatly stimulated. If the Treasury appears to be in a hurry, if it offers loans below the market, and if its own behaviour indicates an expectation that the market will get worse in course of time rather than better, confidence will be quickly destroyed. At present the market does not know what to expect. The volume of Treasury bills is being steadily increased, but there is no sign of an increase in bankers' cash. Thus the tendency is not known for certain.

Yet if the Treasury were to disclose its objective and take the banks and the institutions and the gilt-edged market into its confidence, it could expect whole-hearted collaboration and the battle would be half won already. No one wants to see gilt-edged securities depreciate. It does not suit the institutions or anyone else to leave their accruing resources uninvested at a sacrifice of interest. The only important motive for doing so is the fear that the Bank of England will be reluctant to supply the increased liquidity required partly by the increased scale of operations and partly by the critical times, and that the policy of the Treasury will be such as gradually to work the gilt-edged market downwards. If the opposite were believed, the menace of foreign affairs would not be decisive.

If war is averted, we shall need a low rate of interest to stimulate the huge volume of investment needed to fill the gap caused by the reduction of Government outlays. If it is not, we shall need a low rate to preserve the fabric of our finances. The key to sound public finance in the present emergency is a rigid refusal to fund short-term debt at high interest rates and a stern stiffening of taxation when we have reached the full employment of our productive forces.

Keynes's articles led to two interesting exchanges of correspondence. The first was with 'Lex', a *Financial News* columnist, which continued until the outbreak of war. The correspondence opened after 'Lex' suggested on 27 July that Keynes had underestimated the speed with which Britain was approaching full employment and thus had played down the consequences of this for policy. He echoed this view in a postscript the next day.

To 'LEX', *27 July 1939*

Personal. Not for publication

Dear Mr 'Lex',

In the first of my *Times* articles I wrote 'It now seems certain that it is only a matter of time, and perhaps of a short time, before we reach the point where there are no longer any surplus resources available, so that it is necessary to limit somehow investment that is competitive with the Government's needs.' I wish you read my articles as carefully as I read yours! The whole of my argument was based on the above hypothesis, and the main object of the articles was to produce reasons against the view that the appearance of full employment would make a difference to the low interest policy.

I prefer to adopt this hypothesis because I hope that the Government will continue to increase their programme until they do reach full employment. But I admit to being a little more doubtful than some people whether the *existing* programme is so greatly in excess of our capacity. It seems to me that, after being surprised at the tendency of unemployment to disappear, people are now rushing a little prematurely and a little too violently to the opposite conclusion. It is extremely difficult to say beforehand what our potential maximum capacity is, and I fancy it will turn out to be pretty large.

Yours sincerely,
[copy initialled] J.M.K.

From 'LEX', *28 July 1939*

Dear Mr Keynes,

Thank you very much for your letter of July 27th, which I received this morning. If I had had it last night, I should certainly have omitted my second note from this morning's *Financial News*, even at the sacrifice of a perfectly good epigram.

I *did* read the passage from your first article, which you quote, but I must confess that I assumed that the tenor of your arguments had reference to official policy in the interim period of more or less uncertain duration now left to us before we reach effective full employment.

From your last paragraph (which I read with particular interest) I see that your estimate of the possible duration of this interim is longer than mine; but I should imagine that in any case there is only a few months between us. And there is virtue in the press man's rule: 'Never prophesy the night before', so I will leave that question. Nevertheless, I shall now have to read your articles again with a completely new orientation of mind. I have not only been long convinced myself that your arguments, applied to a near-war economy in a period before full employment, were fundamentally sound, but I have tried, in a Lexian way, to bring that home to the people who live around here. But if, e.g., the programme of credit expansion is designed for application *after* full employment—if the gourmand is to take the same medicine in the *post*– as in the *pre*-repletion stages of the Lord Mayor's Banquet—then I shall have very seriously to think about the matter again before I can conclude that the difference between us is merely one of time.

Yours sincerely,
LEX

To 'LEX', *3 August 1939*

Dear Mr 'Lex',

The point is that the controls on expenditure which will be required when full employment is reached are much the same irrespective of whether interest rates are high or low. In such circumstances, we cannot possibly depend on a high interest rate to protect us from the various impending consequences. Indeed, in such circumstances, the preventive efficacy of a high rate of interest is particularly feeble. Why, therefore, waste our money, when we shall have to depend on other controls to do the trick?

If the amount which the Government is spending is

unchanged, it does not make the slightest difference to inflation whether they finance it by Treasury bills or irredeemable securities. The idea that Treasury bill financing is what you call 'credit expansion' and, therefore, dangerous, and that an identical expenditure financed otherwise is not, is a baseless superstition. Why do you appear to cling to it?

A high rate of interest has no efficacy whatsoever except in so far as it restrains non-Government expenditure. And who can be so silly as to suppose that a moderate rise in the rate of interest (or are you thinking of an immoderate one?) would have much effect in such circumstances compared with the other controls which would be necessary?

Yours very truly,
[copy initialled] J.M.K.

From 'LEX', *4 August 1939*

Dear Mr Keynes,

Thank you for your letter of August 3rd.

I am sure there is no division between us on the fundamental proposition that the test of inflation is not a financial one, but simply and solely whether idle physical resources exist which can be drawn into employment. From this point of view, however, there does seem to be an important distinction between finance by Treasury bills, and finance by long-term securities, since the general assumption is that Treasury bills are to be taken up by the banking system and the longer-dated securities by the public.

Do you not agree that, once a point of effective full employment has been reached, the Government's programme should not be financed by the creation of additional purchasing power (i.e. through Treasury bills and credit expansion) but by the mopping up of funds already in the hands of the public, i.e. by taxation and funding issues? If that is so, it does seem to follow that even the most stringent control of competing demands on the capital market might not suffice to prevent a rise in the rate of interest, however *desirable* it might be to prevent it.

Yours sincerely,
'LEX'

To 'LEX', *14 August 1939*

Dear Mr 'Lex',

I have your letter of August 4th. The point is that, if the additional bank deposits are created to satisfy an increased desire for liquidity on the part of institutions and the public, they do not make any effective increase to purchasing power. So long as the public prefer to keep their savings in the shape of bank deposits, it does not seem to me to matter in the least in what way the Government's expenditure has been financed, or that the banks' holdings of Treasury bills and other investments are enlarged. If and when the public lose their desire for increased liquidity, there will be no difficulty in placing funded securities with them. If and so long as they desire increased liquidity, there is no harm in enlarging bank deposits and bank assets. The only danger would arise in the event of the public losing their desire for liquidity and no steps being taken to supply them with the alternative of funded securities. That is an argument against *never* funding. So far from its being an argument against waiting until their demand for liquidity is satisfied, it is an argument in favour of it.

It is essential to distinguish between increased bank deposits for the purpose of current transactions (though this, of course, is necessary in so far as output can be increased) and inactive deposits required to satisfy an abnormal demand for liquidity.

Yours very truly,
[copy initialled] J.M.K.

From 'LEX', *24 August 1939*

Dear Mr Keynes,

It will be better, I think, if I reply to your letter of August 14th now from this office rather than later from a cellar. In answering it, my chief difficulty is to be quite clear whether we have the same general assumption in mind. It is, of course, obvious that *if* 'additional bank deposits are created to satisfy an increased desire for liquidity...they do not make any effective increase to purchasing power'. Surely this is merely equivalent to saying that *if* the velocity of circulation is declining this can and should be neutralised by an increase in the amount of deposits if one is to do no more than prevent a deflationary spiral. But is this really relevant to the question whether, in a state of full employment, Government expenditure should be financed by the public out of existing savings or by the banking system through the creation of additional credit? In the latter case, one can hardly assume that the beneficiaries of the Government expenditure will leave their new deposits completely inactive. If, instead, they 'save' only a proportion of the additional income, the spending of the new credit must inevitably drive up prices and an inflationary situation will result. It is for this reason that we draw a distinction between Treasury bills and long-term issues, (in the sense of finance by credit expansion and by public subscriptions respectively). Of course, I quite agree that if long-term loans are in fact taken up by the banking system, the effect is the same as if they had taken up bills. I have never argued that there is any distinction in such a case, and so still cannot believe that there is really any fundamental difference between us on this point.

This has been an interesting and, to me, a pleasant correspondence, and I hope that events will not prevent its long continuance!

Yours sincerely,
'LEX'

And now they have raised Bank Rate to 4 per cent![6]

The second exchange was with a member of Pember and Boyle, the stockbrokers.

From S. SCRIMGEOUR, *31 July 1939*

Dear Mr Keynes,

I hope you may excuse my writing to you, and presuming on a very slight acquaintance. Actually we met some years ago with our mutual friend Vernon Malcolmson in a taxi!

My excuse for writing is that I am so very interested in your letters to *The Times* and more particularly in the two which appeared last week in connection with Defence Borrowing. The somewhat detached and grandmotherly attitude of *The Times*, in the leading article of the following day, is

[6] Bank rate rose to 4 per cent on 24 August. It remained there until it was reduced to 2 per cent in two stages on 28 September and 26 October.

rather depressing—in particular the remark that 'The Government have no need to concern itself with the theoretical conjecture' of your arguments! The force and logic of your argument appears to me to amount to rather more than 'theoretical conjecture' and I should have thought that, particularly under present circumstances, it was of paramount importance that the Government should give the most careful study to every side of the question—theoretical or otherwise. I regret, however, that few signs are apparent to my perhaps somewhat limited observation, that the Government are showing any real appreciation of the true situation.

You will gather from the above remarks that I myself—if I may say so without presumption—am in entire agreement with your views and arguments. The only reason I am writing this letter, however, is that I am in some doubt as to whether your policy, in the present state of City and more particularly banking opinion, would have the effect you desire, without some stronger measures by the Treasury than the indirect one—if I may call it so—of providing over-liquidity.

You will I think agree with me that the opinion has been very prevalent, quite wrongly as I think, that war or no war, a return of 3 per cent or under on British Government irredeemable securities was unjustified, and that a normal level should be something much higher. There has, consequently, been a very prevalent feeling that to hold irredeemable securities is an unsound policy, in view of the risk of capital depreciation. The present critical state of international affairs has strengthened this fear, and even at the present level of prices there is, I think, still a fear in many peoples' minds of still further capital depreciation. I am wondering, therefore, whether even the provision of over-liquidity would be sufficient by itself to induce banks and other institutions to overcome this fear and increase their holdings of longer-dated gilt-edged investments; whether they would not prefer to allow their holdings of more liquid assets to rise above the proportion which has previously been considered adequate.

I have, therefore, for some time been turning over in my mind whether the Treasury should not take more direct action to restore confidence to the market for British Government securities, and set up a fund financed by Treasury bills, on analogous lines to the Exchange Equalisation Fund to support the market for the longer-dated stocks. In effect this would merely be changing some of the longer-dated debt into short-term debt at a saving of something like 3 per cent in interest to the Treasury. In practice, however, the amount of longer-dated debt which the Treasury would have to buy would I believe be comparatively small, because would not the very existence of such a fund help to remove the fear of capital depreciation in the case of the longer-dated stocks? With this fear largely eliminated, then the result of greater liquidity owing to the increased issue of Treasury bills would I think have its full effect in raising the price level of British Government securities.

If you can spare time for a reply to this letter I should be very interested to hear what you think of this idea, which by the way is not my own in origin, and also what is your opinion as to the present attitude of the Treasury to the problem involved. It appears on the surface rather as though they were allowing things to drift, and were not bringing what I call up-to-date methods to bear. Is this so or do I misjudge them? If it is so, what steps can be taken to induce a different attitude? I cannot help thinking that the matter is very urgent.

Yours sincerely,
STUART SCRIMGEOUR

To S. SCRIMGEOUR, *3 August 1939*

Dear Mr Scrimgeour,

I am in full agreement with what you say in your letter of July 31st. In the paragraph at the top of page 2 you have touched on the essential difficulty. I have long thought that open market operations in the longer-dated stocks, carried on either by the Bank of England itself, or by something analogous to the Exchange Equalisation Fund is the right solution. I have not much doubt that at long last it will be adopted. I believe I did actually make a proposal on these lines, if my memory does not fail me, in my *Treatise on Money*,[7] which was written as much as ten years ago. At any rate, I do believe the proposal to be an absolutely sound one which would produce a wonderful effect at very small cost.

In reply to the last paragraph of your letter, I have not had a recent opportunity of discussing these matters with Treasury officials. My belief is that the Treasury, though a bit scared of up-to-date methods, have no settled convictions against them and are indeed much more inclined to proceed along such lines than the Bank of England. But the trouble is that they have no really strong convictions in favour of them, with the result that

[7] *JMK*, vol. VI, pp. 331–5.

their action will be half-hearted. And a half-hearted policy may have the disastrous result, not only of failing, but of bringing discredit on a policy which would have been perfectly successful if carried through wholeheartedly. As for the Chancellor of the Exchequer himself, I do not believe that he has ever given ten minutes thought to the subject. It lies entirely outside the ambit of his mind.

I see no harm, quite the contrary, in the ventilation of your suggestion to establish a fund for open market operations in the longer-dated stocks. But I should be surprised if the proposal were to be adopted, in so many words, at this stage. The Treasury would tell the Chancellor of the Exchequer that they are quite in a position to do this, if they want to, with the various funds already in the hands of Government Departments. (So far as I know it would even be legal to use the existing sterling reserves of the Exchange Equalisation Fund for the purpose, without telling us anything about it.) They would say that, if the idea is a good one, it would be much better to apply it quietly in this way, rather than publicly establish such a fund, which might alarm people. Probably, of course, this is opposite the truth. To establish such a fund would not alarm people, but would reassure them. But it is easy to see that the above argument might be felt convincing by a Chancellor who was looking at the matter rather superficially.

Yours very truly,
[copy initialled] J.M.K.

From S. SCRIMGEOUR, *8 August 1939*

Dear Mr Keynes,

Very many thanks for your letter in reply to mine. Your estimates as to the probable attitude of the Treasury, the Bank of England, and the Chancellor of the Exchequer correspond very closely with mine. It is a pity because I fear that the lack of any settled policy is likely to lead to all sorts of difficulties in the future. However, I suppose all one can do is to ventilate the matter, whenever one gets an opportunity.

Here again with one or two exceptions I have not found anyone to express more than a mild interest in the matter and most people appear to look upon it as no more than an interesting theory.

Yours very truly,
S. SCRIMGEOUR

In July Sir Arthur Salter and L. S. Amery made a plea for official reserves of vital imports. Keynes supported it with a letter.

To the Editor of The Times, *5 July 1939*

Sir,

The plea of Mr Amery and Sir Arthur Salter for reserves of vital imports is unanswerable. If prices were high, an anxious Treasury might hesitate; though they would probably go higher in a war. But in fact many commodities are exceptionally low. Wheat is selling within about a shilling a quarter of the lowest price ever recorded. Our ships lie idle in harbour. The producing countries are so eager to sell that we should be able to provide that most of the purchase money is expended in this country. Money spent on stocks is not wasted, even if the emergency passes. It is insane in such circumstances to do nothing.

As your correspondents point out, it does not much matter what is bought. But preference should be given to commodities where heavy shipping tonnage is required and where arrangements can be made for the proceeds to be used for the payment of debts or the purchase of goods in this country. (Why not assist the difficulties of New Zealand by offering Mr Nash to purchase forthwith whatever quantity of goods he can ship to us?) Even when the policy involved us in a loss of gold, the gold will go twice as far as it will in an emergency.

I have never heard of any reason given by the Government for their inactivity. If there exist objections to the policy of buying reserves, we have not been told what they are. Why do they not appoint Mr Amery and Sir Arthur Salter to attend to the matter with an appropriation of £100,000,000? They could not find a pair of more experienced administrators for the purpose.

Yours, etc.,

J. M. KEYNES

Between May and July 1939 the Committee on Economic Information were engaged in preparing what was to be their last report. Their discussions were spread over six meetings, of which Keynes attended the first three. Their topic, 'Defence Expenditure and the Economic and Financial Problems Connected Therewith' naturally concerned Keynes, but most of his energy was directed at the statistical work underlying the report, especially attempts by P. K. Debenham to estimate both investment demand in relation to capacity, and the supply of labour available for new investment. When Keynes was unable to attend meetings he kept up his influence in correspondence.

From a letter to LORD STAMP, *21 June 1939*

I am sorry to say that I am going away to the country for good this week and will not be able, therefore, to come to the meeting of the E.A.C. next Monday, or at any date in the next four weeks. I do not know exactly what you are doing with the original draft dated June 3rd. But if paragraph 2 is being retained (this is a very interesting paragraph) I should like to suggest that the possible expansion of the labour force in war conditions may be seriously overestimated [*sic*]. I should have been inclined to guess that the increase in the labour force under the three headings might easily be as much as 6 millions compared with Debenham's estimate of 4 millions. If so, the result would be extremely significant. An increase of 6 millions (I am deriving 2 millions of this from the increase in the length of the working day compared with present conditions) would mean that 17½ millions would remain for normal activities so that it would not be necessary to contract the volume of consumers' goods and services more than in the proportion of 17½ to 17. This is an illustration of how a comparatively small change in the original assumptions can affect the final result,—a feature with which statisticians are very familiar. There is another illustration of the same sort in the copy I enclose of a letter I have written to Leith-Ross following on his conversation with Moreton.[8]

To P. K. DEBENHAM, *25 June 1939*

Dear Debenham,

I think that the general scheme and arrangement of the new memorandum is very good. This method of analysis is instructive and interesting. But your figures convince me that we ought to be able to get through *this* year's programme—I say nothing of next—without any exceptional measures of a *general* character. Thus your drastic proposals are in my opinion pessimistic.

You show that the demand for investment goods *on your own assumptions* may be about 10 per cent in excess of the supply; and I do not quarrel with that as a rough approximation. But I think that your assumptions contain any amount of give in them and that this 10 per cent can be easily made up from one source or another. I emphasise particularly the two points following:—

(i) You assume that the unemployed in the investment industries will not fall below the 1937 level. It seems to me that we should be able with a little organisation to do much better than that.

(ii) You assume no increase in the hours worked. For your figure of output per head is increased by no more than the technical trend—and is probably insufficient to allow for that. An extra half an hour a day in hours worked would largely solve your problem. E.g. another 100,000 men employed out of your 450,000 assumed unemployed and 7·5 per cent increase in hours worked and an increase in output for technical reasons to £250 in output yields a gross surplus in your last column, table 2, of

[8] Not printed.

about 1,229 or £20,000,000 more than you require. Surely we should first of all aim at that before taking your drastic measures.

(iii) I feel your figure for depreciation, etc., is much too low, when one bears in mind that this has to cover repairs and replacements as well as depreciation reserves set aside. Colin Clark's figure is £386,000,000 for 1934 and would probably be £400,000,000 currently. The last American compilations [were] for not less than 8 per cent of the net refined [?retained] income, which also would yield £400,000,000.

(iv) This probably means that *net* savings in the next part have to be lower than your figure, though not so much lower as if all your other figures are taken as correct. This discrepancy is due to business losses. The avoidance of business losses (100 per cent of which is saved) will be an important source of new *net* savings.

Yours sincerely,

J. M. KEYNES

From P. K. DEBENHAM, *29 June 1939*

Dear Keynes,

I circulated your letter to the Committee at their meeting; and in consequence they decided on a number of modifications in the draft report. They did not seem disposed, however, to retreat from their recommendations, being influenced by Salter, who took the line that if the present programme was possible without their proposed measures it would be better to increase the programme rather than give up the remedies. I have given a brief account of their discussion in the conclusions of the meeting; and the new version of the report, revised in accordance with this discussion, should be circulated soon.

May I make a few comments on your letter on my own account?

(*1*) *The unemployed in the investment industries.* I admit that 450,000 seems a very large number of unemployed for the investment industries, at a time when demand is in excess of supply. Yet I think it can be justified. The bulk of it, (260,000), is in the building and contracting industries and is caused by (i) nearly 100,000 down-and-outs who found refuge there in the slump, and are probably unemployable, (ii) the high seasonal unemployment in building, and (iii) the irregular nature of employment. I don't think it can be put much lower. There is also a rather similar situation in shipbuilding. Owing to the closure of yards, there is a hard core of about 35,000, mostly untransferable older men. This leaves 155,000, about 6 per cent of the insured in other investment industries. I should have thought this a low figure, though of course it might be possible to get lower still. I have assumed the same increase in the insured population in the investment industries as last year, although (i) the militia will take some, (ii) the intake of 16 year olds is less this year than last, and (iii) competition from other industries for available labour will be greater. So I think there is some ground for caution on the unemployment side.

(2) *Output per head, and hours of work.* I am afraid I tripped up on this point. I was under the impression that I was allowing something for overtime; for on the one hand there was probably a good deal of overtime in 1936, and on the other hand output per head had shown a rather startling decline in 1937 and 1938 which I thought might be due to dilution. I have, on enquiry at the Board of Trade, found that their production index for engineering and shipbuilding makes no allowance for increases in naval shipbuilding and aircraft production. I have therefore revised the output figures for those years, using employment figures in the place of the production index. The result is to show a small increase in output per head in 1937 and only a moderate decline in 1938, largely attributable to the decline in steel production. I have now taken £250 as the figure for output per head in 1939. I agree that this allows nothing for longer hours. The effect of this revision, however, does not give ground for optimism, for it suggests that ordinary demand for investment goods was substantially higher in 1938 than I had supposed. As a result, as you will see in the revised draft, I find a fairly substantial deficiency in 1939, even after allowing for another £75 millions of output from longer hours.

(3) *Depreciation.* My figure of depreciation of £115 millions is not of course comparable with Colin's £386 millions. A good deal of that comes under one of my other headings, e.g. roads and other local authority depreciation under (a), and house repairs under (b). Nevertheless, the figure of £60 millions for general depreciation is clearly too low. I have amended this to £165 millions, made up of £130 millions wear and tear allowance, and £35 millions from repairs to land and houses.

(4) *Company reserves and business losses.* I am not sure that I understand the point about business losses. *The Economist*'s figures for reserves are supposed to be *net*, after allowing for business losses, e.g., when businesses make a net loss this is considered a deduction from allocations to reserve. I have had a conversation with the Inland Revenue on the question of net allocations to reserves, and they put them at about £200 millions *gross* (i.e.,

before deduction of tax), and £150 millions *net*, the figure we want. I'm not sure that this isn't a bit low, but I have put it into the Report. The result is to bring private savings down to £110 millions, of which £60 millions is in the form of deposits with the Post Office, etc. I don't think the savings of the rich do much more than pay for their stockbrokers!

Yours sincerely,
P. K. DEBENHAM

To P. K. DEBENHAM, *1 July 1939*

My dear Debenham,

Many thanks for your letter of June 29th.

You may very well be right on points 1 and 2, if we do *not* do anything about it. But I should have thought that the first task could be to organise an increased volume of available labour under these heads.

There is a great deal to be said about points 3 and 4, more than can be put into a letter. I have, in fact, just begun to work at this subject, but need to persevere considerably before I feel that I have anything positive worth saying. I admire your brave pioneer effort in an impracticable country, and I am not prepared at present to offer anything better myself. But I feel that it would be wildly irresponsible of the Committee to print it!

You may be interested in the following figure. In 1936 the increase of funds in the Post Office and Trustee Savings Banks, Treasury Pensions Account, Unemployment and Health Insurance Funds, building societies, insurance companies and sundry small savings agencies, came to £241,000,000. £38,000,000 of this was in the Post Office Savings Bank, cash and stock, leaving £203,000,000 from the other sources. Thus, if your estimate of £50,000,000 for private savings, apart from the Post Office, is correct, private savings from all other sources than those mentioned above, must have come out to

−£153,000,000.* Since the increase in the total assets of building societies do not account for more than about half of the total increased investment in houses, it will not be easy to make the figures cross check. I am not yet clear what the explanation is, but I would emphasise that, at the present stage, the figures are frightfully unreliable.

Yours sincerely,
[copy initialled] J.M.K.

To LORD STAMP, *1 July 1939*

My dear Stamp,

As I shall not be able to come to the meeting of the E.A.C. on Tuesday, I send you herewith my more important comments on the revised document. As I am making so many criticisms I should like to add that I find the draft as a whole a very interesting, all [*sic*] and stimulating document. I am sending a copy to Debenham, so that copies of this letter may be sent out to the Committee, if possible, on Monday.

I. In the first part of the paper the statistics are now much more cautious than before. I believe, however, that it would be wiser to omit the discussion of the sources of saving, which occupy a large part of the latter portion.

This is a matter on which no economist or statistician has felt competent to publish any comprehensive estimate whatever. The Committee is here embarking on an important but excessively difficult piece of original work. It is a brave pioneering effort, but I do not believe the figures are capable of withstanding expert criticism, or that a proper estimate could be compiled by anyone except after many months' work. There is no attempt

* Reduced by an adjustment in respect of life assurance which might reduce it to −£100,000,000. My figure is for *all* insurance after deduction for claims and all other outgoings; yours is life insurance only before deduction for claims.

here to collect any new statistics. It is an estimate based on the partial figures and guesses available. Yet it is a guess which no outside or less responsible authority has had the courage to make. Not even Colin Clark; and for the item in respect of which he has made a guess, namely, depreciation allowances, there is an enormous discrepancy from the present estimate, although, of course, the two figures are not directly comparable. The point I mentioned in my previous letter, namely, the vast unexplored subject of business losses, the recouping of which is almost wholly increased net saving, is untouched.

Do you really think that we are entitled to invent out of our heads a table of this kind and then to base a far-reaching practical proposal on it?

II. Regarded as practical advice to the Government, given at the present stage of things, I feel that the general line taken up is a case of putting the cart before the horse, or rather a case of unloading the cart instead of getting another horse.

It seems to me that the thing to do at this stage is to mobilise our productive resources. Is not this obviously the thing to do before one starts on restrictions? The mobilisation of our resources is particularly important at an early stage because it is extremely difficult and needs long preparation. What we want to do now is to devise methods for drafting into useful jobs men who would otherwise remain unemployed, for dilution, for the greater employment of retired persons and women, and for economising the use of labour in unessential routine purposes of a sort which certainly would not be touched by capital restrictions.

I am quite prepared to believe that all sorts of restrictions will become necessary, and it is useful to explore what form these might take. But when one is discussing immediate measures, the most obvious point is the failure at present to mobilise anything like the whole of our resources. I repeat what I said before, that there is nothing in the programme of production envisaged in this memorandum which could not be met by a proper mobilisation of our resources. That is the first and pressing task.

III. Too much stress is laid on what can be hoped from the regulation of the new issue market. I am not against this proposal, but it would be more helpful to think of it in terms of practice.

Take, for example, the exceptionally heavy new issues of the last month. In each case the purpose of the loan was explained fairly fully. Which of them would the Committee have liked to refuse? If I remember right, they were mainly concerned with Dominion armament expenditure, electricity development, A.R.P., housing and road development; and I should suppose that much the same would apply to all future large-scale issues. Now, if we reach the point, and we well may, when we have, for example, to check housing development, obviously the method is for the Ministry of Health to refuse its consent to the projects of local authorities. It is no good handling the matter via the new issue market, which comes in at much too late a stage.

Or is it the minor issues, amounting only to a few hundred thousand pounds each, at the utmost, which the Committee want to check? There again take the test of recent issues. Which of them would members of the Committee have refused, if they had the choice? E.g. Broadcast Relays?

I believe that the opportunities in this direction are very limited, and that the restrictions have to be imposed at a much earlier state than through the issue market. The obvious measure would be an instruction by the Ministry of Health that no further proposals from local authorities, except those relating to A.R.P. would be allowed. Is the Committee convinced that we have reached the stage when that would be advisable? Or, if we think that all electricity development ought to be stopped, clearly it would be quite easy to do this through the Electricity Commissioners and the Electricity Board, and one would never let things go to the point of a new issue being prepared and then turned down. Does the Committee believe that we have reached the point when further electricity development ought to be stopped?

Or again roads? Nothing is easier than to stop all further expenditure on roads. Do we think it wise?

I would rather think in these particular terms than in general terms. If I was in one of the Government Departments concerned, I should want to know what this Committee was really wanting in terms of particular proposals.

IV. I plead very strongly that the two tentative suggestions of a dear money policy should not be included in this memorandum, and that this problem should be thrashed out by the Committee on a different occasion if we really want to take up this line.

The brief allusions to this subject are not argued and are not really intelligible. One does not know in what order of magnitude the matter is being thought of.

Does the Committee believe that it would do good rather than harm to depreciate War Loan 5 or 10 per cent, or raise the return on Treasury bills to 1 per cent? I should have said that such measures would be of absolutely negligible value from the point of view of restriction, and yet would completely destroy the Government loan programme, and cost the tax-payer in the long run hundreds of millions of pounds. I enclose a couple of articles I have just finished writing, further developing my familiar views on this matter. I do not feel that the Committee is entitled to turn down all this, unargued, in a few *obiter dicta*.

It would, however, be easy to meet me by the following omissions:—

Page 10, paragraph 13. Omit 'exclusive', and in the last sentence of this paragraph omit 'whether or not some hardening of interest rates is allowed to occur'.

Page 12, paragraph 15. For 'moderate tightening of credit

conditions' read 'moderate rationing of bank credit', and omit the two remaining sentences of this paragraph.

Yours ever,
[copy initialled] J.M.K.

I should be interested to see an estimate of how much greater Government-induced expenditure will be at the end of this financial year than it is now. I notice that in the first quarter expenditure has been at an annual rate of £1,184 millions compared with £1,285 millions estimated for the year as a whole. If we raise the estimates for the whole year to £1,350 millions, this leaves £1,054 millions for the remaining three quarters, i.e., annual rate of say £1,400 millions. As against this there is the considerable time lag between production and Exchequer disbursement, and the above figure is for the *average* of the first quarter, not for the last week of June; so that this average rate of expenditure of £1,184 millions in the first quarter may easily cloak a rate of current production of say £1,300 millions or more. If this is right, Government production by the end of the year may be greater by say £2 millions per week than it is now or 2 per cent of the national output, but scarcely more. Allowing for multiplied effects, let us say that the present programme may involve an increase of national output of probably not more than 5 per cent above what it is now. Is that impracticable without restrictions on investment? I should have thought not.

If our point is that our present programme ought to be a great deal bigger than it is, that is another argument. The imposition of immediate restrictions would be taken by Ministers and the public as a reason *against* increasing our present programme, not as an argument in favour. To argue that our resources are already inadequate is not the way to get more done.

I agree whole-heartedly with the memorandum about the balance of trade and the accumulation of stocks. I should like to see the latter taken up more emphatically and in greater detail. The Government seems crack-pot on this subject, even if war is only a remote possibility. The difference between present and probable war prices is worth pointing out.

To LORD STAMP, *1 July 1939*

Dear Stamp,

I do feel that the Committee ought to be a bit cautious about using the statistics which Debenham very bravely invents out of his head. It is very likely that none of us could do much better with a few days' work at the subject. But I am sure that they are wildly unreliable.

As a result of my previous letter, which was the result of a quarter of an hour's thought, he has raised his estimate of output in the investment industries by £75,000,000, and has increased his figures for general depreciation from £60,000,000 to £165,000,000. I am not an expert on these matters, but I fancy that I could in another quarter of an hour make him make about equally large corrections in the figures for savings.

I used to think that Colin Clark deserved the V.C. for statistical courage, but should now certainly depose him in favour of Piers. At any rate, I do feel that it would be wildly irresponsible of the Committee to feed Cabinet Ministers with these guesses.

Yours ever,
[copy initialled] J.M.K.

From P. K. DEBENHAM, *3 July 1939*

Dear Keynes,

Many thanks for your letter of the 1st July, with enclosure which I have had circulated to the Committee for their meeting tomorrow.

In the meantime may I add a note on the reconciliation of your £241 millions of savings with those given in the draft? I think you will find that the bulk of this sum is in fact allowed for in the draft report and that the balance left over, which should be deducted from my £50 millions of private savings (exclusive of working-class savings) is roughly £60 millions leaving a net dissaving of £10 millions, for the private saving of the rich.

The following items already appear:—

	(£ millions)	
	1937	1936
Unemployment funds (Table C page 31)	21	21
Deposits: Post Office, savings banks, building societies and savings certificates (page 19)	60	73
Building societies mortgage repayments (page 18)	75	73
Life insurance (ordinary) premiums (page 18) plus interest less expenses	110	110
	266	277
From these must be deducted claims and surrenders on life policies	70	70
	196	207

The following items are included in your £241 millions but have been left out of my estimates:

	(£ millions)	
	1937	1936
Building societies share capital	37	33
Industrial life assurance (net receipts)	20	20
Health insurance accumulated funds	3	3
Building societies (additional repayments)	10	10
	70	66
Total	266	273

The last item of £10 millions for additional building society repayments is an arbitrary amount which I have deducted from the true figure of building society repayments (given by new mortgages less increase in mortgages outstanding) on the following grounds. The reduction in mortgages outstanding occurs either through weekly repayments or through the repayment of the whole mortgage on the sale of the house. Only the first kind of repayment is regarded by the mortgagor as a charge on his income; the rest is either paid by a new mortgage raised with the building society (in which case it cancels out in the calculation of net repayments), or it is a draft on previously accumulated private savings.

I think that the other items which I have failed to include should have been accounted for somewhere in my draft. Industrial life assurance funds and health insurance funds ought to have been a deduction from private saving, and the increase in building societies share capital should be included with Post Office deposits etc., bringing that figure of £60 millions up to £97 millions.

I am not sure on re-reading your letter whether your £241 millions includes building society mortgage repayments. I should have thought that these plus the new share and deposit capital of the building societies (about £135 millions in 1937) were more than sufficient to finance private house building in 1937. Probably a certain amount of bank loans on house property were repaid by raising building society mortgages in that year. The insurance companies were also in the field.

Yours sincerely,

P. K. DEBENHAM

To P. K. DEBENHAM, *4 July 1939*

Dear Debenham,

In reply to your letter of July 3rd, your re-reading of mine is right, that is to say, I did not include building society mortgage repayments. So there is still rather a large discrepancy. I am sure it cannot easily be explained, though I am not at present prepared to deny that an explanation may be possible. I am also not clear in your reconciliation how you deal with my item from minor saving agencies, which consist of friendly societies, industrial and provident societies, trade unions, workmen's compensation schemes, certified loans societies and railway savings banks. These little items mounted up in 1936 to as much as £36,000,000. The difference between my life assurance figure and yours had nothing to do with industrial life assurance.

My figure was for the actual net increment in the assets of all insurance companies, including fire offices etc. Thus my calculation was on a much more stringent basis than yours, since it assumed that no part of the life insurance claims paid during the year were retained as savings, which is obviously not correct.

Thus the gross figure to be explained away is my figure of £241,000,000 plus building society mortgage repayments plus insurance policies paid to the holder during the year; which brings the total, doesn't it, somewhere in the neighbourhood of £380,000,000? There has to be added to this the positive savings in all the other great variety of ways open to the public; and after that there are all sorts of deductions to be made.

The Research Committee at Cambridge, which is working under Hall's Institute, has been proposing for some time to work at this subject and I hope we shall make more progress during the autumn.[9] Could we associate you with this and get your contributions, both positive and critical.

There is a horrible misprint in the copy of my letter which you have circulated [above, pp. 582–3], namely, £1,900,000,000 instead of £1,400,000,000, which produces rather a confusion. Also on that page, for £1,059,000,000 read £1,054,000,000; and for 'multiplied' read 'multiplier'.

Yours sincerely,
[copy initialled] J.M.K.

From LORD STAMP, *5 July 1939*

My dear Keynes,

Many thanks for the trouble you have been to in giving us your views on the draft. These were fully considered at yesterday's meeting and many of them given effect to, your vote being counted in whenever there was a division.

On the savings question: I was at a Treasury Committee some short time ago, which broke down finally because it could reach no useful conclusion. So the Committee have put a modified form of it in the appendix and the argument now in no way depends upon the validity or the sequence of statistics.

You will get the first proof in print in a few days and will see how far the Committee felt they could take your view.

Yours ever,
STAMP

[9] The Cambridge research scheme was the precursor of the University's Department of Applied Economics. The further work Keynes referred to saw the light in 'How to Pay for the War' and related articles; *JMK*, vol. IX, pp. 367–439 and vol. XXII, pp. 41–81, 124–32.

To LORD STAMP, *25 July 1939*

My dear Stamp,

On the final draft of the report, I sent Debenham one suggestion as to his figures which he no doubt communicated to you. Subject to this, I waived my other criticisms, because I do concur with the rest of the Committee in thinking the document exceedingly able and interesting and approve the various recommendations. Above all I consider that it is all wholesome meat for the authorities and, so far as action is concerned, just what we ought to tell them.

I do feel, however, rather strongly that we ought, another time, to be considerably more critical of statistics before we print them, and that we ought not to give our imprimatur to so many of Debenham's ingenious but rather wild surmises.

So far as the statistics are concerned, the whole of this document is based on his belief that, assuming the national income was about £5,000,000,000 prior to this year, the extent of our additional capacity is measured by an increase of £500,000,000 (price rises excluded); and on the further assumption that out of an increment of £500,000,000 income, one may expect that £100,000,000 will be saved.

For my part, I shall be extremely surprised if our additional capacity is not a great deal higher than that. I should have thought that, in present conditions, it was nearer £6,000,000,000 than £5,000,000,000, and that an increase up to, say, £5,600,000,000 or £5,700,000,000 one could rely on. In war conditions, we might easily expand to £6,500,000,000 or even more. And as regards saving, Debenham is assuming that the multiplier, after allowing for imports and unemployment relief, is as high as 5. This is enormously higher than any estimate I have ever seen made. A figure of even $3\frac{1}{2}$ would be highish. If our income fell to £4,000,000,000, and certainly if it fell to £3,500,000,000, savings would probably be nil or negative. If, therefore, they are £500,000,000 when income rises to

£5,000,000,000, this means that we are saving at least 33 per cent of the increment over £3,500,000,000. Why should we save less than this of the increment over £5,000,000,000?

I believe, therefore, that the problem of the scale assumed in the memorandum solves itself, and it is a fib, however well meant, to pretend otherwise. The reason I consider the document to be wholesome meat for the authorities is because I should like to see our effort considerably higher than the scale envisaged by the memorandum. But that is to put one's case on rather a different basis. I do not believe that the statistics, as actually set forth, are capable of being defended before a competent authority; and it is surely up to us to preserve strict scientific standards. I feel that the Committee have been inclined to swallow whole any statistics which fit in with and seem to support the general line of policy they favour.

Yours ever,
[copy initialled] J.M.K.

From LORD STAMP, *28 July 1939*

My dear Keynes,

Thanks for your letter of the 24th instant, which I am sending to the members, so that they can know your views.

I think we all have much sympathy with the necessity for not being too flamboyant or slipshod in our figures and, while I won't say it can *never* happen again, it is very unlikely!

I hope that you are looking after yourself well, and holding your strength. Everybody is interested in your *Times* articles which, as usual, are right on the spot.

Yours ever,
STAMP

Finally, in the summer of 1939, Keynes returned to an issue he had raised over a decade earlier. The occasion for this return was a letter from his sister Margaret who was a member of the Royal Commission on the Distribution of the Industrial Population under the chairmanship of Sir Montague Barlow.

From MARGARET HILL, *14 June 1939*

My dear Maynard,

There is one question which I should rather like to ask you in connection with the Royal Commission, and that is in connection with the function of a Board, if such constituted, for dealing with the location of industry. I suggested that one of the administrative non-executive functions of this Board should include plans for dealing with unemployment in times of depression, by public works etc.

I think you have written a good deal about this, and I wondered whether there were something which I could read. The argument against this is that it is not possible to find work of a useful and public character, to employ any very large numbers of men. Is this your view, or do you think that in times of boom any preparation can be made for unemployment such as may follow after say a big rearmament scheme is finished?

If you had time to cast your eye over the enclosed paper, and to make any comment on it, I should be extremely grateful as there is a great diversity of opinion as to whether this plan is a good one or not. It is, of course confidential, and is only a suggestion. Some members of the Commission wish to go very much further into granting executive powers to any Board or Authority which should be set up, but personally, from the evidence we have had before us, I feel that there is not enough information to go on at present, apart from London, and I shall probably support Sir Arthur Robinson in his proposal.

Much love

MARG.

To MARGARET HILL, *20 June 1939*

My dear Marg,

I have not written anything recently on the subject of a National Investment Board. My first proposals about this were not published over my own name, but are included in the report of the Liberal Industrial Enquiry, which is some time ago. I rather think that I got something similar in somewhere into the report of the Macmillan Committee. Two rather separate questions arise:

First of all, whether a National Investment Board is advisable. My own feeling is that, when we are ready for reforms, opinion will be found to have hardened a good deal in this direction. Any Government except an ultra-Conservative one might be expected to make a beginning towards introducing it. I am interested that you are meeting with the argument that it is not possible to find work of a useful and public character to employ any very large numbers of men. This used to be the argument of Neville Chamberlain and the Government in the last slump. But most people, I had thought, had quite given it up. It is a wholly untenable position. It is some time since anyone had the face to use such an argument in public. But I know people go on mumbling these sort of things in private long after they have lost the courage to talk such nonsense in public. Anyhow, I should say that practically all reforming minds are in favour of making some move in the direction of the establishment of a National Investment Board.

But it is quite another matter whether this could be appropriately tacked on to a Board which was primarily concerned with the location of industry. I should have said rather strongly that this combination of functions was undesirable. If a National Investment Board were to be set up, it would be most advisable that it should work in close collaboration with a Board for the location of industry. But the functions of the former body would go so very far beyond those of the latter that they could hardly be treated as a subsidiary function of the latter.

I think, therefore, that it would be much better to add a clause to the effect that the proposed authority for the location of industry would find its work very greatly facilitated if there was a Board of National Investment with which it could work in collaboration.

The actual proposals in the enclosed seem to me to be on the right lines. My main criticism would be that it is rather nebulous and passes the buck (to use the American expression) from your Commission to the proposed Board in paragraph 2, dealing with the functions of the Board. I daresay it is all you can do at this stage. But what it rather comes to is that you are proposing the establishment of a Board which should be charged with the duty of preparing and submitting to the Board of Trade precisely those proposals which it was hoped that your Committee might be making itself. I do not necessarily criticise this. It is quite likely that all your Commission can do is to advocate such a Board, and that the body which is to make concrete proposals must be that Board rather than yourselves.

Sorry that Maurice[10] just missed his First. But I gather that he very nearly got it.

Yours ever,
[copy initialled] J.M.K.

From MARGARET HILL, *21 June 1939*

Dear Maynard,

Thank you very much for your letter about the National Investment Board. I rather doubt whether I can get them to do much about it now, but I think your suggestion that a clause be added making some mention of it, is good. I feel that it would make the difficulties of location of industry much easier if a plan were thought out ahead for using the surplus labour, which no amount of planning can prevent from accumulating when international and other situations change.

I rather agree with your criticism that we are handing over, to the proposed Board, the functions which were given us to do. I have however come down on this side, (there is to be a minority report making rather wider suggestions) because I cannot see that from any evidence we have, or from any information we have been able to get, that we can recommend very much beyond an endeavour to stop the growth of London and the south east corner of England. It is impossible to say what is a suitable size for a town. Garden Cities are very slow in growth and are not very popular, and it is not yet evident what the planning schemes which have been got out all over the country are going to achieve. My own opinion is that it seems pretty clear that the people are very gregarious, and like living in large towns with the accompanying excitement and bustle, and that any scheme for distributing them over the country would not only be a dis-satisfaction to them, but would spoil the country as a whole and produce congestion over the whole of England, as opposed to congestion in certain districts. We want a more even

[10] Maurice Hill, Keynes's nephew.

distribution over existing centres *and most important* a rapid improvement in the conditions of all towns.

We were disappointed that Maurice did not get a First, but think that a very good Second will have encouraged him, and at the same time make it clear that he must do a good deal of work before Tripos. I am very glad you stood the term so well. I am going to have ten days in Devon soon.

Yours ever,

MARG.

Further contributions from Keynes's pen were, of course, to come with the outbreak of war. They are the subject of the next volume.

DOCUMENTS REPRODUCED IN THIS VOLUME

Where documents come from the Public Record Office, their call numbers appear before the date.

ARTICLES AND PAPERS *page*

MEMORANDA, NOTES AND COMMENTS

LECTURES, SPEECHES AND BROADCASTS

DOCUMENTS REPRODUCED IN THIS VOLUME

PUBLISHED LETTERS

UNPUBLISHED LETTERS

ACKNOWLEDGEMENTS

The Editors would like to thank the Controller of Her Majesty's Stationery Office for permission to reproduce Crown Copyright material. They are grateful to the Canada Council for financial assistance and to Professors Susan Howson and Donald Winch, and Dr George Peden for advice.

INDEX